KARL MARX

KARL MARX

HIS LIFE AND ENVIRONMENT

ISAIAH BERLIN

THIRD EDITION

A GALAXY BOOK

NEW YORK OXFORD UNIVERSITY PRESS 1963

© Oxford University Press   1963

First Published, 1939
Second Edition, 1948
Third Edition, 1963

Second Edition Published as a Galaxy Book, 1959

First Galaxy Printing of the Third Edition, 1963

Printed in the United States of America

To My Parents

NOTE TO THIRD EDITION

I HAVE taken the opportunity offered by a new edition to correct errors of fact and of judgment, and to repair omissions in the expositions of Marx's views, both social and philosophical, in particular of ideas which were neglected by the first generation of his disciples and his critics and came into prominence only after the Russian Revolution. The most important of these is his conception of the relation between the alienation and the freedom of men. I have also done my best to bring the bibliography up to date (although I have had to confine myself to secondary works in English) and should like to thank Mr. C. Abramsky and Mr. T. B. Bottomore for their valuable help and advice. I should also like to thank Professor S. N. Hampshire for re-reading the first half of the book, and for suggesting many improvements.

OXFORD, 1963   I. B.

NOTE TO FIRST EDITION

MY thanks are due to my friends and colleagues who have been good enough to read this book in manuscript, and have contributed valuable suggestions, by which I have greatly profited; in particular to Mr. A. J. Ayer, Mr. Ian Bowen, Mr. G. E. F. Chilver, Mr. S. N. Hampshire and Mr. S. Rachmilewitch; I am further greatly indebted to Mr. Francis Graham-Harrison for compiling the index; to Mrs. H. A. L. Fisher and Mr. David Stephens for reading the proofs; to Messrs. Methuen for permission to make use of the passage quoted on page 180; and, most of all, to the Warden and Fellows of All Souls College for permitting me to devote a part of the time during which I held a Fellowship of the college to a subject outside the scope of my proper studies.

OXFORD, *May* 1939   I. B.

CONTENTS

Chapter One

INTRODUCTION

Things and actions are what they are, and their consequences will be what they will be: why then should we seek
to be deceived?

BISHOP BUTLER

No thinker in the nineteenth century has had so direct,
deliberate and powerful an influence upon mankind as
Karl Marx. Both during his lifetime and after it he
exercised an intellectual and moral ascendancy over his
followers, the strength of which was unique even in that
golden age of democratic nationalism, an age which saw
the rise of great popular heroes and martyrs, romantic,
almost legendary figures, whose lives and words dominated the imagination of the masses and created a
new revolutionary tradition in Europe. Yet Marx could
not, at any time, be called a popular figure in the ordinary sense: certainly he was in no sense a popular writer
or orator. He wrote extensively, but his works were not,
during his lifetime, read widely; and when, in the late
'seventies, they began to reach the immense public which
several among them afterwards obtained, the desire to
read them was due not so much to a recognition of their
intrinsic qualities as to the growth of the fame and
notoriety of the movement with which he was identified.

Marx totally lacked the qualities of a great popular
leader or agitator; he was not a publicist of genius, like
the Russian democrat Alexander Herzen, nor did he
possess Bakunin's spell-binding eloquence; the greater
part of his working life was spent in comparative obscurity
in London, at his writing-table and in the reading-room
of the British Museum. He was little known to the

general public, and while towards the end of his life he became the recognized and admired leader of a powerful international movement, nothing in his life or character stirred the imagination or evoked the boundless devotion, the intense, almost religious, worship, with which such men as Kossuth, Mazzini, and even Lassalle in his last years, were regarded by their followers.

His public appearances were neither frequent nor notably successful. On the few occasions on which he addressed banquets or public meetings, his speeches were overloaded with matter, and delivered with a combination of monotony and brusqueness, which commanded the respect, but not the enthusiasm, of his audience. He was by temperament a theorist and an intellectual, and instinctively avoided direct contact with the masses to the study of whose interests his entire life was devoted. To many of his followers he appeared in the role of a dogmatic and sententious German schoolmaster, prepared to repeat his theses indefinitely, with rising sharpness, until their essence became irremovably lodged in his disciples' minds. The greater part of his economic teaching was given its first expression in lectures to working men: his exposition under these circumstances was by all accounts a model of lucidity and conciseness. But he wrote slowly and painfully, as sometimes happens with rapid and fertile thinkers, scarcely able to cope with the speed of their own ideas, impatient at once to communicate a new doctrine, and to forestall every possible objection;[1] the

---

[1] Anyone interested in Marx's method of composition would be well advised to read the Rough Draft (see bibliography p. 285) which appears to have remained in manuscript until 1939 and contains the main doctrines both of *Das Kapital* and of earlier studies of social alienation.

published versions were generally turgid, clumsy, and obscure in detail, although the central doctrine is never in serious doubt. He was acutely conscious of this, and once compared himself with the hero of Balzac's *Unknown Masterpiece*, who tries to paint the picture which has formed itself in his mind, touches and retouches the canvas endlessly, to produce at last a shapeless mass of colours, which to his eye seems to express the vision in his imagination. He belonged to a generation which cultivated the emotions more intensely and deliberately than its predecessors, and was brought up among men to whom ideas were often more real than facts, and personal relations meant more than the events of the external world; by whom indeed public life was at times understood and interpreted in terms of the rich and elaborate world of their own private experience. Marx was by nature not introspective, and took little interest in persons or states of mind or soul; the failure on the part of so many of his contemporaries to assess the importance of the revolutionary transformation of the society of their day, due to the swift advance of technology with its accompaniment of sudden increase of wealth, and, at the same time, of social and cultural dislocation and confusion, merely excited his anger and contempt.

He was endowed with a powerful, active, concrete unsentimental mind, an acute sense of injustice, and exceptionally little sensibility, and was repelled as much by the rhetoric and emotionalism of the intellectuals as by the stupidity and complacency of the bourgeoisie; the first often seemed to him aimless chatter, remote from reality and, whether sincere or false, equally irritating; the second at once hypocritical and self-deceived, blinded to the salient features of its time by absorption in the pursuit of wealth and social status.

This sense of living in a hostile and vulgar world, intensified perhaps by his latent dislike of the fact that he was born a Jew, increased his natural harshness and aggressiveness, and produced the formidable figure of popular imagination. His greatest admirers would find it difficult to maintain that he was a sensitive or tender-hearted man, or concerned about the feelings of those with whom he came into contact; the majority of the men he met were, in his opinion, either fools or sycophants, and towards them he behaved with open suspicion or contempt. But if his attitude in public was overbearing and offensive, in the intimate circle composed of his family and his friends, in which he felt completely secure, he was considerate and gentle; his married life was not unhappy, he was warmly attached to his children, and he treated his lifelong friend and collaborator, Engels, with uniform loyalty and devotion. He was a charmless man, and his behaviour was often boorish, but even his enemies were fascinated by the strength and vehemence of his personality, the boldness and sweep of his views, and the breadth and brilliance of his analyses of the contemporary situation.

He remained all his life an oddly isolated figure among the revolutionaries of his time, equally hostile to their persons, their methods and their ends. His isolation was not, however, due merely to temperament or to the accident of time and place. However widely the majority of European democrats differed in character, aims and historical environment, they resembled each other in one fundamental attribute, which made co-operation between them possible, at least in principle. Whether or not they believed in violent revolution, the great majority of them were, in the last analysis, liberal reformers, and appealed explicitly to moral standards common to all mankind. They criticized and condemned the existing condition of humanity in terms of some preconceived ideal, some system, whose desirability at least needed no demonstration, being self-evident to all men with normal moral vision; their schemes differed in the degree to which they could be realized in practice, and could accordingly be classified as less or more utopian, but broad agreement existed between all schools of democratic thought about the ultimate ends to be pursued. They disagreed about the effectiveness of the proposed means, about the extent to which compromise with the existing powers was morally or practically advisable, about the character and value of specific social institutions, and consequently about the policy to be adopted with regard to them. But even the most violent among them—Jacobins and terrorists—and they, perhaps, more than others—believed that there was little which could not be altered by the determined will of individuals; they believed, too, that powerfully held moral ends were sufficient springs of action, themselves justified by an appeal not to facts but to some universally accepted scale of values. It followed that it was proper first to ascertain what one wished the world to be: next, one had to consider in the light of this how much of the existing social fabric should be retained, how much condemned: finally, one was obliged to look for the most effective means of accomplishing the necessary transformation.

With this attitude, common to the vast majority of revolutionaries and reformers at all times, Marx came to be wholly out of sympathy. He was convinced that human history is governed by laws which cannot be altered by the mere intervention of individuals actuated by this or that ideal. He believed, indeed, that the inner experience to which men appeal to justify their ends, so far from revealing a special kind of truth called moral or religious, is merely a faculty which tends to engender myths and illusions, individual and collective. Being conditioned by the material circumstances in which they come to birth, the myths embody in the guise of objective truth whatever men in their misery wish to believe; under their treacherous influence men misinterpret the nature of the world in which they live, misunderstand their own position in it, and therefore miscalculate the range of their own and others' power, and the consequences both of their own and their opponents' acts. In opposition to the majority of the democratic theorists of his time, Marx believed that values could not be contemplated in isolation from facts, but necessarily depended upon the manner in which the facts were viewed. True insight into the nature and laws of the historical process will of itself, without the aid of independently known moral standards, make clear to a rational being what step it is proper for him to adopt, that is, what course would most accord with the requirements of the order to which he belongs. Consequently Marx had no new ethical or social ideal to press upon mankind; he did not plead for a change of heart; a change of heart was necessarily but the substitution of one set of illusions for another. He differed from the other great ideologists of his generation by making his appeal, at least in his own view, solely to reason, to the practical intelligence, denouncing only intellectual vice or blindness, insisting that all that men need, in order to know how to save themselves from the chaos in which they are involved, is to seek to understand their actual condition;

believing that a correct estimate of the precise balance of
forces in the society to which men belong will itself
indicate the form of life which it is rational to pursue.
Marx denounces the existing order by appealing not
to ideals but to history: he denounces it not as unjust, or
unfortunate, or due to human wickedness or folly,
but the effect of laws of social development which
make it inevitable that at a certain stage of history
one class, pursuing its interests with varying degrees
of rationality, should dispossess and exploit another.
The oppressors are threatened not with deliberate retribution on the part of their victims, but with the inevitable destruction which history (in the form of the
interests of an antagonistic social group) has in store
for them, as a class doomed shortly to disappear from
the stage of human events.

Yet, designed though it is to appeal to the intellect,
his language is that of a herald and a prophet, speaking
in the name not of human beings but of the universal
law itself, seeking not to rescue, nor to improve, but to
warn and to condemn, to reveal the truth and, above all,
to refute falsehood. *Destruam et ædificabo* ('I shall destroy and I shall build'), which Proudhon placed at the
head of one of his works, far more aptly describes
Marx's conception of his own appointed task. By 1845
he had completed the first stage of his programme, and
acquainted himself with the nature, history and laws of
the evolution of the society in which he found himself.
He concluded that the history of society is the history
of man seeking to attain to mastery of himself and of
the external world by means of his creative labour.
This activity is incarnated in the struggles of opposed
classes, one of which must emerge triumphant, although
in a much altered form: progress is constituted by the

succession of victories of one class over the other, and that man alone is rational who identifies himself with the progressive class in his society, either, if need be, by deliberately abandoning his past and allying himself with it, or if history has already placed him there, by consciously recognizing his situation and acting in the light of it.

Accordingly Marx, having identified the rising class in the struggles of his own time with the proletariat, devoted the rest of his life to planning victory for those at whose head he had placed himself. This victory the process of history would in any case secure, but human courage, determination and ingenuity could bring it nearer and make the transition less painful, accompanied by less friction and less waste of human substance. His position henceforth is that of a commander, actually engaged in a campaign, who therefore does not continually call upon himself and others to show reason for engaging in a war at all, or for being on one side of it rather than the other: the state of war and one's own position in it are given; they are facts not to be questioned but accepted and examined; one's sole business is to defeat the enemy; all other problems are academic, based on unrealized hypothetical conditions, and so beside the point. Hence the almost complete absence in Marx's later works of discussions of ultimate principles, of all attempts to justify his opposition to the bourgeoisie. The merits or defects of the enemy, or what might have been, if no enemy and no war existed, is of no interest during the battle. To introduce these irrelevant issues during the period of actual fighting is to divert the attention of one's supporters from the crucial issues with which, whether or not they recognize them, they are faced, and so to weaken their power of resistance.

All that is important during the actual war is accurate knowledge of one's own resources and of those of the adversary, and knowledge of the previous history of society, and the laws which govern it, is indispensable to this end. *Das Kapital* is an attempt to provide such an analysis. The almost complete absence from it of explicit moral argument, of appeals to conscience or to principle, and the equally striking absence of detailed prediction of what will or should happen after the victory, follow from the concentration of attention on the practical problems of action. The conceptions of natural rights, and of conscience, as belonging to every man irrespective of his position in the class struggle, are rejected as liberal illusions. Socialism does not appeal, it demands; it speaks not of rights, but of the new form of life before whose inexorable approach the old social structure has visibly begun to disintegrate. Moral, political, economic conceptions and ideals alter with the social conditions from which they spring: to regard any one of them as universal and immutable is tantamount to believing that the order to which they belong—in this case the bourgeois order—is eternal. This fallacy is held to underlie the ethical and psychological doctrines of idealistic humanitarians from the eighteenth century onwards. Hence the contempt and loathing poured by Marx upon the common assumption made by liberals and utilitarians, that since the interests of all men are ultimately, and have always been, the same, a measure of goodwill and benevolence on the part of everyone may yet make it possible to manufacture some sort of general compromise. If the class war is real, these interests are totally incompatible. A denial of this fact can be due only to stupid or cynical disregard of the truth, a peculiarly vicious form of hypocrisy or self-deception repeatedly exposed by history. This fundamental difference of outlook, and no mere dissimilarity of temperament or natural gifts, is the property which distinguishes Marx sharply from the bourgeois radicals and utopian socialists whom, to their own bewildered indignation, he fought and abused savagely and unremittingly for more than forty years.

He detested romanticism, emotionalism, and humanitarianism of every kind, and, in his anxiety to avoid any appeal to the idealistic feelings of his audience, systematically tried to remove every trace of the old democratic vocabulary from the propagandist literature of his movement. He neither offered nor invited concessions at any time, and did not enter into any dubious political alliances, since he declined all forms of compromise. The manifestoes, professions of faith and programmes of action to which he appended his name, contain scarcely any references to moral progress, eternal justice, the equality of man, the rights of individuals or nations, the liberty of conscience, the fight for civilization, and other such phrases which were the stock in trade (and had once genuinely embodied ideals of the democratic movements of his time; he looked upon these as so much worthless cant, indicating confusion of thought and ineffectiveness in action).[1]

The war must be fought on every front, and, since contemporary society is politically organized, a political party must be formed out of those elements which in accordance with the laws of historical development are destined to emerge as the conquering class. They must

[1] His remarks, in a letter to Engels, about his attitude to such expressions in the draft of the declaration of its principles which the First International Workingmen's Association submitted to him, are highly instructive in this connection.

ceaselessly be taught that what seems so secure in existing society is, in reality, doomed to swift extinction, a fact which men may find it difficult to believe because of the immense protective façade of moral, religious, political and economic assumption and beliefs, which the moribund class consciously or unconsciously creates, blinding itself and others to its own approaching fate. It requires both intellectual courage and acuteness of vision to penetrate this smoke-screen and perceive the real structure of events. The spectacle of chaos, and the imminence of the crisis in which it is bound to end, will of itself convince a clear-eyed and interested observer—for no one who is not virtually dead or dying, can be a disinterested spectator of the fate of the society with which his own life is bound up —of what he must be and do in order to survive. Not a subjective scale of values revealed differently to different men, determined by the light of an inner vision, but knowledge of the facts themselves, must, according to Marx, determine rational behaviour. A society is judged to be progressive, and so worthy of support, if it is one whose institutions are capable of further development in its initial direction without subversion of its entire basis. A society is reactionary when it is inevitably moving into an impasse, unable to avoid internal chaos and ultimate collapse in spite of the most desperate efforts to survive, efforts which themselves create irrational faith in its own ultimate stability, the anodyne with which all dying orders necessarily delude themselves. Nevertheless, what history has condemned, will be inevitably swept away: to say that something ought to be saved, even when that is not possible, is to deny the rational plan of the universe. To denounce the process itself—the painful conflicts

through and by which mankind struggles to achieve the
full realization of its powers—was for Marx a form of
childish subjectivism, due to a morbid or shallow view
of life, to some irrational prejudice in favour of this or
that virtue or institution; it revealed attachment to the
old world and was a symptom of incomplete emancipation from its values. It seemed to him that under the
guise of earnest philanthropic feeling there throve,
undetected, seeds of weakness and treachery, due to a
fundamental desire to come to terms with the reaction,
a secret horror of revolution based on fear of reality, of
the full light of day. With reality there could, however,
be no compromise: and humanitarianism was but a
softened, face-saving form of compromise, due to a
desire to avoid the perils of an open fight and, even
more, the risks and responsibilities of victory. Nothing
stirred his indignation so much as cowardice: hence the
furious and often brutal tone with which he refers to it,
the beginning of that harsh 'materialist' style which
struck an entirely unfamiliar note in the literature of
revolutionary socialism. This fashion for 'naked ob-
jectivity' took the form, particularly among Russian
writers of a later generation, of searching for the
sharpest, most unadorned, most shocking form of
statement in which to clothe what were sometimes not
very startling propositions.

Marx had, by his own account, begun to build his
new instrument from almost casual beginnings: because,
in the course of a controversy with the government
on the economic question of purely local importance, in which he was involved in his capacity as editor
of a radical newspaper, he became aware of his almost
total ignorance of the history and principles of economic
development. This controversy occurred in 1843. By

1848 his education as a political and economic thinker was complete. With prodigious thoroughness he had constructed a complete theory of society and its evolution, which indicated with precision where and how the answers to all such questions must be sought and found. Its originality has often been questioned. It is original, not indeed in the sense in which works of art are original when they embody some hitherto un-expressed individual experience, but as scientific theories are said to be original, where they provide a new solution to a hitherto unsolved problem, which they may do by modifying and combining existing views to form a new hypothesis. Marx never attempted to deny his debt to other thinkers: 'I am performing an act of historical justice, and am rendering to each man his due', he loftily declared. But he did claim to have provided for the first time a wholly adequate answer to questions which had been previously either misunder-stood, or answered wrongly or insufficiently or ob-scurely. The characteristic for which Marx sought was not novelty but truth, and when he found it in the works of others, he endeavoured, at any rate during the early years in Paris in which his thought took its final shape, to incorporate it in his new synthesis. What is original in the result is not any one component element, but the central hypothesis by which each is connected with the others, so that the parts are made to appear to follow from each other and to support each other in a single systematic whole.

To trace the direct source of any single doctrine advanced by Marx is, therefore a relatively simple task which his numerous critics have been only too anxious to perform. It may well be that there is not one among his views whose embryo cannot be found in some

previous or contemporary writer. Thus the doctrine of
communal ownership founded upon the abolition of
private property, has probably, in one or other form,
possessed adherents at most periods during the last two
thousand years. Consequently the often debated question whether Marx derived it directly from Mably, or
Babeuf and his followers, or from some German
account of French Communism, is too purely academic
to be of great importance. As for more specific doctrines, historical materialism of a sort is to be found
fully developed in a treatise by Holbach printed almost
a century before, which in its turn owes much to
Spinoza; a modified form of it was restated in Marx's
own day by Feuerbach. The view of human history as
the history of war between social classes is to be found
in Linguet and Saint-Simon, and was to a large extent
adopted by such contemporary liberal French historians
as Thierry and Mignet, and equally by the more conservative Guizot. The scientific theory of the inevitability of the regular recurrence of economic crises was
probably first formulated by Sismondi; that of the rise
of the Fourth Estate was certainly held by the early
French communists, popularized in Germany in Marx's
own day by Stein and Hess. The dictatorship of
the proletariat was adumbrated by Babeuf in the
last decade of the eighteenth century, and was explicitly
developed in the nineteenth in different fashions by
Weitling and Blanqui; the present and future position
and importance of workers in an industrial state was
more fully worked out by Louis Blanc and the French
State Socialists than Marx is prepared to admit. The
labour theory of value derives from Locke, Adam
Smith, Ricardo and the other classical economists; the
theory of exploitation and surplus value is found in

Fourier, and of its remedy by deliberate State control in the writings of early English socialists, such
as Bray, Thompson and Hodgskin; the theory of the
alienation of the proletarians was enunciated by Max
Stirner at least one year before Marx. The influence
of Hegel and German philosophy is the deepest and
most ubiquitous of all; the list could easily be continued
further.

There was no dearth of social theories in the eighteenth century. Some died at birth, others, when the
intellectual climate was favourable, modified opinion
and influenced action. Marx sifted this immense mass
of material and detached from it whatever seemed to
him original, true and important; and in the light of it
constructed a new instrument of social analysis, the
main merit of which lies not in its beauty or consistency,
nor in its emotional or intellectual power—the great
utopian systems are nobler works of the speculative
imagination—but in the remarkable combination of
simple fundamental principles with comprehensiveness,
realism and detail. The environment which it assumed
actually corresponded to the personal, first-hand
experience of the public to which it was addressed; its
analyses, when stated in their simplest form, seemed
at once novel and penetrating, and the new hypotheses
which represent a peculiar synthesis of German
idealism, French rationalism, and English political
economy, seemed genuinely to co-ordinate and account
for a mass of social phenomena hitherto thought of in
comparative isolation from each other. This provided
a concrete meaning for the formulae and popular
slogans of the new communist movement. Above all, it
enabled it to do more than stimulate general emotions
of discontent and rebellion by attaching to them, as

Chartism had done, a collection of specific but loosely connected political and economic ends. It directed these feelings to systematically interconnected, immediate, feasible objectives, regarded not as ultimate ends valid for all men at all times, but as objectives proper to a revolutionary party representing a specific stage of social development.

To have given clear and unified answers in familiar empirical terms to those theoretical questions which most occupied men's minds at this time, and to have deduced from them clear practical directives without creating obviously artificial links between the two, was the principal achievement of Marx's theory, and endowed it with that singular vitality which enabled it to defeat and survive its rivals in the succeeding decades. It was composed largely in Paris during the troubled years between 1843 and 1850, when, under the stress of a world crisis, economic and political tendencies normally concealed below the surface of social life, increased in scope and in intensity, until they broke through the framework which was secured in normal times by established institutions, and for a brief instant revealed their real character during the luminous interlude which preceded the final clash of forces, in which all issues were obscured once more. Marx fully profited by this rare opportunity for scientific observation in the field of social theory; to him, indeed, it appeared to provide full confirmation of his hypotheses.

The system as it finally emerged was a massive structure, heavily fortified against attack at every strategic point, incapable of being taken by direct assault, containing within its walls elaborate resources to meet every conceivable contingency of war. Its influence has been immense on friend and foe alike,

and in particular on social scientists, historians and
critics. It has altered the history of human thought in
the sense that after it certain things could never again
be plausibly said. No subject loses, at least in the long
run, by becoming a field of battle, and the Marxist
emphasis upon the primacy of economic factors in
determining human behaviour led directly to an intensified study of economic history, which, although it
had not been entirely neglected in the past, did not
attain to its present prominent rank, until the rise of
Marxism gave an impulse to exact historical scholarship in that sphere—much as in the previous generation Hegelian doctrines acted as a powerful stimulus to
historical studies in general. The sociological treatment
of historical and moral problems, which Comte and
after him, Spencer and Taine, had discussed and
mapped, became a precise and concrete study only
when the attack of militant Marxism made its conclusions a burning issue, and so made the search for
evidence more zealous and the attention to method
more intense.

In 1849 Marx was forced to leave Paris, and came
to live in England. To him London meant little more
than the library of the British Museum, 'the ideal
strategic vantage point for the student of bourgeois
society', an arsenal of ammunition whose importance its
owners did not appear to grasp. He remained almost
totally unaffected by his surroundings, living encased in
his own, largely German, world, formed by his family
and a small group of intimate friends and political
associates. He met few Englishmen and neither understood nor cared for them or their mode of life. He was a
man unusually impervious to the influence of environment: he saw little that was not printed in newspapers

or books, and remained until his death comparatively
unaware of the quality of the life around him or of its
social and natural background. So far as his intellectual
development was concerned, he might just as well have
spent his exile on Madagascar, provided that a regular
supply of books, journals and government reports
could have been secured: certainly the inhabitants of
London could hardly have taken less notice of his
existence if he had. The formative, psychologically
most interesting, years of his life were over by 1851:
after this he was emotionally and intellectually set and
hardly changed at all. He had, while still in Paris,
conceived the idea of providing a complete account
and explanation of the rise and imminent fall of the
capitalist system. His work upon it was begun in the
spring of 1850, and continued, with interruptions,
caused by day-to-day tactical needs and the journalism
by which he tried to support his household, until his
death in 1883.

His pamphlets, articles and letters during the next
thirty years form a coherent commentary on contemporary political affairs in the light of his new method
of analysis. They are sharp, lucid, mordant, realistic,
astonishingly modern in tone, and aimed deliberately
against the prevailing optimistic temper of his time.

As a revolutionary he disapproved of conspiratorial
methods which he thought obsolete and ineffective,
and liable to irritate public opinion without altering its
foundations, instead he set himself to create an open
political party dominated by the new view of society.
His later years are occupied almost exclusively with
the task of gathering evidence for, and disseminating,
the truths which he had discovered, until they filled the
entire horizon of his followers, and became consciously

woven into the texture of their every thought and word
and act. For a quarter of a century he concentrated his
entire being upon the attainment of this purpose, and,
towards the end of his life, achieved it.

The nineteenth century contains many remarkable
social critics and revolutionaries no less original, no less
violent, no less dogmatic than Marx, but not one so
rigorously single-minded, so absorbed in making every
word and every act of his life a means towards a
single, immediate, practical end, to which nothing was
too sacred to be sacrificed. If there is a sense in which he
was born before his time, there is an equally definite
sense in which he embodies one of the oldest of European traditions. For while his realism, his empiricism,
his attacks on abstract principles, his demand that every
solution must be tested by its applicability to, and
emergence out of, the actual situation, his contempt for
compromise or gradualism as modes of escape from the
necessity of drastic action, his belief that the masses are
infinitely gullible and must at all costs be rescued, if
necessary by force, from the knaves and fools who
impose upon them, make him the precursor of the
severer generation of practical revolutionaries of the
next century: his rigid belief in the necessity of a complete break with the past, in the need for a wholly new
social system as alone capable of saving the individual,
who, if left to himself, will lose his way and perish,
places him among the great authoritarian founders of
new faiths, ruthless subverters and innovators who
interpret the world in terms of a single, clear, passionately held principle, denouncing and destroying all that
conflicts with it. His faith in his own synoptic vision of
an orderly, disciplined, self-directing society, destined to
arise out of the inevitable self-destruction of the irrational

and chaotic world of the present, was of that boundless, absolute kind which puts an end to all questions
and dissolves all difficulties; which brings with it a
sense of liberation similar to that which in the sixteenth
and seventeenth centuries men found in the new Protestant faith, and later in the truths of science, in the
principles of the great Revolution, in the systems of the
German metaphysicians. If these earlier rationalists
are justly called fanatical, then in this sense Marx too
was a fanatic. But his faith in reason was not blind: if
he appealed to reason, he appealed no less to empirical
evidence. The laws of history were indeed eternal and
immutable—and to grasp this fact a quasi-metaphysical
intuition was required—but what they were could be
established only by the evidence of empirical facts. His
intellectual system was a closed one, everything that
entered was made to conform to a pre-established
pattern, but it was grounded in observation and experience. He was obsessed by no fixed ideas. He
betrays not a trace of the notorious symptoms which
accompany pathological fanaticism, that alternation of
moods of sudden exaltation with a sense of loneliness
and persecution, which life in wholly private worlds
often engenders in those who are detached from reality.

The main ideas of his principal work appear to have
matured in his mind as early as 1847. Preliminary
sketches had appeared in 1849 and again seven years
later, but he was incapable of beginning to write before
satisfying himself that he had mastered the entire
literature of his subject. This fact, together with the
difficulty of finding a publisher and the necessity of
providing for his own and his family's livelihood, with
its accompaniment of overwork and frequent illness,
put off its publication year by year. The first volume

finally appeared twenty years after its conception, in 1867, and is the crowning achievement of his life. It is an attempt to give a single integrated account of the process and laws of social development, containing a complete economic theory treated historically, and, less explicitly, a theory of history as determined by economic factors. It is interrupted by remarkable digressions consisting of analyses and historical sketches of the condition of the proletariat and its employers, in particular during the period of transition from manufacture to large-scale industrial capitalism, introduced to illustrate the general thesis, but in fact demonstrating a new and revolutionary method of historical writing and political interpretation: and all in all constitutes the most formidable, sustained and elaborate indictment ever delivered against an entire social order, against its rulers, it supporters, its ideologists, its willing and unwilling instruments, against all whose lives are bound up with its survival. His attack upon bourgeois society was made at a moment when it had reached the highest point of its material prosperity, in the very year in which Gladstone in a budget speech congratulated his countrymen on the 'intoxicating augmentation of their wealth and power' which recent years had witnessed, during a mood of buoyant optimism and universal confidence. In this world Marx is an isolated and bitterly hostile figure, prepared, like an early Christian, or a French *enragé*, to reject boldly everything that it had to offer, calling its ideals worthless and its virtues vices, condemning its institutions not because they were bad but because they were bourgeois, because they belonged to a corrupt, tyrannous and irrational society which must be annihilated totally and for ever. In an age which destroyed its adversaries by methods not less efficient because they were dignified and slow, which forced Carlyle and Schopenhauer to seek escape in remote civilizations or an idealized past, and drove its arch-enemy Nietzsche to hysteria and madness, Marx alone remained secure and formidable. Like an ancient prophet performing a task imposed on him by heaven, with an inner tranquillity based on clear and certain faith in the harmonious society of the future, he bore witness to the signs of decay and ruin which he saw on every side. The old order seemed to him to be patently crumbling before his eyes; he did more than any man to hasten the process, seeking to shorten the final agony which precedes the end.

Chapter Two

CHILDHOOD AND ADOLESCENCE

Nimmer kann ich ruhig treiben
Was die Seele stark befasst,
Nimmer still behaglich bleiben
Und ich stürme ohne Rast.[1]

KARL MARX, *Juvenilia*

KARL HEINRICH MARX, eldest son of Heinrich and
Henrietta Marx, was born on 5 May 1818 in Trier, in
the German Rhineland, where his father practised as a
lawyer. Once the seat of a Prince-Archbishop, it had,
some fifteen years before, been occupied by the French
and was incorporated by Napoleon in the Confederation of the Rhine. After his defeat ten years later it was
assigned by the Congress of Vienna to the rapidly
expanding Prussian kingdom.

The kings and princes of the German states whose
personal authority had recently been all but destroyed
by the successive French invasion of their territories,
were at this time busily engaged in repairing the dam-
aged frabric of hereditary monarchy, a process which
demanded the obliteration of every trace of the dangerous ideas which had begun to rouse even the placid
inhabitants of the German provinces from their
traditional lethargy. Napoleon's defeat and exile had
finally destroyed the illusions of those German radicals
who hoped that the result of Napoleon's centralizing

---

[1] Never can I pursue in quiet that which holds my soul in
thrall, never rest at peace contented, and I storm without
cease.

policy would be, if not the liberty, at any rate the unity of Germany. The *status quo* was re-established wherever this was possible; Germany was once more divided into feudally organized kingdoms and principalities, whose restored rulers, resolved to compensate themselves for the years of defeat and humiliation, set about reviving the old régime in every detail, anxious to exorcize once and for all the spectre of democratic revolution whose memory was sedulously kept alive by the more enlightened among their subjects. The king of Prussia, Frederick William III, was particularly energetic in this respect. Helped by the feudal squirearchy and such land-owning aristocracy as there was in Prussia, and following the example set by Metternich in Vienna, he succeeded in arresting the normal development of the majority of his countrymen for many years, and induced an atmosphere of profound and hopeless stagnation, beside which even France and England during the reactionary years seemed liberal and alive. This was felt most acutely by the more progressive elements in German society—not merely by the intellectuals, but by the bulk of the bourgeoisie and of the liberal aristocracy of the towns, particularly in the west, which had always preserved some contact with general European culture. It took the form of economic, social and political legislation designed to retain, and in some cases to restore, a multitude of privileges, rights and restrictions, many of them dating from the Middle Ages, sordid survivals that had long ceased to be even picturesque; and since they were in direct conflict with the needs of the new age, they needed and obtained an elaborate and ruinous structure of tariffs to keep them in being. This led to a policy of systematic discouragement of trade and industry and, since the obsolete structure had to be preserved against popular pressure, to the creation of a despotic officialdom, whose task it was to insulate German society from the contaminating influence of liberal ideas and institutions.

The increased power of the police, the introduction of rigid supervision over all departments of public and private life, provoked a literature of protest which was rigorously suppressed by the government censors. German writers and poets went into voluntary exile, and from Paris or Switzerland conducted passionate propaganda against the régime. The general situation was reflected particularly clearly in the condition of that section of society which throughout the nineteenth century tended to act as the most sensitive barometer of the direction of social change—the small but widely scattered Jewish population.

The Jews had every reason to feel grateful to Napoleon. Wherever he appeared he set himself to destroy the traditional edifice of social rank and privilege, of racial, political and religious barriers, putting in its place his newly promulgated legal code, which claimed as the source of its authority the principles of reason and human equality. This act, by opening to the Jews the doors of trades and professions which had hitherto remained rigidly barred to them, had the effect of releasing a mass of imprisoned energy and ambition, and led to the enthusiastic—in some cases over-enthusiastic—acceptance of general European culture by a hitherto segregated community, which from that day became a new and important factor in the evolution of European society.

Some of these liberties were later withdrawn by Napoleon himself, and what was left of them was for the most part revoked by the restored German princes, with the result that many Jews who had eagerly broken away from the traditional mode of life led by their fathers toward the prospects of a wider existence, now found that the avenue which had so suddenly been half-opened before them had as suddenly become barred again, and consequently were confronted with a difficult choice. They had either to retrace their steps and pain-fully re-enter the Ghetto in which their families for the most part still continued to live, or else, altering their names and religion, to start new lives as German patriots and members of the Christian Church. The case of Herschel Levi was typical of a whole generation. His father, Marx Levi, and his father before him, were Rabbis in the Rhineland, who, like the great majority of their fellow Jews, had passed their entire existence within the confines of a pious, inbred, passionately self-centred community, which, faced with the hostility of its Christian neighbours, had taken refuge behind a defensive wall of pride and suspicion, which had for centuries almost wholly preserved them from contact with the changing life outside. The enlightenment had, nevertheless, begun to penetrate even this artificial enclave of the Middle Ages, and Herschel, who had received a secular education, became a disciple of the French rationalists and their disciples, the German *Aufkläner*, and was early in life converted to the religion of reason and humanity. He accepted it with candour and naïveté, nor did the long years of darkness and reaction succeed in shaking his faith in God and his simple and optimistic humanitarianism. He detached himself completely from his family, changed his sur-name to Marx, and acquired new friends and new interests. His legal practice was moderately successful, and he began to look to a settled future as the head of a respectable German bourgeois family, when the anti-Jewish laws of 1816 suddenly cut off his means of livelihood.

He probably felt no exceptional reverence for the established church, but he was even less attached to the Synagogue, and, holding vaguely deist views, saw no moral or social obstacle to complete conformity with the mildly enlightened Lutheranism of his Prussian neighbours. At any rate if he did hesitate, it was not for long. He was officially received into the Church early in 1817, a year before the birth of his eldest son, Karl. The hostility of the latter to everything connected with religion, and in particular with Judaism, may well be partly due to the peculiar and embarrassed situation in which such converts sometimes found themselves. Some escaped by becoming devout and even fanatical Christians, others by rebelling against all established religion. They suffered in proportion to their sensitiveness and intelligence. Both Heine and Disraeli were all their lives obsessed by the personal problem of their peculiar status; they neither renounced nor accepted it completely, but alternately mocked at and defended the religion of their fathers, incapable of a single-minded attitude towards their ambiguous position, perpetually suspicious of latent contempt or condescension concealed beneath the fiction of their complete acceptance by the society in which they lived.

The elder Marx suffered from none of these complications. He was a simple, serious, well-educated man, but he was neither conspicuously intelligent nor abnormally sensitive. A disciple of Leibnitz and Voltaire, Lessing and Kant, he possessed in addition a gentle, timid and accommodating temper, and ultimately became a passionate Prussian patriot and monarchist, a position which he sought to justify by pointing to the figure of Frederick the Great—a tolerant and enlightened prince who compared favourably with Napoleon with his notorious contempt for ideologists. After his baptism he adopted the Christian name of Heinrich, and educated his family as liberal protestants, faithful to the existing order and to the reigning King of Prussia. Anxious as he was to identify that ruler with the ideal prince depicted by his favourite philosophers, the repulsive figure of Frederick William III defeated even his loyal imagination. Indeed, the only occasion on which this tremulous and retiring man is known to have behaved with courage was a public dinner at which he made a speech on the desirability of moderate social and political reforms worthy of a wise and benevolent ruler. This swiftly drew upon him the attention of the Prussian police. Heinrich Marx at once retracted everything, and convinced everyone of his complete harmlessness. It is not improbable that this slight but humiliating *contretemps*, and in particular his father's craven and submissive attitude, made a definite impression on his oldest son Karl Heinrich, then sixteen years old, and left behind it a smouldering sense of resentment, which later events fanned into a flame.

His father had early become aware that while his other children were in no way remarkable, in Karl he had an unusual and difficult son; with a sharp and lucid intelligence he combined a stubborn and domineering temper, a truculent love of independence, exceptional emotional restraint, and over all a colossal, ungovernable intellectual appetite. The timorous lawyer, whose life was spent in social and personal compromise, was puzzled and frightened by his son's intransigeance which, in his opinion, was bound to antagonize important persons, and might, one day, lead him into serious trouble. He frequently and anxiously begged him in his letters to moderate his enthusiasms, to impose some sort of discipline on himself, not to waste time on subjects likely to prove useless in later life, to cultivate polite, civilized habits, not to neglect possible benefactors, above all not to estrange everyone by violently refusing to adapt himself—in short to satisfy the elementary requirements of the society in which he was to live his life. But these letters, even at their most disapproving, remained gentle and affectionate; in spite of growing uneasiness about his character and career, Heinrich Marx treated his son with an instinctive delicacy, and never attempted to oppose or bully him on any serious issue. Consequently their relations continued to be warm and intimate until the death of the older Marx in 1838.

It seems certain that the father had a definite influence on his son's intellectual development. The elder Marx believed with Condorcet that man is by nature both good and rational, and that all that is needed to ensure the triumph of these qualities is the removal of unnatural obstacles from his path. They were disappearing already, and disappearing fast, and the time was rapidly approaching when the last citadels of reaction, the Catholic Church and the feudal nobility, would melt away before the irresistible march of reason. Social, political, religious, racial barriers were so many artificial products of the deliberate obscurantism of priests and rulers; with their disappearance a new day would dawn for the human race, when all men would be equal, not only politically and legally, in their formal, external relations, but socially and personally, in their most intimate daily intercourse.

His own history seemed to him to corroborate this triumphantly. Born a Jew, a citizen of inferior legal and social status, he had attained to equality with his more enlightened neighbours, had earned their respect as a human being, and had become assimilated into what appeared to him as their more rational and dignified mode of life. He believed that a new day was dawning in the history of human emancipation, in the light of which his children would live their lives as free-born citizens in a just and liberal state. Elements of this belief are clearly apparent in his son's social doctrine. Karl Marx did not, indeed, believe in the power of rational argument to influence action, but there is, nevertheless, a definite sense in which he remained both a rationalist and a perfectibilian to the end of his life. He believed in the complete intelligibility of the process of social evolution; he believed that society is inevitably progressive, that its movement from stage to stage is a forward movement, that each successive stage represents development, is nearer the rational ideal than its precursors. He detested, as passionately as any eighteenth-century thinker, emotionalism, belief in supernatural causes, visionary fantasy of every kind, and systematically under-estimated the influence of such non-rational forces as nationalism, and religious and racial solidarity. Although, therefore, it remains true that the Hegelian philosophy is the greatest single formative influence in his life, the principles of philosophical rationalism, which were planted in him by his father and his father's friends, performed a definite work of inoculation, so that when later he encountered the metaphysical systems developed by the romantic school, he was saved from that total surrender to their fascination which undid so many of his contemporaries. It was this pronounced taste, acquired early in life, for lucid argument and an empirical approach, that enabled him to preserve a measure of independence in the face of the prevalent philosophy, and later to alter it to his own more positivist pattern. This may perhaps account for the realistic and concrete quality of his thought, even when it is influenced by romantic ideas, as contrasted with the outlook of such leading radicals of his time as Börne, Heine, or Lassalle, whose origins and education are in many respects closely analogous to his own.

Little is known of his childhood and early years in Trier. His mother played a singularly small part in his life; Henrietta Philips belonged to a family of Hungarian Jews settled in Holland, where her father was a Rabbi, and was a solid and uneducated woman entirely absorbed in the cares of her large household, who did not at any time show the slightest understanding of her son's gifts or inclinations, was shocked by his radicalism, and in later years appears to have lost all interest in his existence. Of the eight children of Heinrich and Henrietta Marx Karl was the second; apart from a mild affection as a child for his eldest sister Sophia, he showed little interest in his brothers and sisters either then or later. He was sent to the local High School where he obtained equal praise for his industry and the high-minded and earnest tone of his essays on moral and religious topics. He was moderately proficient in mathematics and theology, but his main interests were literary and artistic: a tendency due principally to the influence of two men from whom he learned most and of whom all his life he spoke with affection and respect. The first of these was his father; the other was their neighbour, Freiherr Ludwig von Westphalen, who was on friendly terms with the amiable lawyer and his family. Westphalen was a distinguished Prussian government official, and belonged to that educated and liberal section of the German upper class whose representatives were to be found in the vanguard of every enlightened and progressive movement in their country in the first half of the nineteenth century. An open-minded, attractive, and cultivated man, he belonged to the generation dominated by the great figures of Goethe, Schiller and Hölderlin, and under their influence he had wandered beyond the aesthetic frontiers so strictly established by the literary mandarins in Paris, and shared in the growing German passion for the rediscovered genius of Dante, Shakespeare, Homer and the Greek tragedians. He was attracted by the striking ability and eager receptiveness of Heinrich Mark's son, encouraged him to read, lent him books, took him for walks in the neighbouring woods and talked to him about Æschylus, Cervantes, Shakespeare, quoting long passages to his enthusiastic listener. Karl, who reached maturity at a very early age, became a devoted reader of the new romantic literature: the taste he acquired during these impressionable years remained unaltered until his death. He was in later life fond of recalling his evenings with Westphalen, during what seemed to him to have been the happiest period his life. He had been treated by a man much older than himself on terms of equality at a time when he was in particular need of sympathy and encouragement; when one tactless or insulting act might have left a lasting mark, he was received with rare courtesy and hospitality. His doctorate thesis contains a glowing dedication to Westphalen, full of gratitude and admiration. In 1837 Marx asked for the hand of his daughter in marriage and obtained his consent without difficulty; an act which, owing to the great difference in their social condition, is said to have dismayed her relations. Speaking of Westphalen in later life Marx, whose judgments of men are not noted for their generosity, grew almost sentimental. Westphalen had humanized and strengthened that belief in himself and his own powers which was at all periods Marx's single most outstanding characteristic. He is one of the rare revolutionaries who were neither thwarted nor persecuted in their early life. Consequently, in spite of his abnormal sensitiveness, his *amour-propre*, his vanity, his aggressiveness and his arrogance, it is a singularly unbroken, positive and self-confident figure that faces us during forty years of illness, poverty and unceasing warfare.

He left the Trier school at the age of seventeen, and, following his father's advice, in the autumn of 1835 became a student in the faculty of law in the University of Bonn. Here he seems to have been entirely happy. He announced that he proposed to attend at least seven courses of weekly lectures, among them lectures on Homer by the celebrated Schlegel, lectures on mythology, on Latin poetry, on modern art. He lived the gay and dissipated life of the ordinary German student, played an active part in university societies, wrote Byronic poems, got into debt and on at least one occasion was arrested by the authorities for riotous behaviour. At the end of the summer term of 1836 he left Bonn and in the autumn was transferred to the University of Berlin.

This event marks a sharp crisis in his life. The

conditions under which he had lived hitherto had been comparatively provincial: Trier was a small and pretty town which had survived from an older order, untouched by the great social and economic revolution which was changing the contour of the civilized world. The growing industrial development of Cologne and Düsseldorf seemed infinitely remote; no urgent problems, social, intellectual, or material, had troubled the peace of the gentle and cultivated milieu of his father's friends, a placid preserve of the eighteenth century which had artificially survived into the nineteenth. By comparison with Trier or Bonn, Berlin was an immensely large and populous city, modern, ugly, pretentious and intensely serious, at once the centre of the Prussian bureaucracy and the meeting-place of the discontented radical intellectuals who formed the nucleus of the growing opposition to it. Marx retained all his life a considerable capacity for enjoyment and a strong if rather ponderous sense of fun, but no one could even at that time describe him as superficial or frivolous. He was sobered by the tense and tragic atmosphere in which he suddenly felt himself, and with his accustomed energy began at once to explore and criticize his new environment.

Chapter Three

THE PHILOSOPHY OF THE SPIRIT

Was Ihr den Geist der Zeiten heisst
Das ist im Grund der Herren eigner Geist
In dem die Zeiten sich bespiegeln.

(What you call the spirit of the age is in reality one's own
spirit, in which the age is mirrored.)
                                        GOETHE

La Raison a toujours raison.
(Reason is always right.)

I

THE dominant intellectual influence in the University
of Berlin, as indeed in every other German university
at this time, was the Hegelian philosophy. The soil for
this had been prepared by gradual revolt from the
beliefs and idiom of the classical period, which had
begun in the seventeenth, and was consolidated and
reduced to a system, in the eighteenth century. The
greatest and most original figure in this movement
among the Germans was Gottfried Wilhelm Leibnitz,
whose ideas were developed by his followers and interpreters into a coherent and dogmatic metaphysical
system, which, so their popularizers claimed, was
logically demonstrated by deductive steps from simple
premises, in their turn self-evident to those who could
use that infallible intellectual intuition with which all
thinking beings were endowed at birth. This rigid
intellectualism was attacked in England, where no form
of pure rationalism had ever found a congenial soil, by

the most influential philosophical writers of the age,
Locke, Hume, and, towards the end of the century,
Bentham and the philosophical radicals, who agreed in
denying the existence of any such faculty as an intellectual intuition into the real nature of things. No
faculty other than the familiar physical senses could provide that initial empirical information on which all other
knowledge of the world is ultimately founded. Since all
information was conveyed by the senses, reason could
not be an independent source of knowledge, and was
responsible only for arranging, classifying and fitting
together such information, and drawing deductions
from it, operating upon material obtained without its
aid. In France the rationalist position was attacked by
the materialist school in the eighteenth century, and
while Voltaire and Diderot, Condillac and Helvétius
freely acknowledged their debt to the free-thinking
English, they constructed an independent system,
whose influence on European thought and action continues into the present day. Some did not go to the
length of denying the existence of knowledge obtained
otherwise than by senses, but claimed that, though such
innate knowledge itself exists and indeed reveals valuable truth, it provides no evidence for the propositions
whose incontrovertible truth the older rationalists
claimed to know, a fact which careful and scrupulous
mental self-examination would show to any open-
minded man not blinded by religious dogmatism or
political and ethical prejudice. Too many abuses had
been defended by appeals to authority, or to a special
intuition: thus Aristotle, appealing to reason for confirmation, had maintained that men were by nature
unequal, that some were naturally slaves, others free
men; and so too the Bible, which taught that truth

could be revealed by supernatural means, afforded texts which could be invoked to prove that man was naturally vicious and must be curbed—theses used by reactionary governments to support the existing state of political, social, even moral inequality. But experience and reason, properly understood, combined to show the precise opposite of this. Arguments could be produced to show beyond any possible doubt that man was naturally good, that reason existed equally in all sentient beings, that the cause of all oppression and suffering was human ignorance, produced partly by social and material conditions which arose in the course of natural historical development, partly through the deliberate suppression of the truth by ambitious tyrants and unscrupulous priests, most frequently by the interplay of both. These evil influences could, by the action of an enlightened and benevolent government, be exposed and thereby annihilated. Left to themselves, with no obstacles to obscure their vision and to frustrate their endeavours, men would pursue virtue and knowledge; justice and equality would take the place of authority and privilege, competition would yield to co-operation, happiness and wisdom would become universal possessions. The central tenet of this semi-empirical rationalism consisted in boundless faith in the power of reason to explain and improve the world, all previous failure to do so being explained as ultimately caused by ignorance of the laws which regulate the behaviour of nature, animate and inanimate. Misery is the complex result of ignorance, not only of nature but of the laws of social behaviour. To abolish it one measure is both necessary and sufficient: the employment of reason, and of reason alone, in the conduct of human affairs.

This task is admittedly far from easy; men have lived too long in a world of intellectual darkness to be able to move unblinkered in the sudden light of day. A process of gradual education in scientific principles is therefore required: the growth of reason and the advance of truth, while in themselves sufficient to conquer the forces of prejudice and ignorance, cannot occur until enlightened men are found ready to devote their whole lives to the task of educating the vast benighted mass of mankind.

But here a new obstacle arises: whereas the original cause of human misery, neglect of reason and intellectual indolence, was not deliberately brought about, there exists in our own day, and has existed for many centuries past, a class of men who, perceiving that their own power rests on ignorance, which blinds men to injustice, promote unreason by every invention and means in their power. By nature all men are rational, and all rational beings have equal rights before the natural law of reason. But the ruling classes, the princes, the nobility, the priests, the generals, realize only too well that the spread of reason would soon open the eyes of the peoples of the world to the colossal fraud by which in the name of such hollow figments as the sanctity of the church, the divine right of kings, the claims of national pride or possession, they are forced to give up their natural claims and labour uncomplainingly for the maintenance of a small class which has no shadow of right to exact such privilege. It is therefore in the direct personal interest of the upper class in the social hierarchy to thwart the growth of natural knowledge, wherever it threatens to expose the arbitrary character of its authority, and in its place to substitute a dogmatic code, a set of unintelligible mysteries expressed in high-sounding phrases, with which to confuse the feeble intelligences of their unhappy subjects, and to keep them in a state of blind obedience. Even though some among the ruling class may be genuinely self-deceived and come themselves to believe in their own inventions, some there must be who know that only by systematic deception, propped up by the occasional use of violence, could so corrupt and unnatural an order be preserved. It is the first duty, therefore, of an enlightened ruler to break the power of the privileged classes, and to allow natural reason, with which all men are endowed, to re-assert itself; and since reason can never be opposed to reason, all private and public conflict is ultimately due to some irrational element, to some simple failure to perceive how an harmonious adjustment of apparently opposed interests may be made.

Reason is always right. To every question there is only one true answer which with sufficient assiduity can be infallibly discovered, and this applies no less to questions of ethics or politics, of personal and social life, than to the problems of physics or mathematics. Once found, the putting of a solution into practice is a matter of mere technical skill; but the traditional enemies of progress must first be removed, and men taught the importance of acting in all questions on the advice of disinterested scientific experts, whose knowledge is founded on reason and experience. Once this has been achieved, the path is clear to the millennium.

But the influence of environment is no less important than that of education. If you should wish to foretell the course of a man's life, you must consider such factors as the character of the region in which he lives, its climate, the fertility of its soil, its distance from the sea, in addition to his physical characteristics and the nature of his daily occupation. Man is an object in nature, and the human soul, like material substance, is swayed by no supernatural influences and possesses no occult properties; its entire behaviour can be adequately accounted for by means of ordinary verifiable physical hypotheses. The French materialist, La Mettrie, developed this empiricism to, and indeed, beyond its fullest limits in a celebrated treatise, *L'Homme Machine*, which caused an immense scandal at the time of its publication. His views were an extreme example of opinions shared in various degrees by the editors of the Encyclopaedia, Diderot and d'Alembert, by Holbach, Helvétius and Condillac, who, whatever their other differences, were agreed that man's principal difference from the plants and lower animals lies in his possession of self-consciousness, in his awareness of certain of his own processes, in his capacity to use reason and imagination, to conceive ideal purposes and to attach moral values to any activity or characteristic in accordance with its tendency to forward or retard the ends which he desires to realize. A serious difficulty which this view involved was that of reconciling the existence of free-will on the one hand, with complete determination by character and environment on the other; this was only the old conflict between free-will and divine foreknowledge in a new form, with Nature in the place of God. Spinoza had observed that if a stone falling through the air could think, it might well imagine that it had freely chosen its own path, being unaware of the external causes, such as the aim and force of the thrower and the natural medium, which determine its fall. Similarly, it is only his ignorance of the natural causes of his behaviour that makes man suppose himself in some fashion different from the falling stone: omniscience would quickly dispel this vain delusion, even though the feeling of freedom to which it gives rise may itself persist, but without its power to deceive. So far as extreme empiricism is concerned, this deterministic doctrine can be made consistent with optimistic rationalism: but it carries the very opposite implications with regard to the possibility of reform in human affairs. For if men are made saints or criminals solely by the movement of matter in space, the educators are as rigorously determined to act as they do, as are those whom it is their duty to educate. Everything occurs as it does as a result of unalterable processes of nature; and no improvement can be effected by the free decisions of individuals, however wise, however benevolent and powerful, since they, no more than any other entity, can alter natural necessity. This celebrated crux, stripped of its old theological dress, emerged even more sharply in its secular form; it presented equal difficulties to both sides, but became obscured by the larger issues at stake. Atheists, sceptics, deists, materialists, rationalists, democrats, utilitarians, belonged to one camp; theists, metaphysicians, supporters and apologists of the existing order to the other. The rift between enlightenment and clericalism was so great, and the war between them so savage, that doctrinal difficulties within each camp passed relatively unperceived.

It is the first of the two theses that became the fundamental doctrine of the radical intellectuals of the next century. They emphasized the natural or potential goodness of men unspoiled by a bad or ignorant government, and emphasized the immense power of rational education to rescue the masses of mankind from their present miseries, to institute a juster and more scientific distribution of the world's goods, and so to lead humanity to the limits of attainable happiness. The imagination of the eighteenth century was dominated by the phenomenal strides made by the mathematical and physical sciences during the previous century, and it was a natural step to apply the method which had proved so successful in the hands of Kepler and Galileo, Descartes and Newton, to the interpretation of social phenomena and to the conduct of life. If any single individual may be said to have created this movement, it is unquestionably Voltaire. If he was not its originator, he was its greatest and most celebrated protagonist for more than half a century. His books, his pamphlets, his mere existence did incomparably more to destroy the hold of absolutism and catholicism than any other single factor. Nor did his death arrest his influence. Freedom of thought was identified with his name: its battles were fought under his banner: no popular revolution from his day to ours has failed to draw some of its most effective weapons from that inexhaustible armoury, which two centuries have not rendered obsolete. But if Voltaire created the religion of man, Rousseau was the greatest of its prophets. His conception of man was different from, and ultimately subversive of, that of the radicals of his time. But he was a preacher and a propagandist of genius, and gave the movement a new eloquence and ardour, a richer, vaguer and more emotionally charged language, which profoundly affected the writers and thinkers of the nineteenth century. Indeed, he may be said to have created the new modes of thought and of feeling, a new idiom, which glorified the will at the expense of reason and observation, an idiom which was adopted as their natural vehicle of self-expression by the artistic and social rebels of the nineteenth century—that first generation of romantics who sought inspiration in the revolutionary history and literature of France and in her name raised the banner of revolt in their own backward lands.

One of the most fervent and certainly the most effective among the advocates of this doctrine in England was the idealistic Welsh manufacturer, Robert Owen. His creed was summarized in the sentence inscribed at the head of his journal, *The New Moral World*: 'Any general character, from the best to the worst, from the most ignorant to the most enlightened, may be given to any community, even the world at large, by the application of proper means, which means are to a great extent at the command and under the control of those who have influence in the affairs of men.' He had triumphantly demonstrated the truth of his theory by establishing model conditions in his own cotton mills in New Lanark, limiting working hours, and creating provision for health and a savings fund. By this means he increased the productivity of his factory and raised immensely the standard of living of his workers, and, what was even more impressive to the outside world, trebled his own fortune. New Lanark became a centre of pilgrimage for kings and statesmen, and, as the first successful experiment in peaceful co-operation between labour and capital, had a considerable influence on the history both of socialism and of the working class. His later attempts at practical reform were less successful. Owen, who died in deep old age in the middle of the nineteenth century, was the last survivor of the classical period of rationalism, and, his faith unshaken by repeated failures, until the end of his life he believed in the omnipotence of education and the perfectibility of man.

The effect which the victorious advance of the new ideas had upon European culture is hardly inferior to that of the Italian Renaissance. The spirit of free inquiry into personal and social issues, of calling all things in question before the bar of reason, acquired a formal discipline and an increasingly enthusiastic acceptance in wide sections of society. Intellectual courage, and even more, intellectual disinterestedness, became fashionable virtues. Voltaire and Rousseau were universally fêted and admired, Hume was magnificently received in Paris. This was the climate of opinion which formed the character of the revolutionaries of 1789, a severe and heroic generation which yields to none in the clearness and purity of its convictions, in the robust and unsentimental intelligence of its humanism—above all, in its absolute moral and intellectual integrity securely founded upon the belief that the truth must ultimately prevail because it is the truth, a belief which years of exile and persecution did not weaken. Their moral and political ideas, and their words of praise and blame have long since become the common inheritance of democrats of all shades and hues; socialists and liberals, utilitarians and believers in natural rights, speak their language and profess their faith, not so naïvely, nor with such utter confidence, but also less eloquently, less simply and less convincingly.

The counter-attack came with the turn of the century. It grew on German soil, but soon spread over the whole civilized world, checking the advance of empiricism from the west, and putting in its place a profoundly metaphysical view of nature and of the individual, the effects of which are with us still, and growing in strength and influence. Germany, spiritually and materially crippled by the Thirty Years' War, was, at the end of a long and sterile period, beginning to produce once more, towards the end of the eighteenth century, an indigenous culture of its own, influenced by, but fundamentally independent of, the French models which all Europe vied in imitating. Both in philosophy and in criticism the Germans began to produce works which were in form clumsier, but more ardently felt, more vehemently expressed, and more disquieting than anything written in France outside the pages of Rousseau. The French saw in this rich disarray only a grotesque travesty of their own limpid style and exquisite symmetry. The Napoleonic Wars, which added to the Germans' wounded intellectual pride the humiliation of military defeat, made the rift still wider, and the strong patriotic reaction which began during these wars and rose to a wild flood of national feeling after Napoleon's defeat, became identified with the new, so-called romantic philosophy of Kant's successors, Fichte, Schelling and the brothers Schlegel; their philosophy thus obtained national significance and became broadened and popularized into an almost official German faith. Against the scientific empiricism of the French and English, the Germans put forward the metaphysical historicism of Herder and of Hegel. Founded on the criticism of its rivals, it offered a bold alternative, the influence of which altered the history of civilization in Europe and left an ineffaceable impression on its imagination and modes of feeling.

The classical philosophers of the eighteenth century had asked: Given that man is neither more nor less than an object in nature, what are the laws which govern his behaviour? If it is possible to discover by empirical means under what conditions bodies fall, planets rotate, trees grow, ice turns into water and water into steam, it must be no less possible to find out under what conditions men are caused to eat, drink, sleep, love, hate, fight one another, constitute themselves into families, tribes, nations, and again into monarchies, oligarchies, democracies. Until this is discovered by a Newton or a Galileo, no true science of society can come into being. This radical empiricism appeared to Hegel to embody a scientific dogmatism even more disastrous than the theology which it wished to displace, involving the fallacy that only methods successful in the natural sciences can be valid in every other department of experience. He was sceptical of the new method even in the case of the material world, and quite groundlessly suspected natural scientists of arbitrarily selecting the phenomena which they discussed and no less arbitrarily limiting themselves to certain kinds of reasoning alone. But if his attitude towards empiricism in the sciences was unsympathetic, he spoke with even greater violence of its ruinous consequences when applied to the subject of human history. If history were written in accordance with scientific rules, as the word was understood by Voltaire or by Hume, a monstrous distortion of the facts would result, which the best historians of the immediate past, Hume and Voltaire themselves, indeed, when they were not theorizing, but writing history, had unconsciously avoided by a sure historical intuition. He conceived of history as it were in two dimensions: the horizontal, in which the phenomena of different spheres of activity, occurring among different peoples belonging to the same stage of development, are seen to be broadly interconnected in some unitary pattern, which gives each period its own individual, 'organic', recognizably unique character; and the vertical dimension, in which the same cross-section of events is viewed as part of a temporal succession, as a necessary stage in a developing process, in some sense contained and generated by its predecessor in time, which is itself seen already to embody, although in a less developed state, those very tendencies and forces whose full emergence makes the later age that which it ultimately comes to be. Hence every age, if it is to be genuinely understood, must be considered in relation not to the past alone; for it contains within its womb seeds of the future, foreshadowing the contour of what is yet to come; and this relation, no historian, however scrupulous, however anxious to avoid straying beyond the bare evidence of the facts, can allow himself to ignore. Only so can he represent in correct perspective the elements which compose the period with which he is dealing, distinguishing the significant from the trivial, the central determining characteristics of an age from those accidental, adventitious elements in it, which might have happened anywhere and at any time, and consequently have no deep roots in its particular past, and no appreciable effects on its particular future.

The conception of growth by which the acorn is said potentially to contain the oak, and to be adequately described only in terms of such development, is a doctrine as old as Aristotle and indeed older. In the Renaissance it came to light once more and was developed to its fullest extent by Leibnitz, who taught that the universe was compounded of a plurality of independent individual substances, each of which is to be conceived as composed of its own whole past and its own whole future. Nothing was accidental; no object could be described as the empiricists wished to describe it, namely as a succession of continuous or discontinuous phenomena or states, connected at best only by the external relation of mechanical causation. The only true definition of an object was in terms which explained why it necessarily developed as it did in terms of its individual history, as a growing entity, each stage of which was, in the words of Leibnitz ,'*chargé du passé et gros de l'avenir*'. Leibnitz made no detailed attempt to apply this metaphysical doctrine to historical events, and yet that seemed to Hegel to be the sphere to which it best applied. For unless some relation other than that of scientific causation be postulated, history becomes nothing but a succession of externally related events. To explain is to give rational grounds and not merely antecedents. To explain a sequence of episodes, in this sense, is to attribute them to a rationally intelligible process—the purposive activity of a being or beings—God or men. Without this the events remain unexplained, groundless, 'meaningless'. A mechanical model may enable one to predict or control the behaviour of objects, but it cannot give a rational explanation; and unexplained events in human lives do not add up to human history. Similarly it seems impossible to account for, even to express, the individual character of a particular personality or period of history, the individual essence, that is the purpose, embodied in a particular work of art or of science, by the methods of natural science, since its characteristics may indeed closely resemble something that has occurred before or after it, but whose totality is in some sense unique, and exists only once; this cannot therefore be accounted for by a scientific method whose successful application depends upon the occurrence of the precise opposite, namely, that the same phenomenon, the same combination of characteristics should repeat itself, regularly recur, again and again.

The new method was first triumphantly applied by Herder, who, perhaps under the influence of the growth of national and racial self-consciousness in Europe, and moved by hatred of the levelling cosmopolitanism and universalism of the prevailing French philosophy, applied the concept of organic development (as it later came to be called) to the history of entire cultures and nations as well as to individuals. Indeed, he represented it as more fundamental in the case of the former, since individuals can only properly be viewed as occurring at a particular stage of the development of a society, which, in the thought and action of its greatest sons, reaches its most typical conscious expression. He immersed himself therefore in the study of national German culture, its barbarian beginnings, its philology and archaeology, its medieval history and institutions, its traditional folklore and antiquities. From this he attempted to draw a portrait of the living German spirit, as a formative force responsible for the unity of its own peculiar national development, which cannot be accounted for by the crudely mechanistic relation of more loose before-and-afterness in time, by which the uniform, monotonous cycle of caused events, the rotation of the crops or the yearly revolutions of the earth, which are not history because they are not ways of human expression, may perhaps be satisfactorily explained.

Hegel developed this theme still more widely and ambitiously. He taught that the explanation offered by French materialism afforded at best a hypothesis for explaining static but not dynamic phenomena, differences but not change. Given such and such material conditions, it may be possible to predict that the men born in them will develop certain characteristics, directly attributable to physical causes and to the education given to them by previous generations, themselves affected by the same conditions. But even if this is so, how much does it really tell us? The physical conditions of Italy, for example, were much the same in the first as they were in the eighth and fifteenth centuries, and yet the ancient Romans differ widely from their Italian descendants, and the men of the Renaissance showed certain marked characteristics, which Italy in decline was losing or had totally lost. It cannot therefore be these relatively invariant conditions, with which alone the natural scientists are competent to deal, that are responsible for the phenomena of historical change, for progress and reaction, glory and decline. Some dynamic factor must be postulated to account both for change as such, and for the single, ultimately perceptible, direction which it has. Such change is plainly not repetitive: each age inherits something new from its predecessors, in virtue of which it differs from every preceding period; the principle of development excludes the principle of uniform repetition which is the foundation on which Galileo and Newton built. If history possesses laws, these laws must evidently be different in kind from what has passed for the only possible pattern of scientific law so far: and since everything that is, persists, and has some history, the laws of history must for that very reason be identical with the laws of being of everything that exists.

Where is this principle of historical motion to be found? It is a confession of human failure, of the defeat of reason, to declare that this dynamic principle is that notorious object of the empiricist's gibes, a mysterious and occult power which men cannot expect ever to detect. It would be strange if that which governs our normal lives were not more present to us, a more familiar experience than any other that we have. For we need only take our own lives as the microcosm and pattern of the universe. We speak familiarly enough of the character, of the temper, of the purposes, motives, aims of a man as accounting for his acts and thoughts, not as some independent thing totally distinct from them, but as the common pattern which they express: and the better we know a man, the better we may be said to understand his moral and mental activity in its relation to the external world. Hegel transferred the concept of the personal character of the individual, the aims, logic, quality of his thoughts, his choices—his whole activity and experience as it unfolds itself throughout a man's life—to the case of entire cultures and nations. He referred to it variously as the Idea or Spirit, distinguished stages in its evolution, and pronounced it to be the motive, dynamic factor in the development of specific peoples and civilizations and so of the sentient universe as a whole. Further, he taught that the error of all previous thinkers was to assume the relative independence of different spheres of activity at a given period, of the wars of an age from its art, of its philosophy from its daily life. We should not naturally make this separation in the case of individuals; in the case of those with whom we are best acquainted, we half-unconsciously correlate all their acts as different manifestations of a single stream of purposive activity; we are affected by innumerable data drawn from this or that phase of their careers, which collectively influence our mental portrait of them. This, according to Hegel, applies no less to our concept of a culture or of a particular historical period. The historians of the past have tended to write monographs on the history of this or that city or campaign, of the acts of this or that king or commander, as if they could be represented in isolation from the other phenomena of their time. But just as the acts of an individual are the acts of the whole individual, so the cultural phenomena of an age, the particular pattern of events that constitute it, are expressions of the whole age and of its whole personality, of a particular phase of the questing human spirit, seeking to understand, to control whatever it meets: that is, in its pursuit of complete self mastery, which is Hegel's notion of freedom. This unitary character of an age, as expressing an integral outlook, is a fact which we do indeed tacitly recognize in speaking of a phenomenon as typical of the ancient rather than the modern world, or of an age of chaos rather than of one of settled peace.

This should be recognized explicitly. In writing, for instance, the history of seventeenth-century music, and in considering the rise of a particular form of polyphony, it is at least relevant to ask whether a development of a similar pattern may not be observed in the history of science at this time; whether, for example, the discovery of the differential calculus simultaneously by Newton and Leibnitz was purely accidental, or due to certain general characteristics of that particular stage of European culture, which produced a not dissimilar genius in Bach and Leibnitz, in Milton and Poussin. Obsession with rigorous scientific method might lead historians, as it does natural scientists, to build walls between their fields of inquiry and treat each branch of human activity as functioning in relative isolation, like so many parallel streams which cross rarely and without effect; whereas, if the historian is fully to realize his task, to rise above the chronicler and the antiquary, he must endeavour to paint a portrait of an age in movement, to collect that which is characteristic, distinguish between its component elements, between the old and the new, the fruitful and the sterile, the dying survivals of a previous age and the heralds of the future, born before their time.

This command to look for the most vivid expression of the universal in the particular, the concrete, the differentiated, the individual, to emulate the art and the realism of the biographer and the painter rather than the photographer and the statistician, is the peculiar legacy of German historicism. If history is a science, it must not be beguiled by the false analogy of physics or mathematics, which, looking for the widest obtainable, least varying, common characteristics, deliberately ignores what specifically belongs to only one time and one place, seeking to be as general, as abstract, as formal, as possible. The historian, on the contrary, must see and describe phenomena in their fullest context, against the background of the past and the foreground of the future, as being organically related to all other phenomena which spring from the same cultural impulse.

The effect of this doctrine, at once a symptom and a cause of a change of outlook on the part of an entire generation, and now grown so familiar, is inestimably great. Our habit of attaching particular characteristics to particular periods and places and of seeing individuals or their acts as typical of nations or of times: of bestowing almost a personality of their own, active causal properties, upon certain periods or peoples, or even on widely felt social attitudes, in virtue of which acts are described as expressions of the spirit of the Renaissance or of the French Revolution, of German romanticism or of the Victorian Age, springs from this new historicism of outlook. Hegel's specifically logical doctrines and his view of the method of the natural sciences were barren and their effects were on the whole disastrous. His true importance lies in his influence in the field of social and historical studies, in the creation of new disciplines, which consist in the history and criticism of human institutions, viewed as great collective quasi-personalities, which possess a life and character of their own, and cannot be described purely in terms of the individuals who compose them. This revolution in thought has bred irrational and dangerous myths—the treatment of state, race, history, epoch, for example, as super-persons exercising influence; but its effect on humane studies has been very fruitful. It was largely due to its influence that there came into existence a new school of German historians whose work made all writers who explained events as the outcome of the character or intentions, the personal defeat of triumph of this or that king or statesman, seem naïve and unscientific.

If history is the development of the impersonal Spirit, which Hegel did not identify solely with the human spirit, since he denied any essential divorce between mind and matter, it is necessary to rewrite it as the history of the achievement of the Spirit. The horizon suddenly seemed immensely widened. Legal history ceased to be a remote and special preserve of archaeologists and antiquaries and was transformed into Historical Jurisprudence, wherein contemporary legal institutions were interpreted as an orderly evolution from Roman or earlier law, embodying the Spirit of the Law in itself, of society in its legal aspect, inter-woven with political, religious, social aspects of its life.

Henceforth the history of art and the history of philosophy began to be treated as complementary and indispensable elements in the general history of culture: facts previously thought trivial or sordid were accorded sudden importance as being hitherto un-explored domains of the activity of the Spirit—the history of trade, of dress, of fashion, of language, of folklore, of the useful arts were seen to be essential elements in the complete, 'organic', institutional history of mankind.

There was one respect, however, in which Hegel sharply diverged from the Leibnitzian conception of development as a smooth progression of an essence gradually unfolding itself from potentiality into actu-ality. He insisted on the reality and necessity of con-flicts and wars and revolutions, of the tragic waste and destruction in the world. He declared (following Fichte) that every process is one of necessary tension between incompatible forces each straining against the other, and by this mutual conflict advancing their own development. This struggle is sometimes concealed and sometimes open, and can be traced in all provinces of conscious activity as the clash between so many rival physical, moral and intellectual attitudes and move-ments, each of which claims to provide total solutions and breeds new crises by its very onesidedness; it grows in strength and sharpness until it turns into an open conflict, which culminates in a final collision, the violence of which destroys all the contenders. This is the point at which the hitherto continuous development is broken, a sudden leap takes place to a new level, whereupon the tension between a new cluster of forces begins once more. Certain among those leaps, those, namely, which occur on a sufficiently large and noticeable scale, are termed political revolutions. But, on a more trivial scale, they occur in every sphere of activity, in the arts and sciences, in the growth of physical organisms studied by biologists and in the atomic processes studied by chemists, and finally in ordinary argument between two opponents, when, in the conflict between two partial falsehoods, new truth is discovered, itself only relative, itself assaulted by a counter-truth, the destruction of each by the other leading once more to a new level in which the antagonistic elements are transfigured into a new organic whole—a process which continues without end. He called this process dialectical. The notion of struggle and of tension provides precisely that dynamic principle which is required to account for movement in history. Thought is reality become conscious of itself, and its processes are the processes of nature in their clearest form. The principle of perpetual absorption and resolution (*Aufhebung*) in an ever higher unity occurs in nature as in discursive thought, and demonstrates that its processes are not purposeless, like the mechanical movements postulated by materialism, but possess an inner logic and lead in the direction of greater and greater perfection. Each major transition is marked by a large-scale revolutionary leap, such as, for example, the rise of Christianity, the destruction of Rome by the barbarians, or the great French Revolutions and the new Napoleonic world. In each case the Spirit or universal idea advances a step nearer to complete realization, humanity is carried a stage forward, but never strictly in the direction anticipated by any of the movements engaged in the preliminary conflict, that side being more deeply and more irrationally disappointed, which believed most firmly in its own peculiar ability to shape the world by its own efforts.

The new methods of research and interpretation which had suddenly been revealed produced a startling, and even intoxicating, effect on enlightened German society, and to a lesser extent on its cultural dependencies, the Universities of St. Petersburg and Moscow. Hegelianism became the official creed of almost every man with intellectual pretensions: the new ideas were applied in every sphere of thought and action with an uncontrolled enthusiasm which an age more sceptical of ideas may find it difficult to conceive. Academic studies were entirely transformed: Hegelian logic, Hegelian jurisprudence, Hegelian ethics and aesthetics, Hegelian theology, Hegelian philology, Hegelian historiography, surrounded the student of the humanities wherever he turned. Berlin, where Hegel's last years were spent, was the headquarters of the movement. Patriotism and political and social reaction lifted their heads again. The advance of the doctrine that all men were brothers, that national, racial and social differences were the artificial products of defective education, was arrested by the Idealist counter-thesis, according to which such differences, for all their apparent irrationality, express the peculiar historical role of a given race or nation, and are grounded in some metaphysical necessity. They are needed for the development of the Idea, of which the nation is a partial incarnation, and they cannot be made to vanish overnight by the mere application of reason by individual reformers. Reform must spring from historically prepared soil; otherwise it is doomed to failure, condemned in advance by the forces of history which move in accordance with their own logic in their own time and at their own pace. To demand freedom from these forces and seek to rise above them, is to wish to escape from one's logically necessary historical position, from the society of which one is an integral part, from the complex of relations, public and private, by which every man is made to be what he is, which are the man, are what he is; to wish an escape from this is to wish to lose one's proper nature, a self-contradictory demand, which could be made only by one who does not understand what he is demanding, one whose idea of personal liberty is childishly subjective.

True freedom consists in self-mastery, escape from external control. This can be achieved only by discovering what one is and can become; that is, by the discovery of the laws to which, in the particular time and place in which one lives, one is necessarily subject, and by the attempt to make actual those potentialities of one's rational, that is, one's law-abiding nature, the realization of which advances the individual and thereby the society to which he 'organically' belongs, and which expresses itself in him and in others like him. When a man in the name of some subjective ideal attempts to destroy a tradition instead of modifying it, he opposes the laws of history, attempts the impossible, and thereby reveals his own irrationality. Such behaviour is condemned, not only because it is necessarily doomed to failure and therefore futile: for situations might occur in which it might be thought to be nobler to perish quixotically than to survive. It is condemned because it is irrational, since the laws of history which it opposes are the laws of the Spirit, which is the ultimate substance of which everything is composed, and are therefore necessarily rational; indeed if they were not, they would not be amenable to human explanation.

The Spirit approaches its perfection by gradually attaining to greater self-consciousness with every generation: and the highest point of its development is reached in those who at any time see themselves most clearly in their relation to their universe, that is, in the profoundest thinkers of every epoch. The thinkers for him include the artists and the philosophers, the scientists and the poets, all those sensitive and inquiring spirits who are more acutely and more profoundly conscious than the rest of their society of the stage of development which humanity has reached, of what has been gained in their time and partly by their effort.

The history of philosophy is the history of the growth of this self-awareness, in which the spirit becomes conscious of its own activity; and the history of humanity, on this view, is itself nothing other than the story of the progress of the spirit in the process of its growing self-awareness. All history is thus the history of thought, that is, the history of philosophy; which is identical with the philosophy of history, since that is but a name for the awareness of this awareness. The celebrated Hegelian epigram, 'the philosophy of history is the history of philosophy', is, for anyone who accepts the Hegelian metaphysic, not an obscure paradox, but a platitude, quaintly expressed—with the important and peculiar corollary that all true progress is progress of the spirit—most conscious in men, not conscious in nature—since that is the substance of which all else is compounded. Hence the sole method by which those who have the good of society at heart can improve society, is to develop in themselves and in others the power of analysing themselves and their environment, an activity later called criticism, the growth of which is identical with human progress. From this it follows that changes involving physical violence and bloodshed are due solely to the recalcitrance of brute matter, which, as Leibnitz had taught, is itself but spirit, at a lower, less conscious level. The revolutions instituted by Socrates, or by Jesus, or by Newton, was therefore far more truly a revolution than events which are commonly so called, although they occurred without battles; all genuine conquest, all true victory is literally, and not in metaphor, gained always in the realm of the Spirit. Thus the French Revolution was in effect over when the philosophers had transformed men's consciousness of their world before the guillotine began its work.

This doctrine appeared to solve at last the great problem which vexed men's minds throughout the early nineteenth century; the question to which all its leading political theories are so many different answers. The French Revolution had been made in order to secure liberty, equality and fraternity among men; it was the greatest attempt in modern history to embody a wholly new revolutionary ideology in concrete institutions by the violent and successful seizure of power on the part of the ideologues themselves: it failed and its purpose, the establishment of human freedom and equality, was as remote from realization as ever. What answer was there to those who, bitterly disillusioned, fell into cynical apathy, proclaiming the impotence of good over evil, of truth over falsehood, affirming the total inability of mankind to improve its lot by its own efforts? To this problem, with which the social thought of the period of political reaction in Europe is preoccupied, Hegel provided an impressive solution by his doctrine of the inevitable character of the historical process, which involves the predestined

failure of any attempt to deflect it or hasten it by violence,—a sign of fanaticism, that is, one-sided exaggeration of some one aspect of the dialectic—a view
directly opposed to the rival technological hypotheses
then being advanced in France by Saint-Simon and
Fourier. The problem of social freedom, and of the
causes of the failure to attain it, is therefore quite naturally the central subject of all Marx's early writings.
His approach to the problem and his solution are in
spirit purely Hegelian. His early training and his natural
instincts inclined him towards empiricism: and the
modes of thought which belong to this outlook are
sometimes visible below the metaphysical structure
beneath which they are for the most part concealed.
This emerges most clearly in his passion for exposing
irrationalism and myths in every shape and guise; often
in his argument he uses the methods and examples of
eighteen-century materialism: but the form in which it
is expressed, and the theses it is designed to prove are
wholly Hegelian; the ascent of humanity which by its
labours transforms itself and the external nature to
which it is organically related by subjugating all it
deals with to rational control. He was converted to the
new outlook in his youth and for many years, despite his
vehement attack on the idealist metaphysic, remained
a convinced, consistent and admiring follower of the
great philosopher.

Chapter Four

THE YOUNG HEGELIANS

They [the Germans] will never rise. They would sooner die than rebel . . . perhaps even a German, when he has been driven to absolute despair, will cease to argue, but it needs a colossal amount of unspeakable oppression, insult, injustice and suffering to reduce him to that state.

MICHAEL BAKUNIN

THE years which Marx spent as a student in the University of Berlin were a period of profound depression among the radical intelligentsia of Germany. In 1840 a new king from whom much was expected had ascended the throne of Prussia. Before his accession he had spoken more than once of a natural alliance of patriotism, democratic principles and the monarchy; he had spoken of granting a new constitution; ecstatic references began to appear in the liberal press to Don Carlos and The Crowned Romantic. These promises came to less than nothing. The new monarch was no less reactionary, but more astute and less bound by routine than his father; the methods of suppression employed by his police were more imaginative and more efficient than those in use in the days of Frederick William III; otherwise his accession made little difference. There was no sign of reform, either political or social; the July Revolution in France, which was greeted with immense enthusiasm by German radicals, had merely caused Metternich to set up a central commission to suppress dangerous thought in all German lands, a measure zealously welcomed by the Prussian landowning gentry, whose continued power paralysed every effort towards freedom. The governing class did all that was in its power to obstruct—it could not entirely suppress—the growing class of industrialists and bankers, which, even in backward and docile Prussia, began to show unmistakable signs of restiveness. Open expression in the Press or at public meetings was unthinkable: the official censorship was far too efficient and too ubiquitous; the Diet was packed with the King's supporters; the gathering feeling of resentment against the landlords and officials, increased by the growing sense of its own strength on the part of the middle class, finally poured itself out in the traditional form of German self-expression, in a flood of words, a philosophy of opposition.

If orthodox Hegelianism was a reactionary movement, and the answer of wounded German nationalism to the French attempt to impose its new principle of universal reason upon the world, the secession of its younger members represents an effort to find some progressive interpretation for the formulae of natural development, to detach the Hegelian philosophy from its preoccupation with past history and to identify it with the future, to adapt it to the new social and economic factors which were everywhere coming into being. Both camps, the right and the left, the old, and as they came to be called, the Young Hegelians, based themselves on their founder's famous dictum according to which the real is the rational and the rational is the real; and both agreed that this was to be interpreted as meaning that the true explanation of any phenomenon was equivalent to the demonstration of its logical— which to them meant historical or metaphysical (for all these were in some sense identical)—necessity, which was tantamount to its rational justification. Nothing could be both evil and necessary, for whatever is real is justified because it is real: *Die Weltgeschichte ist das Weltgericht* (world history is world justice). So much was accepted by both sides. The schism arose over the relative emphasis to be placed on the crucial terms, 'rational' and 'real'.

The conservatives, proclaiming that only the real was rational, declared that the measure of rationality was actuality, or capacity for survival—that the stage reached by social or personal institutions, as they existed at any given moment, was the sufficient measure of their excellence. So, for example, Germanic (i.e. western) culture, as Hegel did in fact declare, was a higher, and probably ultimate, synthesis of its pre-decessors, Oriental and Graeco-Roman cultures. From which it followed (for some of the master's disciples) that the last stage being of necessity the best, the most perfect political framework yet attained by men consisted in the highest incarnation to date of western values—the modern i.e. the Prussian State. To wish to alter this State or subvert it was morally bad, because directed against the rational will embodied in it, and in any case futile, because set against a decision already made by history. This is a form of argument with which Marxism later familiarized the world.

The radicals, stressing the converse, protested that only the rational was real. The actual, they insisted, is often full of inconsistencies, anachronisms and blind unreason: it cannot therefore be regarded in any genuine, that is metaphysical, sense, as being real. Basing themselves on numerous texts from Hegel, they pointed out that the master recognized that mere occur-rence in space or time was by no means equivalent to being real: the existent might well be a tissue of chaotic institutions, each frustrating the purposes of the other, and so from the metaphysical point of view contradictory and therefore utterly illusory. Degree of reality was measured by their tendency to form a rational whole, which may necessitate a radical transformation of given institutions in accordance with the dictates of reason. These are best known to those who have emancipated themselves from the tyranny of the merely actual, and have revealed its inadequacy to its historic role, as deduced from a correct interpretation of the character and direction of the past and present. This critical activity directed against the social institutions of his time, on the part of the individual who lifts himself above them, is the noblest function of man; the more enlightened the critic, the more searching his criticism, the more rapid will be the actual progress towards the real. For, as Hegel had indubitably said, reality is a process—a universal effort to attain to self-consciousness, and grows more perfect in the very growth of critical self-consciousness among men. Nor was there any reason to suppose that such progress must be gradual and painless. Citing again the texts undeniably to be found in Hegel, the radicals reminded their opponents that progress was the result of tension between opposites, which grew to a crisis and then burst into open revolution: then and only then did the leap into the next stage occur. These were the laws of development found equally in the obscurest processes of brute nature and in the affairs of men and societies.

The plain duty of the philosopher who carries the burdens of civilization on his shoulders is, therefore, to promote revolution by the special technical skill which he alone commands, that is by intellectual warfare.

It is his task to stir men from their indolence and torpor, to sweep away obstructive and useless institutions with the aid of his critical weapons much as the French philosophers had undermined the *ancien régime* by the power of ideas alone. No resort must be had either to physical violence or to the brute force of the masses: to appeal to the mob, which represents the lowest level of self-consciousness reached by the Spirit among men, is to make use of irrational means, which could only produce irrational consequences: a revolution of ideas will of itself bring about a revolution in practice: *Hinter die Abstraktion stellt sich die Praxis von selbst* (Behind the abstract theory practice materializes of its own accord). But since open political pamphleteering was forbidden, the opposition was driven into less direct methods of attack: the first battles against orthodoxy were fought in the field of Christian theology, whose professors had hitherto tolerated, if not encouraged, a philosophy which had shown every disposition to support the existing order. In 1835 David Friedrich Strauss published a critical life of Jesus written in accordance with the new Hegelian method, in which he rejected some portions of the Gospels as pure invention, regarding others as representing not facts, but semi-mythological beliefs, entertained in the early Christian communities, as a stage in the self-awareness of mankind, and treating the whole subject as an exercise in the critical treatment of a historically important but unreliable text. His book caused an immediate storm not in orthodox circles only, but also among the Young Hegelians, whose most prominent representative, Bruno Bauer, then a lecturer in theology in the University of Berlin, published several attacks upon it from the point of view of an even extremer Hegelian atheism, wholly denying the historical existence of Jesus, and attempting to explain the Gospels as works of pure fiction, as the literary expression of the 'ideology' prevalent in its time, as the highest point reached at this period by the development of the Absolute Idea. The Prussian authorities were not in general interested in sectarian controversies among philosophers, but in this quarrel both sides appeared to hold views subversive of religious, and so, in all likelihood, of political orthodoxy. Hegelianism, which had previously been left in peace as a harmless, and even a loyal and patriotic philosophical movement, was suddenly accused of demagogical tendencies. Hegel's greatest opponent, Schelling, by then a pious and bitterly reactionary old romantic, was brought to Berlin in order to refute these doctrines publicly, but his lectures failed to produce the desired result. The censorship was tightened, and the Young Hegelians found themselves driven into a position in which they were given the choice of capitulating completely or of moving farther to the political left than the majority wished to go. The only arena where the issue could be still raised were the universities, where a curtailed, but nevertheless genuine, academic freedom continued to survive. The University of Berlin was the chief seat of Hegelianism and it was not long before Marx became immersed in its philosophical politics.

He began his academic career as a student of the faculty of law by attending Savigny's lectures on jurisprudence and those of Gans on criminal law. Savigny, the founder and the greatest theorist of the Historical School of Jurisprudence, and a convinced and rabid anti-liberal, was by far the most distinguished defender of Prussian absolutism in the nineteenth century. He

was not a Hegelian in the strict sense, but agreed
with the school in rejecting equally the theory of
natural rights and of utilitarianism, and he interpreted
law historically, as a continuous, orderly, traditional
development springing from, and justified by, the
ideals and character of a given nation in its historical
surroundings.

Marx attended Savigny's lectures for two terms with
great regularity, and the immense erudition and power
of close historical argument for which the latter was
notable was probably Marx's first contact with the new
method of historical research, which demanded minute
knowledge of facts as a basis for broad general theses.
Savigny's chief professional opponent was the professor
of criminal law, Eduard Gans, whose effect on Marx
was more considerable. Gans was one of Hegel's
favourite disciples: he was by birth a Jew, a friend of
Heine, and like him a humanitarian radical who did not
share his teacher's low opinion of the French enlightenment. His lectures, models, it seems, both of eloquence
and of courage, were widely attended; his free criticism
of legal institutions and of methods of legislation in the
light of reason, with no trace of mysticism about the
past, affected Marx profoundly, and inspired him
with a conception of the proper purpose and method
of theoretical criticism which he never completely
lost.

Under the influence of Gans he saw in jurisprudence
the natural field for the application and verification of
every type of philosophy of history. Hegelianism at
first repelled his naturally positivist intelligence. In a
long and intimate letter to his father he described his
efforts to construct a rival system; after sleepless nights
and disordered days spent in wrestling with the

adversary, he fell ill and left Berlin to recuperate. He returned with a sense of failure and frustration, equally unable to work or to rest. His father wrote him a long paternal letter, begging him not to waste his time on barren metaphysical speculation when he had his career to think of. His words fell on deaf ears. Marx resolutely plunged into an exhaustive study of Hegel's work, read night and day, and after three weeks announced his complete conversion. He sealed it by becoming a member of the *Doktorklub* (Graduates' Club), an association of free-thinking university intellectuals, who met in beer cellars, wrote mildly seditious verse, professed violent hatred of the King, the church, the bourgeoisie, and above all argued endlessly on points of Hegelian theology. Here he met, and was soon on terms of intimacy with, the leading members of this bohemian group, the brothers Bruno, Edgar and Egbert Bauer, Köppen, one of the earliest students of Tibetan lamaism and the author of a history of the French Terror, Max Stirner who preached an ultra-individualism of his own, and other free spirits (as they called themselves).

He abandoned his legal studies, and became entirely absorbed in philosophy. No other subject seemed to him to possess sufficient contemporary significance. He planned to become a lecturer in philosophy in one of the universities, and together with Bauer to launch a violent atheistic campaign which should put an end to the timorous, half-hearted toying with dangerous doctrines to which the milder radicals confined themselves. It was to take the form of an elaborate hoax, appearing as an anonymous diatribe against Hegel by a pious Lutheran charging him with atheism and subversion of public order and morality, and armed with copious quotations from the original text. This joint work actually appeared and caused some stir; a few reviewers were genuinely taken in, but the authors were discovered, and the episode ended by Bauer's removal from his academic post. As for Marx, he frequented social and literary salons, met the celebrated Bettina von Arnim, the friend of Beethoven and Goethe, who was attracted by his audacity and wit; wrote a conventional philosophical dialogue, and composed a fragment of a Byronic tragedy and several volumes of bad verse which he dedicated to Jenny von Westphalen, to whom he had in the meantime become secretly engaged. His father, frightened by this intellectual dissipation, wrote letter after letter full of anxious and affectionate advice, begging him to think of the future and prepare himself to be a lawyer or a civil servant. His son sent soothing answers, and went on with his previous mode of life.

He was now twenty-four years of age, an amateur philosopher of no fixed occupation, respected in advanced circles for his erudition and for his powers as an ironical and bitter controversialist. He soon began to be increasingly irritated by the prevailing literary and philosophical style of his friends and allies, an extraordinary compound of pedantry and arrogance, full of obscure paradoxes and laboured epigrams, embedded in elaborate, alliterative, punning prose which can never have been intended to be fully understood. Marx was to some extent infected by it himself, particularly in his early polemical pieces; yet his prose is compact and luminous in comparison with the mass of neo-Hegelian patter which at this time was let loose upon the German public. Some years later he wrote a description of the condition of German philosophy at this time: 'According to the reports of our ideologists', he wrote, 'Germany has, during the last decade, undergone a revolution of unexampled proportions . . . a revolution in comparison with which the French Revolution was mere child's play. With unbelievable rapidity one empire was supplanted by another, one mighty hero was struck down by another still bolder and more powerful in the universal chaos. During three years, from 1842 to 1845, Germany went through a cataclysm more violent in character than anything which had happened in any previous century. All this, it is true, took place only in the region of pure thought. For we are dealing with a remarkable phenomenon—the decomposition of the Absolute Spirit.

'When the last spark of life disappeared from its body, its various constituents disintegrated and entered into new combinations and formed new substances. Dealers in philosophy, who had previously made a living by exploiting the Absolute Spirit, now threw themselves avidly on the new combinations. Each busily began to dispose of his share of it. Plainly this could not be done without competition. At first it possessed a solidly commercial, respectable character; but later when the German market became glutted, and the world market, in spite of all efforts, proved incapable of assimilating further goods, the whole business—as usual in Germany—was spoilt by mass production, lowering of quality, adulteration of raw material, forged labels, fictitious deals, financial chicanery, and a credit structure which lacked all real basis. Competition turned into an embittered struggle, which is now represented to us in glowing colours as a revolution of cosmic significance, rich in epoch-making achievements and results.'

This was written in 1846: in 1841 Marx might perhaps have continued to live in this fantastic world, himself taking part in the inflation and mass production of words and concepts, if his circumstances had not suffered a sudden catastrophic change: his father, on whom he financially depended, died, leaving a barely sufficient competence to his widow and youngest children. At the same time, the Prussian Minister of Education finally decided to condemn the Hegelian Left officially, and expelled Bauer from his post. This effectually closed the possibility of an academic career to Marx who was heavily compromised in the Bauer affair, and it forced him to look for another occupation. He did not have long to wait. Among his warmest admirers was a certain Moses Hess, a Jewish publicist from Cologne, a sincere and enthusiastic radical, who was even then far in advance of even the Hegelian Left. He had visited Paris and had there met the leading French socialist and communist writers of the day, to whose views he became a passionate convert. Hess, who was a curious blend of ardent traditional Judaism with idealist humanitarianism and Hegelian ideas, preached the primacy of economic over political factors and the impossibility of emancipating mankind without previously liberating the wage-earning proletariat. Its continued slavery, he declared, made all the efforts of intellectuals to establish a new moral world unavailing, since justice cannot exist in a society which tolerates economic inequality and exploitation. The institution of private property was the source of all evil; men could be freed only by the abolition of both private and national property, which must involve the removal of national frontiers, and the reconstitution of a new international society on a rational, collectivist economic basis. His meeting with Marx overwhelmed him: in a letter to a fellow radical he declared: 'He is the greatest, perhaps the one genuine philosopher now alive and will soon . . . draw the eyes of all Germany . . . Dr. Marx—that is my idol's name—is still very young (about twenty-four at most) and will give medieval religion and politics their *coup de grâce*. He combines the deepest philosophical seriousness with the most biting wit. Imagine Rousseau, Voltaire, Holbach, Lessing, Heine and Hegel fused into one person—I say fused, not thrown together in a heap—and you have Dr. Marx.'

Marx thought Hess's enthusiasm endearing but ridiculous, and adopted a patronizing tone which Hess was at first too amiable to resent. Hess was a disseminator of ideas, a fervent missionary rather than an original thinker, and converted more than one of his contemporaries to communism, among them a young radical named Friedrich Engels who had not at this time met Marx. Both learnt from association with him far more than either was ready to admit in later years, when they tended to treat Hess, who remained a dedicated Marxist, but added 'to it a fervent belief in Zionism, and, in any case, was not a man of action, as a harmless but tedious fool. At this time, however, Marx found him a useful ally, since Hess, who was a tireless agitator, had managed to persuade a group of liberal industrialists in the Rhineland to finance the publication of a radical journal which should contain articles on political and economic subjects directed against the economically reactionary policy of the Berlin government, and in general sympathy with the needs of the rising bourgeois class. It was issued at Cologne and was called the *Rheinische Zeitung*.

Marx was invited, and eagerly consented, to contribute regular articles to this journal; ten months later he became its chief editor. It was his first experience of practical politics: he conducted his paper with immense vigour and intolerance: his dictatorial nature asserted itself early in the venture, and his subordinates were only too glad to let him do entirely as he pleased, and write as much of the paper as he wished. From a mildly liberal paper it rapidly became a vehemently radical one: more violently hostile to the Government than any other German newspaper. It published long and scurrilous attacks on the Prussian censorship, on the Federal Diet, on the landowning class in general: its circulation rose, its fame grew throughout Germany, and the Government was at last forced to take notice of the surprising behaviour of the Rhineland bourgeoisie. The shareholders were, indeed, scarcely less surprised than the authorities, but as the number of subscribers was steadily increasing, and the economic policy pursued by the paper was scrupulously liberal, advocating free trade and the economic unification of Germany, they did not protest. The Prussian authorities, anxious not to irritate the newly annexed western provinces, also refrained from interference. Emboldened by this toleration, Marx intensified the attack and added to the discussion of general political and economic subjects two particular issues over which there was much bitter feeling in the province: the first was the distressed condition of the Moselle vine-growing peasantry; the second, the harsh law punishing thefts by the poor of decayed timber in the neighbouring forests. Marx used both these as texts for a particularly violent indictment of the government of landlords. The government, after cautiously exploring feeling in the district, decided to apply its power of censorship, and did so with increasing severity. Marx used all his ingenuity to circumvent the censors who were mostly men of limited intelligence, and he managed to publish a quantity of thinly veiled democratic and republican propaganda, which more than once led to the reprimand of the censor and his replacement by another and stricter official. The year 1842 was spent in this elaborate game, which might have continued indefinitely if Marx had not inadvertently overstepped the limit. The Russian Government throughout the nineteenth century represented the greatest embodiment of obscurantism, barbarism and oppression in Europe, the inexhaustible reservoir whence the reactionaries of other nations were able to draw strength, and consequently became the bugbear of Western liberals of all shades of opinion. It was at this time the dominant partner in the Russo-Prussian alliance, and as such was fiercely attacked by Marx in successive editorial articles: a war against the Russians seemed to him both then and later the best blow that could be struck on behalf of European liberty. The Emperor Nicholas I himself happened to come upon a copy of one of these philippics, and expressed angry surprise to the Prussian Ambassador. A severe note was sent by the Russian Chancellor upbraiding the King of Prussia for the inefficiency of his censors. The Prussian Government, anxious to appease its powerful neighbour, took immediate steps; the *Rheinische Zeitung* was suppressed without warning in April 1843, and Marx was free once more. One year had sufficed to turn him into a brilliant political journalist of notorious views, with a fully developed taste for baiting reactionary governments, a taste which his later career was to give him full opportunity of satisfying.

Meanwhile he had been working with restless energy: he had taught himself French by reading the works of the Paris socialists, Fourier, Proudhon, Dézami, Cabet and Leroux. He read recent French and German history and Machiavelli's *Prince*. For a month he was absorbed in the histories of ancient and modern art in order to gather evidence to demonstrate the basically revolutionary and disruptive character of Hegel's fundamental categories; like the young Russian radicals of this period he looked upon them as being, in Herzen's phrase, 'The algebra of revolution'. 'Too frightened to apply them openly', wrote Herzen, 'in the storm-tossed ocean of politics, the old philosopher set them afloat in the tranquil inland lake of aesthetic theory'. Marx's view of their proper interpretation had lately been affected, however, by a book which had appeared during that year—the *Theses on the Hegelian Philosophy*, by Ludwig Feuerbach, which had been sent him to be reviewed.

Feuerbach is one of those authors, not infrequently met with in the history of thought, who, mediocrities themselves, nevertheless happen to provide men of genius with the sudden spark which sets on fire the long-accumulated fuel. His own contribution to philosophy is uninspired, but he was a materialist at a time when Marx was reacting violently against the subtleties of the decadent idealism in which he had been immersed during the past five years. Feuerbach's simpler style, for all its woodenness and perhaps because of it, seemed suddenly to open a window into the real world. The neo-Hegelian scholasticism of the Bauers and their disciples suddenly seemed to him like a heavy nightmare which had but lately lifted, and the last memories of which he was determined to shake off.

Hegel had asserted that the thoughts and acts of men who belong to the same period of a given culture are determined by the working in them of an identical spirit which manifests itself in all the phenomena of the period. Feuerbach vehemently rejected this. 'What', he inquired in effect, 'is the spirit of an age or a culture other than a compendious name for the totality of the phenomena which compose it?' To say, therefore, that the phenomena were determined to be what they were by it, was to assert that they were determined by the totality of themselves,—the emptiest and silliest of tautologies. Nor was the case improved, he went on to point out, by substituting for this totality the concept of a pattern, for patterns cannot cause events; a pattern was a form, an attribute of events, which could themselves be caused only by other events. The Greek genius, the Roman character, the spirit of the Renaissance, the spirit of the French Revolution, what were these but abstractions, labels to describe compendiously a given complex of qualities and historical events, general terms invented by men for their own convenience, but in no sense real objective inhabitants of the world, capable of effecting this or that alteration in human affairs. The older view according to which it is the decision and action of individuals that is responsible for change was fundamentally less absurd: for individuals at least exist and act in a sense in which general notions and common names do not. Hegel had rightly stressed the inadequacy of this view, because it failed to give an explanation of how the total result emerged from the interplay of a colossal number of individual lives and acts, and he showed genius in looking for some single common force responsible for giving a definite direction to these wills, some general law in virtue of which history can be made a systematic account of the progress of whole societies; but in the end he failed to be rational, and ended in an obscure mysticism; for the Hegelian Idea, if it was not a tautological re-formation of what it was intended to explain, was but a disguised name for the personal God of Christianity, and so lifted the subject beyond the confines of rational discussion.

Feuerbach's next step was to declare that the motive force of history was not spiritual, but the sum of material conditions at any given time which determine the men who live in them to think and act as they do. Their material distress caused them, however, to seek solace in an immaterial ideal world of their own, albeit unconscious, invention, where as a reward for the unhappiness of their lives on earth, they would enjoy eternal bliss hereafter. All that they lack on earth— justice, harmony, order, goodness, unity, permanence— they transform into transcendent attributes of a transcendent world, which alone they call real and turn into an object of worship. If this illusion was to be exposed, it must be analysed in terms of the material maladjustments which psychologically give rise to it. Like Holbach and the author of *L'Homme Machine*, Feuerbach's hatred of transcendentalism often led him to seek for the crudest and simplest explanation in purely physical terms. *Der Mensch ist was er isst* (Man is what he eats) is his own Hegelian caricature of his doctrine: human history is the history of the decisive influence of physical environment on men in society; therefore knowledge of physical laws alone can make Man master of these forces by enabling him to adapt his life consciously to them.

His materialism, and in particular his theory that all

'ideologies' whether religious or secular are often an attempt to provide ideal compensation for real miseries, and hence at once disclose and obscure their existence, made a profound impression both on Marx and on Engels, as it later did on Lenin, who read it during his Siberian exile. Feuerbach's treatise is a badly written, unhistorical, naïve book, yet after the absurdities of the unbridled Hegelianism of the thirties, its very *terre à terre* quality must have seemed refreshingly sane. Marx, who was still a radical and an idealist at this period, was roused by it from his dogmatism. The Hegelian Idea had turned out to be a meaningless expression: Hegel now seemed to him to have built a specious edifice of words about words, and one which it was the duty of his generation, armed with the valuable Hegelian method, to replace by symbols denoting real objects in time and space, in their observable empirical relations to each other. He still believed in the efficacy of the appeal to reason and was opposed to violent revolution. He was a dissident idealist, but an idealist still: a year previously he had obtained a doctor's degree in the University of Jena, with a highly conventional thesis on the contrast between the views of Democritus and Epicurus, both viewed inevitably as precursors of Hegel. In it he defends a materialism far more nebulous than much of what he later himself condemned as typical idealist nonsense.

In April 1843, he married Jenny von Westphalen, against the wishes of the greater part of her family. This hostility only served to increase the passionate loyalty of the serious and profoundly romantic young woman: her existence had been transformed by the revelation to her of a new world by her husband, and she dedicated her whole being to his life and his work.

She loved, admired, and trusted him, and was, emotionally and intellectually, entirely dominated by him.
He leaned on her unhesitatingly in all times of crisis
and disaster, remained all his life proud of her beauty,
her birth and her intelligence. The poet Heine, who
knew them well in Paris, paid eloquent tribute to her
charm and wit. In later years, when they were reduced
to penury, she displayed great moral heroism in
preserving intact the framework of a family and a
household, which alone enabled her husband to continue his work.

Together they decided to emigrate to France. He
knew that he had an original contribution to make to
the agitating questions of the day, and that in Germany
it was impossible to speak openly on any serious topic.
Nothing held him back: his father was dead, for his
family he cared nothing. He had no fixed source of
income in Germany. His old associates of Berlin now
seemed to him to be a collection of intellectual mounte-
banks who wished to cover the poverty and confusion
of their thought by violent language and scandalous
private lives. All his life he detested two phenomena
with peculiar passion: disorderly life and histrionic
display. It seemed to him that bohemianism and
deliberate flouting of conventions was but inverted
philistinism, emphasizing and paying homage to the
very same false values by exaggerated protest against
them, and exhibiting therefore the same fundamental
vulgarity. Köppen he still respected, but he lost all personal touch with him, and formed a new and tepid
friendship with Arnold Ruge, a gifted Saxon journalist
who edited a radical periodical to which Marx had
contributed. Ruge was a pompous and irritable man, a
discontented Hegelian romantic, who after 1848

gradually became transformed into a reactionary nationalist. As a writer he had a wider outlook and surer taste than many of his fellow radicals in Germany, and appreciated the gifts of greater men, such as Marx and Bakunin, with whom he came into contact. He saw no possibility of continuing his journal on German soil in the teeth of the censor and the Saxon police, and decided to establish it in Paris. He invited Marx to assist him in editing a new journal to be called *Deutsch-Französische Jahrbücher*; Marx accepted the offer with alacrity. 'The atmosphere here is really too intolerable and asphyxiating', he wrote to Ruge in the summer of 1843. 'It is not easy to cringe even for the sake of liberty, armed with pins instead of a sword: I am tired of this hypocrisy and stupidity, of the boorishness of officials, I am tired of having to bow and scrape and invent safe and harmless phrases. In Germany there is nothing I can do . . . in Germany one can only be false to oneself.' Marx left Prussian territory in November 1843, and two days later arrived in Paris. His reputation had to some extent preceded him: at that date he was principally thought of as a liberal journalist with a mordant pen, who was forced to leave Germany because he had too violently advocated democratic reform. Two years later he was known to the police of many lands as an uncompromising revolutionary communist, a sworn enemy of reformist liberalism, the notorious leader of a subversive movement with international ramifications. The years 1843-5 are the most decisive in his life: in Paris he underwent his final intellectual transformation. At the end of it he had arrived at a clear position personally and politically: the remainder of his life was devoted to its development and practical realization.

Chapter Five

PARIS

The time will come when the sun will shine only upon a
world of free men who recognize no master except their
reason, when tyrants and slaves, priests, and their stupid
or hypocritical tools, will no longer exist except in history
or on the stage.

CONDORCET

THE social, political and artistic ferment of Paris in
the middle of the nineteenth century is a phenomenon
without parallel in European history. A remarkable
concourse of poets, painters, musicians, writers, reformers and theorists had gathered in the French
capital, which, under the comparatively tolerant
monarchy of Louis Philippe, gave asylum to exiles and
revolutionaries of many lands. Paris had long been
notable for wide intellectual hospitality; the thirties and
forties were years of profound political reaction in the
rest of Europe, and artists and thinkers in growing
numbers flocked to the circle of light from the sur-
rounding darkness, finding that in Paris they were
neither, as in Berlin, bullied into conformity by the
native civilization, nor yet, as in London, left coldly to
themselves, clustering in small isolated groups, but
rather were welcomed freely and even enthusiastically,
and given free entry into the artistic and social *salons*
which had survived the years of monarchist restoration.
The intellectual atmosphere in which these men talked
and wrote was excited and idealistic. A common mood
of passionate protest against the old order, against kings

and tyrants, against the Church and the army, above all against the uncomprehending philistine masses, slaves and oppressors, enemies to life and the rights of the free human personality, produced an exhilarating sense of emotional solidarity, which bound together this tumultuous and widely heterogeneous society. The emotions were intensely cultivated, individual feelings and beliefs were expressed in ardent phrases, revolutionary and humanitarian slogans were repeated with fervour by men who were prepared to stake their lives upon them; it was a decade during which a richer international traffic in ideas, theories, personal sentiments, was carried on than during any previous period; there were alive at this time, congregated in the same place, attracting, repelling and transforming each other, men of gifts more varied, more striking and more articulate than at any time since the Renaissance. Every year brought new exiles from the territories of the Emperor and the Czar. Italian, Polish, Hungarian, Russian, German colonies throve in the atmosphere of universal sympathy and admiration. Their members formed international communities, wrote pamphlets, addressed assemblies, entered conspiracies, but above all talked and argued ceaselessly in private houses, in the streets, in cafés, at public banquets; the mood was exalted and optimistic.

The revolutionary writers and radical politicians were at the height of their hopes and power, their ideals not yet killed, nor the revolutionary phrases tarnished by the débâcle of 1848. Such international solidarity for the cause of freedom had never before been achieved in any place: the poets and musicians, the historians and social theorists felt that they wrote not for themselves but for humanity. In 1830 a victory had been achieved over the forces of reaction. They continued to live on its fruits; the suppressed Blanquist conspiracy of 1839 had been ignored by the majority of romantic liberals as an obscure *émeute*, yet it was no isolated outbreak: for this seething and nervous artistic activity took place against a background of hectic financial and industrial progress accompanied by ruthless corruption, in which vast sudden fortunes were made and lost again in colossal bankruptcies. A government of disillusioned realists was controlled by the new ruling class of great financiers and railway magnates, large industrialists who moved in a maze of intrigue and bribery, in which shady speculators and sordid adventurers controlled the economic destiny of France. The frequent riots of the industrial workers in the south indicate a state of turbulent unrest due as much to the unscrupulous behaviour of particular employers of labour, as to the industrial revolution which was transforming the country more rapidly and more brutally, although on a far smaller scale, than in England. Acute social discontent, together with the universal recognition of the weakness and dishonesty of the Government, added to the general sense of crisis and transition, which made anything seem attainable to one who was sufficiently gifted, unscrupulous and energetic; it fed the imagination, and produced full-blooded, ambitious opportunists of the type to be found in the pages of Balzac, and in Stendhal's unfinished novel, *Lucien Leuwen*; while the laxity of the censorship, and the tolerance exercised by the July monarchy, permitted that sharp and violent form of political journalism, sometimes rising to noble eloquence, which, at a time when printed words had a greater power to move, stirred the intellect and the passions, and served still further to intensify the already electric atmosphere. The memoirs and letters left by writers, painters, musicians—Musset, Heine, Tocqueville, Delacroix, Wagner, Berlioz, Gautier, Herzen, Turgenev, Victor Hugo, George Sand, Liszt—convey something of the enchantment which surrounds those years marked by the acute and conscious sensibility and heightened vitality of a society rich in genius, by a preoccupation with self-analysis, morbid and self-dramatizing, but proud of its novelty and strength, by a sudden freedom from ancient fetters, a new sense of spaciousness, of room in which to move and to create. By 1851 this mood was dead; but a great legend had been created, which has survived to our own day, and has made Paris a symbol of revolutionary progress in its own and other's eyes.

Marx had not, however, come to Paris in quest of novel experience. He was a man of unemotional, even frigid nature, upon whom environment produced little effect, and who rather imposed his own unvarying form on any situation in which he found himself: he distrusted all enthusiasm, and in particular one which fed on gallant phrases. Unlike his compatriot, the poet Heine, or the Russian revolutionaries Herzen and Bakunin, he did not experience that sense of emancipation, when in ecstatic letters they proclaimed that they had found in this centre all that was most admirable in European civilization. He chose Paris rather than Brussels, or some town in Switzerland, for the more practical and specific reason that it seemed to him the most convenient place from which to issue the *Deutsch-Französische Jahrbücher*, which was intended as much for the non-German as for the German public. Moreover, he still wished to find an answer to the question to which he had found no satisfactory solution either in the Encyclopaedists, or in Hegel, or in Feuerbach, or in the mass of political and historical literature which he consumed so rapidly and impatiently in 1843. What ultimately was responsible for the failure of the French Revolution? What fault of theory or of practice made the Directoire, the Empire, and finally the return of the Bourbons possible? What errors must be avoided by those who half a century later still sought to discover the means of founding a free and just society? Are there no laws which govern social change, knowledge of which might have saved the great revolution? The more extreme among the Encyclopaedists had doubtless grossly over-simplified human nature by representing it as capable of being made overnight wholly rational and wholly good by enlightened education. Nor was the problem brought nearer solution by the Hegelian answer that the revolution had failed because the Absolute Idea had not then reached the appropriate stage, since no criterion of appropriateness was given, save the occurrence of the stage itself; nor did the substitution for the orthodox answer of such new formulae as human self-realization, or embodied reason, or critical criticism, appear to make it any more concrete, or indeed to add anything at all.

Faced with the question, Marx acted with characteristic thoroughness: he studied the facts, and read the historical records of the revolution itself; he also plunged headlong into the colossal mass of the polemical literature written in France upon this and kindred questions, and with characteristic thoroughness accomplished both tasks within a year. His leisure, since his schooldays, had been mainly spent in reading, but the extent of his appetite in Paris surpassed all limits. As in the days of his conversion to Hegelianism, he read night and day in a kind of frenzy, filling his notebooks with extracts and abstracts and lengthy comments on which he largely drew in his later writings. By the end of 1844 he had made himself familiar with the political and the economic doctrines of the leading French and English thinkers, examined them in the light of his own still semi-orthodox Hegelianism, and finally established his own position by sharply defining his attitude towards these two irreconcilable tendencies. He read principally the economists, beginning with Quesnay and Adam Smith, and ending with Sismondi, Ricardo, Say, Proudhon and their followers. Their lucid, cool, unsentimental style contrasted favourably with the confused emotionalism and rhetoric of the Germans; the combination of practical shrewdness and emphasis on empirical investigation with bold and ingenious general hypotheses, attracted Marx and strengthened his natural tendency to avoid all forms of romanticism and to accept only such naturalistic explanations of phenomena as could be supported by the evidence of scientific observation. The influence of French socialist writers and English economists had begun to dispel the all-enveloping mist of Hegelianism.

He compared the general condition of France with that of his native land and was impressed by its infinitely higher level of intelligence and capacity for political thought: 'in France every class is tinged with political idealism', he wrote in 1843, 'and feels itself a representative of general social needs . . . whereas in Germany, where practical life is unintelligent, and intelligence unpractical, men are driven to protest only by the material necessity, the actual chains themselves . . . but

revolutionary energy and self-confidence are not sufficient by themselves to enable a class to be the liberator
of society—it must identify another class with the
principle of oppression . . . as in France the nobility and
priesthood were identified. This dramatic tension is
absent in German society . . . there is only one class
whose wrongs are not specific but those of the whole of
society—the proletariat.' He declares that the Germans
are the most backward of western peoples. The past of
England and of France is faithfully mirrored in the
German present: the real emancipation of the Germans, who stand to more advanced peoples as the
proletariat to other classes, will necessarily entail the
emancipation of the whole of European society from
political and economic oppression.

But if he was impressed by the political realism of
those writers, he was no less shocked by their lack of
historical sense. This alone, it seemed to him, made
possible their easy and shallow eclecticism, the remarkable unconcern with which they introduced modifications and additions into their systems with no apparent
intellectual discomfort. Such tolerance seemed to him
to show a lack either of seriousness or of integrity. His
own view was at all times clear cut and violent, and was
deduced from premises which permitted of no vagueness in the conclusions; such intellectual elasticity, it
seemed to him, could be due only to insufficient grasp
of the rigorous framework of the historical process.
The assumption made by the classical economists that
the contemporary categories of political economy
held good of all times and all places struck him as
particularly absurd. As Engels later put it, 'the economists of the day speak as if Richard Coeur de Lion, had
he only known a little economics, might have saved six

centuries of bungling, by setting up free trade, instead of wasting his time on the crusades', as if all previous economic systems were so many blundering approximations to capitalism, by the standards of which they must be classified and assessed. Such inability to grasp the fact that every period can be analysed only in terms of concepts and categories peculiar to itself is responsible for Utopian socialism, for those elaborate schemes which turn out to be so many idealized versions of bourgeois or feudal society, with the 'bad' aspects left out; whereas the question to ask is not what one would wish to happen, but what history will permit to happen, which tendencies in the present are destined to develop and which to perish; one must build solely in accordance with the results of this strictly empirical method of investigation.

Nevertheless Marx found the moral taste of these writers sympathetic. They, too, distrusted innate intuitions and appeals to sentiments which transcend logic and empirical observation: they, too, saw in this the last defence of reaction and irrationalism; they, too, were passionately anti-clerical and anti-authoritarian. Many of them held oddly outmoded views about the natural harmony of all human interests, or believed in the capacity of the individual freed from the interference of states and monarchs to secure his own and others' happiness. Such views his Hegelian education had made wholly unacceptable; but in the last resort these men were the enemies of his enemies, ranged on the side of progress, fighters for the advance of reason.

II

If Marx derived from Hegel his view of the historical structure—that is, of the formal relations between

the elements of which human history consists, he
obtained his knowledge of the elements themselves
from Saint-Simon and his disciples, notably Thierry
and Mignet. Saint-Simon was a thinker of bold and
original views: he was the first writer to assert that the
development of economic relationships is the determining factor in history—and to have done this in his day
in itself constitutes a sufficient claim to immortality—
and further to analyse the historical process as a continuous conflict between economic *classes*, between
those who, at any given period, are the possessors of
the main economic resources of the community, and
those who lack this advantage and come to depend upon
the former for their subsistence. According to Saint-
Simon, the ruling class is seldom sufficiently able or disinterested to make rational use of its resources, or to
institute an order in which those most capable of
doing so apply and increase the resources of the community, and seldom flexible enough to adapt itself, and
the institutions which it controls, to the new social
conditions which its own activity brings about. It
therefore tends to pursue a short-sighted and egoistic
policy, to form a close caste, accumulate the available
wealth in a few hands, and by means of the prestige and
power thus obtained, to reduce the dispossessed majority to social and economic slavery. The unwilling subjects naturally grow restive and devote their lives to the
overthrow of the tyrannical minority; this, when the
conjunction of circumstances favours them, they
eventually succeed in doing. But they grow corrupted
by the long years of servitude, and become incapable of
conceiving ideals higher than those of their masters, so
that when they acquire power, they use it no less irrationally and unjustly than their own former oppressors;

in their turn they create a new proletariat, and so at a new level the struggle continues. Human history is the history of such conflicts: due ultimately—as Adam Smith and the eighteenth-century French philosophers would have said—to the blindness of both masters and subjects to the coincidence of the best interests of both under a rational distribution of economic resources. Instead of this the ruling classes attempt to arrest all social change, lead idle and wasteful lives, obstructing economic progress in the form of technical invention, which, if only it were properly developed, would, by creating unlimited plenty and distributing it scientifically, swiftly ensure the eternal happiness and prosperity of mankind. Saint-Simon, who was a far better historian than his encyclopaedist predecessors, took a genuinely evolutionary view of human society, and estimated past epochs, not in terms of their remoteness from the civilization of the present, but in terms of the adequacy of their institutions to the social and economic needs of their own day; with the result that his account of, for example, the Middle Ages is far more penetrating and sympathetic than that of the majority of his liberal contemporaries. He saw human progress as the inventive, creative activity of men in society, whereby they transform and enlarge their own nature and its needs and the means of satisfying them, both spiritual and material; human nature is not, as the eighteenth century had assumed, a fixed entity, but a process of growth, the direction of which is determined by its own failures and successes. Hence he noted that a social order which responded to genuine needs in its own day might tend to hamper the movements of a later time, becoming a straitjacket, the nature of which is concealed by the classes protected by its existence. The army and the Church, organic and progressive elements in the mediaeval hierarchy, are now obsolete survivals, whose functions are performed in modern society by the banker, the industrialist, and the scientist; with the consequence that priests, soldiers, *rentiers*, can survive only as idlers and social parasites, wasting the substance and holding up the advance of the new classes; they must therefore be eliminated. In their place industrious and skilful experts, chosen for their executive ability, must be placed at the head of society: the financiers, engineers, organizers of large, rigorously centralized, industrial and agricultural enterprises, must constitute the government. The Saint-Simonians taught that the laws of inheritance which lead to undeserved inequalities of wealth must be abolished: but on no account must this be extended to private property in general: every man has a right to the fruit of his own personal labour. Like the makers of the Revolution, and Fourier and Proudhon after them, Saint-Simon and his disciples firmly believed that the ownership of property furnished at the same time the sole incentive to energetic labour and the foundation of private and public morality. Bankers, company promoters, industrialists, inventors, scientists, engineers, thinkers, artists, poets, must be adequately rewarded by the State in proportion to the efficiency: once the economic life of the society is rationalized by the experts, the natural virtue of progressive human nature, the natural harmony of the interests of all, will guarantee universal justice, security, contentment and equality of opportunity for all men alike.

Saint-Simon lived at a time when the last relics of feudalism in Western Europe were finally disappearing before the advance of the bourgeois *entrepreneur* and his new mechanical devices. He had endless faith in the immense possibilities of technical invention and in its naturally beneficent effect on human society: he saw in the rising middle class able and energetic men animated by a sense of justice and disinterested altruism, hampered by the blind hostility of the land-owning aristocracy and of the Church, which trembled for their own privileges and possessions, and so became enemies to all justice and to all scientific and moral progress.

This belief was not so naïve then as it may now seem to be. As Marx was himself later to repeat, in the actual moment of struggle for social emergence, the vanguard of the rising class in a nation naturally identifies its own cause with the whole mass of the oppressed, and feels, and to a certain degree is, the disinterested champion of a new ideal, fighting at the furthest outposts of the progressive front. Saint-Simon was the most eloquent prophet of the rising bourgeoisie in its most generous and idealistic mood. He naturally set the highest value on industry, initiative, inventiveness, and the capacity for large-scale planning: but he also sharply formulated the theory of the class struggle, little knowing to what application this portion of his doctrine would one day be put. He was himself a landed nobleman of the eighteenth century, ruined by the Revolution, who had chosen to identify himself with the advancing power, and so to explain and justify the supersession of his own class.

His most celebrated ideological rival, Charles Fourier, was a commercial traveller who lived in Paris during those first decades of the new century, when the financiers and industrialists, upon whom Saint-Simon had placed all his hopes, so far from effecting social reconciliation, proceeded to sharpen class antagonism by the creation of strongly centralized monopolist concerns. By obtaining control of credit, and employing labour on an unprecedented scale, they created the possibility of mass production and mass distribution of goods, and so competed on unequal terms with the smaller traders and artisans, whom they systematically drove out of the open market, and whose children they absorbed into their factories and mines. The social effect of the Industrial Revolution in France was to create a rift and a state of permanent bitterness between the *grande* and the *petite bourgeoisie*, which dominates the history of that country from that date. Fourier, a typical representative of the ruined class, inveighs bitterly against the illusion that capitalists are the predestined saviours of society. His older contemporary, the Swiss economist Sismondi, had defended, with an immense mass of historical evidence, at a period when it required something akin to genius to have perceived it, the view that, whereas all previous class struggles occurred as a result of the scarcity of goods in the world, the discovery of new mechanical means of production would flood the world with excessive plenty, and would themselves, unless checked, lead to a class war before which previous conflicts would pale into insignificance. The necessity of marketing the ever-growing produce would lead to a continual competition between the rival capitalists, who would be forced systematically to lower wages and increase the working hours of the employees in order to secure even temporary advantage over a slower rival, which in turn would lead to a series of acute economic crises, ending in social and political chaos, due to the internecine wars between groups of capitalists. Such artificial poverty growing in direct proportion with the increase of goods, above all the monstrous trampling on those very fundamental human rights, to guarantee which the great revolution was made, could only be prevented by State intervention, which must curtail the right of accumulating capital and of the means of production. But whereas Sismondi was an early 'New Dealer', who believed in the possibility of a centrally organized, rationally and humanely conducted society, and confined himself to general recommendations, Fourier distrusted all central authority, and declared that bureaucratic tyranny is bound to develop, if the government units are too large; he proposed that the earth should be divided into small groups which he called phalansteries, each self-governing and federated into larger and larger units; all machinery, land, buildings, natural resources should be owned in common. His vision, an odd blend of eccentricity and genius, at its most apocalyptic moments remains elaborate and precise: a great central electric plant will by its power do all the mechanical labour of the phalanstery: profits should be divided between labour, capital and talent in the strict proportion 5 : 3 : 2, and its members, with no more than a few hours of daily work, will thus be free to occupy themselves with developing their intellectual, moral and artistic faculties to an extent hitherto unprecedented in history. The exposition is at times interrupted by bursts of pure fantasy, such as the prophecy of the emergence in the immediate future of a new race of beasts, not dissimilar in appearance to existing species, but more powerful and more numerous—'anti-lions', 'anti-bears', 'anti-tigers', as friendly and attached to man as their present ancestors are hostile and destructive, and doing much of his work with the skill, intelligence and foresight wanting to mere machines. The thesis is at its best at its most destructive. In the remorseless exactness of its analysis of the self-destructive effects of free competition; in the intense quality of its indignation and its sense of genuine horror at the wholesale disregard for the life and liberty of the individual by the monstrous régime of financiers and their hirelings, the judges, the soldiers, the administrators, Fourier's indictment is the prototype of all later attacks on the doctrine of the unchecked *laissez-faire*, of the great denunciations of Marx and Carlyle, of Daumier's cartoons and Büchner's plays, no less than of the communist, fascist, and Christian protests against the substitution of new forms of privilege for old, and against the enslavement of the individual by the very machinery designed to set him free.

The Revolution of 1830, which expelled Charles X and brought Louis Philippe to the throne of France, revived public interest in social questions once more. During the decade which followed, an endless succession of books and pamphlets poured from the presses, attacking the evils of the existing system, and suggesting every kind of remedy, from the mildly liberal proposals of Lamartine or Crémieux to the more radical semi-socialist demands of Marrast or Ledru Rollin, and the developed State socialism of Louis Blanc, and ending with the drastic programmes of Barbès and Blanqui, who in their journal *L'Homme Libre*, advocated a violent revolution and the abolition of private property. Fourier's disciple Considérant proclaimed the imminent collapse of the existing system of property relations; and well-known socialist writers of the time, Pecqueur, Louis Blanc, Dézami, and the most independent and original figure among

them, Proudhon, published their best known attacks on
the capitalist order between 1839 and 1842, and were
in their turn followed by a host of minor figures who
diluted and popularized their doctrines. In 1834, the
Catholic priest Lamennais published his Christian
socialist *Words of a Believer*, and in 1840 appeared the
Bible of Freedom by the Abbé Constant, fresh evidence
that even in the Church there were men unable to resist
the great popular appeal of the new revolutionary
theories.

The sensational success of Louis Blanc's *Ten Years*,
a brilliant and bitter analysis of the years 1830–40,
indicated the trend of opinion. Literary and philosophical communism began to come into fashion:
Cabet wrote a highly popular communist utopia called
Voyage to Icaria. Pierre Leroux preached a mystical
egalitarianism to the novelist George Sand, and Heine
discussed it with sympathy in his celebrated vignettes
of social and literary life in Paris during the July
monarchy.

The subsequent fate of these movements is of small
importance. The Saint-Simonists, after some years of
desultory existence, disappeared as a movement: some
of them became highly prosperous railway magnates
and *rentiers*, fulfilling at least one aspect of their
master's prophecy. The more idealistic Fourierists
founded communist settlements in the United States,
some of which, like the Oneida community, lasted for
some decades and attracted leading American thinkers
and writers; in the sixties they had considerable influence through their newspaper, the *New York Tribune*.

Marx familiarized himself with these theories, and
his own doctrines owe much to them. Saint-Simon's
vision of vast new productive possibilities, and of their

revolutionary effect on society, spoke (and speaks still) to those who see that only bold industrialization holds out the prospects of rapid advance towards power and the expansion and realization to the fullest degree of human capacities in all spheres. Fourier spoke to those who, on the contrary, saw the unbridled drive towards production heedless of distribution, as breaking natural human relations, turning men into commodities, mocking justice, twisting men's faculties into channels in which they are blocked or turned against men's most natural needs, creating a hideous, mutually destructive field of jungle warfare, curbed only by ruthless centralization, which equally crushed its victims and which the frenzied expansion of productive enterprises seemed to make inescapable. Marx accepted both theses; he attempted to show that men were progressing—through seas of mud and blood—to a society in which men's most optimistic prophecies of unchecked productivity were conjoined with social control which saved men from waste, oppression, frustration, atomization. To show this and give concrete evidence for it, he tested the social theories of the French thinkers as best he could, by acquiring knowledge of the details of recent social history from all available sources, from books, from newspapers, by meeting writers and journalists, and by spending his evenings among the small revolutionary groups composed of German journeymen which, under the influence of communist agitators, met to discuss the affairs of their scattered organization and more vaguely the possibility of a revolution in their native country. In conversation with these artisans he discovered something of the needs and hopes of a class, of which a somewhat abstract portrait had been drawn in the works of Saint-Simon and his epigoni. Marx had given little thought to the precise parts which the *petite bougeoisie* and the proletariat were to play in the advance of reason and the improvement of society. There was in addition the unstable, *déclassé* element, composed of marginal figures, members of odd trades, bohemians, unemployed soldiers, actors, intellectuals, neither masters nor slaves, independent and yet precariously situated on the very edge of the subsistence level, whose existence had hardly been recognized by social historians, still less accounted for or analysed. His interest in the economic writings of the socialists who formed the left wing of the French party of reform turned his attention to these questions. Ruge had commissioned him to write an essay for his periodical on Hegel's *Philosophy of Right*. He wrote it together with an essay on the Jewish question, early in 1844. The essay on the Jews was intended as an answer to Bruno Bauer's articles on this topic. Bauer had declared that the Jews, lagging historically one stage behind the Christians, must be baptized before they could reasonably claim full civil emancipation. Marx in his reply declared that Jews were no longer a religious or racial entity, but a purely economic one, forced into usury and other unattractive professions by the treatment they received from their neighbours; they could, therefore, be emancipated only with the emancipation of the rest of European society; to baptize them would be but to substitute one set of chains for another; to give them solely political liberties would play into the hands of those liberals who see in these all that any human being can hope, and indeed ought, to possess. It is a dull and shallow composition, but it shows Marx in a typical mood: he was determined that the sarcasms and insults, to which some of the notable

Jews of his generation, Heine, Lassalle, Disraeli, were all their lives a target, should, so far as he could effect it, never be used to plague him. Consequently he decided to kill the Jewish problem once and for all so far as he was concerned, declaring it to be an unreal subject, invented as a screen for other more pressing questions: a problem which offered no special difficulty, but arose from the general social chaos which demanded to be put in order. He was baptized a Lutheran, and was married to a Gentile: he had once been of assistance to the Jewish community in Cologne: during the greater part of his life he held himself aloof from anything remotely connected with his race, showing open hostility to all its institutions.

The critique of Hegel is more important: the doctrine which it expounds is unlike anything he had published before. In it he had begun, as he himself declared, to settle his account with the idealist philosophy. It was the beginning of a lengthy, laborious, and thorough process which, when it reached its culminating point four years later, proved to have created the foundations of a new movement and a new outlook, and to have grown into a dogmatic faith and a plan of action, which dominates the political consciousness of Europe until this day.

III

If what Marx required was a complete plan of action, based on the study of history and observation of the contemporary scene, he must have found himself singularly out of sympathy with the reformers and prophets who gathered in the *salons* and cafés of Paris at the time of his arrival. They were, indeed, more intelligent, more politically influential and more responsible than the café philosophers of Berlin, but to him they seemed either gifted visionaries like Robert Owen, reformist liberals like Ledru Rollin, or, like Mazzini, both at once, unprepared, in the last resort, to do anything for the working-class; or else they were sentimental *petit bourgeois* idealists in disguise, sheep in wolves' clothing, like Proudhon or Louis Blanc, whose ideals might indeed be at least partially attainable, but whose gradualist, unrevolutionary tactics showed them to be radically mistaken in their estimates of the enemy's strength, and who were, consequently, to be fought all the more assiduously as the internal, often quite unconscious, enemies of the Revolution. Nevertheless, he learnt much from them which he did not acknowledge, notably from Louis Blanc, whose book on the organization of labour influenced him in his view of the evolution and correct analysis of industrial society.

He was attracted far more strongly to the party, which, to distinguish itself from the moderates who came to be called socialists, adopted the name of communists. Neither was a party in the modern sense of the word: both consisted of loosely associated groups and individuals. But whereas the former consisted predominantly of intellectuals, the latter was almost entirely composed of factory workers and small artisans, the majority of whom were simple and self-educated men, exasperated by their wrongs and easily converted to the necessity of a revolutionary conspiracy to abolish privilege and private property, a doctrine preached by Babeuf's disciple Filippo Buonarotti, and inherited by the lifelong conspirator, the Jacobin-communist Blanqui, who was implicated in the abortive rising of 1839. Marx was impressed in particular by Auguste

Blanqui's organizing capacity and by the boldness and violence of his convictions; but he thought him lacking in ideas, and excessively vague as to the steps to be taken after the successful result of the *coup d'état*. He found a similarly irresponsible attitude among the other advocates of violence, the most notable of whom, the itinerant German tailor Weitling and the Russian exile Bakunin, he knew well at this time. Only one among the communists whom he met in Paris seemed to him to display a genuine understanding of the situation. This was a certain Friedrich Engels, a well-to-do young German radical, the son of a cotton manufacturer in Barmen. They met in Paris over the publication of economic articles by Engels in Marx's journal. The meeting proved decisive for both. It was the beginning of a remarkable career of friendship and collaboration which lasted during the remainder of their lives.

Engels began life as a radical poet and journalist and ended it, after the death of Marx, as the acknowledged leader of international socialism, which, in his own lifetime, had grown into a world movement. He was a man of solid and robust, but hardly creative, mind; a man of exceptional integrity and strength of character, of many varied gifts, but in particular endowed with a remarkable capacity for the rapid assimilation of knowledge. He possessed a shrewd and lucid intellect and a sense of reality, which few, if any, among his radical contemporaries could claim; himself little capable of original discovery, he had an exceptional talent for sifting, assessing and perceiving the practical applicability of the discoveries of others. His knack of writing rapidly and clearly, his unbounded loyalty and patience, made him an ideal ally and collaborator for the inhibited and difficult Marx, whose own writing was often clumsy, overcharged and obscure. In his own lifetime Engels desired no better fate than to live in the light of Marx's teaching, perceiving in him a spring of original genius which gave life and scope to his own peculiar gifts; with him he identified himself and his work, to be rewarded by sharing in his master's immortality. Before they met he had independently arrived at a position not unlike that of Marx, and in later years he understood his friend's new, only half articulated, ideas sometimes more clearly than he understood them himself, and clothed them (at times at the cost of drastic simplification) in language more attractive and intelligible to the masses than Marx's often tortuous style. Most important of all, he possessed a quality essential for permanent intercourse with a man of Marx's temperament, a total uncompetitiveness in relation to him, absence of all desire to resist the impact of that powerful personality, to preserve and retain a protected position of his own; on the contrary, he was only too eager to receive his whole intellectual sustenance from Marx unquestioningly, like a devoted pupil, and he repaid him by his sanity, his enthusiasm, his vitality, his gaiety, and finally, in the most literal sense, by supplying him with means of livelihood at moments of desperate poverty. Marx, who, like many dedicated intellectuals, was himself haunted by a perpetual feeling of insecurity, and was morbidly thin-skinned and jealously suspicious of the least signs of antagonism to his person or his doctrines, required at least one person who understood his outlook, in whom he could confide completely, on whom he could lean as heavily and as often as he wished. In Engels he found a devoted friend and intellectual ally, whose very pedestrianism restored his sense of perspective and his belief in himself and his purpose. Throughout the greater part of his life his actions were performed with the knowledge that this massive and dependable man was always at hand to support the burden in every contingency. For this he paid him with an affection, and a sense of pride in his qualities, which he gave to no one else beside his wife and children.

They met in the autumn of 1844 after Engels had sent him for publication in his periodical a sketch of a critique of the doctrines of the liberal economists. Marx had hitherto vaguely counted Engels among the Berlin intellectuals, an impression which their only previous meeting had failed to dispel. He now wrote to him at once: the result was a meeting in Paris in the course of which the similarity of their views on the fundamental issues became clear to both. Engels, who had been travelling in England and had published a vivid description of the condition of the English working class, disliked social humanitarianism of the school of Sismondi even more acutely than Marx. He provided that for which Marx had long been looking, a rich supply of concrete information about the actual state of affairs in a progressive industrial community, to act as the material evidence for the broad historical thesis which was rapidly crystallizing in Marx's mind. Engels, on the other hand, found that Marx gave him what he had been lacking, a solid framework within which to fit his facts, so as to make of them a weapon against the prevalent abstractions upon which, in his opinion, no serious revolutionary philosophy could be based. The effect which the meeting with Marx had upon him must have resembled that which it had made earlier on the more impressionable Hess. It heightened his vitality, clarified his hitherto undeveloped political ideas, provided him with a sense of definite orientation, an ordered view of society within which he could work with the assurance of the concrete, attainable character of the revolutionary goal. This, after aimless wandering in the intricate maze of the young Hegelian movement, must have resembled the beginning of a new life, and, indeed, such for him it proved to be. Their immense correspondence, which lasted for forty years, was, from the very beginning, at once familiar and businesslike in tone; neither was greatly given to introspection; both were entirely occupied with the movement which they were engaged in creating and which became for them the most solid reality of their lives. Upon this firm and reliable foundation was built a unique friendship, free from all trace of possessiveness, patronage or jealousy. Neither ever referred to it without a certain shyness and embarrassment; Engels was conscious of receiving far more than he gave, living in a mental universe created and furnished by Marx out of his own inner resources. When Marx died, he looked upon himself as its appointed guardian, jealously protecting it against all attempts at reform by the reckless and impatient younger generation of socialists.

The two years which Marx passed in Paris were the first and last occasion in his life on which he met, and was on terms of friendly intercourse with, men who were his equals, if not always in intelligence, at any rate in the originality of their personalities and their lives. After the débâcle of 1848, which broke the spirit of all but the strongest characters amongst the radicals, decimated them by death, imprisonment and transportation, and left the majority listless or disillusioned, he withdrew into an attitude of aggressive isolation, preserving contact only with men who had proved their personal loyalty to the cause with which he was identified. Henceforth Engels was his chief of staff; the rest he treated openly as rivals, subordinates.

The portrait of him that emerges from the memoirs of those who were his friends at this time, Ruge, Freiligrath, Heine, Annenkov, is that of a bold and energetic figure, a vehement, eager, contemptuous controversialist, applying to everything his cumbrous and heavy Hegelian weapons, but, in spite of the clumsiness of the mechanism, revealing an acute and powerful intellect, the quality of which even those who were most hostile to him—and there were few prominent radicals whom he had failed to wound and humiliate in some fashion—in later years acknowledged freely.

He met and formed a warm friendship with the poet Heine, by whom he may have been influenced, and in whom, despite his anti-democratic views, he saw a more genuinely revolutionary poet than Herwegh or Freiligrath, both, at this time, idolized by the radical youth of Germany. He was also on good terms with the circle of Russian liberals, some among them genuine rebels, others cultivated aristocratic dilettanti, connoisseurs of curious men and situations. One of these, a shrewd and agreeable man of letters, Paul Annenkov, for whom, Marx conceived a liking, has left a brief description of him at this time: 'Marx belonged to the type of men who are all energy, force of will and unshakeable conviction. With a thick black mop of hair on his head, with hairy hands and a crookedly buttoned frock coat, he had the air of a man used to commanding the respect of others. His movements were clumsy but self-assured. His manners defied the accepted conventions of social intercourse and were haughty and almost contemptuous. His voice was disagreeably harsh, and he spoke of men and things in the tone of one who would tolerate no contradiction, and which seemed to express his own firm conviction in his mission to sway men's minds and dictate the laws of their being.' Another, and far more remarkable member of this circle, was the celebrated Michael Bakunin, upon whom his meeting with Marx in Paris at this time had a more lasting effect. Bakunin had left Russia at approximately the same time as Marx had left Germany and for much the same reason. He was at this time an ardent 'critical' left-wing Hegelian, a passionate enemy of Czarism and all absolutist government. He had a generous, extravagant, wildly impulsive character, a rich, chaotic, unbridled imagination, a passion for the violent, the immense, the sublime, a hatred of all discipline and institutionalism, total lack of all sense of personal property, and, above all, a savage and overwhelming desire to annihilate the narrow society of his time, in which, like Gulliver in Lilliput, the human individual was suffocating for want of room to realize his faculties to their fullest and noblest extent. His friend and compatriot Alexander Herzen, who at once admired him and was intensely irritated by him, said of him in his memoirs:

'Bakunin was capable of becoming anything—an agitator, a tribune, a preacher, the head of a party, of a sect, a heresy. Put him where you like, so long as it always is the most extreme point of a movement, and he will fascinate the masses and sway the destinies of peoples . . . but in Russia this Columbus without America and without a ship, having served, greatly against his will, a year or two in the artillery, and after that another year or so in the Moscow Hegelians, longed desperately to tear himself away from a land where every form of thought was prosecuted as evil-mindedness, and independence of judgment or speech was looked upon as an insult to public morality.'

He was a marvellous mob orator, consumed with a genuine hatred of injustice and a burning sense of his mission to rouse mankind to some act of magnificent collective heroism which would set it free for ever; and he exercised a personal fascination over men, blinding them to his irresponsibility, his mendacity, his fundamental frivolity, in the overwhelming revolutionary enthusiasm which he communicated. He was not an original thinker, and easily absorbed the views of others; but he was an inspired teacher, and, although his entire creed amounted to no more than a passionate egalitarian belief in the need for destruction of all authority and the freeing of the oppressed, mingled with a short-lived Panslavism, he built on this alone a movement which lived on long after his death.

Bakunin differed from Marx as poetry differs from prose; the political connexion between them rested on inadequate foundations and was very shortlived. Their main bond was a common hatred of every form of reformism; but this hatred sprang from dissimilar roots. Gradualism to Marx was always a disguised attempt on the part of the ruling class to deflect their enemies' energy into ineffective and harmless channels: a policy which the clearer heads among them knew to be a deliberate stratagem, while the rest were themselves deceived by it, as much taken in as the radical reformers, whose fear of violence was itself a form of unconscious sabotage of their professed ends. Bakunin detested reform because he held that all frontiers limiting personal liberty were intrinsically evil, and all destructive violence, when aimed against authority, was good in itself, inasmuch as it was a fundamental form of creative self-expression. On this ground he was passionately opposed to the aim accepted by both Marx and the reformists—the replacement of the *status quo* by a centralized socialism—since, according to him, this was a new form of tyranny at once meaner and more absolute than the personal and class despotism it was intended to supplant. This attitude had as its emotional basis a temperamental dislike of ordered forms of life in normal civilized society, a discipline taken for granted in the ideas of western democrats, which to a man of his luxuriant imagination, chaotic habits and hatred of all restraints and barriers, seemed colourless, petty, oppressive and vulgar. An alliance built on an almost complete absence of common aims could not last: the orderly, rigid, unimpressionable Marx regarded Bakunin as half charlatan, half madman, and his views as absurd and barbarian. He saw in Bakunin's doctrine a development of the wild individualism for which he had already condemned Stirner: but whereas Stirner was an obscure instructor in a High School for girls, a politically ineffective intellectual, neither capable nor ambitious of stirring the masses, Bakunin was a resolute man of action, an adroit and fearless agitator, a magnificent orator, a dangerous megalomaniac consumed by a fanatical desire for power fully equal to that which possessed Marx himself.

Bakunin recorded his view of Marx many years later in one of his political tracts. 'M. Marx', he wrote, 'is by origin a Jew. He unites in himself all the qualities and defects of that gifted race. Nervous, some say, to the point of cowardice, he is immensely malicious, vain, quarrelsome, as intolerant and autocratic as Jehovah, the

God of his fathers, and like Him, insanely vindictive.

'There is no lie, no calumny, which he is not capable of using against anyone who has incurred his jealousy or his hatred; he will not stop at the basest intrigue if, in his opinion, it will serve to increase his position, his influence and his power.

'Such are his vices, but he also has many virtues. He is very clever, and widely learned. In about 1840 he was the life and soul of a very remarkable circle of radical Hegelians—Germans whose consistent cynicism left far behind even the most rabid Russian nihilists. Very few men have read so much and, it may be added, have read so intelligently, as M. Marx. . . .

'Like M. Louis Blanc, he is a fanatical authoritarian —triply so, as a Jew, a German and a Hegelian—but where the former, in place of argument, uses declamatory rhetoric, the latter, as behoves a learned and ponderous German, has embellished this principle with all the tricks and fancies of the Hegelian dialectic, and with all the wealth of his many-sided learning.'

Their mutual hatred became more and more evident as time went on: outwardly friendly relations continued uneasily for some years, saved from complete rupture by the reluctant and apprehensive respect which each had for the formidable qualities of the other. When the conflict ultimately did break out, it all but destroyed the work of both, and did incalculable damage to the cause of European socialism.

If Marx treated Bakunin as an equal, he did not conceal his contempt for the other famous agitator, Wilhelm Weitling, whom he met at this time. A tailor by profession, a wandering preacher by calling, this earnest and fearless German visionary was the last and most eloquent descendant of the men who raised peasant

revolts in the late Middle Ages, and whose modern
representatives, for the most part artisans and journeymen, congregated in secret societies dedicated to the
cause of revolution; there were branches in many
industrial towns in Germany and abroad, scattered
centres of political disaffection round which there
accumulated many victims and casualties of the social
process, men violently embittered by their wrongs and
confused as to their cause and remedy, but united by
a common sense of grievance and a common desire to
eradicate the system which had destroyed their lives.
In his books, *A Poor Sinner's Gospel* and *Guarantees of
Harmony and Freedom*, Weitling advocated a class war
of the poor against the rich, with open terrorism as its
chief weapon; and, in particular, the formation of shock
troops out of the most deeply wronged and, therefore,
the most abandoned and fearless elements in society—
the outlaws and criminals—who would fight desperately to avenge themselves on the class which had dispossessed them, for a new and uncompetitive world in
which they would begin new lives. Weitling's belief in
the solidarity of the workers of all lands, his personal
stoicism, the years which he spent in various prisons
and, above all, the fervent evangelical zeal of his
writings, attracted to him many devoted followers
among his fellow-artisans, and made him, for a brief
period, a figure of European magnitude. Marx, who
cared nothing for sincerity when it was misdirected,
and particularly disliked itinerant prophets and the
vague emotionalism with which they inevitably infected
serious revolutionary work, nevertheless conceded
Weitling's importance. His conception of an open
declaration of war against the ruling class by desperate
men who had nothing to lose and everything to gain

by the total destruction of existing society,[1] the personal
experience which lay behind his denunciations and
moved his audiences, his emphasis on the economic
realities, and attempt to penetrate the deceptive façade
of political parties and their official programmes, above
all, his practical achievement in creating the nucleus of
an international communist party, impressed Marx
profoundly. Weitling's detailed doctrines, however, he
treated with open contempt, and, justly believing him
to be muddled, hysterical and a source of confusion in
the party, set himself to expose his ignorance publicly
and lower his prestige in every possible fashion. An
account has been preserved of a meeting in Brussels in
1846 in the course of which Marx demanded to be told
Weitling's concrete proposals to the working class.
When the latter faltered, and murmured something
about the uselessness of criticism carried on in the
study, far from the suffering world, Marx struck the
table and shouted, 'Ignorance has never yet helped
anyone', after which the gathering rapidly came to
an end. They never met again.

His relation to Proudhon was altogether more com-
plicated. While still in Cologne he had read the book
which first made Proudhon's name famous, *What is
Property?*, and praised the brilliance of its style and the
courage of its author. In 1843 everything appealed to
him which revealed a revolutionary spark, anything
which sounded clear and resolute and openly advocated
the overthrow of the existing system. Soon, however,

[1] The thesis that only the ruined and the outcasts can be
relied on to carry through the revolution to its conclusion,
since others will inevitably stop short when their own interests
are threatened, influenced Bakunin decisively, and through
him the conception of a ruthless revolutionary *élite* familiar in
our own day.

he became convinced that Proudhon's approach to social problems, for all his declared admiration for Hegel, was ultimately not historical but moral, that his praise and condemnation was directly based on his own absolute ethical standards, and that he ignored altogether the historical importance of institutions and systems. From this moment he conceived him as merely another French philistine moralist, a conscious or unconscious defender of the social ideals of *petit-bourgeois* victims of industrialism, and lost all respect for his person and his doctrines.

At the time of Marx's arrival in Paris, Proudhon was at the height of his reputation. By origin a peasant from Besançon, by profession a typesetter, he was a man of narrow, obstinate, fearless, puritanical character, a typical representative of the French lower middle class which, after playing an active part in the final overthrow of the Bourbons, found it had merely succeeded in changing masters, and that the new government of bankers and large industrialists, from whom Saint-Simon had taught them to expect so much, had merely increased the tempo of their destruction.

The two forces which Proudhon conceived as fatal to social justice and the brotherhood of man were the tendency towards the accumulation of capital, which led to the continual increase of inequalities of wealth, and the tendency directly connected with it, which openly united political authority with economic control, and so was designed to secure a growth of a despotic plutocracy under the guise of free liberal institutions. The state became, according to him, an instrument designed to dispossess the majority for the benefit of a small minority, a legalized form of robbery, which systematically deprived the individual of his natural right to property by giving to the rich sole control of social legislation and financial credit, while the *petit bourgeoisie* was helplessly expropriated. Proudhon's best known book, which opens with the statement that all property is theft, has misled many as to his mature views. Early in life he held that all property was misappropriation; later, however, he taught that a minimum of property was required by every man in order to maintain his personal independence, his moral and social dignity: a system, under which this minimum was lost, under whose laws a man could, by a commercial transaction, barter it away, and so, in effect, sell himself into economic slavery to others, was a system that legalized and encouraged theft, theft of the individual's elementary rights without which he had no means of pursuing his proper ends. The principal cause of this process Proudhon perceived in the unchecked economic struggle between individuals, groups, social orders, which necessarily leads to the domination of the ablest and best organized, and of those least restrained by a sense of moral or social duty, over the mass of the community. This represents the triumph of unscrupulous force allied to tactical skill over reason and justice; but for Proudhon, who was not a determinist, there was no historical reason why this situation should continue indefinitely. Competition, the favourite panacea of enlightened thinkers of the previous century, which appeared to nineteenth-century liberals and rationalists in an almost sacred light, as the fullest and richest expression of the individual's strenuous idealism, his triumph over the blind forces of nature and over his own undisciplined appetites, was to Proudhon the greatest of all evils, the perversion of all the faculties towards the unnatural promotion of an acquisitive and, therefore, unjust society, in which the advantage of each depended on, even consisted in, his ability to outwit, defeat, or exterminate the others. The evil was identical with that attacked earlier by Rousseau, Fourier and Sismondi, but it was differently expressed and differently accounted for. Fourier was heir to both the thought and the style of the eighteenth century, and interpreted the calamities of his time as the results of the suppression of reason by deliberate conspiracy on the part of those who feared its application, the priests, the well born, the rich. Proudhon did not accept this simple view; he was to some extent affected by the historicism of his age: he knew no German, but had had Hegelianism poured into him by Bakunin and later by German exiles. Proudhon's attempt to adapt the new theory to his own doctrine with its stress on justice and human rights, led to results which to Marx seemed a crude caricature of Hegelianism.

The method, indeed, by which everything was described in the form of two antithetical conceptions, which made every statement seem at once realistic and paradoxical, suited Proudhon's talent for coining sharp and arresting phrases, his love of epigram, his desire to move, to startle and to provoke. Everything is contradictory; property is theft; to be a citizen is to be deprived of rights; capitalism is at once the despotism of the stronger over the weaker, and of the lesser over the greater; to accumulate wealth is to rob; to abolish it is to undermine the foundations of morality. Proudhon's remedy for this is the suppression of competition and the introduction in its place of a 'mutualist' co-operative system under which limited private property should be permitted, and indeed enforced, but not the accumulation of capital. Whereas competition evokes the worst and most brutal qualities in men, co-operation, besides promoting greater efficiency, moralizes and civilizes them by revealing the true end of communal life. The state may be endowed with certain centralizing functions, but its activity must be severely controlled by the associations by trades, professions, occupations, and again of consumers and producers, under which society would be organized. Organize society into a single economic whole on non-competitive 'mutualist' lines, and the antinomies will be resolved, the good remain, the evil disappear. Poverty, unemployment, the frustration of men forced into uncongenial tasks as a result of the class maladjustments of an unplanned society, will disappear, and men's better natures will find it possible to assert themselves; for there is no lack of idealism in human nature, but under the existing economic order it is rendered ineffectual or, through misdirection, dangerous. But, for Proudhon, it is useless to preach to the rich; their generous instincts became atrophied long ago. The enlightened prince dreamt of by the encyclopaedists and, at times by Saint-Simon and Fourier too, will not be born, being himself a social contradiction. Only the real victims of the system, the small farmers, the small bourgeoisie and the urban proletariat can be appealed to. They alone can alter their own condition, since, being at once the most numerous and the most indispensable members of society, they alone have the power to transform it. To them consequently Proudhon addressed himself. He warned the workers against organizing themselves politically, since by imitating the ruling class they will inevitably place themselves at its mercy. The enemy, being more experienced in

political tactics, will, by bullying, or by financial or
social bribes, succeed in luring over the weaker or less
astute among the revolutionary leaders, and so render
the movement impotent. In any case, even if the rebels
were victorious, they would, by acquiring control over,
and so preserving the political forms of authoritarian
government, give a new lease of life to the very contradiction from which they seek to escape. The workers
and small bourgeoisie must therefore seek, by purely
economic pressure, to impose their own pattern on the
rest of society; this process should be gradual and
peaceful. Again and again Proudhon declared that the
workers must on no account have recourse to coercion;
not even strikes were to be permitted, since this would
infringe upon the individual worker's right to the free
disposal of his labour.

Proudhon had the unwisdom to submit his book, *La
Philosophie de la Misère* (the Philosophy of Poverty) to
Marx for criticism. Marx read it in two days and pronounced it fallacious and superficial, but written attrac-
tively and with sufficient eloquence and sincerity to
mislead the masses. 'To leave error unrefuted', he
declared in a similar situation many years later, 'is to
encourage intellectual immorality.' For ten workers
who might go further, ninety may stop with Proudhon
and remain in darkness. He, therefore, determined to
destroy it, and with it Proudhon's reputation as a
serious thinker, once and for all.

In 1847 in answer to *La Philosophie de la Misère* there
appeared *La Misère de la Philosophie*, containing the
bitterest attack delivered by one thinker upon another
since the celebrated polemics of the Renaissance. Marx
took immense trouble to demonstrate that Proudhon
was totally incapable of abstract thought, a fact which he

vainly attempted to conceal by a use of pseudo-Hegelian terminology. Marx accused Proudhon of radically mis-understanding the Hegelian categories by naïvely interpreting the dialectical conflict as a simple struggle between good and evil, which leads to the fallacy that all that is needed is to remove the evil, and the good will remain. This is the very height of superficiality: to call this or that side of the dialectical conflict good or bad is a sign of unhistorical subjectivism out of place in serious social analysis. Both aspects are equally indispensable for the development of human society. Genuine progress is constituted not by the triumph of one side and the defeat of the other, but by the duel itself which necessarily involves the destruction of both. In so far as Proudhon continually expresses his sympathy for this or that element in the social struggle, he remains, however sincerely he may think himself convinced of the necessity and value of the struggle itself, hopelessly idealist, that is, committed to evaluating objective reality in terms of his own *petit bourgeois* desires and preferences disguised as eternal values—itself an absurdity—without reference to the stage of evolution which the class war has reached. This is followed by a laborious refutation of Proudhon's economic theory, which Marx declared to rest on a fallacious conception of the mechanism of exchange: Proudhon had mis-understood Ricardo no less profoundly than he had misunderstood Hegel, and confused the proposition that human labour determines economic value, with the proposition that it ought to do so. This leads in its turn to a total misrepresentation of the relation of money to other commodities, which vitiates his entire account of the contemporary economic organization of capitalist society. The fiercest attack is directed against Proudhon's

crypto-individualism, against his obvious hatred of
any tendency to collective organization, his nostalgic
faith in the sturdy yeoman farmer and his morality, his
belief in the indestructible value of the institution of
private property, in the sanctity of marriage and of the
family, in the absolute moral and legal authority of its
head over his wife and children; which was indeed the
basis of his own life and was responsible for his deep-
seated fear of any form of violent revolution, of anything likely to destroy the fundamental forms of life on
a small farm, in which his ancestors were born and
bred, and to which, in spite of his brave revolutionary
phrases, he remained immovably loyal. In effect Marx
accused Proudhon of wishing to remedy the immediate
wrongs of the existing system without destroying the
system itself, because, like all Frenchmen of his class,
he was emotionally attached to it; of not believing, in
spite of his veneer of Hegelianism, that the historical
process is either inevitable or irreversible, nor that it
advances by revolutionary leaps, nor yet that the
present evils are themselves as strictly necessitated by
the laws of history as the stage which will one day
supersede them. For it is only on the assumption that
such evils are accidental blemishes that it is plausible to
urge their removal by courageous legislation which
need not involve the destruction of the social forms of
which they are the historical product. In a rhetorical
passage Marx exclaims: 'It is not enough to desire the
collapse of these forms, one must know in obedience to
what laws they came into being, in order to know how
to act within the framework of these laws, since to act
against them, whether deliberately or not, in blind
ignorance of the causes and character, would be a
futile and suicidal act and would, by creating chaos,

defeat and demoralize the revolutionary class, and so prolong the existing agony.' This is the criticism which he used against all Utopians who claimed to have a new message for the working class.

Marx was convinced that Proudhon was constitutionally incapable of grasping the truth; that, despite an undoubted gift for telling phrases, he was a fundamentally stupid man; the fact that he was brave and fanatically honest, and attracted a growing body of devoted followers, only made him and his fantasies more dangerous; hence this attempt to annihilate his doctrine and his influence with one tremendous blow. His brutality over-reached itself, however, and created indignant sympathy for its victim. Proudhon's system survived this and many subsequent Marxist onslaughts, and its influence increased in the following years.

Proudhon was not primarily an original thinker. He had a gift for absorbing and crystallizing the radical ideas current in his time: he wrote well, sometimes with brilliance, and his eloquence was felt to be genuine by the masses for whom he wrote, springing from wants and ambitions which he had in common with them. The tradition of political non-participation, industrial action, and of decentralized federalism, of which he was the most eloquent advocate, survive powerfully amongst French radicals and socialists, and found support in the individualist tendency, most pronounced in Latin countries the vast majority of whose inhabitants were small farmers, artisans, professional men, living at a distance from the industrial life of great cities. Proudhonism is the direct ancestor of modern syndicalism. It was affected by Bakunin's anarchism, and, half a century later, by the doctrine that, since economic categories were the most fundamental, therefore the units out of which the anti-capitalist force must be constituted, should contain men connected not by common convictions,—a mere intellectual superstructure—but by the actual occupations which they pursue, since this is the essential factor which determines their acts. Wielding as its most formidable weapon the threat of disorganizing social life by suspending all vital services by a general strike, it became the most powerful left wing doctrine in many parts of France, Italy and Spain, wherever indeed, industrialism had not gone too far, and an agrarian-craftsmen's individualist tradition still survived. Marx, who had an infallible sense of the general direction and political flavour of a movement or a doctrine whatever its ostensible appearance, at once recognized the individualistic, and therefore for him reactionary substratum of this attitude: and consequently attacked it no less violently than avowed liberalism. *La Misère de la Philosophie* is now, like the specific views which it attacked, largely out of date. But it represents a definite stage in its author's mental development: one of the elements in his lifelong attempt to synthesize his economic, social and political views into the unified body of doctrine, capable of application to every aspect of the social situation, which came to be known as the Materialist Conception of History.

Chapter Six

HISTORICAL MATERIALISM

A certain person once took it into his head that people drown in water only because they are obsessed by the *notion* of weight. If only, he thought, they could rid themselves of this idea, by calling it, for instance, superstitious or religious, they would thereby be saved from all danger of drowning. All his life he fought against the illusion of weight, concerning whose deleterious consequences statistics continually provided him with fresh evidence. This figure is the prototype of the German revolutionary philosophers of our day.

KARL MARX *The German Ideology*

No formal exposition of historical materialism was ever published by Marx himself. It occurs in a fragmentary form in all his early work written during the years 1843–8, and is taken for granted in his later thought. He did not regard it as a new philosophical system so much as a practical method of social and historical analysis, and a basis for political strategy. Later in life he often complained of the use made of it by his followers, some of whom appeared to think that it would save them the labour of historical study by providing a kind of algebraic 'table', from which, given enough factual data, automatic answers to all historical questions could be mechanically 'read off'. In a letter which, towards the end of his life, he wrote to a Russian correspondent, he gave as an example of dissimilar development, despite analogous social conditions, the history of the Roman plebs and of the European industrial proletariat. 'When one studies these forms of evolution separately', he wrote, 'and then compares them, one can easily find the clue to this phenomenon; but one will never get there by the universal *passe partout* of particular historico-philosophical theory which explains everything because it explains nothing, the supreme virtue of which consists in being super-historical.'

The theory matured gradually in his mind. It is possible to trace its growth in the essays on the *Hegelian Philosophy of Right* and on the *Jewish Question;* in these the proletariat is for the first time identified as the agent destined to change society in the direction adumbrated by philosophy, which because it is as yet philosophy divorced from action, is itself a symptom and an expression of impotence. It is further developed in *The Holy Family*—an amalgam of polemical outbursts against the 'critical critics', i.e. the young Hegelians— principally the brothers Bauer and Stirner—interspersed with fragments on the philosophy of history, social criticism of literature, and other oddities; it is most fully stated in a volume, over six hundred pages in length, which he composed with Engels in 1846, entitled *The German Ideology*, but never published. This, for the most part, confused, verbose and ponderous work, which deals with authors and views long dead and justly forgotten, contains in its lengthy introduction the most sustained, imaginative and impressive exposition of Marx's theory of history. Like the terse and brilliant *Theses on Feuerbach* which belong to the same period, and the *Philosophico-economic Manuscripts* of 1844 with their new application of Hegel's concept of alienation, the greater part of *The German Ideology* did not see the light until the present century. It is philosophically far more interesting than any other work by Marx, and represents a submerged, but a most crucial and original stage of his thought, the total ignorance or neglect of which by his immediate followers (including the makers of the Russian Revolution) led to an exclusive emphasis on the historical and economic aspects, and defective understanding of the sociological and philosophical content, of his ideas. This fact is responsible for the clear, half positivist, half Darwinian interpretation of Marx's thought, which we owe mainly to Kautsky, Plekhanov, and above all to Engels—a tradition that has decisively influenced both the theory and the practice of the movement which goes by Marx's name.

The framework of the new theory is undeviatingly Hegelian. It recognizes that the history of humanity is a single, non-repetitive process, which obeys discoverable laws. These laws are different from the laws of physics or of chemistry, which being unhistorical, record unvarying conjunctions and successions of interconnected phenomena, whenever or wherever these may repeat themselves; they are similar rather to those of geology or botany, which embody the principles in accordance with which a process of continuous change takes place. Each moment of this process is new in the sense that it possesses new characteristics, or new combinations of known characteristics; but unique and unrepeatable though it is, it nevertheless follows from the immediately preceding state in obedience to the same laws, as this last state from its own predecessor. But whereas according to Hegel the single substance in the succession of whose states history consists, is the eternal universal Spirit, the internal conflict of whose elements is made concrete, e.g. in religious conflicts or the wars of national states, each being the embodiment of the self-realizing Idea which it requires a supersensible intuition to perceive, Marx, following

Feuerbach, denounces this as a piece of mystification on which no knowledge could be founded. For if the world were a metaphysical substance of this type; its behaviour could not be tested by the only reliable method in our power, namely, empirical observation; and an account of it could not, therefore, be verified by the methods of any science. The Hegelian can, of course, without fear of refutation, attribute anything he wishes to the unobservable activity of an impalpable world-substance, much as the believing Christian or theist attributes it to the activity of God, but only at the cost of explaining nothing, of declaring the answer to be an empirically impenetrable mystery. It is such translation of ordinary questions into less intelligible language that makes the resultant obscurity look like a genuine answer. To explain the knowable in terms of the unknowable is to take away with one hand what one affects to give with the other. Whatever value such procedure may have, it cannot be regarded as equivalent to a scientific explanation, that is, to the ordering by means of a comparatively small number of inter-related laws of the great variety of distinct, *prima facie* unconnected, phenomena. So much for orthodox Hegelianism.

But the solutions of the 'critical' schools of Bauer, Ruge, Stirner, even Feuerbach, are in principle no better. After having so mercilessly unmasked the defects of their master, they thereupon themselves proceeded to fall into worse illusions: for Bauer's 'spirit of self-criticizing criticism', Ruge's 'progressive human spirit', the 'individual self' and 'its inalienable possessions' apostrophized by Stirner, and even the human being of flesh and blood whose evolution Feuerbach traces, are all generalized abstractions no less empty, no more capable of being appealed to as something beyond the phenomena, as that which causes them, than the equally insubstantial but far more magnificent and imaginative edifice—shadowy, but rich and comprehensive, not contracted into some single bleak abstraction—offered by orthodox Hegelianism.

The only possible region in which to look for the principles of historical motion must be one that is open to scientific, that is empirical, inspection. Marx maintains that since the phenomena to be explained are those of social life, the explanation must in some sense reside in the nature of the social environment which forms the context in which men spend their lives, in that network of private and public relationships, of which the individuals form the terms, of which they are, as it were, the focal points, the meeting-places of the diverse strands whose totality Hegel called civil society. Hegel had shown his genius in perceiving that its growth was not a smooth progression, arrested by occasional setbacks, as Saint-Simon and his disciple Comte taught, but the product of continual tension between opposing forces which guarantee its unceasing forward movement: that the appearance of regular action and reaction is an illusion caused by the fact that now the first, now the second, of the conflicting tendencies makes itself most violently felt. In fact progress is discontinuous, for the tension, when it reaches the critical point, precipitates a cataclysm; the increase in quantity of intensity becomes a change of quality; rival forces working below the surface grow and accumulate and burst into the open; the impact of their encounter transforms the medium in which it occurs; as Engels was later to say, ice becomes water and water steam; slaves become serfs and serfs free men; all evolution ends in creative revolution in nature and society alike. In nature these forces are physical, chemical, biological: in society they are specifically economic and social.

What are the forces between which social conflict arises? Hegel had supposed that in the modern world they were embodied in nations which represented the development of a specific culture or incarnation of the Idea. Marx, following Saint-Simon and Fourier, and not unaffected perhaps by Sismondi's theory of crises, replied that these forces were predominantly socio-economic. 'I was led,' he wrote twelve years later, 'to the conclusion that legal relations, as well as forms of state, could neither be understood, by themselves, nor explained by the so-called general progress of the human mind, but that they are rooted in the material conditions of life which Hegel calls . . . civil society. The anatomy of civil society is to be sought in political economy.' The conflict is always a clash between economically determined classes, a class being defined as a group of persons in a society, whose lives are determined by their position in the productive arrangements which determine the structure of that society. The status of an individual is determined by the part which he plays in the process of social production, and this in its turn directly depends upon the character of the productive forces and their degree of development at any given stage. Men act as they do in virtue of the economic relationships in which they in fact stand to the other members of their society, whether they are aware of them or not. The most powerful of these relationships is based, as Saint-Simon had taught, on ownership of the means of subsistence: the most pressing of all needs is the need for survival.

The central Hegelian conception remains at the basis

of Marx's thought, although it is transposed into semi-empirical terms. History is not the succession of the effects on men of external environment or of their own unalterable constitutions, or even the interplay between these factors, as earlier materialists had supposed. Its essence is the struggle of men to realize their full human potentialities; and, since they are members of the natural kingdom (for there is nothing that transcends it), man's effort to realize himself fully is a striving to escape from being the plaything of forces that seem at once mysterious, arbitrary and irresistible, that is, to attain to the mastery of them and of himself, which is freedom. Man attains this subjugation of his world not by increase in knowledge obtained by contemplation (as Aristotle had supposed)—but by activity— by labour—the conscious moulding by men of their environment and of each other—the first and most essential form of the unity of will and thought and deed, of theory and practice. Labour transforms man's world, and himself too, in the course of its activity. Some needs are more basic than others—bare survival comes before more sophisticated wants. But man differs from the animals, with whom he shares essential physical needs, in possessing the gift of invention: thereby he alters his own nature and its needs, and escapes from the repetitive cycles of the animals, who remain unaltered, and therefore have no history. The history of society is the history of the inventive labours that alter man, alter his desires, habits, outlook, relationships both to other men and to physical nature, with which man is in perpetual physical and technological metabolism. Among man's inventions—conscious or unconscious—is the division of labour, which arises in primitive society, and vastly increases his productivity, creating wealth beyond his immediate needs. This accumulation in its turn creates the possibility of leisure, and so of culture; but thereby also of the use of this accumulation—of these hoarded necessities of life—as a means of withholding benefits from others, and so of bullying them, of forcing them to work for the accumulators of wealth, of coercing, exploiting and thereby of dividing men into classes—into controllers and controlled. This last is perhaps the most far-reaching of all the unintended results of invention, technical advance and the resultant accumulation of goods. History is the interaction between the lives of the actors, the men engaged in the struggle for attaining self-direction, and the consequences of their activities. Such consequences may be intended or unintended; their effect upon men or their natural environment may be foreseen or not; they may occur in the material sphere, or that of thought or feeling, or at unconscious levels of the lives of men; they may affect only individuals, or take the form of social institutions or movements; but the complex web can only be understood and controlled if the central dynamic factor responsible for the direction of the process is grasped. Hegel, who was the first to see the matter in so illuminating and profound a fashion, found it in the Spirit seeking to understand itself in the institutions—abstract or concrete—which it has itself, at various levels of consciousness, created. Marx accepted this cosmic scheme, but charged Hegel and his disciples with giving a mythical account of the ultimate forces at work—a myth which is itself one of the unintended results of the process of externalizing the work of human personality —that is, of giving the appearance of independent, external objects or forces to what are, in fact, products of human labour. Hegel had spoken of the march of the Objective Spirit. Marx identified the chief factor with human beings seeking intelligible human ends—no single goal such as pleasure, or knowledge, or security, or salvation beyond the grave, but the harmonious realization of all human powers in accordance with the principles of reason. In the course of this quest men transform themselves, so that the predicaments and the values which determine and explain the conduct of one group or generation or civilization to others who seek to understand it, themselves in the course of their partial realization, and inevitable partial frustration, alter the predicaments and values of their successors. This constant self-transformation which is the heart of all work and all creation, renders absurd the very notion of fixed timeless principles, unalterable universal goals, and an eternal human predicament. The character of the age with which he was dealing was, in Marx's view, determined by class war; the behaviour and outlook of individuals and societies was decisively determined by this factor; this was the central historical truth about a culture which rests on accumulation, and on the battles for the control of this accumulation, by those who strive to realize their powers, often in useless or self-destructive ways. But precisely because it was a historical predicament, it was not eternal. It had been different in the past; and it would not last for ever. Indeed the symptoms of its approaching doom were all too visible for those who had eyes to see. The only permanent factor in the history of man was man himself, intelligible only in terms of the struggle which he had not chosen—the struggle which was part of his essence (this is the metaphysical moment in Marx), the struggle to master nature and organize his productive powers in a rational pattern in which inner and outer harmony consisted. Work in the cosmic vision of Marx is what cosmic love had been for Dante—that which makes men and their relationships what they are, given the relatively invariant factors of the external world into which they are born; its distortion by the division of labour and the class war leads to degradation, dehumanization, perverted human relationships and conscious and unconscious falsification of vision to maintain this, and conceal the real state of affairs. When this has been understood, and action, which is the concrete expression of such understanding, takes place, labour, instead of dividing and enslaving men, unites and liberates them: gives full expression to their creative capacities in the only form in which men's nature is wholly itself, wholly free—common endeavour, social co-operation in a common, rationally understood and accepted, cause. Yet Marx's attitude towards this most central of all the concepts of his system remained curiously uncertain: sometimes he speaks of labour as identical with that free creation which is the fullest expression of untrammelled human nature, the essence of happiness, emancipation, frictionless rational harmony within and between men. At other times he contrasts labour with leisure: and promises that with the abolition of the class war labour will be reduced to a minimum, but not wholly eliminated; it will not be the labour of exploited slaves but of free men building their own socialized lives in accordance with self-imposed rules freely adopted, but it will still be a disagreeable necessity imposed on man by the inescapable fact of physical nature, which it is mere Utopianism to hope to conjure away. There is no final reconciliation between these views. The same ambivalence affects his

combination of evolutionary determinism and libertar-
ian belief in free choice; both are present in his thought,
a 'dialectical' contradiction that remained to plague his
followers, and divide them, especially in Eastern
Europe, where it vitally affected their revolutionary
practice.

Feuerbach for all his crudeness correctly saw that
men eat before they reason. The satisfaction of this
need can be fully guaranteed only by the control of the
means of material production, that is of human strength
and skill, of natural resources, of land and water, tools,
machine, slaves. There is a natural scarcity of these in
the beginning, and they are therefore the objects of
violent competition, all the more so because those who
secure them are able to control the lives and actions of
those who lack them; until they, in their turn, lose
possession of them to their subjects, who, grown powerful and cunning in their service, oust them and enslave
them, only to be ousted and expropriated by others in
their turn. Immense institutions, social, political,
cultural, have been created to conserve their possessions in the hands of their present owners, not indeed
by deliberate policy, but arising unconsciously out of
the general attitude to life of those who govern a given
society. But whereas Hegel had declared that what
gave its specific character to any given society was its
national character, the nation (in the large sense of
civilization) being for him the embodiment of a given
stage in the development of the world Spirit, for Marx
it was the system of economic relations which governed
the society in question. In a celebrated passage, written
a decade after he had arrived at this position, he summarized this view as follows:

'In the social production which men carry on, they

enter into definite relations that are indispensable and independent of their will; these relations of production correspond to a definite stage of development of their material powers of production. The sum total of these productive relations constitutes the economic structure of society—the real foundation on which rise legal and political superstructures, and to which correspond definite forms of social consciousness. The mode of production in material life determines the general character of the social, political and spiritual processes of life. It is not the consciousness of men that determines their existence, but on the contrary their social existence determines their consciousness. At a certain stage of their development, the material forces of production in society come into conflict with the existing relations of production, or—what is but a legal expression for the same thing—with the property relations within which they had been at work before. From forms of development of the productive forces these relations turn into their fetters. Then comes the period of social revolution. With the change of the economic foundation the whole vast superstructure is sooner or later entirely transformed. But in considering such transformations the distinction should always be made between the material transformation of the economic conditions of production, which can be determined with the precision of natural science, and the legal, political, religious, aesthetic or philosophical—in short the ideological forms in which men become conscious of the conflict and fight it out.

'Just as it would be impossible to arrive at a correct judgment about an individual by noting only his own view of himself, so it is impossible to judge whole revolutionary periods by the conscious way in which

they see themselves, for, on the contrary, such consciousness must be explained as the product of the
contradictions of material life, of the conflict between
the forces of social production and their actual relations. No social order ever disappears before all the
productive forces, for which there is room in it, have
developed, and the new higher relations of production
never appear before the conditions of their existence
have matured in the womb of the old society . . . the
problem itself only arises when the material conditions
necessary for its solution already exist or are at least in
the process of formation.'[1]

Bourgeois society is the last form which these an-
tagonisms take. After its disappearance the conflict will
disappear for ever. The pre-historic period will be
completed, the history of the free human individual
will at last begin.

The single operative cause which makes one people
different from another, one set of institutions and
beliefs opposed to another is, so Marx now came to
believe, the economic environment in which it is set,
the relationship of the ruling class of possessors to
those whom they exploit, arising from the specific
quality of the tension which persists between them. The
fundamental spring of action in the life of a man, he
believed, all the more powerful for not being recognized
by him, is his relationship to the alignment of classes
in the economic struggle: the factor, knowledge of
which would enable anyone to predict successfully a
given individual's basic line of behaviour, is that
individual's actual social position—whether he is
outside or inside the ruling class, whether his personal
welfare depends on its success or failure, whether he is

---

[1] *Critique of Political Economy*, trans. by N. I. Stone, pp. 11 ff.

placed in a position to which the preservation of the existing order is or is not essential. Once this is known, his particular personal motives and emotions become comparatively irrelevant to the investigation: he may be egoistic or altruistic, generous or mean, clever or stupid, ambitious or modest. His natural qualities will be harnessed by his circumstances to operate in a similar way, whatever their natural tendency. Indeed, it is misleading to speak of 'a natural tendency' or an unalterable 'human nature'. Tendencies may be classified either in accordance with the subjective feeling which they engender (and this is, for purposes of scientific prediction, unimportant), or in accordance with their actual aims, which are socially conditioned. One behaves before one starts to reflect on the reasons for, or the justification of, one's behaviour; the majority of the members of a community will act in a similar fashion, whatever the subjective motives for which they will appear to themselves to be acting as they do. This is obscured by the fact that in the attempt to convince themselves that their acts are determined by reason or by moral or religious beliefs, men have tended to construct elaborate rationalizations of their behaviour. Nor are these rationalizations wholly powerless to affect action, for, growing into great institutions like moral codes or religious organizations, they often linger on long after the social pressures, to explain away which they arose, have disappeared. Thus these great organized illusions themselves become part of the objective social situation, part of the external world which modifies the behaviour of individuals, functioning in the same way as the invariant factors, climate, soil, physical organism, already function in their interplay with social institutions.

Marx's immediate successors tended to minimize
Hegel's influence upon him; but his vision of the world
crumbles and yields only isolated insights if, in the
effort to represent him as he conceived himself, as the
rigorous, severely factual social scientist, the great
unifying metaphysical pattern in terms of which he
thought, is left out or whittled down.

Like Hegel, Marx treats history as a phenomenology.
In Hegel the Phenomenology of the human Spirit is
an attempt to show, often with great insight and
ingenuity, an objective order in the development of
human consciousness and in the succession of civilizations that are its concrete embodiment. Influenced by a
notion prominent in the Renaissance, but reaching back
into earlier mystical cosmogony, Hegel looked upon the
development of mankind as being similar to that of an
individual human being. Just as in the case of a man a
particular capacity, or outlook, or way of dealing with
reality cannot come into being until and unless other
capacities have first become developed—that is, indeed
the essence of the notion of growth or education in the
case of individuals—so races, nations, churches,
cultures, succeed each other in a fixed order, determined by the growth of the collective faculties of mankind expressed in arts, sciences, civilization as a whole.
Pascal had perhaps meant something of this kind when
he spoke of humanity as a single, centuries old, being,
growing from generation to generation. For Hegel all
change is due to the movement of the dialectic, that
works by a constant logical criticism, that is, struggle
against, and final self-destruction of, ways of thought
and constructions of reason and feeling, which, in their
day, had embodied the highest point reached by the
ceaseless growth (which for Hegel is the logical self-

realization) of the human spirit; but which, embodied in rules or institutions, and erroneously taken as final and absolute by a given society or outlook, thereby become obstacles to progress, dying survivals of a logically 'transcended' stage, which by their very one-sidedness breed logical antinomies and contradictions by which they are exposed and destroyed. Marx accepted this vision of history as a battlefield of incarnate ideas, but translated it into social terms, of the struggle between classes. For him alienation (for that is what Hegel, following Rousseau and Luther and an earlier Christian tradition, called the perpetual self-divorce of men from unity with nature, with each other, with God, which the struggle of thesis against antithesis entailed) is intrinsic to the social process, indeed it is the heart of history itself. Alienation occurs when the results of men's acts contradict their true purposes, when their official values, or the parts they play, misrepresent their real motives and needs and goals. This is the case, for example, when something that men have made to respond to human needs—say, a system of laws, or the rules of musical composition—acquires an independent status of its own, and is seen by men, not as something created by them to satisfy a common social want (which may have disappeared long ago), but as an objective law or institution, possesssing eternal, impersonal authority in its own right, like the unalterable laws of Nature as conceived by scientists and ordinary men, like God for a believer. For Marx the capitalist system is precisely this kind of entity, a vast instrument brought into being by intelligible material demands—a progressive improvement and broadening of life in its own day, that generates its own intellectual, moral, religious beliefs, values and forms of life.

Whether those who hold them know it or not, such values are simply props to the power of the class whose interests the capitalist system embodies; nevertheless, they come to be viewed by all sections of society as being objectively valid for all mankind. Thus, for example, industry and the capitalist mode of exchange are not timelessly valid institutions, but were generated by the mounting resistance by peasants and artisans to dependence on the blind forces of nature.

Production is a social activity. Any form of co-operative work or division of labour, whatever its origin, creates common purposes and common interests, not analysable as the mere sum of the individual aims or interests of the human beings involved. If, as in capitalist society, the product of the total social labour of a society is appropriated by one section of that society for its own exclusive benefit, as a result of an inexorable historical development, which Engels, more explicitly (and much more mechanistically) than Marx, attempts to describe, this goes against the 'natural' needs of human society—against what men, whose essence, as human beings, is to be social, require, in order to develop freely and fully. According to Marx, those who accumulate in their hands the means of production, and thereby also its fruits in the form of capital, forcibly deprive the majority of the producers—the workers—of what they create, and so split society into exploiter and exploited; the interests of these classes are opposed; the survival of each class depends on its ability to defeat its adversary in a continuous war, a war that determines all the institutions of that society. In the course of the struggle technological skills develop, the culture of the class-divided society becomes more complex, its products grow richer, and the needs which its material progress breeds, more varied and more artificial—that is, more 'unnatural'. Unnatural, because both the warring classes became 'alienated', by the conflict which has replaced co-operation for common ends, from the integrated common life and creation, that, according to this theory, is demanded by the social nature of man. The monopoly of the means of production held by a particular group of men, enables it to bind its will on the others and to force them to perform tasks alien to their own needs. Thereby the unity of society is destroyed, and the lives of both classes become distorted. The majority—that is the propertyless proletarians—now work for the benefit, and according to the ideas, of others: the fruit of their labour as well as its instruments are taken from them; their mode of existence, their ideas and ideals correspond not to their own real predicament—that of human beings artificially prevented from living as their natures demand (namely as members of a unified society, capable of understanding the reasons for doing what they do, and of enjoying the fruits of their own united, free and rational activity)— but to the aims of their oppressors. Hence their lives rest on a lie. Their masters, in their turn, whether consciously or not, cannot help seeking to justify their own parasitic existence as being both natural and desirable. In the course of this, they generate ideas, values, laws, habits of life, institutions (a complex which Marx sometimes calls 'ideology'), the whole purpose of which is to prop up, explain away, defend, their own privileged, unnatural, and therefore unjustified, status and power. Such ideologies—national, religious, economic and so on, are forms of collective self-deception; the victims of the ruling class—the proletarians and peasants—imbibe it as part of their

normal education, of the general outlook of the unnatural society, and so come to look upon it, and accept
it, as objective, just, necessary, a part of the natural
order which pseudo-sciences are then created to
explain. This, as Roussseau had taught, serves to
deepen still further human error, conflict and frustration.

The symptom of alienation is the attribution of
ultimate authority, either to some impersonal power
—say the laws of supply and demand—from which the
rationality of capitalism is represented as being logically
deducible, or to imaginary persons or forces—divinities,
churches, the mystical person of the king or priest, or
interims of other oppressive myths, whereby men, torn
from a 'natural' mode of life (which alone makes it
possible for entire societies to perceive the truth and
live harmoniously), seek to explain their unnatural
condition to themselves. If men are ever to liberate
themselves, they must be taught to see through these
myths. The most oppressive of all, in Marx's demono-
ology, is bourgeois economic science, which represents
the movement of commodities or of money—indeed the
process of production, consumption and distribution—
as an impersonal process, similar to those of nature, an
unalterable pattern of objective forces before which men
can only bow, and which it would be insane to resist.[1]
Deterministic as he was, Marx nevertheless resolved to
show that the conception of any given economic or
social structure as a part of an unchangeable world

[1] For Marx classical economics or sociology are so many
attempts to disguise transient and largely irrational arrangements, as the operations of universally valid laws: a quasi
religion of which bourgeois economists, sociologists, philosophers and so forth, are the priests.

order was an illusion brought about by man's alienation from the form of life natural to him—a typical 'mystification', the effects of purely human activities masquerading as a law of nature; it would be removed only by other, equally human activities—the application of 'demystifying' reason and science; ultimately by the weapon of revolution. These liberating activities may themselves be determined by objective laws, but what these laws determine is the activity of human thought and will (particularly of men taken in the mass), and not merely the movement of material bodies, obeying their own inexorable patterns that are independent of human decisions and actions. If, as Marx believed, human choices can affect the course of events, then, even if these choices are themselves ultimately determined and scientifically predictable, such a situation is one in which Hegelians and Marxists think it legitimate to call men free, since such choices are not, like the rest of nature, mechanically determined. Indeed this kind of determination, according to thinkers of this school, is all that can be meant by the notion of freedom.

Because the historical function of capitalism, and its relation to the interests of a specific class, are not understood, it comes not to enrich but to crush and distort the lives of millions of workers, and indeed of their oppressors too, like everything that is not rationally grasped and therefore blindly worshipped as a fetish. Money for instance, which played a progressive role in the days of liberation from barter, has now become an absolute object of pursuit and reverence for its own sake, brutalizing and destroying man whom it was invented to liberate. Men are divorced from the products of their own toil and from the instruments with which they produce: these acquire a life and status of their own, and in the name of their survival or improvement, living human beings are oppressed and treated like cattle or saleable commodities. This is true of all institutions, churches, economic systems, forms of government, moral codes, which, through being misunderstood, become more powerful than their inventors, monsters worshipped by their makers—the blind, unhappy Frankensteins whose lives they frustrate and twist. At the same time, merely to see through or criticize this predicament, which the young Hegelians thought sufficient, will not destroy it. To be effective, the weapons with which one fights, among them ideas, must be those called for by the historical situation— neither those that served a previous period, nor those for which the historical process has not yet called. Men must ask themselves, first and foremost, what stage the class war—which is the dialectic at work—has reached, and then act accordingly. This is to be 'concrete' and not timeless, or idealistic or 'abstract'. Alienation—the substitution of imaginary relations between, or worship of, inanimate objects or ideas for real relations between, or respect for, persons—will come to an end only when the final class—the proletariat—defeats the bourgeoisie. Then the ideas which this victory will generate, will automatically be those expressive of, and beneficial to, a classless society, that is, all mankind. Neither institutions nor ideas which rest on falsifying the character of any section of the human race, and so leading to (or expressive of) their oppression, will survive. Capitalism, under which the labour of human beings is bought and sold, and the workers are treated merely as sources of labour power, is plainly a system which distorts the truth about what men are and can be, and seeks to subordinate history to a class interest (which is injustice), and is therefore due to be superseded by the gathering power of its indignant victims which its own victories call into existence. All frustration, for Marx, is the product of alienation—the barriers and distortions that are created by the inevitable war of classes, and shut out this or that body of men from the harmonious co-operation with one another for which their nature craves.

In the *German Ideology* the claims of the neo-Hegelians are examined one by one, and 'awarded' their due. The brothers Bruno, Edgar and Egbert Bauer are dealt with briefly and savagely here as in the published, though little read, 'Holy Family'. They are represented as three sordid peddlers of inferior metaphysical wares, who believe that the mere existence of a fastidious critical *élite*, raised by its intellectual gifts above the philistine mob, will itself effect the emancipation of such sections of humanity as are worthy of it. This belief in the power of a frigid detachment from the social and economic struggle to effect a transformation of society, is regarded as academicism run mad, an ostrich-like attitude which will be swept away, like the rest of the world to which it belongs, by the real revolution which could not, it was clear, now be long in coming. Stirner is treated at greater length. Under the title of St. Max he is pursued through five hundred pages of heavy-handed mockery and insult. Stirner believed that all programmes, ideals, theories as well as political, social and economic orders are so many artifically built prisons for the mind and the spirit, means of curbing the will, of concealing from the individual the existence of his own infinite creative powers, and that all systems must therefore be destroyed, not because they are evil, but because they are systems; only when this has been achieved, would man, released from his unnatural fetters become truly master of himself and attain to his full stature as a human being. This doctrine, which had a great influence on Nietzsche and probably on Bakunin, is (perhaps because it anticipated Marx's own economic theory of alienation too precisely) treated as a pathological phenomenon, the agonized cry of a persecuted neurotic, belonging to the province of medicine rather than to that of political theory.

Feuerbach is more gently treated. He is held to have written more soberly, and to have made an honest, if crude, attempt to expose the mystifications of idealism. In the *Eleven Theses on Feuerbach* which he composed during the same period, Marx declared that while Feuerbach had correctly perceived that men are largely the product of circumstances and education, he had not gone on to see that circumstances are themselves altered by the activity of men, and that the educators themselves are children of their age. Feuerbach's doctrine artifically divides society into two parts: the masses, which, being helplessly exposed to every influence, must be freed; and the teachers, who contrive somehow to remain immune from the effect of their environment. But the relation of mind and matter, of men and nature, is reciprocal; otherwise history becomes reduced to physics. Feuerbach is praised for showing that in religion men delude themselves by inventing an imaginary world to redress the balance of misery in real life,—it is a form of escape, a golden dream, or, in a phrase made celebrated by Marx, the opium of the people; the criticism of religion must therefore be anthropological in character, and take the form of exposing and analysing its secular origins.

But Feuerbach is accused of leaving the major task untouched: he sees that religion is the anodyne to soften the pain caused by the contradictions of the material world, but then fails to see that these contradictions must, in that case, be removed: otherwise they will continue to breed comforting and fatal delusions: the revolution which alone can do so, must occur not in the super-structure—the world of thought—but in its material substratum, the real world of men and things. Philosophy has hitherto treated ideas and beliefs as possessing an intrinsic validity of their own; this has never been true; the real content of a belief is the action in which it is expressed. The real convictions and principles of a man or a society are expressed in their acts, not their words. Belief and act are one; if acts do not correspond to avowed beliefs, the beliefs are lies—ideologies, conscious or not, to cover the opposite of what they profess. 'Philosophers have previously offered various interpretations of the world. Our business is to change it.'

The so-called 'True Socialists', Grün and Hess, fare no better. It is true that they wrote about the actual situation; but, placing ideals before interests in order of importance, they are equally far removed from a clear view of the facts. They believed correctly that the political inequality, and the general emotional *malaise* of their generation, were both traceable to economic contradictions which could only be removed by the total abolition of private property. But they also believed that the technological advance which made this possible was not an end but a means; that action could be justified only by appeal to moral ideals; that the use of force, however noble the purpose for which it was employed, defeated its own end, since it brutalized both parties in the struggle, and made them both incapable of true freedom after the struggle was over. If men were to be freed, it must be by peaceful and civilized means alone, to be effected as rapidly and painlessly as possible, before industrialization had spread so widely as to make a bloody class war inevitable. Indeed, unless this was done, only violence would be left, and this would, in the end, defeat itself; for a society set up by the sword, even if justice initially were on its side, could not fail to develop into a tyranny of the victorious class—even though it be that of the workers—over the rest and this would be incompatible with that human equality which true socialism seeks to create. The 'True Socialists' opposed the doctrine of the necessity of open class war on the ground that it blinded the workers to those rights and ideals for the sake of which they fought. Only by treating men as equal from the beginning, by dealing with them as human beings, that is, by renouncing force, and appealing to the sense of human solidarity, of equal justice and the generous sentiments of mankind, could a lasting harmony of interests be obtained. Above all, the burden of the proletariat must not be removed by being shifted on to the shoulders of some other class. Marx and his party, they maintained, merely desired to reverse the roles of the existing classes, to deprive the bourgeoisie of its power only to ruin and enslave it. But this, besides being morally unacceptable, would leave the class war itself in existence and so would fail to reconcile the existing contradiction in the only way possible by fusing conflicting interests into one common ideal.

Marx looked upon all this as so much idiocy or cant. The whole argument, he wearily points out, rests

on the premiss that men, even capitalists, are amenable
to a rational argument, and under suitable conditions
will voluntarily give up the power which they have
acquired by birth or wealth or ability, for the sake of a
moral principle, to create a juster world. To Marx this
was the oldest, most familiar, most outworn of all the
rationalist fallacies. He had met it in its worst form in
the belief of his own father and his contemporaries
that in the end reason and moral goodness were bound
to triumph, a theory which was utterly discredited
by events during the dark aftermath of the French
Revolution. To preach it now, as if one were still living
in the eighteenth century, was to be guilty either of
boundless stupidity, or of a cowardly escape into mere
words, or else of deliberate Utopianism, when what was
needed was a scientific examination of the actual situation. Marx was careful to point out that he did not himself fall into the opposite error: he did not simply
contradict this thesis about human nature, and say that
whereas these theorists assumed man to be fundamentally generous and just, he found him rapacious, self-
seeking and incapable of disinterested action. That
would have been an hypothesis as subjective and
unhistorical as that of his opponents. Each was vitiated
by the fallacy that men's acts were in the end determined by their moral character, which could be
described in comparative isolation from their environment. Marx, true to the method, if not to the conclusions, of Hegel, maintained that a man's purposes
were made what they were by the social, that is economic, situation in which he was in fact placed
whether he knew it or not. Whatever his opinions, a
man's actions were inevitably guided by his real
interests, by the requirements of his material situation;

the conscious aims of at any rate the bulk of mankind did not clash with their real interests, although they sometimes appeared disguised as so many independent, objective, disinterested ends, political, moral, aesthetic, emotional and the like. Most individuals concealed their own dependence on their environment and situation, particularly on their class affiliation, so effectively even from themselves, that they quite sincerely believed that a change of heart would result in a radically different mode of life. This was much the profoundest error made by modern thinkers. It arose partly as a result of Protestant individualism, which, arising as the 'ideological' counterpart of the growth of freedom of trade and production, taught men to believe that the individual held the means for his happiness in his own hands, that faith and energy were sufficient to secure it, that every man had it in his power to attain to spiritual or material well-being, that for his weakness and misery he ultimately had only himself to blame. Marx maintained, against this, that liberty of action was severely curtailed by the precise position which the agent occupied on the social map. All notions of right and wrong, justice and injustice, altruism and egoism were beside the point, as referring exclusively to the mental states, which, while in themselves quite genuine, were never more than symptoms of the actual condition of their owner. Acts—particularly the objective behaviour of a group, whatever the subjective motives of its members—these alone counted. Sometimes, when the patient was himself acquainted with the science of pathology, he could accurately diagnose his own condition; this is indeed what was meant by genuine insight on the part of a social philosopher. But more frequently the symptom would pose as the only true reality, occupying the whole attention of the sufferer. Since the symptoms in this case were mental states, it was this that bred the otherwise inexplicable fallacy that reality was mental or spiritual in character, or that history could be altered by the isolated decisions of unfettered human wills. Principles and causes, unless allied to real interests which caused action, were so many empty phrases; to lead men in their name, was to feed them on air, reduce them to a state in which their very failure to apprehend their true situation, would involve them in chaos and destruction.

To alter the world, one must first understand the material with which one deals. The bourgeoisie which wishes not to alter it, but to preserve the *status quo*, acts and thinks in terms of concepts, which, being products of a given stage in its development, themselves serve, whatever they pretend to be, as instruments of its temporary preservation. The proletariat, in whose interest it is to alter it, blindly accepts the entire intellectual paraphernalia of middle-class thought, born of middle-class needs and conditions, although there is an utter divergence of interest between the two classes. Phrases about justice or liberty represent something more or less definite when they are uttered by the middle-class liberal, namely, his attitude, however deluded, to his own mode of life, his actual or desired relation to members of other social classes. But they are empty sounds when repeated by the 'alienated' proletarian, since they describe nothing real in his life, and only betray his muddled state of mind, the result of the hypnotic power of phrases, which, by confusing issues, not only fail to promote, but hinder and sometimes paralyse his power to act. Mutualists, True

Socialists, mystical Anarchists, however pure their motives, are thus even more dangerous enemies of the proletariat than the bourgeoisie: for the latter is at least an open enemy whose words and deeds the workers can be taught to distrust. But these others, who proclaim their solidarity with the workers, and assume that there always exist universal interests of mankind as such, common to all men—that men have interests independent of, or transcending their class affiliation—spread error and darkness in the proletarian camp itself, and thus weaken it for the coming struggle. The workers must be made to understand that the modern industrial system, like the feudal system before it, like every other social system, is, so long as the ruling class requires it for its continuance as a class, an iron despotism imposed by the capitalist system of production and distribution, from which no individual, whether he be master or slave, can escape. All visionary dreams of human liberty, of a time when men will be able to develop their natural gifts to their fullest extent, living and creating spontaneously, no longer dependent on others for the freedom to do or think as they will, remain an unattainable utopia so long as the fight for control of the means of production continues. It is no longer a struggle strictly for the means of subsistence, for modern inventions and discoveries have abolished natural scarcity: it is now an artificial scarcity, created by the very struggle for securing new instruments itself, a process which necessarily leads to the centralization of power by the creation of monopolies at one end of the social scale, and the increase of penury and degradation at the other. The war between economically determined groups alone divides men from each other, blinds them to the real facts of their situation, makes them slaves to customs and rules which they dare not question, because they would crumble at the touch of historical explanation; only one remedy—the disappearance of the class struggle—can achieve the abolition of this widening gulf. But the essence of a class is to compete with other classes. Hence this end can be achieved not by creating equality between classes—a utopian conception—but by the total abolition of classes themselves.

For Marx, no less than for earlier rationalists, man is potentially wise, creative and free. If his character has deteriorated beyond recognition, that is due to the long and brutalizing war in which he and his ancestors have lived ever since society ceased to be that primitive communism out of which, according to the current anthropology, it has developed. Until this state is reached again, embodying, however, all the conquests, technological and spiritual, which mankind has won in the course of its long wandering in the desert, neither peace nor freedom can be obtained. The French Revolution was an attempt to bring this about by altering political forms only—which was no more than the bourgeoisie required, since it already possessed the economic reality: and, therefore, all it succeeded in doing (as indeed was its appointed historical task at the stage of development at which it occurred) was to establish the bourgeoisie in a dominant position by finally destroying the corrupt remnant of an obsolete feudal régime. This task could not but be continued by Napoleon whom no one could suspect of wishing consciously to liberate humanity; whatever his personal motive for acting as he did, the demands of his historical environment inevitably made him an instrument of social change; by his agency, as Hegel had indeed perceived, Europe advanced yet another step towards the realization of its destiny.

The gradual freeing of mankind has pursued a definite, irreversible direction: every new epoch is inaugurated by the liberation of a hitherto oppressed class; nor can a class, once it has been destroyed, ever return. History does not move backwards, or in cyclical movements: all its conquests are final and irrevocable. Most previous ideal constitutions were worthless because they ignored actual laws of historical development, and substituted in their place the subjective caprice or imagination of the thinker. A knowledge of these laws is essential to effective political action. The ancient world gave way to the medieval, slavery to feudalism, and feudalism to the industrial bourgeoisie. These transitions were not peaceful, but sprang from wars and revolutions, for no established order gives way to its successor without a struggle.

And now only one stratum remains submerged below the level of the rest, one class alone remains enslaved, the landless, propertyless proletariat, created by the advance of technology, perpetually assisting classes above itself to shake off the yoke of the common oppressor, always, after the common cause has been won, condemned to be oppressed by its own former allies, the new victorious class, by masters who were themselves but lately slaves. The proletariat is on the lowest possible rung of the social scale: there is no class below it; by securing its own emancipation the proletariat will therefore emancipate mankind. It has, unlike other classes, no specific claim, no interests of its own which it does not share with all men as such: for it has been stripped of everything but its bare humanity: its very destitution causes it to represent human beings as such—what it is entitled to, is the minimum to which all men are entitled. Its fight is thus not a fight for the natural rights of a particular section of society: for natural rights are but the ideal aspect of the bourgeois attitude to the sanctity of private property; the only real rights are those conferred by history, the right to act the part which is historically imposed upon one's class. The bourgeoisie, in this sense, has a full right to fight its final battle against the masses, but its task is hopeless: it will necessarily be defeated, as the feudal nobility was defeated in its day. As for the masses, they fight for freedom not because they choose, but because they must, or rather they choose because they must: to fight is the condition of their survival; the future belongs to them, and in fighting for it, they, like every rising class, are fighting against a foe doomed to decay, and thereby fighting for the whole of humanity. But whereas all other victories placed in power a class itself doomed to ultimate disappearance, this conflict will be followed by no other, being destined to end the condition of all such struggles, by abolishing classes as such; by dissolving the state itself, hitherto the instrument of a single class, into a free, because classless, society. The proletariat must be made to understand that no real compromise with the enemy is possible: that, while it may conclude temporary alliances with him in order to defeat some common adversary, it must ultimately turn against him. In backward countries, where the bourgeoisie itself is still fighting for power, the proletariat must throw in its lot with it, asking itself not what the ideals of the bourgeoisie may be, but what it is *compelled* to do in the particular situation: and must adapt its tactics to this. And while history is determined —and the victory will, therefore, be won by the rising class whether any given individual wills it or not—how rapidly this will occur, how efficiently, how far in accordance with the conscious popular will, depends on human initiative, on the degree of understanding of their task by the masses and the courage and efficiency of their leaders.

To make this clear, and to educate the masses for their destiny is, therefore, according to Marx, the whole duty of a contemporary philosopher. But, it has often been asked, how can a moral precept, a command to do this or that, be deduced from the truth of a theory of history? Historical materialism may account for what does in fact occur, but cannot, precisely because it is concerned solely with what is, provide the answer to moral questions, that is, tell us what ought to be. Marx, like Hegel, flatly rejected this distinction. Judgments of fact cannot be sharply distinguished from those of value: all one's judgments are conditioned by practical activity in a given social milieu which, in its turn, are functions of the stage reached by one's class in its historical evolution: one's views as to what one believes to exist and what one wishes to do with it, modify each other. If ethical judgments claim objective validity— and unless they do so, they cannot, according to Marx, be either true or false—they must be definable in terms of empirical activities and be verifiable by reference to them. He rejected any notion of a non-empirical, purely contemplative or specifically moral intuition or moral reason. The only sense in which it is possible to show that something is good or bad, right or wrong, is by demonstrating that it accords or discords with the historical process i.e. the collective acitivity of men, that it assists it or thwarts it, will survive or will inevitably perish. All causes permanently lost or doomed to fail, are, by that very fact, made bad and wrong, and indeed this is what constitutes the meaning of these terms. But this is a dangerous empirical criterion, since causes which may appear lost may, in fact, have suffered only a temporary setback, and will in the end prevail.

His view of truth in general derives directly from this position. He is sometimes accused of maintaining that, since a man is wholly determined to think as he does by his social environment, even if some of his statements are objectively true, he cannot know it, being conditioned to think them true by material causes, not by their truth. Marx's statements on this subject are vague to a degree; but in general it may be said that he would have accepted the normal interpretation of what is meant by saying that a theory or a proposition of natural science or of ordinary sense experience is true or false. But he was scarcely interested in this, the most common, type of truth discussed by philosophers. He was concerned with the reasons for which social, moral, historical verdicts are thought true or false, where arguments between opponents can so easily not be settled by direct appeal to empirical facts accessible to both. He might have agreed that the bare proposition that Napoleon died in exile, would have been accepted as equally true by a bourgeois and a socialist historian. But he would have gone on to say that no true historian confines himself to a list of events and dates: that the plausibility of his account of the past, its claim to be more than a bare chronicle, depends, at the very least, upon his choice of fundamental concepts, his power of emphasis and arrangement, that the very process of selection of material betrays an inclination to stress this or that event or act as important or trivial, adverse or favourable to human progress, good or bad.

And in this tendency the social origin and environment and class affiliation and interests of the historian tell only too clearly.

This attitude underlies his purely Hegelian view of rationality as identical with the knowledge of the laws of necessity. If you know in what direction the world process is working, you can either identify yourself with it or not; if you do not, if you fight it, you thereby compass your own certain destruction, being necessarily defeated by the forward advance of history. To choose to do so deliberately is to behave irrationally. Only a wholly rational being is wholly free to choose between alternatives: where one of these irresistibly leads to his own destruction, he cannot choose it freely, because to say that an act is free, as Marx employs the term, is to deny that it is contrary to reason. The bourgeoisie as a class is indeed fated to disappear, but individual members of it may follow reason and save themselves (as Marx might have claimed to have done himself) by leaving it before it finally founders. True freedom is unattainable until society has been made rational, that is, has overcome the contradictions which breed illusions and distort the understanding of both masters and slaves. But men can work for the free world by discovering the true state of the balance of forces, and acting accordingly; the path to freedom thus entails knowledge of historical necessity. Marx's use of words like 'right', or 'free', or 'rational', whenever he does not slip insensibly into ordinary usage, owes its eccentric air to the fact that it derives from his metaphysical views; and therefore diverges widely from that of common speech, which is largely intended to record and communicate something scarcely of interest to him—the subjective experience of class-perverted individuals, their states of mind or of body as revealed by the senses or in self-consciousness.

Such in outline is the theory of history and society which constitutes the metaphysical basis of communism. It is a wide and comprehensive doctrine which derives its structure and basic concepts from Hegel and the Young Hegelians, and its dynamic principles from Saint-Simon, its belief in the primacy of matter from Feuerbach, and its view of the proletariat from the French communist tradition. Nevertheless it is wholly original; the combination of elements does not in this case lead to syncretism, but forms a bold, clear, coherent system, with the wide range and the massive architectonic quality that is at once the greatest pride and the fatal defect of all forms of Hegelian thought. But it is not guilty of Hegel's reckless and contemptuous attitude towards the results of the scientific research of his time; on the contrary, it attempts to follow the direction indicated by the empirical sciences, and to incorporate their general results. Marx's practice did not always conform to this theoretical ideal, and that of his followers sometimes did so even less: while not actually distorted, the facts are sometimes made to undergo peculiar transformations in the process of being fitted into the intricate dialectical pattern. It is by no means a wholly empirical theory, since it does not confine itself to the description of the phenomena and the formulation of hypotheses concerning their structure and behaviour; the Marxist doctrine of movement in dialectical collisions is not a hypothesis liable to be made less or more probable by the evidence of facts, but a pattern, uncovered by a non-empirical, historical method, the validity of which is not questioned. To deny this would be tantamount, according to Marx, to a return to 'vulgar' materialism, which, ignoring the crucial discoveries of Hegel and indeed Kant, recognizes only those connexions as real, for which there is the corrigible evidence of the physical senses.

In the sharpness and the clarity with which this theory formulates its questions, in the rigour of the method by which it proposes to search for the answers, in the combination of attention to detail and power of wide comprehensive generalization, it is without parallel. Even if all its specific conclusions were proved false, its importance in creating a wholly new attitude to social and historical questions, and so opening new avenues of human knowledge, would be unimpaired. The scientific study of historically evolving economic relations, and of their bearing on other aspects of the lives of communities and individuals, began with the application of Marxist canons of interpretation. Previous thinkers—for example, Vico, Hegel, Saint-Simon—drew up general schemata, but their direct results, as embodied, for instance, in the gigantic systems of Comte or Spencer, are at once too abstract and too vague, and as little remembered in our day as they deserve to be. The true father of modern economic history, and, indeed, of modern sociology, in so far as any one man may claim that title, is Karl Marx. If to have turned into truisms what had previously been paradoxes is a mark of genius, Marx was richly endowed with it. His achievements in this sphere are necessarily ignored in proportion as their effects have become part of the permanent background of civilized thought.

Chapter Seven

1848

Gegen Demokraten Helfen nur Soldaten.
(Against democrats, only soldiers help.)
Prussian Song.

Liberty, Equality, Fraternity . . . when what this republic really means is Infantry, Cavalry, Artillery. . . .
KARL MARX, *Eighteenth Brumaire of Louis Bonaparte*

MARX was expelled from Paris in the beginning of 1845 by the Guizot government as a result of representations from Prussia, which had demanded the suppression of the socialist *Vorwärts* in which offensive comments had appeared concerning the character of the reigning Prussian king. The order of expulsion was originally intended to apply to the entire group, including Heine, Bakunin, Ruge and several other lesser foreign exiles. Ruge, being a Saxon citizen, was left unmolested; the French government itself did not venture to press the order against Heine, a figure of European fame, then at the height of his powers and influence. Bakunin and Marx were duly expelled in spite of vigorous protests in the radical press. Bakunin went to Switzerland; Marx, with his wife and one-year-old daughter Jenny, to Brussels where shortly afterwards he was joined by Engels who had returned from England for this purpose. In Brussels he lost no time in establishing contact with the various German communist workers' organizations which contained members of the dissolved League of the Just, an international society of proletarian revolutionaries with a vague, but violent, programme, influenced by Weitling; it had branches in various European cities. He entered into relations with Belgian socialists and radicals, carried on an active correspondence with members of similar bodies in other countries, and established regular machinery for the exchange of political information, but the chief sphere of his activity lay among the German workmen in Brussels itself. To these he attempted by means of lectures, and of articles in their organ, the *Brüsseler Zeitung*, to explain their proper part in the coming revolution, which he, like the majority of European radicals, believed to be imminent.

As soon as he concluded that the establishment of communism could only be achieved by a rising of the proletariat, his entire existence turned into an attempt to organize and discipline it for its task. This personal history which up to this point can be regarded as a series of episodes in the life of an individual, now becomes inseparable from the general history of socialism in Europe. An account of one is necessarily to some degree an account of the other. Attempts to distinguish the part which Marx played in directing the movement from the movement itself obscure the history of both. The task of preparing the workers for the revolution was for him a scientific task, a routine occupation, something to be performed as solidly and efficiently as possible, and not a direct means of personal self-expression. The external circumstances of his life are therefore as monotonous as those of any other devoted expert, as those of Darwin or Pasteur, and offer the sharpest possible contrast to the restless, emotionally involved, lives of the other revolutionaries of his time.

The middle decades of the nineteenth century form

a period in which an enormous premium was placed on sensibility. What had begun by being the isolated experience of exceptional individuals, of Rousseau and Chateaubriand, Schiller and Jean Paul, Byron and Shelley, by insensible degrees became part of the general attitude of European society. For the first time a whole generation became fascinated by the personal experience of men and women, as opposed to the external world composed of interplay of the lives of whole groups or societies. This tendency obtained public expression in the lives and doctrines of the great democratic revolutionaries, and in the passionate adoration with which they were regarded by their followers: Mazzini, Kossuth, Garibaldi, Bakunin, Lassalle, were admired not only as heroic fighters for freedom, but for their romantic, poetical properties as individuals. Their achievements were looked upon as the expression of profound inner experience, the intensity of which gave their words and gestures a moving personal quality wholly different from the austerely impersonal heroism of the men of 1789, a quality which constitutes the distinguishing character-istic, the peculiar temper and outlook of the age. Karl Marx belonged in spirit to an earlier or a later genera-tion; but certainly not to his own time. He lacked psychological insight, and poverty and hard work did not increase his emotional receptiveness; this extreme blindness to the experience and character of persons outside his immediate range made his intercourse with the outside world seem singularly boorish; he had had a brief sentimental period as a student in Berlin: this was now over and done with. He looked upon moral or emotional suffering, and spiritual crises, as so much bourgeois self-indulgence unpardonable in time of war;

like Lenin after him, he had nothing but contempt for those who, during the heat of the battle, while the enemy gained one position after another, were pre-occupied with the state of their own souls.

He set to work to create an international revolution-ary organization. He received the warmest response in London, from a society called the German workers' Educational Association, headed by a small group of exiled artisans, whose revolutionary temper was beyond suspicion: the type-setter Schapper, the watch-maker Moll and the cobbler Bauer were his first reliable political allies. They had affiliated their society to a federation called the Communist League which succeeded the dissolved League of the Just. He met them in the course of a journey to England with Engels, and found them men after his own heart, determined, capable and energetic. They looked on him with con-siderable suspicion as a journalist and an intellectual: and their relations for some years preserved a severely impersonal and business-like character. It was an association for immediate practical ends, and this he approved. Under his guidance, the Communist League grew fast and began to embrace groups of radical workers, scattered for the most part in the industrial areas in Germany, with a sprinkling of army officers and professional men. Engels wrote glowing reports of the increase in their numbers and their revolutionary zeal in his own native province. For the first time Marx found himself in the position which he had long desired, the organizer and leader of an active and expanding revolutionary party. Bakunin, who had in his turn arrived in Brussels, and was on equally good terms with the foreign radicals and members of the local aristocracy, complained that Marx preferred the society of artisans and workmen to that of intelligent people, and was spoiling good and simple men by filling their heads with abstract theories and obscure economic doctrines, which they did not begin to understand, and which only made them intolerably conceited. He saw no point in lecturing to, and organizing small groups of ill-educated and hopelessly limited German artisans, who understood little of what was so elaborately expounded to them, drab, underfed creatures who could not conceivably turn the scale in any decisive conflict. Marx's attack on Proudhon still further estranged them; Proudhon was an intimate friend and, in Hegelian matters, a disciple of Bakunin; and the attack was aimed no less at Bakunin's own habit of indulging in vague and exuberant eloquence in place of detailed political analysis.

The events of 1848 altered the view of both on the technique of the coming revolution, but in precisely opposed directions. Bakunin in later years turned to secret terrorist groups, Marx to the foundation of an open, official, revolutionary party proceeding by recognized political methods. He set himself to destroy the tendency to rhetoric and vagueness among the Germans, nor was he wholly unsuccessful, as may be seen in the efficient and disciplined behaviour of the members of his organization in Germany during the two revolutionary years and after.

In 1847 the London centre of the Communist League showed its confidence in him by commissioning him to compose a document containing a definitive statement of its beliefs and aims. He eagerly embraced this opportunity for an explicit summary of the new doctrine which had lately assumed its final shape in his head. He delivered it into their hands early in 1848. It was published a few weeks before the outbreak of the Paris revolution under the title of *The Manifesto of the Communist Party*.

Engels wrote the first draft in the form of questions and answers, but since this was not thought sufficiently forcible, Marx completely re-wrote it. According to Engels the result was an original work which owed hardly anything to his own hand; but he was excessively modest wherever their collaboration was concerned, but the draft shows how great a share he had in its composition. The result is the greatest of all socialist pamphlets. No other modern political movement or cause can claim to have produced anything comparable with it in eloquence or power. It is a document of prodigious dramatic force; in form it is an edifice of bold and arresting historical generalizations, mounting to a denunciation of the existing order in the name of the avenging forces of the future, much of it written in prose which has the lyrical quality of a great revolutionary hymn, whose effect powerful even now, was probably greater at the time. It opens with a menacing phrase which reveals its tone and its intention: 'A spectre is wandering over Europe today—the spectre of communism. All the forces of Europe have united to exorcise it: the Pope and the Czar, Metternich and Guizot, French radicals and German policemen . . . it is recognized as a real force by all the European powers.' It proceeds as a succession of interconnected theses which are developed and brilliantly embroidered, and ends with a famous and magnificent invocation addressed to the workers of the world.

The first of these theses is contained in the opening sentence of the first section: 'The history of all previous society is the history of class struggles.' At all periods within recorded memory mankind has been divided into exploiter and exploited, master and slave, patrician and plebeian, and in our day proletarian and capitalist. The immense development of discovery and invention has transformed the economic system of modern human society: guilds have given way to local manufacture, and this in its turn to great industrial enterprises. Each stage in this expansion is accompanied by political and cultural forms peculiar to itself. The structure of the modern State reflects the domination of the bourgeoisie —it is in effect a committee for managing the affairs of the bourgeois class as a whole. The bourgeoisie fulfilled a highly revolutionary role in its day; it overthrew the feudal order and in so doing destroyed the old, picturesque, patriarchal, relations which connected a man to his 'natural masters' and left only one real relation between them—the cash nexus, naked self-interest. It has turned personal dignity into a negotiable commodity, to be bought and sold; in place of ancient liberties, secured by writs and charters, it has created freedom of trade; for exploitation disguised by religious and political masks, it has substituted exploitation, direct, cynical and unashamed. It has turned professions formerly thought honourable, as being forms of service to the community, into mere hired labour: acquisitive in its aims, it has degraded every form of life. This was achieved by calling immense new natural resources into existence: the feudal framework could not contain the new development, and was split asunder. Now the process has repeated itself. The frequent economic crises due to over-production are a symptom of the fact that capitalism can in its turn no longer control its own resources. When a social order is forced to destroy its own products, to prevent its own facilities from expanding too rapidly and too far, that is a certain sign of its approaching bankruptcy and doom. The bourgeois order has created the proletariat which is at once its heir and its executioner. It has succeeded in destroying the power of all other rival forms of organization, the aristocracy, the small artisans and leaders, but the proletariat it cannot destroy, for it is necessary to its own existence, is an organic part of its system, and constitutes the great army of the dispossessed, whom in the very act of exploiting it inevitably disciplines and organizes. The more international capitalism becomes—and as it expands, it inevitably grows more so—the wider and more international the scale on which it automatically organizes the workers, whose union and solidarity will eventually overthrow it. The international of capitalism breeds inevitably, as its own necessary complement, the international of the working class. This dialectical process is inexorable, and no power can arrest it or control it. Hence it is futile to attempt to restore the old medieval idyll, to build utopian schemes on a nostalgic desire to return to the past, for which the ideologists of peasants, artisans, small traders so ardently long. The past is gone, the classes which belonged to it have long been decisively defeated by the march of history; their hostility toward the bourgeoisie, often falsely called socialism, is a reactionary attitude, a futile attempt to reverse the advance of human evolution. Their only hope of triumph over the enemy lies in abandonment of their independent existence and fusion with the proletariat whose growth corrodes the bourgeoisie from within; for the increases of crises and of unemployment forces the bourgeoisie to exhaust itself in feeding its servants instead of feeding on them, which is its natural function.

From attack the Manifesto passes to defence. The enemies of socialism declare that the abolition of private property will destroy liberty and subvert the foundations of religion, morality and culture. This is admitted. But the values which it will thus destroy will be only those which are bound up with the old order—bourgeois liberty and bourgeois culture, whose appearance of absolute validity for all times and places is an illusion due solely to their function as a weapon in the class struggle. True personal freedom is possession of the power of independent action, of which the artisan, the small trader, the peasant, has long been deprived by capitalism. As for culture, 'the culture the loss of which is lamented is, for the enormous majority, a mere training to act as a machine'. With the total abolition of the class struggle these illusory ideals will necessarily vanish and be succeeded by the new and wider form of life founded upon a classless society. To mourn their loss is to lament the disappearance of an old familiar ailment.

The revolution must differ in differing circumstances, but its first measures everywhere must be the nationalization of land, credit, transport, the abolition of rights of inheritance, the increase of taxation, the intensification of production, the destruction of the barriers between town and country, the introduction of compulsory work and of free education for all. Only then can serious social reconstruction begin. The rest of the Manifesto exposes and refutes various forms of pseudo-socialism—the attempts of various enemies of the bourgeoisie, the aristocracy, or the Church, to gain the proletariat to its cause by specious pretence of common interest. Into this category enters the ruined *petite bourgeoisie*, whose writers, adept as they are at exposing the chaos of capitalist production, the pauperization and degradation caused by the introduction of machinery, the monstrous inequalities of wealth, offer remedies which, being conceived in obsolete terms, are utopian. Even this cannot be said of the German 'True Socialists',[1] who by translating French platitudes into the language of Hegelianism, produce a meaningless collection of nonsense phrases which cannot long deceive the world. As for Proudhon, Fourier or Owen, their followers draw up schemes to save the bourgeoisie, as if the proletariat did not exist, or else could be drawn upwards into capitalist ranks, leaving only exploiters and no exploited. This endless variety of views represents the desperate plight of the bourgeoisie unable or unwilling to face its own impending death, concentrating upon vain efforts to survive under the guise of a vague and opportunist socialism. The communists are not a party or a sect, but the self-conscious vanguard of the proletariat itself, obsessed by no mere theoretical ends, but seeking to fulfil their historical destiny. They do not conceal their aims. They openly declare that these can be gained only when the entire social order is overthrown by force of arms, and they themselves seize all political and economic power. The Manifesto ends with the celebrated words: 'The workers have nothing to lose but their chains. They have a world to win. Workers of all lands, unite!'

Later scholars have convincingly shown how much familiar material from earlier programmes—especially Babouvist—has been incorporated in the Manifesto;

---

[1] I.e. Hess, Grün and the rest whose error is to advocate socialism not because it is historically due, but because it is just and demanded by human nature conceived as an absolute essence, an entity not radically transformed by history or class war.

nevertheless it has been fused into an unbroken unity. No summary can convey the quality of its opening or its closing pages. As an instrument of destructive propaganda it has no equal anywhere; its effect upon succeeding generations is unparalleled outside religious history; had its author written nothing else, it would have ensured his lasting fame. Its most immediate effect, however, was upon his own fortunes. The Belgian Government, which behaved with considerable tolerance to political exiles, could not overlook this formidable publication, and brusquely expelled him and his family from its territory. On the next day the long expected revolution broke out in Paris. Flocon, a radical member of the new French Government, in a flattering letter, invited Marx to return to the revolutionary city. He set off immediately and arrived a day later.

He found the city in a state of universal and uncritical enthusiasm. The barriers had fallen once more, this time it seemed for ever. The king had fled, declaring that 'he had been driven out by moral forces', a new Government had been appointed containing representatives of all the friends of humanity and progress: the great physicist Arago and the poet Lamartine received portfolios, the workers were represented by Louis Blanc and Albert. Lamartine, composed an eloquent manifesto which was read, quoted, declaimed everywhere. The street were filled with an immense singing, cheering throng of democrats of all hues and nationalities. The opposition showed no sign of life. The Church published a manifesto in which it asserted that Christianity was not inimical to individual liberty, that on the contrary it was its natural ally and defender; its kingdom was not of this world, and consequently such support as it had been accused of giving to the reaction, sprang neither from its principles nor from its historical position in European society, and could be radically modified without doing violence to the essence of its teaching. These announcements were received with enthusiasm and credulity. The German exiles vied with the Poles and the Italians in their predictions of the imminent and universal collapse of the reaction, and of the immediate appearance on its ruins of a new moral world. News presently arrived that Naples had revolted; and after it Milan, Rome, Venice and other Italian cities. Berlin, Vienna, and Budapest had risen in arms. Europe was ablaze at last. Excitement among the Germans in Paris rose to fever pitch. To support the insurgent republicans a German Legion was formed, which the poet Georg Herwegh and a Prussian communist ex-soldier named Willich were to lead. It was to start at once. The French Government, not un-willing, perhaps, to see so many foreign agitators leave its soil, encouraged the project. Engels was greatly attracted by the scheme and would almost certainly have enlisted, but was dissuaded by Marx, who viewed the proceeding with the greatest mistrust and hostility. He saw no sign of any large-scale revolt of the German masses: here and there autocratic governments were overthrown, and the princes were forced to promise constitutions and appoint mildly liberal governments, but the Prussian army was still largely loyal to the king, while the democrats were scattered, badly led, and unable to reach agreement among themselves on vital points. The elected popular congress which met in Frankfurt to decide the future government of Germany was a failure from the first, and the sudden appearance of a legion of untrained *émigré* intellectuals on German soil appeared to Marx a needless waste of revolutionary energy, likely to have a ludicrous or a pitiful end, and to be followed by a paralysing mood of shame and disillusionment. Consequently, Marx opposed the formation of the legion, took no interest in it after it had left Paris for its inevitable defeat by the royal army, and went to Cologne to see what could be done by propaganda in his native Rhineland. He was there largely instrumental in persuading a group of liberal industrialists and communist sympathizers to found a new *Rheinische Zeitung*, in succession to the journal of that name which had been suppressed five years before, and to appoint him its editor. Cologne was then the scene of an uneasy balance of power between the local democrats, who controlled the local militia, and a garrison under orders from Berlin. Acting in the name of the Communist League, Marx sent his agents to agitate among the German industrial masses, and used their reports as the material for his leading articles. There was at this time no formal censorship in the Rhineland, and his inflammatory words reached an ever-widening public. The *Neue Rheinische Zeitung* was well informed, and alone in the left-wing press possessed a clear policy of its own. Its circulation increased rapidly and it began to be widely read in other German provinces.

Marx had come armed with a complete political and economic plan of action founded on the solid theoretical basis which he had built carefully during the preceding years. He advocated a conditional alliance between the workers and the radical bourgeoisie for the immediate purpose of overthrowing a reactionary government, declaring that whereas the French had freed themselves from the yoke of feudalism in 1789, and were by this enabled to take the next step forward in 1848, the

Germans had so far achieved their revolutions in the region of pure thought alone; as thinkers they had far outstripped the French in the radicalism of their sentiments: politically they still inhabited the eighteenth century. The most backward of western nations, they thus had two stages to achieve before they could hope to attain to that of developed industrialism, thenceforth to march in step with the neighbouring democracies. The dialectical movement of history permits no leaps, and the representatives of the proletariat did ill to overlook the claims of the bourgeoisie which, in working for its own emancipation, was furthering the general cause, and was economically and politically far better organized and capable of ruling than the ignorant, scattered, badly organized masses of the working class. Hence the proper step for the workers was to conclude an alliance with their fellow victims among the middle and lower middle class and then, after the victory, to seek to control, and if necessary, obstruct the work of their new allies (who by this time would doubtless be anxious to end their compromising association) by the sheer weight of their numbers and economic power. He opposed the extreme Cologne democrats, Anneke and Gottschalk, who advocated absolute abstention from such opportunism and indeed from all political action, as likely to compromise and weaken the pure proletarian cause. This seemed to him a typically German blindness to the true balance of forces. He demanded direct intervention and the sending of delegates to Frankfurt, as the only effective practical course. Political aloofness seemed to him the height of tactical folly, since it was likely to leave the workers isolated, and at the mercy of the victorious class. In foreign policy he was something of a pan-German and a rabid Russophobe. Russia had for many years occupied the same position in relation to the forces of democracy and progress and evoked the same emotional reaction as the fascist powers in the twentieth century. It was hated and feared by democrats of all persuasions as the great champion of reaction, able and willing to crush all attempts at liberty within and without its borders.

As in 1842, Marx demanded an immediate war with Russia, because no attempt at democratic revolution could succeed in Germany in view of the certainty of Russian intervention, and as a means of welding the German principalities into a united democratic whole in opposition to a power whose entire influence was ranged on the side of the dynastic element in European politics; perhaps also in order to aid those scattered revolutionary forces within Russia itself to the existence of which Bakunin used to make constant mysterious references. Marx was prepared to sacrifice many other considerations to the ends of German unity—since in its disunion he, no less than Hegel and Bismarck, saw the cause at once of its weakness, its inefficiency and its political backwardness. He was neither a romantic, nor a nationalist, and regarded small nations as so many obsolete survivals impeding social and economic progress. He therefore acted quite consistently in publicly approving the cold-blooded German invasion of the Danish province of Schleswig-Holstein; an act the open support of which by most of the leading German democrats caused considerable embarrassment to their allies among the liberals and constitutionalists of other lands.

He denounced the succession of short-lived liberal Prussian governments which, easily and, it seemed to him, almost with relief, allowed power to slip from their grasp back into that of the king and his party. There were furious outbursts against 'empty chatter' and 'parliamentary cretinism' in Frankfurt, which ended in a storm of indignation hardly paralleled in *Das Kapital* itself. He did not either then or later despair of the ultimate outcome of the conflict, but his conception of revolutionary tactics, and his view of the intelligence and reliability of the masses and their leaders, changed radically: he declared their own incurable stupidity to be a greater obstacle to their progress than capitalism itself. His own policy, as it turned out, proved as impracticable as that of the intransigent radicals whom he denounced. In his subsequent analysis he attributed the disastrous result of the revolution to the weakness of the bourgeoisie, the ineffectiveness of the parliamentary liberals, but principally to the political blindness of the infinitely gullible masses, obstinately loyal to the agents of their own worst enemy who deceived and flattered them and led them only too easily to their destruction. If the rest of his life was spent as much over purely tactical problems and consideration of what method it was best for revolutionary leaders to adopt in the interests of their uncomprehending flock, as in the analysis of actual conditions, this was largely due to the lesson of the German revolution. In 1849, after the failure of the risings in Vienna and in Dresden, he wrote violent diatribes against liberals of all persuasions as being cowards and *saboteurs*, still hypnotized by the king and his drill sergeants, frightened by the thought of too definite a victory, prepared to betray the revolution for fear of the dangerous forces which it might unleash, and so virtually defeated before they began. He declared that, even if the bourgeoisie succeeded in making its

corrupt deal with the enemy at the expense of its allies
among the *petite bourgeoisie* and the workers, at best it
would not gain more than had been won by French
liberals under the July monarchy in France, while at
worst the bargain would be repudiated by the king and
become the prelude to a new monarchist terror. No
other journal in Germany dared to go as far in denouncing the government. The uncompromising directness
of these analyses, and the audacity of the conclusions
which Marx drew from them, fascinated his readers
against their will, although unmistakable signs of
panic began to show themselves among the shareholders.

By June 1848 the heroic phase of the Paris revolution
had spent itself, and the conservative forces began to
rally their strength. The socialist and radical members
of the Government, Louis Blanc, Albert, Flocon, were
forced to resign. The workers rebelled against the right-
wing republicans who remained in power, threw up
barricades, and after three days' hand-to-hand fighting
in the streets, were dispersed and routed by the
National Guard and troops which remained loyal to
the Government. The June *émeute* may be considered
as the first purely socialist rising in Europe, consciously
directed against liberals no less than against legitimists.
The followers of Blanqui (who was in prison) called
upon the people to seize power and establish an armed
dictatorship: the spectre of the Communist Manifesto
acquired substance at last; for the first time revolutionary socialism revealed itself in that savage and menacing
aspect in which it has appeared ever since to its opponents in every land.

Marx reacted at once. Against the frantic protests of
the owners of his newspaper, who looked upon all

forms of bloodshed and violence with profound horror, he published a long and fiery leading article, taking as his subject the funeral accorded by the State to the soldiers killed during the riots in Paris:

'The fraternity of the two opposing classes (one of which exploits the other) which in February was inscribed in huge letters upon all the façades of Paris, upon all the prisons and all the barracks ... this fraternity lasted just so long as the interests of the bourgeoisie could fraternize with the interests of the proletariat. Pedants of the old revolutionary tradition of 1793, socialist systematizers who begged the bourgeoisie to grant favours to the people, and were allowed to preach long sermons ... needed to lull the proletarian lion to sleep, republicans who wanted the whole of the old bourgeois system, minus the crowded figurehead, legitimists who did not wish to doff their livery but merely to change its cut—these had been the people's allies in the February revolution! Yet what the people hated was not Louis Philippe, but the crowded dominion of a class, capital enthroned. Nevertheless, magnanimous as ever, it fancied it had destroyed its own enemies when it had merely overthrown the enemy of its enemies, the common enemy of them all.

'The clashes that spontaneously arise out of the conditions of bourgeois society must be fought to the bitter end; they cannot be conjured out of existence. The best form of State is the one in which opposed social tendencies are not slurred over . . . but secure free expression, and are thus resolved. But we shall be asked: "Have you then no tears, no sighs, no words of sympathy for the victims of popular frenzy?"

'The State will take due care of the widows and orphans of these men. They will be honoured in decrees: they will be given a splendid public funeral: the official press will proclaim their memories immortal ... but the plebeians, tormented by hunger, reviled in the newspapers, abandoned by even the surgeons, stigmatized by all "decent" people as thieves, incendiaries, convicts, their wives and their children plunged in greater misery than ever, the best among the survivors transported—surely the democratic press may claim the right to crown with laurel their grim and sombre brow?'

This article (not dissimilar to his tribute to the Paris Commune more than twenty years later) caused alarm among the subscribers and the paper began to lose money. Presently the Prussian Government, by this time convinced it had nothing to fear from popular sentiment, ordered the dissolution of the democratic assembly. The latter replied by declaring all taxes imposed by the government illegal. Marx vehemently supported this decision and called upon the people to resist attempts to collect the tax. This time the government acted promptly and ordered the immediate suppression of the *Neue Rheinische Zeitung*. The last issue was printed in a red type, containing an inflammatory article by Marx and a magnificent poem by Freiligrath, and was bought up as a collector's curiosity. Marx was arrested for incitement to sedition and tried before a Cologne jury. He turned the occasion into the opportunity of delivering a speech of great length and erudition in which he analysed in detail the social and political situation in Germany and abroad. The result was unexpected: the foreman of the jury in announcing the acquittal of the accused said that he wished to thank him in his own name and that of the jury for an unusually instructive and interesting lecture by which they had all greatly profited. The Prussian Government, which had annulled his Prussian citizenship four years previously, unable to reverse the verdict itself, in July 1849 expelled him from the Rhineland. He went to Paris, where the Bonapartist agitation in favour of the first Napoleon's nephew had made the political situation even more confused than before, and it looked as if something of importance might occur at any moment. His collaborators scattered in various directions: Engels, who disliked inactivity, and declared he had nothing to lose, joined the Paris legion commanded by Willich, a single-minded communist and capable commander, whom Marx detested as a romantic adventurer, and Engels admired for his sincerity, coolness and personal courage. The legion was defeated in Baden by the royal forces without difficulty, and retired in good order to the frontier of the Swiss Confederation, where it dispersed. The majority of the survivors crossed into Switzerland, among them Engels, who preserved the pleasantest memories of his experiences on this occasion, and in later life used to enjoy telling the history of the campaign, which he represented as a gay and agreeable episode of no particular importance. Marx, whose capacity for enjoyment was more limited, found Paris a melancholy place. The revolution had patently failed. Legitimist, Orleanist and Bonapartist intrigue were undermining whatever remained of the democratic structure: such socialists and radicals as had not fled were either in prison or liable to find themselves there at any moment. The appearance of Marx, who was by this time a figure of European notoriety, was highly unwelcome to the government. Soon after his arrival he was presented with the alternative of leaving France or retiring to the

Morbihan in Brittany. Of free countries Belgium was closed to him; Switzerland, which had expelled Weitling and showed little friendliness to Bakunin, was unlikely to permit him to stay: only one European country was likely to place no obstacle in his path. Marx arrived in Paris from the Rhineland in July; a month later a subscription among his friends, among whom Lassalle's name occurs for the first time, enabled him to pay his fare to England. He arrived in London on 24 August 1849; his family followed a month later, and Engels, after dallying in Switzerland, and making a long and enjoyable sea voyage from Genoa, came in the beginning of November. He found Marx convinced that the revolution might at any moment break out once more, and engaged on a pamphlet against the conservative French republic.

Chapter Eight

EXILE IN LONDON: THE FIRST
PHASE

There is only one antidote to mental suffering, and that is
physical pain.

KARL MARX, *Herr Vogt*

MARX arrived in London in 1849 expecting to stay in
England for a few weeks, perhaps months: and in the
event lived there uninterruptedly until his death in
1883. The isolation of England intellectually and socially from the main currents of continental life had
always been great, and the middle years of the nineteenth century offered no exception. The issues which
shook the Continent took many years to cross the
English Channel, and when they did, did so in some
new and peculiar shape, transformed and anglicized in
the process of transition. Foreign revolutionaries were
on the whole left unmolested, provided they behaved
themselves in an orderly and inconspicuous manner,
but neither was any kind of contact established with
them. Their hosts treated them with correctness and
civility, mingled with a mild indifference to their affairs
which at once irritated and amused them. Revolutionaries and men of letters, who for many years had spent
their lives in a ferment of intellectual and political
activity, found the London atmosphere inhumanly
cold. The sense of total isolation and exile was brought
home to them even more sharply by the benevolent,
distant, often slightly patronizing manner in which
they were treated by the few Englishmen with whom

they came into contact; and while this tolerant and civilized attitude did indeed create a vacuum, in which it was possible to recover physically and morally after the nightmare of 1849, the very distance from events which created this feeling of tranquillity, the immense stability which the capitalist *régime* appeared to possess in England, the complete absence of any symptom of revolution, at times tended to induce a sense of hopeless stagnation which demoralized and embittered all but very few of the men engaged in it. In the case of Marx desperate poverty and squalor were added factors in desiccating his never unduly romantic or pliant character. While these years of exile benefited him as a thinker and a revolutionary, they caused him to retire almost entirely into the narrow circle composed of his family, Engels, and a few intimate friends, such as Liebknecht, Wolff and Freiligrath. As a public personality his natural harshness, aggressiveness, and jealousy, his desire to crush all rivals, increased with years; his dislike of the society in which he lived became more and more acute and his personal contact with individual members of it more and more difficult: he was more amiable to 'bourgeois' strangers than to socialists outside his orbit; he quarrelled easily and disliked reconciliation. While he had Engels to lean on he required no other help, and towards the end of his life when the respect and admiration which he received were at their highest, no one else dared to approach him too closely for fear of some particularly humiliating rebuff. Like many great men he liked flattery, and even more, total submission: in his last years he obtained both in full measure, and died in greater honour and material comfort than he had enjoyed during any previous period of his life.

These were the years in which romantic patriots, like Kossuth or Garibaldi, were fêted and publicly cheered in the streets of London; they were regarded as picturesque figures from whom heroic behaviour and noble words were to be expected, rather than as interesting or distinguished men with whom human relations could be established. The majority of their followers were looked upon as harmless eccentrics, as indeed many of them were. Marx, who did not possess sufficient fame or charm to attract such attention, found himself with few friends, and practically penniless, in a country which, although he had visited it less than three years previously, he knew superficially. He remained in this isolated condition all his life. Living as he did in the midst of an immensely variegated and thriving society, then in the very heyday of the phenomenal growth of its economic and political power, he remained all his life personally insulated from it, treating it solely as an object of scientific observation. The collapse of militant radicalism abroad left him no choice, at any rate for a time, but that of a life of observation and scholarship. The important consequence of this was that, since the material upon which he drew was largely English, he relied for the evidence for his hypotheses and generalizations almost entirely on English authors and experience. Those pieces of detailed social and historical research, which form the best and most original chapters in *Das Kapital*, are chiefly occupied with periods for which most of the evidence could be obtained from the financial columns of the *Economist* newspaper, from economic histories, from statistical material to be found in government Blue Books (which he was the first scholar to put to serious scientific use) and other sources to which access could be had without leaving the confines of London, or indeed of the Reading Room of the British Museum. It was done in the midst of a life spent in ceaseless agitation and practical organizing activity, but with an air of extreme aloofness, as if the writer were situated many miles from the scene of his discussion, a fact which sometimes causes an entirely false impression of Marx, as having grown, during the years of exile, into a remote and detached man of learning who at the age of thirty-two had left the life of action behind him to engage in purely theoretical inquiries.

The moment at which Marx arrived in England was singularly unfavourable to any prospects of the revolution. The mass movement to which continental socialists looked as a model of organized proletarian action among the most highly industrialized and therefore the most socially advanced European nation—Chartism—had lately suffered an overwhelming defeat: foreign observers, including Engels, had seriously over-estimated its strength. It was a loose congeries of heterogeneous interests and persons, and included romantic Tories, advanced radicals influenced by continental models, evangelical reformers, philo-sophical radicals, dispossessed farmers and artisans, apocalyptic visionaries. They were united by a common horror of the growing pauperization and social degradation of the lower middle class which marked every advance of the industrial revolution; many of them recoiled from all thought of violence and belonged to the class so contemptuously referred to in the Communist Manifesto as 'economists, philanthropists, humanitarian improvers of the conditions of the working class, organizers of charity, members of societies for the prevention of cruelty to animals, temperance fanatics, hole-and-corner reformers of every imaginable kind'.

The movement was badly organized. Its leaders neither agreed among themselves nor possessed individually, and still less collectively, clear beliefs as to the ends to be set before their followers, or the means to be adopted for their realization. The most steadfast members of the movement were those trade unionists of the future, who were principally anxious to improve the conditions and wages of labour, and were interested in wider questions only so far as they concerned their particular cause. It is doubtful whether a serious revolutionary movement could under any circumstances have been created out of this peculiar amalgam. As it was, nothing happened. It may have been the specious relief afforded by the great Reform Bill, or the power of Nonconformity which originally stemmed the tide. At any rate by 1850 the great crisis which had begun in 1847 was over. It was succeeded by the first consciously recognized economic boom in European history, which enormously increased the rate of development of industry and commerce and extinguished the last embers of the Chartist conflagration. Organizers and agitators remained to fight the workers' wrongs, but the exasperated years of Peterloo and the Tolpuddle martyrs, which, in the grim and moving pamphlets of Hodgskin and Bray, and the savage irony of William Cobbett, have left a bitter record of stupid oppression and widespread social ruin, were insensibly giving way to the milder age of John Stuart Mill and the English positivists with their socialist sympathies, the Christian Socialism of the sixties, and the essentially non-political trade-unionism of such prudent and cautious opportunists as Cremer or Lucraft, who distrusted the attempts of foreign doctrinaires to teach them their own business.

Marx naturally began by establishing contact with the German exiles. London at this time contained a conflux of German *émigrés*, members of the dissolved revolutionary committees, exiled poets and intellectuals, vaguely radical German artisans who had settled in England long before the revolution and active communists lately expelled from France or Switzerland, who attempted to reconstitute the Communist League and to renew relations with sympathetic English radicals. Marx followed his usual tactics and kept rigidly to the society of the Germans: he believed firmly that the revolution was not over: indeed he remained convinced of this until the *coup d'état* which placed Louis Napoleon on the throne of France. Meanwhile he spent what he regarded as a mere lull during the battle in pursuing the normal activities of political exile, attending meetings of refugees, and quarrelling with those who incurred his suspicion. The cultured and fastidious Herzen, who was in London at this time, conceived a violent dislike for him, and in his memoirs gave a malicious and brilliant description of the position occupied by Marx and his followers, then and later, among the other political *émigrés*. The Germans in general were notoriously incapable of co-operating with the other exiles, Italians, Russians, Poles, Hungarians, whose lack of method and passion for intense personal relations shocked and disgusted them. The latter, for their part found the Germans equally unattractive; they disliked their woodenness, their coarse manners, their colossal vanity, above all their sordid and unceasing internecine feuds, in the course of which it was not unusual for intimate details of private life to be dragged into the open and brutally caricatured in the public Press.

The disasters of 1848 did not indeed shake Marx's theoretical beliefs, but they forced him seriously to revise his political programme. In the years 1847–8 he was so far influenced by the propaganda of Weitling and Blanqui as to begin to believe, against his natural, Hegelian, inclination, that a successful revolution could be made by means of a *coup d'état*, carried out by a small and resolute body of trained revolutionaries, who, having seized power, would hold it, constituting themselves the executive committee of the masses in whose name they acted. This body would function as the spear-head of the proletarian attack. The broad masses of the working class after years of bondage and darkness could not be expected to be ripe either for self-government, or for the control and liquidation of the forces they had displaced. A party must therefore be formed to function as a political, intellectual, and legislative *élite* of the people, enjoying its confidence in virtue of its disinterestedness, its superior training and its practical insight into the needs of the immediate situation, able to guide the people's uncertain steps during the first period of its new freedom. This necessary interlude he termed the state of permanent revolution, guided by the revolutionary class dictatorship of the proletariat over the rest 'as a necessary intermediate step to the abolition of all class distinctions, to the abolition of all the existing productive relations upon which these distinctions rest, to the abolition of all social relations which correspond to these productive relations, and to the complete reversal of all ideas which derive from these social relations'. But here, although the end was clear, the means were left comparatively vague. The 'permanent revolution' was to be brought about by the dictatorship of the proletariat: but how was this stage to be effected and what form was it to take? There is no doubt that by 1848 Marx thought of it in terms of a self-appointed *élite*: not indeed working in secret, as Blanqui insisted, or headed by a single dictatorial figure, as occasionally advocated by Bakunin, but as Babeuf had conceived it in 1796, a small body of convinced and ruthless individuals, who were to wield dictatorial power and educate the proletariat until it reached a level at which it comprehended its proper task. It was as a means to this that he advocated in Cologne in 1848–9 a temporary alliance with the leaders of the radical bourgeoisie. The *petite bourgeoisie* struggling against the pressure of the classes immediately above it was the workers' natural ally at this stage: but being unable to rule by its own strength, it would become more and more dependent on the workers' support, until the moment arrived at which the workers, already economic masters of the situation, acquire the official forms of political power, whether by a violent *coup*, or by gradual pressure. This doctrine (the clearest formulation of which is to be found in Marx's Address to the Communist League in 1850) is familiar to the world because it was urged by Trotsky in 1905, adopted by Lenin, and put into practice with the most literal fidelity by them in Russia in 1917. Marx himself, however, in the light of the events in 1848, abandoned it, at any rate in practice, in vital respects. He gradually discarded the whole conception of the seizure of power by an *élite*, which seemed to him powerless to effect anything in the face of a hostile regular army and a supine and untrained proletariat. The leaders of the workers were devoid neither of courage nor of practical sense, yet it would plainly have been quite impossible for them to remain in power in 1848 against the combined force of the royalists, the army and the upper middle class. Unless the proletariat as a whole was made conscious of its historic part, its leaders must remain helpless. They might provoke an armed rising, but could not hope to retain its fruits without conscious and intelligent support from the majority of the working class. Consequently, the vital lesson which the events of 1848 contain is, according to Marx, that the first duty of a revolutionary leader is to disseminate among the masses the consciousness of their destiny and their task. Inevitably this is a lengthy and laborious process, but unless it is performed, nothing will be achieved, save the squandering of revolutionary energy in sporadic outbursts led by adventurers and hot-heads, which, having no real basis in the popular will, must inevitably be defeated after a short period of triumph by the recovered forces of reaction, and be followed by brutal repression which cripples the proletariat for many years to come. On this ground he refused to support, on the eve of its occurrence, the revolution which resulted in the Paris Commune of 1871: although later, and largely for tactical motives, he wrote it a moving and eloquent epitaph.

The second point on which he changed his views was the possibility of collaboration with the bourgeoisie. Theoretically, he still believed that the dialectic of history necessitated a *bourgeois* régime as a prelude to complete communism; but the strength of this class in Germany and France, and its open determination to protect itself against its proletarian ally, convinced him that a compact with it would militate against the workers as the weaker power: the plan to govern from behind the scenes could not be realized yet. This had been the chief point of difference between him and the Cologne communists who had opposed alliance with the liberals as being suicidal opportunism. He now embraced their point of view himself, although not for their reasons: not, that is to say, because opportunism as such was morally degrading or necessarily self-defeating, but because it was in this particular case bound to be unsuccessful, to confuse issues in a party not too securely organized, and so lead to internal weakness and defeat. Hence his continued insistence in later years on preserving the purity of the party, and its freedom from any compromising entanglements. The policy of gradual expansion and the slow conquest of political power through recognized parliamentary institutions, accompanied by systematic pressure on an international scale upon employers through trade unions and similar organizations, as a means of securing improved economic conditions for their workers, which characterizes the tactics of socialist parties in the late nineteenth and early twentieth centuries, was the legitimate product of Marx's analysis of the causes of the catastrophe of the revolutionary year 1848.

His main objective—the creation of conditions in which the dictatorship of the proletariat, 'the permanent revolution', might be realized—was left unaffected: the bourgeoisie and all its institutions were inevitably doomed to extinction. The process might take longer than he had originally supposed; if so, the proletariat must be taught patience; not until the situation itself is ripe for intervention must the leaders call for action: in the meanwhile it must devote itself to husbanding, organizing and disciplining its forces into readiness for the decisive crisis. History has offered a ironical commentary on this conclusion: the makers of

the communist revolution in Russia (to which, let it
be admitted, Marx did not think his theory to be
applicable), by acting in accordance with the earlier
and discarded view of 1850, and striking while the
popular masses were palpably unripe for their task, did,
at any rate, succeed in averting the consequences of
1848 and 1871: while the orthodox German and
Austrian social democrats, faithful to the master's later
doctrine, by moving carefully and with caution, and
expending their energy upon the education of the masses
to a sense of their mission, were duly overwhelmed
by the re-organized reactionary class, whose strength the
march of history, and constant sapping on the part of the
proletariat, should long before have fatally undermined.

Meanwhile no sign of revolution could be detected
anywhere, and the mood of irrational optimism was
succeeded by one of profound depression. 'One cannot
recollect those days without acute pain', wrote Herzen
in his memoirs. '. . . France was moving with the
velocity of a falling star towards the inevitable *coup
d'état*. Germany lay prostrate at the feet of Czar
Nicholas, dragged down by wretched, betrayed
Hungary. . . . The revolutionaries carried on empty
agitation. Even the most serious persons are sometimes
overcome by the fascination of mere forms, and
manage to convince themselves that they are in fact
doing something if they hold meetings with a mass of
documents and protocols, conferences at which facts
are recorded, decisions are taken, proclamations are
printed, and so forth. The bureaucracy of the revolution is capable of losing itself in this sort of thing just
as much as real officialdom: England teems with hundreds of associations of this sort: solemn meetings take
place which dukes and peers of the realm, clergymen

and secretaries, ceremoniously attend: treasurers collect funds, journalists write articles, all are busily engaged in doing nothing at all. These philanthropic or religious gatherings fulfil the double function of serving as a form of amusement and acting as a sop to the troubled consciences of these somewhat worldly Christians. . . . The whole thing was a contradiction in terms: an open conspiracy, a plot concocted behind open doors.'

In the sultry atmosphere of continual intrigue, suspicion and recrimination which fills the early years of any large politicial emigration whose members are bound to each other by circumstances rather than by any clearly conceived common cause, Marx spent his first two years in London. He resolutely declined to have any dealings with Herzen, Mazzini and their associates, but he was not inactive. He transformed the *Neue Rheinische Zeitung* into a review, organized committees to help refugees, published a successful denunciation of the methods of the police in the Cologne trials of his associates, tracking down and exposing the gross forgeries and perjury perpetrated by its agents; which, if it did not free his comrades, made trials of the same kind more difficult in the future; carried on a vendetta against Willich within the Communist League, and, believing that an institution which promotes half-truths is more dangerous than total inactivity and is better dead, by remorseless intrigue brought about its dissolution. Having thus successfully torpedoed his own former associates, and feeling nothing but contempt for the rest of the emigration as a collection of ineffective and harmless chatterers, he constituted himself and Engels as an independent centre of propaganda, a personal union round which the broken and scattered remnants of German Communism would gradually be gathered into a force once more. The plan was completely successful.

His most important writings of this period are concerned with the recent events in France: his style, often opaque and obscure when dealing with abstract issues, is luminous when dealing with facts. The essays on the *Class Struggle in France*, and the articles reprinted under the title *The Eighteenth Brumaire of Louis Bonaparte*, are models of penetrating and cruel pamphleteering. The two pamphlets cover much of the same ground and give a brilliant, polemical description of the revolution and the second republic, analysing in detail the relations and interplay of the political, economic and personal factors, in terms of the alignment of classes whose needs they embody. There is a brilliant analysis of the role of the French state which functions less as the committee of the ruling class (the formula of *Communist Manifesto*) than as an independent source of power supported by, but at times overriding the wishes of, the bourgeoisie, in order to preserve the social and political *status quo*. In a series of sharp, epigrammatic sketches the leading representatives of the various parties are classified and assigned to the classes on whose support they depend. The evolution of the political situation from vague liberalism to the conservative republic, and thence to the open class-struggle, ending in naked despotism, is represented as a travesty of the events of 1789: then every successive phase was more violent and revolutionary than the last; in 1848 the exact reverse occurred: in June the proletariat was deserted and betrayed by its *petit bourgeois* allies; later those were in their turn abandoned by the middle class; finally they too were outmanoeuvred by

the great landowners and financiers and delivered into
the hands of the army and Louis Napoleon. Nor could
this have been prevented by a different policy on the
part of individual politicians since it was the inescapable result of the stage of historical development
reached by French society at this time.

Marx's other activities at this period included popular lectures on political economy to the German
Workers' Educational Union, and finally a considerable
correspondence with the German revolutionaries now
scattered everywhere, and notably with Engels, who
reluctantly and unhappily, having no other means of
supporting himself, made his peace with his parents and
settled down in Manchester to work in the office of his
father's firm of cotton-spinners. The comparative
security which he obtained by this means he used to
support Marx, materially and intellectually, during the
remainder of his life. Marx's own financial position was
for many years desperate: he had no regular source of
income, a growing family, and a reputation which
precluded the possibility of employment by any
respectable concern. The squalid poverty in which he
and his family lived during the next twenty years, and
the unspeakable humiliation which this entailed, have
often been described: at first the family wandered from
one hovel to another, from Chelsea to Leicester Square
and thence to the disease-ridden slums of Soho; often
there was no money to pay the tradesmen and the
family would literally starve until a loan or the arrival
of a pound note from Engels temporarily eased the
situation; sometimes the entire clothing of the family
was in pawn, and they were forced to sit for hours
without light or food, interrupted only by the visits of
dunning creditors, who were met on the doorstep by

one or other of the children with the unvarying and automatic answer, 'Mr. Marx ain't upstairs.'

A lively description of the conditions in which he lived during the first seven years of exile survives in the report of a Prussian spy who somehow contrived to worm his way into the Dean Street establishment: '. . . He lives in one of the worst and cheapest neighbourhoods in London. He occupies two rooms. There is not one clean or decent piece of furniture in either room, everything is broken, tattered and torn, with thick dust over everything . . . manuscripts, books and newspapers lie beside the children's toys, bits and pieces from his wife's sewing basket, cups with broken rims, dirty spoons, knives, forks, lamps, an inkpot, tumblers, pipes, tobacco ash—all piled up on the same table. On entering the room smoke and tobacco fumes make your eyes water to such an extent that at first you seem to be groping about in a cavern—until you get used to it, and manage to make out certain objects in the haze. Sitting down is a dangerous business. Here is a chair with only three legs, there another which happens to be whole, on which the children are playing at cooking. That is the one that is offered to the visitor, but the children's cooking is not removed, and if you sit down you risk a pair of trousers. But all these things do not in the least embarrass Marx or his wife. You are received in the most friendly way and are cordially offered pipes, tobacco, and whatever else there may happen to be. Presently a clever and interesting conversation arises which repays for all the domestic deficiencies and this makes the discomfort bearable...'[1]

A man of genius forced to live in a garret, to go into

[1] Quoted from *Karl Marx, Man and Fighter*, by B. Nicolaievsky and O. Maenchen-Helfen.

hiding when his creditors grow importunate, or to lie in bed because his clothes are pawned, is a conventional subject of gay and sentimental comedy. Marx was not a bohemian, and his misfortunes affected him tragically. He was proud, excessively thin-skinned, and made great demands upon the world: the petty humiliations and insults to which his condition exposed him, the frustration of his desire for the commanding position to which he thought himself entitled, the repression of his colossal natural vitality, made him turn in upon himself in paroxysms of hatred and of rage. His bitter feeling often found outlet in his writings and in long and savage personal vendettas. He saw plots, persecution, and conspiracies everywhere; the more his victims protested their innocence, the more convinced he became of their duplicity and their guilt.

His mode of living consisted of daily visits to the British Museum reading-room, where he normally remained from nine in the morning until it closed at seven; this was followed by long hours of work at night, accompanied by ceaseless smoking, which from a luxury had become an indispensable anodyne; this affected his health permanently and he became liable to frequent attacks of a disease of the liver sometimes accompanied by boils and an inflammation of the eyes, which interfered with his work, exhausted and irritated him, and interrupted his never certain means of livelihood. 'I am plagued like Job, though not so God-fearing', he wrote in 1858. 'Everything that these gentlemen [the doctors] say boils down to the fact that one ought to be a prosperous *rentier* and not a poor devil like me, as poor as a church mouse.' In other moods he would swear that the bourgeoisie would one day pay dearly for every one of his carbuncles. Engels, whose annual income during those years does not appear to have exceeded one hundred pounds, with which, as his father's representative, he had to keep up a respectable establishment in Manchester, could not, with all his generosity, afford much systematic help at first: occasionally, friends in Cologne, or generous German socialists like Liebknecht or Freiligrath, managed to collect small sums for him, which, together with fees for occasional journalism, and occasional 'loans' from his rich uncle Philips in Holland and small legacies from relatives, enabled him to continue on the very brink of subsistence. It is not therefore difficult to understand that he hated poverty and the vicious slavery and degradation which it entails at least as passionately as servility. The descriptions scattered in his works of life in industrial slums, in mining villages or plantations, and of the attitude of civilized opinion towards them, are given with a combination of violent indignation and frigid, wholly unhysterical bitterness, which, particularly when his account grows detailed and his tone grows unnaturally quiet and flat, possess a frightening quality and induce intolerable anger and shame in readers left unmoved by the fiery rhetoric of Carlyle, the dignified and humane pleading of J. S. Mill, or the sweeping eloquence of William Morris and the Christian Socialists. During these years three of his children, his two sons Guido and Edgar, and his daughter Franziska died, largely as a result of the conditions in which they lived. When Franziska died he had no money to pay for a coffin, and was rescued only by the generosity of a French refugee. The incident is described in harrowing details in a letter written by Frau Marx to a fellow exile. She was herself often ill, and the children were looked after by their family servant, Helene Demuth, who remained with them until the end.

'I could not and cannot fetch the doctor', he wrote to Engels on one of these occasions, 'because I have no money for the medicine. For the last eight or ten days I have fed my family on bread and potatoes, and today it is still doubtful whether I shall be able to obtain even these.'

He was uncommunicative by nature, and less than anyone who has ever lived given to self-pity; indeed, in his letters to Engels he sometimes satirized his own misfortunes with a grim irony which may conceal from the casual reader the desperate condition in which he frequently found himself. But when in 1856, his son Edgar, of whom he was very fond, died at the age of six, it broke through even his iron reserve: 'I have suffered every kind of misfortune,' he wrote to his friend, 'but I have only just learnt what real unhappiness is . . . in the midst of all the suffering which I have gone through in these days the thought of you, and your friendship, and the hope that we may still have something reasonable to do in this world, has kept me upright. . . .

'Bacon says that really important people have so many contacts with nature and the world, have so much to interest them, that they easily get over any loss. I am not of those important people. My child's death has affected me so greatly that I feel the loss as bitterly as on the first day. My wife is also completely broken down.'

The only form of pleasure which the family could allow itself was an occasional picnic on Hampstead Heath during the summer months. They used to set out on Sunday morning from the house in Dean Street, and, accompanied by Lenchen Demuth (to whom Marx became much attached) and one or two friends, carrying a basket of food and newspapers bought on the

way, walked to Hampstead. There they would sit under
the trees, and while the children played or picked
flowers, their elders would talk or read or sleep. As the
afternoon wore on, the mood grew gayer and gayer,
particularly when the jovial Engels was present. They
made jokes, sang, ran races. Marx recited poetry, which
he was fond of doing, took the children for rides on his
back, entertained everyone, and as a final turn, would
solemnly mount and ride a donkey up and down in front
of the party: a sight which never failed to give general
pleasure. At nightfall they would walk back often singing patriotic German or English songs on their way
home to Soho. These agreeable occasions were, however, few and rare, and did little to lighten what Marx
himself in one of his letters to Engels called the sleepless night of exile.

To this condition some slight relief was brought by
the sudden invitation to write regular articles on affairs
in Europe for the *New York Daily Tribune*. The offer
was made by Charles Augustus Dana, its foreign
editor, who had been introduced to Marx by Freiligrath in Cologne in 1849, and was greatly impressed by
his political shrewdness. The *New York Tribune* was a
radical newspaper, founded by a group of American
followers of Fourier, which had at this period a circulation of over 200,000 copies, then probably the greatest
of any newspaper in the world; its outlook was broadly
progressive: in internal affairs it pursued an anti-
slavery, free trade policy, while in foreign affairs it
attacked the principle of autocracy, and so found itself
in opposition to virtually every government in Europe.
Marx, who stubbornly refused offers of collaboration
with Continental journals the tendency of which he
thought reactionary, accepted this offer with alacrity.

The new correspondent was to be paid one pound sterling per article. For nearly ten years he wrote weekly dispatches for it roaming over a wide field of subjects, which are of some interest even now. Dana's first request to him was to write a series of articles on the strategy and tactics of both armies during the civil war in Germany and Austria, together with general comments on the art of modern warfare. As Marx was entirely ignorant of the latter subject and had at this period very little English, he found the request far from easy to fulfil: but to refuse anything which offered a steady if meagre source of income was unthinkable. In his perplexity he turned to Engels, who, as on so many occasions in later life, readily and obligingly wrote the articles and signed them with Marx's name. Henceforward, whenever the subject was unknown or uncongenial to him, or he was prevented from working by absence or ill-health, Engels was called upon, and performed his task with such efficiency that the *Tribune's* London correspondent soon acquired a considerable popularity in America as an exceptionally versatile and well-informed journalist, with a definite public of his own.

Engels's articles on the German revolution were reprinted as a pamphlet by Marx called *The German Revolution and Counter Revolution*, and end with the assurance that the revolution is about to break out with even greater violence in the near future. Later the friends admitted they were over-optimistic. Marx formulated the celebrated generalization that only an economic slump could lead to a successful revolution; thus the revolution of 1848 was nurtured in the economic collapse of 1847, and the boom of 1851 removed all hope of imminent political conflagration.

Henceforth the attention of both is concentrated upon detecting symptoms of a major economic crisis. Engels from his office in Manchester filled his letters with information about the state of world markets; gold losses by the Bank of England, the bankruptcy of a Hamburg bank, a bad harvest in France or America, are noted exultantly as indicating that the great crisis cannot be far off. In 1857 a genuine slump did at last occur on the required scale. It was not, however, except in agricultural Italy, followed by any revolutionary developments. After this there is less mention of inevitable crises, and more discussion of the organization of a revolutionary party. The acute disappointment had left its effect.

While Engels dealt with the military intelligence required by the American public, Marx published a rapid succession of articles on English politics, internal and external, on foreign policy, on Chartism, and the character of the various English ministries, which he became expert at summing up in a few malicious sentences, usually at the expense of *The Times*, which always remained his bugbear. He wrote a good deal about the English rule in India and in Ireland. India was, he declared, bound in any case to have been conquered by a stronger power:

'The question is not whether the English had any right to conquer India, but whether we should have preferred her to have been conquered by Turks or Persians, or Russians. . . . Of course it is impossible to compel the English bourgeoisie to want the emancipation or improvement of the social condition of the Indian masses, which depends not only on the development of the forces of production, but on the ownership of them by the people. But what it can do is to create the material conditions for the realization of this double need.'

And again: 'However melancholy we may find', he wrote in 1853, 'the spectacle of the ruin and desolation of these tens of thousands of industrious, peaceful patriarchal, social groups . . . suddenly cut off from their ancient civilization and their traditional means of existence, we must not forget that these idyllic village communities . . . always provided a firm basis to oriental despotism, confining the human intelligence within the narrowest limits, making of it the obedient traditional instrument of superstition, stunting its growth, robbing it . . . of all capacity of historical activity; let us not forget the egoism of barbarians who, concentrated on an insignificant portion of earth's surface, watched unmoved while immense empires crumbled, unspeakable cruelties were committed, the populations of entire cities were butchered—observed this as if they were events in nature, and so themselves became the helpless victims of every invader who happened to turn his attention to them. . . . In causing social revolution in India, England was, it is true, guided by the lowest motives, and conducted it dully and woodenly. But that is not the point. The question is whether humanity can fulfil its purpose without a complete social revolution in Asia. If not, then England, in spite of all her crimes, was the unconscious instrument of history in bringing about this revolution.'

Of Ireland he said that the cause of English labour was inextricably bound up with the liberation of Ireland, whose cheap labour was a continual threat to the English unions; her economic subjection, as in the analogous cases of serfdom in Russia and slavery in the United States, must be abolished before Ireland's English masters, among whom the English working class (who treated the Irish much as the 'poor whites' of the Southern states of America treated the negroes) must be included, could hope to emancipate themselves and create a free society. In both cases he consistently underestimated the force of rising nationalism: his hatred of all separatism, as of all institutions founded on some purely traditional or emotional basis, blinded him to their actual influence. In a similar spirit Engels, writing of the Czechs, observed that the nationalism of the Western Slavs was an artificially preserved, unreal phenomenon, which could not long resist the advance of the superior German culture. Such absorption was a fate inevitably in store for all small and local civilizations, in virtue of the force of historical gravitation which causes the smaller to be merged in the greater: a tendency which all progressive parties should actively encourage. Both Marx and Engels believed that nationalism, together with religion and militarism, were so many anachronisms, at once the by-products and the bulwarks of the capitalist order, irrational, counter-revolutionary forces which, with the passing of their material foundation, would automatically disappear. Marx's own tactical policy with regard to them was to consider whether in a given case they operated for or against the proletarian cause, and to decide in accordance with this criterion alone, whether they were to be supported or attacked. Thus he favoured it in India and in Ireland, because it was a weapon in the fight against imperialism, and attacked the democratic nationalism of Mazzini or Kossuth because in such countries as Italy, Hungary or Poland, it seemed to him to work merely for the replacement of a foreign by a native system of capitalist exploitation, and so to obstruct the social revolution. Among English politicians he attacked Russell as a pseudo-radical who betrayed his cause at every step, but his *bête noire* was undoubtedly Palmerston, whom he accused of being a disguised Russian agent, and mocked for his sentimental support of small nationalities in Europe. He was, however, a connoisseur of political skill in all its forms, and confessed to a certain admiration of the *élan* and adroitness with which that cynical and light-hearted statesman carried off his most unscrupulous strokes.

His attacks on Palmerston brought him into contact with an exceedingly odd and remarkable figure. David Urquhart had in his youth been in the diplomatic service, and after becoming a warm Philhellene in Athens had been transferred to Constantinople, where he conceived a violent and life-long passion for Islam and the Turks. He celebrated the "purity" of their constitution, and the spiritual and physical effects of their steam baths to which he introduced his country-men. He equally admired the Church of Rome, with which he remained on excellent terms, although he was born and died a Calvinist; with this he combined an equally violent hatred for Whigs, free trade, the Church of England, industrialism, and, in particular, the Russian Empire, whose malevolent and omnipotent influence he regarded as responsible for all the evils in Europe. This eccentric figure, a picturesque survival from a more spacious age, sat in Parliament as an Independent for many years, and published a newspaper and numerous tracts devoted almost entirely to the single purpose of exposing Palmerston, whom he accused of being a hired agent of the Czar, engaged in a life-long attempt to subvert the moral order of Western Europe in his master's interest. Even Palmerston's attitude during the Crimean War did not shake him: he explained it as a

cunning ruse to cloak the nature of his real activities;
hence his deliberate sabotage of the entire campaign,
which was clearly designed to do Russia as little
damage as possible. Marx, who had somehow arrived
at the same curious conclusion, seemed to be no less
genuinely convinced of Palmerston's venality. The two
men met and formed an alliance; Urquhart published
anti-Palmerstonian pamphlets by Marx while Marx became an official Urquhartite, contributed to Urquhart's
paper and appeared on the platforms of his meetings.
His articles were later published as pamphlets. The
most peculiar are *Palmerston, What Has He Done?* and
The Secret Diplomatic History of the Eighteenth Century,
both of which were devoted to exposing the hidden
hand of Russia in all major European disasters. Each
was under the impression that he was skilfully using the
other for his own ends: Marx thought Urquhart a
harmless monomaniac of whom use might be made;
Urquhart, for his part, thought highly of Marx's
abilities as a propagandist, and on one occasion congratulated him on possessing an intelligence worthy of a
Turk. This bizarre association continued harmoniously, if intermittently, for a number of years. After the
deaths of Palmerston and Czar Nicholas, the alliance
was gradually dissolved. Marx obtained a good deal of
amusement, and as much financial help as he could
extract, from his relationship with his strange patron,
of whom he soon grew quite fond; indeed, the latter was
unique among his political allies in that their relation
continued to be entirely friendly until Urquhart's death.

Marx found few sympathizers among the trade
union leaders. The ablest of them either held views not
very dissimilar to those of Owen, who by the shining
example of his own achievements, sought to prove the

wicked baselessness of the doctrine of class war: or else were busy local labour leaders working for the immediate needs of this or that trade or industry, dead to wider issues, prepared to welcome all radicals equally in a federation called 'The Fraternal Democrats', the very name of which revolted Marx. He tolerated radicals like the voluble and energetic George Harvey whom he and Engels called 'Citizen Hip Hip Hurrah'. The only Englishman who stood at all close to him in those days was Ernest Jones, a revolutionary Chartist, who made a vain attempt to revive that dying movement. Jones was born and brought up in Germany and resembled more closely than anyone else in England the type of continental socialist familiar to Marx; his views were, especially in later years, too similar to those of the 'True Socialists' Hess and Grün to please Marx entirely, but he needed allies, the choice was limited, and he accepted Jones as the best and most advanced that England had to offer. Jones, who conceived a great admiration and affection for Marx and his household, supplied him with a great deal of information about English conditions; it was he who turned Marx's attention to the land enclosures which still went on in Scotland where many hundreds of small tenants and crofters had been evicted to make room for deer parks and pasture. The result was a vitriolic article by Marx in the *New York Tribune* on the private affairs of the Duchess of Sutherland, who had expressed sympathy for the cause of the Negro slaves in America. The article, which is a sketch for the longer passage in *Kapital*, is a masterpiece of bitter and vehement eloquence, directly descended from the masterpieces of Voltaire and Marat, and a model for many later pieces of socialist invective. The attack is not so much personal as directed at the system under which a capricious old woman no more deranged, heartless, and vindictive than the majority of her immediate society, has it in her absolute power, with the full approval of her class and of public opinion, to humiliate, uproot and ruin an entire population of honest and industrious men and women, rendered destitute overnight in a land which was rightfully theirs, since all that was man-made in it they and their ancestors had created by their labour.

Such pieces of social analysis and polemic pleased the American public no less than Marx's dry and ironical articles on foreign affairs. The articles were well-informed, shrewd and detached in tone: they showed no particular power of prescience, nor were there any attempts to give a comprehensive survey of contemporary affairs as a whole: as a commentary on events they were less candid and less interesting than the letters which their author wrote to Engels at this period, but as journalism they were in advance of their time. Marx's method was to present his readers with a brief sketch of events or characters, emphasizing hidden interests and the sinister activities likely to result from them, rather than the explicit motives furnished by the actors themselves, or the social value of this or that measure or policy. This gives his journalism a highly twentieth-century flavour, and exhibits more vividly than his theoretical writings, the genuine difference between his naturalistic, acid, distrustful, ethically pragmatic attitude, and that of the great majority of the more or less humanitarian and idealistic social historians and critics of his time. At the same time he was engaged in gathering material for the economic treatise which should serve as a weapon against the vague idealism of the loosely connected radical groups, which, in his view, led to confusion both of thought and of action, and paralysed the efforts of such few clear-headed leaders as the workers possessed. He applied himself to the task of establishing, in the place of this, a rigorous doctrine, unambiguous in theory and definite in practice, adherence to which would become at once the test, the reason and the guarantee of a united, and, above all, active body of social revolutionaries. Their strength would derive from their unity, and their unity from the coherence of the practical beliefs which they had in common.

The foundations of his doctrine were embodied in his previous writings, notably in the *Communist Manifesto*. In a letter written in 1852 he carefully stated what he regarded as original in it: 'What I did that was new was to prove (1) that the *existence of classes* is only bound up with particular, historic phases in the development of production; (2) that the class struggle necessarily leads to the *dictatorship of the proletariat*; (3) that this dictatorship itself only constitutes the transition to the *abolition of all classes* and to a classless society.' On these foundations the new movement was to be built.

In a sense he succeeded more rapidly than he could have hoped: the rise and swift growth upon the ruins of 1848 of a new and militant party of socialist workers in Germany created for him a sphere of new practical activity in which the latter half of his life was spent. This party was not indeed created by him, but his ideas, and above all a belief in the political programme which he had elaborated, inspired its leaders. He was consulted and approached at every turn; everyone knew that he, and he alone, had inspired the movement and created its basis; to him all questions of theory and practice were instinctively referred; he was admired, feared, suspected and obeyed. Yet the German workers did not look to him as their foremost representative and champion: the man who had organized them into a party and ruled it with absolute power was Marx's junior by several years, born and brought up under similar conditions, but in temper and in outlook more unlike, and even opposed to, him than at the time either explicitly admitted.

Ferdinand Lassalle, who created German Social Democracy and led it during its first heroic years, was one of the most ardent public personalities of the nineteenth century. By birth a Silesian Jew, by profession a lawyer, by temperament a romantic revolutionary, he was a man whose outstanding characteristics were his intelligence, his vanity, his boundless energy and self-confidence. Since most of the normal avenues of advancement were barred to him on account of his race and his religion, he threw himself with immense passion into the revolutionary movement, where his exceptional ability, his enthusiasm, but most of all his genius as an agitator and a popular orator swiftly raised him to leadership. During the German revolution he delivered inflammatory speeches against the Government, for which he was tried and imprisoned. During the years which followed the period of recantations and dishonour, when Marx and Engels were in exile, and Liebknecht alone among the original leaders who remained in Germany remained faithful to the cause of socialism, Lassalle took upon himself the task of creating a new and better organized proletarian party upon the ruins of 1848. He conceived himself in the part of its sole leader and inspirer, its intellectual, moral and political dictator. He accomplished this task with brilliant success. His beliefs were derived in equal parts from Hegel and from Marx: from the latter he derived the doctrines of economic determinism, of the class struggle, of the inevitability of exploitation in capitalist society. But he rejected the condemnation of the state in the name of society, refusing to follow Proudhon and Marx in regarding the former as a mere coercive instrument of the ruling class, and accepting the Hegelian thesis, according to which the state, even in its present condition, constitutes the most progressive and dynamic function of a collection of human beings assembled to lead a common life. He strongly believed in centralization and, up to a point, in internal national unity: in later years he began to believe in the possibility of an anti-bourgeois coalition between the king, the aristocracy, the army, and the workers, culminating in an authoritarian collectivist state, headed by the monarch, and organized in the interests of the only true productive, i.e. the labouring, class.

His relations with Marx and Engels had never been wholly easy: he declared that Marx was in theoretical matters his master, and treated him with nervous respect. He heralded him everywhere as a man of genius, arranged for the German publication of his books, and otherwise strove to be of service to him in many ways. Marx grudingly recognized the value of Lassalle's energy, and his organizing ability, but was repelled by him personally, and was deeply suspicious of him politically. He disliked his ostentation, his extravagance, his vanity, his histrionic manners, his loud public profession of his tastes, his opinions and his ambitions; he detested the very brilliance of his impressionistic surveys of social and political facts, which seemed to him flimsy, superficial, and fallacious by comparison with his own painful and laborious thoroughness: he disliked and distrusted the temperamental and capricious control which Lassalle exercised over the workers, and, even more, his absorbed flirtation with the enemy. Finally, he felt jealous and possessive about a movement which owed to him both its practical policy and its intellectual foundations, and now seemed to have deserted him, infatuated by a political *femme fatale*, a specious, glittering adventurer, an avowed opportunist both in private life and in public policy, guided by no fixed plan, attached to no principle, moving towards no clear goal. Nevertheless, a certain intimacy of relations existed between them, or if not intimacy, a mutual appreciation. Lassalle was born and brought up under intellectual influences similar to his own, they fought against the same enemy, and on all fundamental issues spoke the same language, which Proudhon, Bakunin, and the English trade unionists had never done, and the former young Hegelians had long ceased to do. Moreover, he was a man of action, a genuine revolutionary, and absolutely fearless. Each recognized that with, perhaps, the exception of Engels, the other possessed a higher degree of political intelligence, penetration, and practical courage than any other member of their party. They understood each other instinctively, and found communication both easy and exhilarating: when Marx went to Berlin, he stayed quite naturally with Lassalle. When Lassalle came to London, he stayed with Marx, and maddened his proud and sensitive host, then in the last stage of penury, by the mere fact of being a witness of his condition, and even more by his gay patter and easy extravagance, spending more on cigars and buttonholes than Marx and his family spent on a week's livelihood. There was some difficulty, too, about a sum of money which Marx had borrowed from him. Of all this Lassalle, it seemed, was totally unaware, being exceptionally insensitive to his surroundings, as vigorous and flamboyant natures often are. Marx never forgot his humiliation, and after Lassalle's London visit their relations deteriorated abruptly.

Lassalle created the new party by a method still novel in his day, and employed only sporadically by the English Chartists, although familiar enough later: he undertook a series of highly publicized political tours through the industrial areas of Germany, making fiery and seditious speeches which overwhelmed his proletarian audiences and roused them to immense enthusiasm. There and then he formed them into sections of the new workers' movement, organized as an official, legally constituted party, thus breaking openly with the old method of small revolutionary cells which met in secret and carried on underground propaganda. His last journey among his followers was a triumphal tour over conquered territory: it strengthened his already unique influence upon German workers of all types, ages and professions.

The theoretical foundations of the programme were borrowed, largely from Marx, and perhaps to some extent from the radical Prussian economist Rodbertus-Jagetzow, but the party had many strongly non-Marxist characteristics: it was not specifically organized for a revolution; it was opportunist, and prepared for alliance with other anti-bourgeois parties; it was nationalistic and largely confined to German conditions and needs. One of its foremost ends was the development of a workers' co-operative system, not indeed as an alternative to, but as an intrinsic element in, political action, to be organized or financed by the state, yet still sufficiently similar to Proudhon's anti-political mutualism, and the politically sluggish English trade unionism, to incur open hostility from Marx. Moreover, it had been created by means of the personal ascendancy of one individual. There was a strong emotional element in the unquestioned dictatorship which Lassalle exercised in his last years, a form of hero-worship which Marx, who disliked every form of unreason, and distrusted spell-binders in politics, instinctively abhorred. Lassalle introduced into German socialism the theory that circumstances might occur in which something like a genuine alliance might be formed with the absolutist Prussian government against the industrial bourgeoisie. This was the kind of opportunism which Marx must have considered the most ruinous of all possible defects; the experience of 1848, if it taught no other lesson, had conclusively demonstrated the fatal consequence to a young, and as yet comparatively defenceless, party of an alliance with a well-established older party, fundamentally hostile to its demands, in which each attempts to exploit the other, and the better armed force inevitably wins. Marx, as was made evident from his address to the Central Communist Committee in 1850, considered himself to have erred seriously in supposing that an alliance with the radical bourgeoisie was possible and even necessary before the final victory of the proletariat. But even he had never dreamed of an alliance with the feudal nobility for the purpose of delivering an attack on individualism as such, merely for the sake of attaining some kind of state control. Such a move he regarded as a typical Bakuninist caricature of his own policy and aspirations.

Both Marx and Engels were fundamentally solid

German democrats in their attitude to the masses, and instinctively reacted against the seeds of romantic élitism which can now be so clearly discerned in Lassalle's beliefs and acts and speeches, particularly in his passionate patriotism, his self-dramatization as the dedicated leader, his belief in a state-planned economy controlled, at any rate for a time, by the military aristocracy, his advocacy of armed intervention by Germany on the side of the French Emperor in the Italian campaign (which he defended against Marx and Engels on the ground that only a war would precipitate a German revolution), his unconcealed sympathy with Mazzini and the Polish nationalists, finally his belief, on which the economic policies of the fascist régimes of our century offer a curious commentary, that the existing machinery of the Prussian state can be used to aid the *petite bourgeoisie* as well as the proletariat of Germany against the growing encroachment of merchants, industrialists and bankers. He actually went to the length of negotiating with Bismarck on these lines, each being under the impression that, when the time came, he could use the other as a cat's-paw for his own ends: each recognized and admired the other's audacity, intelligence, and freedom from petty scruple; they vied with each other in the candour of their political realism, in their open contempt for their mediocre followers, and in their admiration for power and success as such. Bismarck liked vivid personalities, and in later years used to refer to these conversations with pleasure, saying that he never hoped to meet so interesting a man again. How far Lassalle had in fact gone in this direction was subsequently revealed by the discovery in 1928 of Bismarck's private record of the negotiations. They were cut short by Lassalle's early death in a duel, which arose out of a casual love-affair. If he had lived, and Bismarck had chosen to continue to play on his almost megalomaniac vanity, Lassalle would in the end almost certainly have lost, and the newly created party might have foundered long before it did; indeed, as a theorist of state supremacy and as a demagogue, Lassalle should be counted among the founders not only of European socialism, but equally of the doctrine of leadership and romantic authoritarianism; it may have been this fascist streak that had attracted Bismarck.

In the subsequent conflict between the Marxists and the Lassalleans, Marx won a formal victory which saved the purity of his own doctrine and political method, not, oddly enough, for Germany, for which it was primarily intended, but for application in far more primitive countries which scarcely entered his thoughts, Russia, China, and, up to a point, Spain, Mexico, and Cuba. The report of Lassalle's death in the spring of 1864 roused little sympathy in either Marx or Engels. To both it seemed a typically foolish end to a career of absurd vanity and ostentation. Lassalle, had he lived, might well have proved an obstacle of the first magnitude. Yet the relief, at least in the case of Marx, was not unmixed with a certain sentimental regret for the passing of so familiar a figure on whom he looked, in spite of of his failings, with something not wholly unlike affection. Lassalle was a German and a Hegelian, inextricably connected with the events of 1848, and his own revolutionary past: a man who, in spite of all his colossal defects, stood head and shoulders above the pygmies among whom he moved, creatures into whom he had for a brief hour infused his own vitality, and who would soon sink exhausted into their old apathy, appearing even smaller, pettier, meaner than before.

'He was, after all, one of the old stock,' he wrote, 'the enemy of our enemies . . . it is difficult to believe that so noisy, stirring, pushing a man is now as dead as a mouse, and must hold his tongue altogether . . . the devil knows, the crowd is getting smaller and no new blood is coming forward.'

The news of Lassalle's death sent him into one of his rare moods of personal melancholy, almost of despair, very different from the cloud of anger and resentment in which he normally lived. He suddenly became overwhelmed by the sense of his own total isolation, and the hopelessness of all individual endeavour in the face of the triumphant European reaction, a feeling which the tranquillity and monotony of life in England sooner or later introduced in all the exiled revolutionaries. Indeed the very respect, and even admiration with which many of them spoke of English life and English institutions, were an implicit acknowledgement of their own personal failure, their loss of faith in the power of mankind to achieve its own emancipation. They saw themselves gradually sinking into a cautious, almost cynical, quietism which they themselves knew to be an admission of defeat and a complete stultification of a life spent in warfare, the final collapse of the ideal world in which they had invested beyond recovery everything that they themselves possessed, and much that belonged to others. This mood, with which Herzen, Mazzini, Kossuth were intimately acquainted, was with Marx uncommon: he was genuinely convinced that the process of history was both inevitable and progressive, and this intense belief excluded all possibility of doubt or disillusionment on fundamental issues; he had never relied on reason or the idealism of individuals or of the masses as decisive factors in

social evolution, and having staked nothing, lost nothing in the great intellectual and moral bankruptcy of
the 'sixties and 'seventies. All his life he strove to
destroy or diminish the influence of popular leaders
and demagogues who believed in the power of the
individual to alter the destinies of nations. His savage
attacks on Proudhon and Lassalle, his later duel with
Bakunin, were not mere moves in the struggle for
personal supremacy on the part of an ambitious and
despotic man resolved to destroy all possible rivals. It
is true that he was by nature almost insanely jealous:
nevertheless, mingled with his personal feelings there
was genuine indignation with the gross errors of
judgment of which these men seemed to him too often
guilty: and, even more strongly felt, ironical as it may
seem when his own position is remembered, a violent
disapproval of the influence of dominant individuals as
such, of the element of personal power, which, by
creating a false relation between the leader and his
followers, is, sooner or later, bound to blind both to the
demands of the objective situation.

Yet it remains the case that the unique position of
authority which he himself occupied in international
socialism during the last decade of his life, did more to
consolidate and ensure the adoption of his system than
mere attention to his works, or the consideration of
history in the light of them, could ever have achieved.
His writings published during these years make depres-
ing reading: apart from journalism in German and
American papers, and literary hackwork forced on him
by his poverty, he confined himself almost entirely to
polemical tracts, the longest of which, *Herr Vogt*,
written in 1860, was designed to clear his own name
from the imputation of having brought his friends into

unnecessary danger during the Cologne trials, and to counter-attack his accuser, a well-known Swiss naturalist and radical politician, Karl Vogt, by alleging that he was in the pay of the French Emperor. It is of interest only for the melancholy light which it throws on ten years of frustration, filled with squabbles and intrigues, which succeeded the heroic age. In 1859 he finally published his *Critique of Political Economy*, yet despite the fact that its introductory pages contain the clearest statement of his theory of history, it was little read: its main theses were much more impressively stated eight years later, in the first volume of *Das Kapital.*

His faith in the ultimate victory of his cause remained unaffected even during the darkest years of the reaction. Speaking in the early 'fifties at a dinner given to the compositors and staff of *The People's Paper*, in answer to the toast 'The proletarians of Europe' he declared: 'In our days everything seems pregnant with its contradiction. Machinery gifted with the wonderful power of shortening and fructifying human labour we behold starving and overworking it. The victories of art seem bought by the loss of character. Even the pure light of science seems able to shine only against the dark background of ignorance. . . . This antagonism between modern industry and science on the one hand, and modern misery and dissolution on the other, this antagonism between the productive forces and the social relations of our epoch is a fact, palpable and overwhelming. Some may bewail it, others may wish to get rid of modern arts in order to get rid of modern conflicts. . . . For our part we do not mistake the shape of the shrewd spirit that continues to mark these contradictions . . . we recognize our old friend, Robin

Goodfellow, the old mole that can work in the earth so fast ... the Revolution.' This thesis must have sounded singularly unplausible to the majority of his listeners: certainly the events of the years which followed did little to bear out his prophecy.

In 1860 Marx's fame and influence were confined to a narrow circle: interest in communism had died down since the Cologne trials in 1851; with the phenomenal development of industry and commerce, faith in liberalism, in science, in peaceful progress, began to mount once more. Marx himself was almost beginning to acquire the interest of a historical figure, to be regarded as the formidable theorist and agitator of a former generation, now exiled and destitute and supporting himself by casual journalism in an obscure corner of London. Fifteen years later all this had altered. Still comparatively unknown in England, he had grown abroad into a figure of vast fame and notoriety, regarded by some as the instigator of every revolutionary movement in Europe, the fanatical dictator of a world movement pledged to subvert the moral order, the peace, happiness and prosperity of mankind. By these he was represented as the evil genius of the working class, plotting to sap and destroy the peace and morality of civilized society, systematically exploiting the worst passions of the mob, creating grievances where none existed, pouring vinegar in the malcontents' wounds, exacerbating their relations with their employers in order to create the universal chaos in which everyone would lose, and so finally all would be made level at last, the rich and the poor, the bad and the good, the industrious and the idle, the just and the unjust. Others saw in him the most indefatigable and devoted strategist and tactician of labouring classes everywhere, the infallible authority on all theoretical questions, the creator of an irresistible movement designed to overthrow the prevailing rule of injustice and inequality by persuasion or by violence. To them he appeared as an angry and indomitable modern Moses, the leader and saviour of all the insulted and the oppressed, with the milder and more conventional Engels at his side, an Aaron ready to expound his words to the benighted, half-comprehending masses of the proletariat. The event which more than any other was responsible for this transformation was the creation of the first Workers' International in 1864, which radically altered the character and history of European socialism.

Chapter Nine

THE INTERNATIONAL

The French Revolution is the precursor of another, more magnificent revolution which will be the last.
GRACCHUS BABEUF, *Manifeste des Egaux*, 1796

THE First International came into being in the most casual possible fashion. In spite of the efforts of various organizations and committees to co-ordinate the activities of the workers of various countries, no genuine ties between them had been established. This was due to several causes. Since the general character of such bodies was conspiratorial, only a small minority of radically minded, fearless and 'advanced' workers were attracted to them; moreover, it was generally the case that before anything concrete could be achieved, a foreign war, or repressive measures by governments, put an end to the existence of the secret committees. To this must be added the lack of acquaintance and sympathy between the workers of different nations, working under totally different conditions. And finally the increased economic prosperity which succeeded the years of hunger and revolt, by raising the general standard of living, automatically made for greater individualism, and stimulated the personal ambition of the bolder and more politically minded workers towards local self-improvement and the pursuit of immediate ends, and away from the comparatively nebulous ideal of an international alliance against the bourgeoisie. The development of the German workers, led by Lassalle, is a typical example of such a purely internal movement, rigorously centralized but confined to a single land, spurred on by an optimistic hope of gradually forcing the capitalist enemy to terms by the sheer weight of numbers, without having recourse to a revolutionary upheaval or violent seizure of power. This hope was encouraged by Bismarck's anti-bourgeois policy which appeared to weight the scales in favour of the workers. In France the fearful defeat of 1848–9 left the city proletariat broken and for many years incapable of action on a large scale, healing its wounds by forming small local associations more or less Proudhonist in inspiration. Nor were they entirely discouraged in this by the government of Napoleon III. The Emperor himself had in his youth posed as a friend of the peasants, artisans and factory workers against capitalist bureaucracy, and wished to represent his monarchy as a novel and exceedingly subtle form of government, an original blend of monarchism, republicanism and Tory democracy, a kind of New Deal in which political absolutism was tempered by economic liberalism; while the government, although centralized and responsible to the Emperor alone, in theory rested ultimately on the confidence of the people, and was therefore to be an entirely new and thoroughly modern institution, sensitive to new needs, responsive to every nuance of social change.

Part of Napoleon's elaborate policy of social conciliation was the preservation of a delicate balance of power between the classes by playing them off against each other. The workers were therefore permitted to form themselves into unions under strict police supervision, in order to offset the dangerously growing power of the financial aristocracy with its suspected

Orleanist loyalties. The workers, with no alternative choice before them, accepted this cautiously outstretched official hand, and began constituting trade associations, a process half encouraged, half hampered, by the authorities.

When the great Exhibition of Modern Industry was opened in London in 1863, French workers were given facilities for visiting it, and a selected deputation duly came to England, half tourists, half representatives of the French proletariat, theoretically sent to the Exhibition in order to study the latest industrial developments. A meeting was arranged between them and the representatives of English unions. At this meeting, which to begin with, was probably as vague in intention as other gatherings of its kind, and seemed to be mainly stimulated by the desire to help Polish democrats exiled as a result of the abortive Polish uprising in that year, there arose such questions as comparative hours and wages in France and England, and the necessity of preventing employers from importing cheap black-leg labour from abroad with which to break strikes organized by local unions. Another meeting was called in order to form an association which should be confined not merely to holding discussions and comparing notes, but for the purpose of beginning active economic and political co-operation, and perhaps for the promotion of an international democratic revolution. The initiative on this occasion came not from Marx, but from the English and French labour leaders themselves. On their fringe were radicals of various kinds, Polish democrats, Italian Mazzinists, Proudhonists, Blanquists and neo-Jacobins from France and Belgium: anyone, indeed, who desired the fall of the existing order was at first freely welcomed.

This meeting was held in St. Martin's Hall in London, and was presided over by Edward Beesly, a charming and benevolent figure, then professor of ancient history in the University of London, a radical and a positivist, who belonged to the small but notable group that included Frederic Harrison and Compton, which had been deeply influenced by Comte and the early French socialists. Its members could be counted on to support every enlightened measure, and, for many years almost alone among the educated men of their time were aligned with Mill in defending the unpopular cause of trade unionism at a period when it was being denounced in the House of Commons as an instrument deliberately invented to foment ill will between the classes. The meeting resolved to constitute an international federation of working men, pledged not to reform but to destroy the prevalent system of economic relations, and to substitute in its place one in which the workers would themselves acquire the ownership of the means of production, which would put an end to their economic exploitation and cause the fruit of their labour to be communally shared—an end that entailed the ultimate abolition of private property in all its forms. Marx, who had previously held himself coldly aloof from other gatherings of democrats, perceived the solid character of this latest attempt at combination, organized as it was by genuine workers' representatives and advertising definite and concrete purposes in which his own influence was clearly traceable. He rarely took part in any movement which he had not initiated himself. This was to be the exception. The German artisans in London appointed him their representative on the executive committee, and by the time the second meeting was held to vote the constitution, he took entire

charge of the proceedings. After the French and Italian
delegates, to whom the task of drafting the statutes was
entrusted, had failed to produce anything but the usual
faded democratic commonplaces, Marx drew them up
himself, adding an inaugural address which he composed for the occasion. The constitution which, as
framed by the International Committee, was vague,
humanitarian, and tinged with liberalism, emerged
from his hands a tightly drawn, militant document
constituting a rigorously disciplined body whose members were pledged to assist each other not merely in
improving their common condition, but in systematically subverting, and whenever possible overthrowing,
the existing capitalist régime by open political action.
In particular they were to try to enter democratic
parliaments, as the followers of Lassalle were beginning to attempt to do in German countries. Upon a
request being made to include some expressions of
respect for 'right and duty, truth, justice and freedom'
the words were inserted but in a context in which, Marx
wrote to Engels, 'they could do no possible harm'.
The new constitution was passed, and Marx began to
work with his customary feverish rapidity, emerging into
the limelight of international activity after fifteen years,
if not of obscurity, of intermittent light and darkness.

The Inaugural Address of the International is, after
the Communist Manifesto, the most remarkable document of the Socialist Movement. It occupies little over
a dozen octavo pages and opens with the declaration
'. . . That the emancipation of the working class must
be conquered by the working class themselves . . . that
the economic subjection of the man of labour to the
monopolizer of the means of labour . . . lies at the
bottom of servitude in all its forms of social misery,

mental degradation and political dependence. That the economic emancipation of the working class is therefore the great end to which every political movement ought to be subordinate as a means. That all efforts aiming at this great end have hitherto failed from want of solidarity between the manifold divisions of labour in each country, and from the absence of a fraternal bond of union between the working classes of different countries . . . for these means the undersigned . . . have taken the steps necessary for founding the International Working Men's Association.'

It contains a survey of the economic and social conditions of the working class from 1848, and contrasts the rapidly growing prosperity of the propertied classes with the depressed condition of the workers. 1848 is recognized as a crushing defeat for them, yet even so not wholly without benefit to them: as a result of it, the feeling of international solidarity among workers had awoken. This development had made agitation for the legal limitation of the working day not entirely unsuccessful—the first definite victory over a policy of extreme *laissez-faire*. The co-operative movement had proved that high industrial efficiency was compatible with, and even increased by, the elimination of the capitalist slave-driver: wage labour had thus been demonstrated to be not a necessary but a transient and eradicable evil. The workers were at last beginning to grasp that they had nothing to gain and everything to lose by listening to their capitalist advisers who, whenever they could not use force, sought to play on national and religious prejudices, on personal or local interests, on the profound political ignorance of the masses. Whoever might gain by national or dynastic wars, it was the workers on both sides who always lost. Yet their strength was such that by common action they could prevent this exploitation in peace as in war: as, indeed, their success in intervening in England against the sending of help to the Southern states in the American civil war had proved. Against the formidable and in appearance overwhelming power of their enemy they had only one weapon—their numbers, 'but numbers weigh in the scales only when they are united and organized and led consciously towards a single aim'. It was in the political field that their slavery was most manifest. To hold aloof from politics in the name of economic organization, as Proudhon and Bakunin taught, was criminal short-sightedness; they would obtain justice only if they upheld it, if necessary by force, wherever they saw it trampled upon. Even if they could not intervene with armed force, they could at least protest and demonstrate and harass their governments, until the supreme standards of morality and justice, by which relations between individuals were conventionally judged, became the laws governing relations between nations. But this could not be done without altering the existing economic structure of society which, in spite of minor improvements, necessarily worked for the degradation and enslavement of the working class. There was only one class in whose real interest it was to arrest this downward trend and remove the possibility of its occurrence: that was the class which, possessing nothing, was bound by no ties of interest or sentiment to the old world of injustice or misery—the class which was as much the invention of the new age as machinery itself. The Address ended, like the *Communist Manifesto*, with the words, 'Workers of the world unite!'

The tasks of the new organization, as embodied in

this document, were: to establish close relations between the workers of various countries and trades; to collect relevant statistics; to inform the workers of one country of the conditions, needs and the plans of the workers of another; to discuss questions of common interest; to secure co-ordinated simultaneous action in all countries in the event of international crises; to publish regular reports on the work of the associations, and the like. It was to meet in annual congresses and would be convened by a democratically elected general council in which all affiliated countries would be represented. Marx left the constitution as elastic as possible in order to be able to include as many active workers' organizations as possible, however disparate their methods and character. At first he resolved to act cautiously and with moderation, to bind and unify, and eliminate dissidents gradually, as a greater measure of agreement was progressively reached. He carried out his policy precisely as he had planned it. Its consequences proved self-destructive, although it is difficult to see what other tactics Marx could have adopted consistently with his principles.

The International grew rapidly. Union after union of workers in the principal countries of Europe was converted by the prospect of united warfare for higher wages, shorter hours and political representation: it was far better organized than either Chartism or the earlier communist leagues had ever been, partly because tactical lessons had been learnt. Independent activity on the part of individuals was suppressed, popular oratory was discouraged and rigid discipline in all departments was introduced, mainly because it was led and dominated by a single personality. The only man who might have attempted to rival Marx in the early years was Lassalle, and he was dead; even so, the spell of his legend was strong enough to insulate the Germans against full support of the London centre. Liebknecht, a man of mediocre talent, boundlessly devoted to Marx, preached the new creed with enthusiasm and skill, but the continuation of Bismarck's anti-socialist policy, and the tradition of nationalism derived from Lassalle, kept the German workers' activity within the frontiers of their country, preoccupied with problems of internal organization. As for Bakunin, that great disturber of men's spirits had lately returned to Western Europe after a romantic escape from Siberia, but while his personal prestige, both in the International and outside it, was immense, he had no organized following: he had drifted away from Herzen and the liberal agrarian party among the Russian *émigrés*, and no one knew whither he was tending, least of all he himself. In common with the great majority of Proudhonists he and his followers became members of the International, but since it was openly committed to political action, they did so in defiance of their somewhat vaguely formulated anarchist principles. The most enthusiastic members at this time were English and French trade unionists, who were temporarily under the spell of the new experiment with its vast promise of prosperity and power; they were no theorists, nor wished to be, and left all such questions to the General Council of the International. While this mood lasted, Marx had no serious rivals in the organization, being altogether superior in intellect, revolutionary experience and strength of will, to the odd amalgam of professional men, factory workers and stray ideologists who, with the addition of one or two dubious adventurers, composed the First International Working Men's Association.

Marx was now forty-six years of age and in appearance and habits prematurely old. Of his six children three were dead, largely as a result of the material conditions of the life led by the family in their rooms in Soho: they had contrived to move to a more spacious house in Kentish Town, although they were still almost destitute. The great economic crisis, the severest yet experienced in Europe, which began in 1857, was warmly welcomed both by him and by Engels as likely to breed discontent and rebellion, but it also curtailed Engels's income, and so struck a blow at Marx himself at a moment when he could least afford it. The *New York Tribune* and occasional contributions to radical German newspapers saved him from literal starvation; but the margin by which the family survived was for twenty years perilously thin. By 1860 even the American source began to fail; the editor of the *New York Tribune*, Horace Greeley, a fervent supporter of democratic nationalism, found himself in growing disagreement with his European correspondent's sharply worded views. The economic crisis, and the added effect of the civil war, led to the dismissal of many of the *Tribune's* European correspondents: Dana pleaded to be allowed to retain Marx, but in vain. He was gradually edged out of his post during the beginning of 1861; the association finally ended a year later. As for the International, it added to his duties and enlivened his existence, but did not add to his income. In despair he applied for a post of booking clerk in a railway office, but his tattered clothes and his menacing appearance were unlikely to produce a favourable impression on a potential employer of clerical labour, and his application was finally rejected on account of his illegible handwriting. It is difficult to see how, without the support of Engels, he and his family could have survived at all during those fearful years.

Meanwhile branches of the International had been established in Italy and Spain; by the mid-sixties governments began to grow frightened; there was talk of arrests and proscriptions; the French Emperor made a half-hearted attempt to suppress it. This only served to heighten the fame and the prestige of the new body among the workers. For Marx, after the dark tunnel of the 'fifties, this was once more life and activity. The work of the International consumed his nights and days. With the customary devoted help of Engels he took personal possession of the central office, and acted not only as its semi-dictatorial adviser, but as the central drafting office and clearing-house of all correspondence. Everything passed through his hands and moved in the direction which he gave it. The French, a portion of the Swiss, to some degree the Belgian, and later the Italian sections, bred on the anti-authoritarianism of Proudhon and Bakunin, made vague but unavailing protests. Marx, who enjoyed complete ascendancy over the Council, tightened his hold still further: he insisted on rigid conformity to every point of the original programme. His old energy seemed to return. He wrote spirited, almost gay letters to Engels; even his theoretical works bear the imprint of this newly found vigour, and as often happens, intense work in one field stimulated dormant activity in another. A sketch of his economic theory had appeared in 1859: but his major work, which poverty and ill-health had interrupted, now at last began to near its end.

Marx made few personal appearances at the meetings of the congress of the International: he preferred to control its activities from London, where he regularly attended the meetings of the General Council and issued detailed instructions to his followers on it. As always he trusted and relied almost entirely on Germans: he found a faithful mouthpiece in an elderly tailor named Eccarius, long resident in England, a man not burdened with excess of intelligence or imagination, but dependable and thorough. Eccarius, like the majority of Marx's underlings, eventually revolted, and joined the secessionists, but for eight years, as secretary to the Council of the International, he carried out Marx's instructions to the letter. Annual congresses were held in London, Geneva, Lausanne, Brussels, Basle, at which general problems were discussed and definite measures voted upon; common decisions were adopted with regard to hours and wages; such questions as the position of women and children, the type of political and economic pressure most suitable to differing conditions in various European countries, the possibility of collaboration with other bodies, were considered. Marx's chief concern was to arrive at a clear formulation of a concrete international policy in terms of specific demands co-ordinated with each other, and the creation of a rigorous discipline which guaranteed undeviating adhesion to this policy. He therefore successfully resisted all offers of alliance with such purely humanitarian bodies as the League of Peace and Freedom, then newly founded under the aegis of Mazzini, Bakunin and John Stuart Mill. This dictatorial policy was bound, sooner or later, to lead to discontent and rebellion; it crystallized round Bakunin whose conception of a loose federation of semi-independent local bodies began to gain adherents in the Swiss and Italian sections of the International, and to a lesser extent in France. Finally they resolved to constitute themselves, under Bakunin's leadership, into a body to be called the Democratic Alliance, affiliated to the International, but with an internal organization of its own pledged to resist centralization and to support federal autonomy. This was a heresy which even a more tolerant man than Marx could not afford to overlook: the International was not intended to be a mere correspondence society between a loose association of radical committees, but a unified political party pressing for a single end in all the centres of its dispersion. He believed firmly that any connexion with Bakunin—or indeed any Russian—was bound to end by badly betraying the working class, a view which he had acquired after his brief and enjoyable flirtation, and subsequent disillusionment, with the aristocratic Russian radicals of the 'forties. As for Bakunin, while he professed sincerely enough to admire Marx's personal genius, he never concealed either his personal antipathy for him, or his rooted loathing of Marx's belief in author-itarian methods, expressed both in his theories and in his practical organization of the revolutionary party.

'We, revolutionary anarchists', Bakunin declared, 'are the enemies of all forms of state and state organiza-tion . . . we think that all state rule, all governments, being by their very nature placed outside the mass of the people, must necessarily seek to subject it to cus-toms and purposes entirely foreign to it. We therefore declare ourselves to be foes . . . of all state organizations as such, and believe that the people can only be happy and free, when, organized from below by means of its own autonomous and completely free associations, without the supervision of any guardians, it will create its own life.

'We believe power corrupts those who wield it as much as those who are forced to obey it. Under its corrosive influence, some become greedy and ambitious tyrants, exploiting society in their own interest, or in that of their class, while others are turned into abject slaves. Intellectuals, positivists, doctrinaires, all those who put science before life . . . defend the idea of the state and its authority as being the only possible salvation of society—quite logically, since from their false premiss that thought comes before life, that only abstract theory can form the starting-point of social practice . . . they draw the inevitable conclusion that since such theoretical knowledge is at present possessed by very few, these few must be put in control of social life, not only to inspire, but to direct all popular movements, and that no sooner is the revolution over than a new social organization must at once be set up; not a free association of popular bodies . . . working in accordance with the needs and instincts of the people, but a centralized dictatorial power concentrated in the hands of this academic minority, as if they really expressed the popular will. . . . The difference between such revolutionary dictatorship and the modern State is only one of external trappings. In substance both are a tyranny of the minority over the majority in the name of the people—in the name of the stupidity of the many and the superior wisdom of the few—and so they are equally reactionary, devising to secure political and economic privilege to the ruling minority, and the . . . enslavement of the masses, to destroy the present order only to erect their own rigid dictatorship on its ruins.'

Bakunin's attacks on Marx and Lassalle could not pass unnoticed, the more so because they were tinged by anti-semitism, for which his friend Herzen more than once had occasion to reproach him. And yet, when in 1869 Herzen begged him to leave the International, he wrote, with a characteristic burst of magnanimity, that he could not join the opponents of a man 'who has served [the cause of socialism] for twenty-five years with insight, energy, and disinterestedness in which he undoubtedly excelled us all.'

Marx's dislike of Bakunin did not blind him to the need for conceding a certain measure of regional independence for motives of sheer expediency. Thus he successfully foiled the plan to create international trade unions because he believed that this was premature and would lead to an immediate rift with the existing, nationally organized, trade unions from which, at any rate in England, the chief support of the International was drawn. But if he made this concession, he did so not for love of federalism as such, but solely not to endanger what had already been built up, an organization without which he could not create a body the existence of which would make the workers conscious that there stood behind their demands, not, as in 1848, merely sympathizers here and there, prepared to offer moral support or at best occasional contributions—but a well-disciplined, militant force pledged to resist, and when necessary, intimidate and coerce their own governments unless justice were done to their brothers everywhere.

In order to create the permanent possibility of such active solidarity in theory and in practice, a central body in undisputed authority, a kind of general staff responsible for strategy and tactics, seemed to him indispensable. Bakunin, by his attempts to loosen the structure of the International and to encourage varieties of opinion in the local sections, appeared to him to be deliberately aiming to destroy this possibility. If he were successful, it would mean the loss of what had been won, a return to utopianism, the disappearance of the new sober outlook, of the realization that the sole strength of the workers lay in unity, that what delivered them into the hands of their enemies in 1848 was the fact that they were engaged in scattered risings, sporadic emotional outbursts of violence, instead of a single carefully concerted revolution, organized to begin at a moment chosen for its historical appropriateness, directed from a common source and to a common end by men who had accurately studied the situation and their own and their enemy's strength. Bakuninism led to the dissipation of the revolutionary impulse, to the old romantic, noble, futile heroism, rich in saints and martyrs, but crushed only too easily by the more realistic enemy, and necessarily followed by a period of weakness and disillusionment likely to set the movement back for many decades. Marx did not underestimate Bakunin's revolutionary energy and power to stir men's imaginations: indeed, it was for this reason that he regarded him as a dangerously disruptive force likely to breed chaos wherever he went. The workers' cause would rest on volcanic soil if he and his followers were allowed to irrupt into the ranks of its defenders. Hence after some years of desultory skirmishing, he decided upon an open attack. It ended with the excommunication of Bakunin and his followers from the ranks of the International.

Chapter Ten

'THE RED TERRORIST DOCTOR'

> We are what we are because of him: without him we should still be sunk in a slough of confusion.
>
> FRIEDRICH ENGELS, 1883

THE first volume of *Das Kapital* was finally published in 1867. The appearance of this book was an epoch-making event in the history of international socialism and in Marx's own life. It was conceived as a comprehensive treatise on the laws and morphology of the economic organization of modern society, seeking to describe the processes of production, exchange and distribution as they actually occur, to explain their present state as a particular stage in the development constituted by the movement of the class struggle, in Marx's own words, 'to discover the economic law of motion of modern society' by establishing the natural laws that govern the history of classes. The result was an original amalgam of economic theory, history, sociology and propaganda which fits none of the accepted categories. Marx certainly regarded it as primarily a treatise on economic science. The earlier economists, according to Marx, misunderstood the nature of economic laws when they compared them with the laws of physics and chemistry, and assumed that, although social conditions may change, the laws that govern them do not; with the result that their systems either apply to imaginary worlds, peopled by idealized economic men, modelled upon the writer's own contemporaries, and therefore usually compounded of selected characteristics which came into prominence only in the eighteenth and nineteenth centuries; or else describe societies which if they were ever real, have long since vanished. He therefore conceived it as his task to create a new system of concepts and definitions which should have definite application to the contemporary world, and be so constructed as to reflect the changing structure of economic life in relation not only to its past, but also to its future. In the first volume Marx made an attempt at once to provide a systematic exposition of certain basic theorems of economic science, and more specifically to describe the rise of the new industrial system, as a consequence of the new relations between employers and labour created by the effect of technological progress on the methods of production.

The first volume therefore deals with the productive process; that is, on the one hand, the relations between machinery and labour, and on the other those between the actual producers, i.e. the workers and those who employ and direct them. The remaining volumes, published after his death by his executors, deal with the methods in use of marketing the finished product, i.e. the system of exchange and the financial machinery which it involves, and with relations between producers and consumers, which determine prices, the rate of interest and profit.

The general thesis which runs through the entire work is that adumbrated in the *Communist Manifesto* and Marx's earlier economic writings.[1] It rests on three

---

[1] For a more detailed account of Marxist economic doctrine together with the best-known classical criticisms of it, published in this series, the reader is referred to the chapter on 'Communist Economics' in Professor H. J. Laski's *Communism*.

fundamental assumptions: (*a*) that political economy seeks to explain who obtains what goods or services or status and why; (*b*) that it is therefore a science not of inanimate objects—commodities—but of persons and their activities, to be interpreted in terms of motives and not solely of mechanical causes or pseudo-objective laws beyond human control, such as those of supply and demand governing natural objects—objects whose behaviour is governed by laws independent of human will: this he calls 'fetishism of commodities'; (*c*) that the decisive factor in social behaviour in modern times is that of industrialization; with the rider that the earliest and fullest form of it—the industrial revolution in England—offers the student the best example of a process that will, in due course, take place everywhere. Marx traces the rise of the modern proletariat by correlating it with the general development of the technical means of production. When, in the course of their gradual evolution, these means can no longer be created by each man for his own use, and division of labour is born, certain individuals (as Saint-Simon had taught) owing to their superior skill, power and enterprise, acquire sole control of such instruments and tools, and thus find themselves in a position in which they can hire the labour of others by a combination of threats to withhold necessities of life from them and of offering them more in the form of a regular remuneration than they would receive as independent producers, vainly attempting to achieve the same results with the old and obsolete tools which alone they have in their possession. As a result of selling their labour to others, these men themselves become so many commodities in the economic market, and their labour power acquires a definite price which fluctuates precisely like that of other commodities.

A commodity is any object embodying human labour
for which there is a social demand. It is thus a concept
which, Marx is careful to point out, can be applied only
at a relatively late stage of social development: and is
no more eternal than any other economic category. The
commercial value of a commodity is assumed to be
directly constituted by the number of hours of socially
necessary human labour, i.e. what it takes an average
producer to create an average specimen of its kind (a
view derived from a somewhat similar doctrine held by
Ricardo and the classical economists). A day's work by
a labourer may well produce an object possessing a
value greater than the value of the minimum quantity
of commodities which he needs for his own support; he
thus produces something worth more in the market
than he consumes; indeed, unless he did so, his master
would have no economic reason for employing him. As
a commodity in the market, a man's labour power may
itself be acquired for $£x$, which represents the minimum
sum needed to maintain him in sufficient health to
enable him to do his work efficiently; the goods he
produces will sell for $£y$; $£y-x$ represents the extent by
which he has increased the total wealth of society, and
this is the residue which his employer pockets. Even
after the reasonable reward of the employer's own work
in his capacity as the organizer and manager of the
processes of production and distribution is deducted, a
definite residue of the social income remains, which in
the form of rent, interest on investments, or commercial
profit, is shared, according to Marx, not by society
as a whole, but solely by those members of it who
are called the capitalist or bourgeois class, distinguished from the rest by the fact that they alone
in their capacity as sole owners of the means of

production, obtain and accumulate such unearned increment.

Whether Marx's concept of value be interpreted as meaning the actual market price of commodities, or an average norm, round which the actual prices oscillate, or an ideal limit towards which they tend, or that which in a rationally organized society prices ought to be, or an element in the sociological explanation of what constitutes and satisfies the material interests of men in society, or something more metaphysical—an impalpable essence, infused into brute matter by the creativeness of human labour, or, as unsympathetic critics have maintained, a confusion of all these; and again whether the notion of a uniform entity called undifferentiated human labour (which according to the theory constitutes economic value), different manifestations of which can be compared in respect of quantity alone, is, or is not, valid—and it is not easy to defend Marx's use of either concept—the theory of exploitation based on them remains comparatively unaffected. The central thesis which made so powerful an appeal to workers, who did not for the most part begin to comprehend the intricacies of Marx's general argument about the relation of exchange value and actual prices, is that there is only one social class, their own, which produces more wealth than it consumes, and that this residue is appropriated by other men simply by virtue of their strategic position as the sole possessors of the means of production, that is, natural resources, machinery, means of transport, financial credit, and so forth, without which the workers cannot create, while control over them gives those who have it the power of starving the rest of mankind into capitulation on their own terms.

Political, social, religious and legal institutions of the

capitalist era are represented as being so many moral and intellectual weapons designed to organize the world in the interest of the employers. These last employ, over and above the producers of commodities, that is, the proletariat, a whole army of ideologists: propagandists, interpreters and apologists, who defend the capitalist system, embellish it, and create literary and artistic monuments to it, likely to increase the confidence and optimism of those who benefit under it, and make it appear more palatable to its victims, in Rousseau's phrase—'cover their chains with garlands of flowers'. But if the development of technology, as Saint-Simon correctly discovered, has for a period given this unique power to landowners, industrialists and financiers—every type of middle-man—its uncontrollable advance will no less inevitably destroy them.

Already Fourier, and after him Proudhon, had declaimed against the processes by which the great bankers and manufacturers, by means of their superior resources, tend to eliminate small traders and craftsmen from the economic market, creating a mass of discontented, *déclassé* individuals, who are automatically forced into the ranks of the proletariat. The capitalist is, in his day, a historical necessity. He extracts surplus value and accumulates; this is indispensable to industrialization and is history's agency of progress. 'Fanatically bent on increasing value, he ruthlessly forces the human race to produce for the sake of production'. He may do so brutally and for purely selfish motives; but in the course of this 'he creates those material conditions which alone can form the real foundations of a higher form of society, of which the full and free development of every man is the dominant principle.' He had already paid his tribute to the progressive role of industrialization in the *Communist Manifesto*. 'The bourgeoisie' he wrote 'cannot exist without constantly revolutionizing the instruments of production, and thereby the relations of production and with them the entire relations of society.... During it's rule of scarcely one hundred years, it has created more massive and colossal productive forces than all the earlier generations taken together. Subjection of the forces of nature to man, application of chemistry and industry to agriculture, steam navigation, railways, the electric telegraph, clearing entire continents for cultivation, canalization of rivers, whole populations conjured up out of the earth—what earlier age had even a presentiment of such gigantic social forces slumbering in the lap of socialized labour?' but the capitalist will have played his part, and will then be superseded. He will be 'liquidated' by his own essential characteristics as an accumulator. Ruthless competition between individual capitalists, seeking to increase the quantity of surplus value, and the natural necessity arising from this of lowering the cost of production and finding new markets, is bound to lead to greater and greater fusion of rival firms, that is to a ceaseless process of amalgamation, until only the largest and most powerful groups are left in existence, all others being forced into a position of dependence or semi-dependence, in the new centralized industrial hierarchy, ruling over a concentration of productive and distributive machinery, which grows, and will continue to grow, faster and faster. Centralization is a direct product of rationalization: of increased efficiency in production and transport secured by the pooling of resources, of the formation of great monopolistic trusts and combines which are capable of planned co-ordination. The workers previously scattered among many small enterprises, reinforced by continual influx of the sons and daughters of the ruined small traders and manufacturers, automatically become united into a single, ever growing, proletarian army by the very processes of integration at work among their masters. Their power as a political and economic body, increasingly conscious of its historical role and resources, grows correspondingly greater. Already trade unions, developing in the shadow of the factory system, represent a far more powerful weapon in the hands of the proletariat than any that existed before. The process of industrial expansion will tend to organize society more and more into the shape of an immense pyramid, with fewer and increasingly powerful capitalists at its summit and a vast, discontented mass of exploited workers and colonial slaves forming its base. The more machinery replaces human labour, the lower the rate of profit is bound to fall, since the rate of 'surplus value' is determined solely by the latter. The struggle between competing capitalists and their countries, which are in effect controlled by them, will grow more deadly, being wedded to a system of unhampered competition, under which each can only survive by overreaching and destroying his rivals.[1]

[1] If this is really so, why should not the capitalist destroy machines and increase surplus value by returning to slave labour? In the posthumous volume of *Capital* edited by Engels from Marx's manuscripts, it is maintained that machinery does not indeed increase profits, relatively or absolutely: but it helps to eliminate inefficient competitors; the rate of profit continues to fall, but it is divided among increasingly fewer capitalists—the 'fittest' in this jungle warfare. The reader can tell for himself whether, or how far, this has occurred.

Within the framework of capitalism and unchecked private enterprise, these processes cannot be made rational, since the vested interests on which capitalist society rests, depend for their survival on freedom of competition, if not between individual producers, then between combines and monopolies. The inexorable tendency of technological progress to increasingly collective forms of production will conflict more and more violently with individual forms of distribution i.e. private control, private property. Big Business, which Marx was among the few to foresee, with its military allies, will destroy *laissez-faire* and individualism. Marx did not, however, allow for the consequences of the growth of state control or democratic resistance, nor the development of political nationalism as a force cutting across and transforming the development of capitalism itself, either as an obstacle to unchecked exploitation or as a bulwark to the gradually impoverished section of the *bourgeoisie*, which would form an alliance with the reaction in its desperate anxiety to avoid its Marxist destiny of falling into the proletariat below it. In other words, he foresees neither fascism nor the welfare state.

His classification of social strata into the obsolescent military-feudal aristocracy, the industrial *bourgeoisie*, the *petite bourgeoisie*, the proletariat, and that casual riff-raff on the edge of society which he called the *Lumpenproletariat*—a fruitful and original classification for its time—over-simplifies issues when it is too mechanically applied to the twentieth century. A more elaborate instrument is required, if only to deal with the independent behaviour of classes, like the semi-ruined *petite bourgeoisie*, the growing salaried lower middle class, and above all the vast agricultural population, classes which Marx regarded as naturally reactionary, but forced by their growing pauperization either to sink to the level of the proletariat, or to offer their services as mercenaries to its protagonist, the industrial *bourgeoisie*. The history of post-war Europe, at any rate in the West, requires to be considerably distorted before it can be made to fit this hypothesis.

Marx prophesied that the periodic crises due to the absence of planned economies, and unchecked industrial strife, would necessarily grow more frequent and acute. Wars, on a hitherto unprecedented scale, would ravage the civilized world, until finally the Hegelian contradictions of a system, whose continuance depends upon more and more destructive conflicts between its constituent parts, would obtain a violent solution. The ever-decreasing group of capitalists in power would be overthrown by the workers whom they themselves would have so efficiently drilled into a compact, disciplined body. With the disappearance of the last possessing class, the final end would be reached of the war between the classes, which is the sole and sufficient cause of economic scarcity, social strife and individual misery and degradation.

In a celebrated passage in the twenty-second chapter of the first volume of *Das Kapital* he declared: 'While there is a progressive diminution in the number of capitalist magnates, there is of course a corresponding increase in the mass of poverty, enslavement, degeneration and exploitation, but at the same time there is a steady intensification of the role of the working class— a class which grows ever more numerous, and is disciplined, unified and organized by the very mechanism of the capitalist method of production which has flourished with it and under it. The centralization of the means of production and the socialization of labour reach a point where they prove incompatible with their capitalist husk. This bursts asunder. The knell of private property sounds. The expropriators are expropriated.' The State, the instrument whereby the authority of the ruling class is artificially enforced, having lost its function, will disappear; the ideal community, painted in colours at once too simple and too fantastic by the Utopians of the past, will at last be reached—a community in which there will be neither master nor slave, neither rich nor poor, in which the world's goods, being produced in accordance with social demand unhampered by the caprice of individuals, will be distributed not indeed equally—a notion so lamely borrowed by the workers from the liberal ideologists with their utilitarian concept of justice as arithmetical equality—but rationally, that is unequally: for, as a man's capacities and needs are unequal, his reward, if it is to be just, must, in the formula of the *Communist Manifesto*, accrue 'to every one according to his need, from every one according to his capacity'. Men, emancipated at last from the tyranny both of nature and of their own ill-adapted and ill-controlled and therefore oppressive institutions, will begin to develop their capacities to the fullest extent. History will cease to be the succession of one exploiting class after another. Real freedom, so obscurely adumbrated by Hegel, will be realized. Human history in the true sense will only then begin.

The publication of *Das Kapital* had at last provided a definite intellectual foundation for international socialism in the place of a scattered mass of vaguely defined and conflicting ideas. The interdependence of the historical economic and political theses preached by Marx and Engels was revealed in this monumental compilation. It became the central objective of attack and defence. All subsequent forms of socialism here-after defined themselves in terms of their attitude to the position taken in it, and were understood and classified by their resemblance to it. After a brief period of obscurity, its fame began to grow and reached an extraordinary height. It acquired a symbolic signific-ance beyond anything written since the age of faith. It has been blindly worshipped, and blindly hated, by millions who have not read a line of it, or have read without understanding its obscure and tortuous prose. In its name revolutions were made (and are); counter-revolutions concentrated (and concentrate) upon its sup-pression as the most potent and insidious of the enemy's weapons. A new social order has been estab-lished which professes its principles and sees in it the final and unalterable expression of its faith. It has called into existence an army of interpreters and casuists, whose unceasing labours for nearly a century have buried it beneath a mountain of commentary which has outgrown in influence the sacred text itself.

In Marx's own life it marked a decisive moment. He intended it to be his greatest contribution to the emancipation of humanity, and had sacrificed to it fifteen years of his life and much of his public ambition. The labour which had gone towards it was truly prodigious. For its sake he endured poverty, illness and persecution both public and personal, suffering these not gladly indeed, but with a single-minded stoicism whose strength and harshness both moved and fright-ened those who came in contact with it.

He offered to dedicate his book to Darwin, for whom he had a greater intellectual admiration than for any other of his contemporaries, regarding him as having, by his theory of evolution and natural selection, done for the morphology of the natural sciences, what he himself was striving to do for human history. Darwin hastily declined the honour in a polite, cautiously phrased letter, saying that he was unhappily ignorant of economic science, but offered the author his good wishes in what he assumed to be their common end— the advancement of human knowledge. It was dedicated to the memory of Wilhelm Wolff, a Silesian communist, who had been his devoted follower since 1848, and had recently died in Manchester. The published volume was the first part of the projected work, the rest was still a confused mass of notes, references and sketches. He sent copies of it to his old associates, to Freiligrath who congratulated him on having produced a useful work of reference, and to Feuerbach who said that he found it 'rich in undeniable facts of the most interesting, but at the same time most horrible nature'. Ruge gave it more discriminating praise; it obtained at least one critical notice in England, in the *Saturday Review*, which quaintly observed that 'the presentation of the subject invests the driest economic questions with certain peculiar charm'. It was more widely noticed in Germany where Marx's friends Liebknecht and Kugelmann, a Hanover physician who had conceived an immense admiration for him, made vigorous propaganda for it. In particular Joseph Dietzgen, a self-taught German cobbler in St. Petersburg, who became one of Marx's most ardent disciples, did much to popularize it with the German masses.

Marx's scientific appetite had not diminished since his Paris days. He believed in exact scholarship and sternly drove his reluctant followers into the reading-room of the British Museum. Liebknecht, in his memoirs, describes how day after day the 'scum of international communism' might be seen meekly seated at the desks in the reading-room, under the eye of the master himself. Indeed no social or political movement has laid such emphasis on research and erudition. The extent of Marx's own reading is to some degree indicated by the references in his works alone, which explore exceedingly obscure by-ways in ancient, medieval, and modern literature. The text is liberally sprinkled with footnotes, long, mordant and annihilating, which recall Gibbon's classical employment of this weapon. The adversaries at whom they are directed are for the most part forgotten names to-day, but occasionally his shafts are aimed at well-known figures; Macaulay, Gladstone, and one or two well known academic economists of the time, are attacked with a savage concentration which inaugurated a new epoch in the technique of public vituperation, and created the school of socialist polemical writing which has altered the general character of political controversy. There is conspicuously little praise in the book. The warmest tribute is earned by the British factory inspectors, whose fearless and unbiased reports both of the appalling conditions which they witnessed, and of the means adopted by factory owners to circumvent the law, is declared to be a uniquely honourable phenomenon in the history of bourgeois society. The technique of social research was revolutionized by the example set by Marx in the use of Blue Books and official reports: he claimed to base the greater part of his detailed indictment of modern industrialism largely upon them.

After his death, Engels, who edited the second and third volumes of *Das Kapital*, found the manuscript in a far more chaotic condition than he had expected. The year in which the first volume appeared marks not a turning but a breaking-point in Marx's life. His views during the remaining sixteen years of his life altered little; he added, revised, corrected, wrote pamphlets and letters, but published nothing that was new; he reiterated the old position tirelessly, but the tone is milder, a faint note almost of querulous self-pity, totally absent before, is now discernible. His belief in the proximity, even in the ultimate inevitability of a world revolution, diminished. His prophecies had been disappointed too often: he had confidently predicted a great upheaval in 1842, during a weavers' rising in Silesia, and even inspired Heine to write the famous poem upon it which he published in his Paris journal; again in 1851, 1857 and 1872 he expected revolutionary outbreaks which failed to materialize. His prophecies of falling rates of profit, concentration of ownership of industry and land in private hands, decline in the standard of living of the proletariat, the intimate connection of capitalism and nationalism, have not, on the whole, been borne out in this century. On the other hand he saw much that others did not: the concentration and centralization of control of economic resources; the increasing incompatibility between Big Business methods of production and older methods of distribution and the social and political impact of this fact; the effect of industrialization—and science—on the methods of war; and the swift and radical transformation of ways of living that all this would cause. And he remained one of the acutest of political observers: after the annexation of Alsace-Lorraine by Prussia, he foretold that this would throw France into the arms of Russia and so bring about the first great world war. In his later years he allowed that the revolution might be longer in arriving than he and Engels had once estimated, and in some countries, notably in England, where in his day there was no real army and no real bureaucracy, it might actually not occur at all, 'although', he enigmatically added, 'history indicates otherwise'. He was not fifty when he began to subside into conscious old age. The heroic period was over.

Das Kapital created a new reputation for its author. His previous books had been passed over in silence even in German-speaking countries: his new work was reviewed and discussed as far afield as Russia and Spain. In the next ten years it was translated into French, English, Russian, Italian; indeed, Bakunin himself gallantly offered to translate it into Russian. But this project, if it was ever begun, collapsed in circumstances of sordid personal and financial scandal which were partly responsible for the demise of the International five years later. The sudden rise to fame of this organization was due to a major event which two years earlier altered the history of Europe and completely changed the direction in which the working class movement had hitherto developed.

If Marx and Engels sometimes predicted events which failed to happen, they more than once failed to foresee events which did. Thus Marx denied that the Crimean War would occur, and backed the wrong side in the Austro-Prussian War. The Franco-Prussian War of 1870 came to them as something wholly unexpected. For years they had underestimated Prussian strength; the true alliance of cynicism and brute force was in their eyes represented by the Emperor of the French. Bismarck was an able Junker, who served his King and his class; even his victory over Austria did not convince them of his real quality or aims. Marx

may have been to some extent genuinely deceived by
Bismarck's representation of the war as being on his
part purely defensive, for he signed the protest which
the Council of the International immediately published
only after it had been altered to make this clear—a step
for which many socialists in Latin countries never for-
gave him, insisting in later years that it was inspired by
pure German patriotism to which both he and Engels
were always conspicuously prone. The International in
general, and in particular its German members, behaved irreproachably throughout the brief campaign.
The Council in its proclamation, issued in the middle
of the war, warned the German workers against supporting the policy of annexation which Bismarck might
well pursue; it explained in clear terms that the interests
of the French and German proletariat were identical,
being menaced only by the common enemy—the capitalist bourgeoisie of both countries, which had brought
about the war for its own ends, wasting for their sakes the
lives and substance of the working class equally of Germany and of France. In due course it exhorted the French
workers to support the formation of a republic on a
broadly democratic basis. During the wild wave of war
chauvinism which swept over Germany, and engulfed
even the left wing of the Lassallians, only the Marxists,
Liebknecht and Bebel, preserved their sanity. To the
indignation of the entire country they abstained from
voting for war credits and spoke vigorously in the Reich-
stag against the war, and in particular against the annexation of Alsace-Lorraine. For this they were charged with
treason and imprisoned. In a celebrated letter to Engels,
Marx pointed out that the defeat of Germany, which
would have strengthened Bonapartism and crippled the
German workers for many years to come, might have been

even more disastrous than Germany's victory. By trans-
ferring the centre of gravity from Paris to Berlin, Bismarck
was doing their work for them, however unconsciously;
for the German workers, being better organized and
better disciplined than the French, were consequently a
stronger citadel of social democracy than Frenchmen
could have been; while the defeat of Bonapartism
would remove a nightmare from Europe.

In the autumn the French army was defeated at
Sedan, the Emperor taken prisoner, and Paris besieged.
The King of Prussia, who had solemnly sworn that the
war was defensive and directed not against France but
against Napoleon, changed his tactics, and, armed with
an enthusiastic plebiscite from his people, demanded
the cession of Alsace-Lorraine and the payment of an
indemnity of five billion francs. The tide of English
opinion, hitherto anti-Bonapartist and pro-German,
under the influence of continual reports of Prussian
atrocities in France, veered round sharply. The International issued a second Manifesto violently protesting
against the annexation, denouncing the dynastic ambitions of the Prussian King, and calling upon the
French workers to unite with all defenders of democracy against the common Prussian foe. 'If frontiers are
to be fixed by military interests', wrote Marx in 1870,
'there will be no end of claims, because every military
line is necessarily faulty and may be improved by an-
nexing some more outlying territory: they can never be
fixed fairly or finally because they always must be
improved by the conqueror or the conquered, and
consequently carry within them the seeds of fresh wars.
History will measure its retribution, not by the extent
of square miles conquered from France, but by the
intensity of the crime of reviving, in the second half of

the nineteenth century, *the policy of conquest.*' This time war credits were voted against, not by Liebknecht and Bebel alone, but also by the Lassallians, shamed out of their recent patriotism. Marx jubilantly wrote to Engels that for the first time the principles and policy of the International had obtained public expression in a European legislative assembly: the International had become a force to be officially reckoned with: the dream of a united proletarian party with identical ends in all countries was beginning to be realized. Paris was presently starved into submission and capitulated; a national assembly was elected, Thiers was made President of the new Republic, and appointed a provisional government of conservative views. In March the government made an attempt to disarm the Paris National Guard, a volunteer citizen force which showed signs of radical sympathies. It refused to give up its arms, declared its autonomy, deposed the officials of the provisional government, and elected a revolutionary committee of the people as the true government of France. The regular troops were brought to Versailles and invested the rebellious city. It was the first campaign of what both sides immediately recognized to be an open class war.

The Commune, as the new government described itself, was neither created nor inspired by the International: it was not even, in a strict sense, socialist in its doctrines, unless a dictatorship of any popularly elected committee in itself constitutes a socialist phenomenon. It consisted of a highly heterogeneous collection of individuals, for the most part followers of Blanqui, Proudhon, and Bakunin, with an admixture of neo-Jacobin rhetoricians, like Félix Pyat, who knew only that they were fighting for France, the people, and the revolution, and proclaimed death to all tyrants, priests and Prussians. Workmen, soldiers, writers, painters like Courbet, scholars like the geographer Élisée Réclus and the critic Vallès, ambivalent polititicians like Rochefort, foreign exiles of mildly liberal views, bohemians and adventurers of every description were swept up in a common revolutionary wave. It rose at a moment of national hysteria after the moral and material misery of a siege and a capitulation, at a moment when the national revolution which promised to do away finally with the last relics of Bonapartist and Orleanist reaction, abandoned by the middle classes, denounced by Thiers and his ministers, uncertain of support among the peasantry, seemed suddenly threatened with the return of all that it most feared and loathed, the generals, the financiers, the priests. By a great effort the people had shaken off the nightmare first of the Empire, then of the siege; they had hardly awoken yet when the spectres seemed to advance upon them once again: terrified, they revolted. This common sense of horror before the resurgence of the past was almost the sole bond which united the Communards. Their views on political organization (beyond common hatred of the centralized government dear to Marx) were vague to a degree: they announced that the state in its old form was abolished, and called upon the people in arms to govern itself.

Presently, as supplies began to give out, and the condition of the besieged grew more desperate, terror developed: proscriptions began, men and women were condemned and executed, many of them certainly guiltless, and few deserving of death. Among those executed was the archbishop of Paris, who had been held as a hostage against the army at Versailles. The rest of

Europe watched the monstrous events with growing indignation and disgust. The Communards seemed even to enlightened opinion, even to old and tried friends of the people like Louis Blanc and Mazzini, to be a band of criminal lunatics dead to the appeal of humanity, social incendiaries pledged to destroy all religion and all morality, men driven out of their minds by real and imaginary wrongs, scarcely responsible for their enormities. Practically the entire European Press, reactionary and liberal alike, combined to give the same impression. Here and there a radical journal condemned less roundly than the others, and timidly pleaded extenuating circumstances. The atrocities of the Commune did not long remain unavenged. The retribution which the victorious army exacted took the form of mass executions; the white terror, as is common in such cases, far outdid in acts of bestial cruelty the worst excesses of the régime, the misdeeds of which it had come to end.

The International vacillated; composed as it largely was of opponents of the Proudhonists, the Blanquists and neo-Jacobins who formed the majority of the Commune, opposed to the loosely federal Communard programme, and in particular to acts of terrorism, it had, moreover, formally advised against the revolt declaring that 'any attempt at upsetting the new government in the present crisis, . . . would be desperate folly'. The English members were particularly anxious not to compromise themselves by open association with a body which, in the opinion of the majority of their countrymen, was little better than a gang of common murderers. Marx solved their doubts by a very characteristic act. In the name of the International he published an address in which he proclaimed that the moment for analysis and criticism had passed. After giving a swift and vivid account of the events which led to the creation of the Commune, of its rise and fall, he acclaimed it as the first open and defiant manifestation in history of the strength and idealism of the working class—the first pitched battle which it had fought against its oppressors before the eyes of the whole world, an act forcing all its false friends, the radical bourgeoisie, the democrats and humanitarians to show themselves in their true colours, as enemies to the ultimate ends for which it was prepared to live and die. He went further than this: he recognized the replacement of the *bourgeois* state by the Commune as that transitional form of social structure by passing through which alone the workers could gain their ultimate emancipation. The state is revealed as the embodiment of 'the civilization and justice of the *bourgeois* order' legalizing parliamentarism which, once challenged by its victims, 'stands forth as undisguised savagery and lawless revenge'. The state must therefore be destroyed root and branch. To this extent he once more, as in 1850 and 1852, retracted the doctrine of the *Communist Manifesto*, which had asserted, as against the French utopians and early anarchists, that the immediate end of the revolution was not to destroy, but to seize the state ('the proletariat will . . . centralize all instruments of production in the hands of the State') and make use of it to liquidate the enemy.

While he approved many of the measures of the Commune, he blamed it for not being ruthless and radical enough: nor did he believe in its aim of creating immediate social and economic equality. 'Right can never be higher', he wrote some years afterwards, 'than the economic structure of society and the cultural development thereby determined.' These cannot be transformed overnight.

His pamphlet, later entitled *The Civil War in France*, was not primarily intended as a historical study: it was a tactical move, and one of typical audacity and intransigeance. Marx was sometimes blamed by his own followers for allowing the International to be linked in the popular mind with a band of law-breakers and assassins, an association which earned for it an unnecessarily sinister reputation. This was not the kind of consideration which could have influenced him in the slightest degree. He was, all his life, a convinced and uncompromising believer in a violent working class revolution. The Commune was the first spontaneous rising of the workers in their capacity as workers: the June *émeute* of 1848, was, in his view, an attack on, and not by, them. The Commune was not directly inspired by Marx. He regarded it, indeed, as a political blunder: his adversaries the Blanquists and Proudhonists predominated in it to the end; and yet its significance in his eyes was immense. Before it there had indeed been many scattered streams of socialist thought and action; but this rising, with its world repercussions, the great effect which it was bound to have upon the workers of all lands, was the first event of the new era. The men who had died in it and for it, were the first martyrs of international socialism, their blood would be the seed of the new proletarian faith: whatever the tragic faults and shortcomings of the Communards, they were as nothing before the magnitude of the historical role which these men had played, the position which they were destined to occupy in the tradition of proletarian revolution.

By coming forward to pay them open homage he

achieved what he intended to achieve: he helped to create a heroic legend of socialism. More than thirty years later Lenin defended the Moscow rising, which occurred during the abortive Russian revolution of 1905, against the criticisms of Plekhanov, by quoting the attitude of Marx towards the Commune: by pointing out that the emotional and symbolic value of the memory of a great heroic outburst, however ill conceived, however damaging in its immediate results, was an infinitely greater and more permanent asset to a revolutionary movement than the realization of its futility at a moment when what matters most is not to write accurate history, or even to learn its lessons, but to make it.

The publication of the address embarrassed and shocked many members of the International and hastened its ultimate dissolution. Marx attempted to forestall all reproaches by revealing his name as the sole author of the work. 'The Red Terrorist Doctor', as he was now popularly known, became overnight the object of public odium: anonymous letters began to arrive, his life was several times threatened. Jubilantly he wrote to Engels: 'It is doing me good after twenty long and boring years of idyllic isolation like a frog in a swamp. The Government organ—the *Observer*—is even threatening me with prosecution. Let them try it. I snap my fingers at the canaille!' The hubbub died down, but the damage done to the International was permanent: it became indissolubly connected in the minds both of the police and of the general public with the outrages of the Commune. A blow was dealt to the alliance of the English trade-union leaders with the International, which was, in any case, from their point of view entirely opportunist, based on its usefulness in promoting specific union interests. The unions were at this time being strongly wooed by the Liberal Party with promises of support upon these very issues. The prospect of a peaceful and respectable conquest of power made them less than ever anxious to be associated with a notorious revolutionary conspiracy; their sole end was to raise the standard of living and the social and political status of the skilled workers whom they represented. They did not look upon themselves as a political party, and if they subscribed to the programme of the International, this was due partly to the elasticity of its statutes, which skilfully avoided committing its members to definitely revolutionary ends, but most of all to their haziness on political issues. This fact was well appreciated by the Government which, in reply to a circular from the Spanish Government demanding the suppression of the International, replied in the person of the Foreign Secretary, Lord Granville, that in England they felt no danger of armed insurrection: the English members were peaceful men, solely occupied in labour negotiations, and gave the Government no ground for apprehension. Marx himself was bitterly aware of the truth of this: even Harney and Jones were in his eyes preferable to the men he now had to deal with, solid trade-union officials like Odger, or Cremer or Applegarth, who distrusted foreigners, cared little for events outside their country, and took little interest in ideas.

No meetings of the International having been held in 1870–1, a meeting was convened in London in 1872. The most important proposal brought up by this Congress, that the working class henceforth cease to rely in the political struggle upon the assistance of bourgeois parties, and form a party of their own, was, after a stormy debate, carried by the votes of the English delegates. The new political party was not set up during Marx's lifetime, but, in idea at least, the Labour party was born at this meeting, and may be regarded as Marx's greatest single contribution to the internal history of his adopted land. At the same congress the English delegates insisted on, and won, the right to form a separate local organization instead of, as before, being represented by the General Council. This displeased and frightened Marx: it was a gesture of distrust, almost of rebellion; at once he suspected the machinations of Bakunin, whom the recent events in France had put in a proud and ecstatic mood, since he felt that they were overwhelmingly due to his personal influence. A large part of Paris was destroyed by fire during the Commune: this fire seemed to him a symbol of his own life, and a magnificent realization of his favourite paradox: 'The passion for destruction, too, is a creative passion.'

Marx neither understood nor wished to understand the emotional basis of Bakunin's acts and declarations: the influence of this 'Mahomet without a Koran' was a menace to the movement, and must consequently be destroyed.

'The International was founded', he wrote in 1871, 'in order to replace the socialist and semi-socialist sects with a genuine organization of the working class for its struggle. . . . Socialist sectarianism and a real working-class movement are in inverse ratio to each other. Sects have a right to exist only so long as the working class is not mature enough to have an independent movement of its own: as soon as that moment arrives sectarianism becomes reactionary. . . . The history of the International is a ceaseless battle of the

General Council against dilettantist experiments and sects. . . . Towards the end of 1868 the International was joined by Bakunin whose purpose it was to create an International within the International, and to place himself at its head. For M. Bakunin, his doctrine (an absurd patchwork composed of bits and pieces of views taken from Proudhon, Saint-Simon, &c.) was, and still is, something of secondary importance, serving him only as a means of acquiring personal influence and power. But if Bakunin, as a theorist, is nothing, Bakunin, the intriguer, has attained to the highest peak of his profession. . . . As for his political non-participation, every movement in which the working class as such is opposed to the ruling classes, and exercises pressure upon it from without, is *eo ipso* a political movement . . . but when the workers' organization is not so highly developed that it can afford to risk decisive engagement with the dominant political power—then it must be prepared for this by ceaseless agitation against the crimes and follies of the ruling class. Otherwise it becomes a plaything in its hands, as was demonstrated by the September revolution in France, and, to some extent, by the recent successes in England of Gladstone & Co.'

Bakunin at this period had entered upon the last and strangest phase of his bizarre existence. He had completely fallen under the spell of a young Russian terrorist, Nechayev, whose audacity and freedom from scruple he found irresistible. Nechayev, who believed in blackmail and intimidation as essential revolutionary weapons justified by their end, had written an anonymous letter to the agent of the prospective publisher of Bakunin's Russian version of *Das Kapital*, threatening him in general but violent terms, if he should continue to force his wretched hackwork upon men of genius, or pester Bakunin for the return of the advance which had been paid him. The frightened and infuriated agent sent the letter to Marx. It is doubtful whether the evidence of the intrigues conducted by Bakunin's organization, the Democratic Alliance, would in itself have been sufficient to secure his expulsion, since he numbered many personal supporters at the Congress; but the report of the committee instructed to look into this scandal and the dramatic production of the Necha-yev letter, turned the scale. After long and stormy sessions, in the course of which even the Proudhonists had finally been persuaded that no party could pre-serve its unity while Bakunin was in its ranks, he and his closest associates were expelled by a small majority.

Marx's next proposal also came as a bombshell to the uninitiated members of the Congress: it was to transfer the seat of the Council to the United States. Everyone realized that this was tantamount to the dissolution of the International. America was not merely infinitely distant from European affairs, but insignificant in the affairs of the International. The French delegates declared that one might as well remove it to the moon. Marx gave no explicit reason for this proposal, which was formally moved by Engels, but its purpose must have been clear enough to all those present. He could not operate without the loyal and unquestioned obedience of at least some sections of the body over which he ruled: England had seceded; he had thought of moving the Council to Belgium, but there, too, the anti-Marxist element was becoming formidable; in Germany the government would sup-press it; France, Switzerland and Holland were far

from reliable; Italy and Spain were definitely Bakuninist strongholds. Sooner than face a bitter struggle
which could end at best in a Pyrrhic victory and destroy
all hope of a proletarian unity for many generations,
Marx decided, after ensuring that it did not fall into
Bakuninists' hands, to allow the International to die
peacefully.

His critics claim that he judged the merit of all
socialist assemblies solely by the degree to which he
was himself permitted to control them: this equation
was certainly made both by him and by Engels, and
made quite automatically; neither ever showed any
sign of understanding the bewildered indignation which
this attitude excited among broad sections of their
followers. Marx attended the Hague congress in person,
and his prestige was such that, in spite of violent
opposition, the Congress finally by a narrow majority
voted its own virtual extinction. Its later meetings were
sordid travesties: it finally expired in Philadelphia in
1876. The International was, indeed, reconstituted
thirteen years later, but by that time—a period of
rapidly increasing Socialist activity in all countries—its
character was very different. Despite its explicitly
revolutionary aims, it was more parliamentary, more
respectable, more optimistic, essentially conciliatory
in temper, more than half committed to the belief in
the inevitability of the gradual evolution of capitalist
society into moderate socialism under persistent but
peaceful pressure from below.

Chapter Eleven

LAST YEARS

I remarked [to Marx] that as I grew older I became more tolerant. 'Do you,' he said, '*do* you?'
H. M. HYNDMAN, *Record of an Adventurous Life*

THE duel with Bakunin is the last public episode in Marx's life. The revolution seemed dead everywhere, although its embers glowed faintly in Russia and Spain. The reaction was once more triumphant, in a milder form, indeed, than in the days of his youth, prepared to make definite concessions to its adversary, but appearing to possess all the more stability for that reason. The peaceful conquest of political and economic control seemed the workers' best hope of emancipation. The prestige of Lassalle's followers in Germany rose steadily, and Liebknecht, who represented the Marxist opposition, now that the International was dead, was inclined to come to terms with them, in order to form a single united party. He was persuaded that placed as he was inside Germany, he had a better grasp of the tactical exigencies than Marx and Engels, who continued to live in England and would not listen to any suggestion of compromise. The two parties finally held a conference at Gotha in 1875 and formed an alliance, issuing a common programme composed by the leaders of both factions. It was naturally submitted to Marx for approval. He left no doubt as to the impression which it made on him.

A violently worded attack was instantly dispatched

to Liebknecht in Berlin and Engels was commanded to
write in a similar strain. Marx accused his disciples of
straying into the use of the misleading, half-meaning-
less terminology inherited from Lassalle and the True
Socialists, interspersed with vague liberal phrases
which he had spent half his life in exposing and elimin-
ating. The programme itself seemed to him to be
permeated by the spirit of compromise—especially in
accepting the validity of their worst enemy, the state—
and to rest on a belief in the possibility of attaining
social justice by peacefully agitating for such trivial
ends as a 'just' remuneration for labour, and the abolition of the law of inheritance—Proudhonist and Saint-
Simonian remedies for this or that abuse, calculated to
prop up the state and the capitalist system rather than
hasten its collapse. In the form of angry marginal notes
he conveyed for the last time his own conception of
what the programme of a militant socialist party ought
to be. The loyal Liebknecht received this, as everything
else which came from London, meekly, and even
reverently, but made no use of it. The alliance continued and grew in strength. Two years later Liebknecht was again sharply criticized by Engels, who took
an even lower view than Marx of his political capacity.
On this occasion the cause was the appearance in the
pages of the official organ of the German Social Democratic party of articles by, and in support of, a certain
Eugen Dühring, a radical lecturer on economics in the
University of Berlin, a man of violently anti-capitalist
but hardly socialist views, who was acquiring growing
influence in the ranks of the German party. Against
him Engels published his longest and most comprehensive work, the last written in collaboration with
Marx; it contained an authoritative (though flatly

non-Hegelian) version of the materialist view of history,
expounded in the blunt, vigorous, lucid prose which
Engels wrote with great facility. *The Anti-Dühring*, as
it came to be called, is an attack on the undialectical,
positivistic materialism, then increasingly popular
among scientific writers and journalists, which maintained that all natural phenomena could be interpreted
in terms of the motion of matter in space, and advances
against it the principle of the universal working of the
dialectical principle far beyond the categories of human
history, in the realms of biology, physics and mathematics. Engels was a versatile and well-read man, and
had, by sheer industry, acquired some rudimentary
knowledge of these subjects, but his discussions of them
are not illuminating. In particular the over-ambitious
attempt to discover the working of the triad of the
Hegelian dialectic in the mathematical rule by which
the product of two negative quantities is positive,
has proved a source of much embarrassment to later
Marxists, who have found themselves saddled with the
impossible task of defending an eccentric view not
entailed by anything that Marx himself had ever
asserted at any rate in his published writings. Marxist
physics and mathematics of our own day are subjects
which, like Cartesian physics, forms a peculiar and
isolated enclave in the development of a great intellec-
ual movement, of antiquarian rather than scientific
interest. More important, Engels's version of the
materialist conception of history, while it faithfully
develops Marx's attack on liberal or idealist historiography, is far more mechanistic and crudely determinist than most of Marx's writings on the subject,
especially in his early years. In this Engels, perhaps
because he wrote so clearly, was followed by the

overwhelming majority of Marxist writers, with Kautsky, and Plekhanov at their head, for more than half a century. Perhaps when Marx, towards the end of his life, declared that whatever else he might be, he was certainly not a Marxist, he had such extravagances and popularizations in view. The most readable are the chapters later reprinted as a pamphlet under the title *The Evolution from Utopian to Scientific Socialism*. That is written in Engels's best vein, and gives a somewhat Darwinian account of the growth of Marxism from its origins in German idealism, French political theory and English economic science. It is the best brief autobiographical appreciation of Marxism by one of its creators, and has had a decisive influence on both Russian and German Socialism.

The attack on the Gotha Programme was Marx's last violent intervention in the affairs of the party. No similar crisis occurred again in his lifetime, and he was left free to devote his remaining years to theoretical studies and vain attempts to restore his failing health. He had moved from Kentish Town first to one, then to another home in Haverstock Hill, not far from Engels, who had sold his share in the family business to his partner, and had established himself in London in a large, commodious house in St. John's Wood. A year or two before this he had settled a permanent annuity on Marx, which, modest though it was, enabled him to pursue his work in peace. They saw each other nearly every day, and together carried on an immense correspondence with socialists in every land, by many of whom they had come to be regarded with increasing respect and veneration. Marx was now without question the supreme moral and intellectual authority of international socialism; Lassalle and Proudhon had died in the 'sixties, Bakunin, in poverty and neglect, in 1876. The death of his last great enemy evoked no public comment from Marx: perhaps because his harsh obituary notice of Proudhon in a German newspaper had caused a wave of indignation among the French socialists, and he thought it more tactful to remain silent. His sentiments towards his adversaries, living and dead, had not altered, but he was physically less capable of the active campaigns of his youth and middle years; overwork and a life of poverty had finally undermined his strength; he was tired, and often ill, and began to be preoccupied by his health. Every year, generally accompanied by his younger daughter Eleanor, he would visit the English seaside, or a German or Bohemian spa, where he would occasionally meet old friends and followers, who sometimes brought with them young historians or economists anxious to meet the celebrated revolutionary.

He rarely spoke of himself or of his life, and never about his origin. The fact that he was a Jew neither he nor Engels ever mentions. His references to individual Jews, particularly in his letters to Engels, are virulent to a degree: his origin was evidently a personal stigma which he was unable to avoid pointing out in others; his denial of the importance of racial categories, his emphasis upon the international character of the proletariat, takes on a peculiar sharpness of tone, directed as it is against misconceptions of which he himself had been a conspicuous victim. His impatience and irritability increased with old age, and he took care to avoid the society of men who bored him or disagreed with his views. He became more and more difficult in his personal relations; he broke off all connexion with one of his oldest friends, the poet Freiligrath, after his patriotic odes in 1870; he deliberately insulted his devoted adherent Kugelmann to whom some of his most interesting letters were written, because the latter insisted on joining him in Karlsbad after he had made it clear that he wished for no company. On the other hand, when he was tactfully approached, his behaviour could be friendly and even gracious, particularly to the young revolutionaries and radical journalists who came to London in growing numbers to pay homage to the two old men. Such pilgrims were agreeably received at his house, and through them he established contacts with his followers in countries with which he had had no previous relations, notably with Russia, where a vigorous and well-disciplined revolutionary movement had at last taken root. His economic writings, and in particular *Das Kapital*, had had a greater success in Russia than in any other country: the censorship—ironically enough—permitted its publication on the ground that 'although the book has a pronounced socialist tendency . . . it is not written in a popular style . . . and is unlikely to find many readers among the general public'. The reviews of it in the Russian press were more favourable and more intelligent than any others, a fact which surprised and pleased him, and did much to change his contemptuous attitude to 'the Russian clodhoppers' into admiration for the new generation of austere and fearless revolutionaries whom his own writings had done so much to educate.

The history of Marxism in Russia is unlike its history in any other country. Whereas in Germany and in France, unlike other forms of positivism and material-ism, it was primarily a proletarian movement, marking a sharp revulsion of feeling against the ineffectiveness of the liberal idealism of the bourgeoisie in the first half of the century, and represented a mood of deflationary realism, in Russia, where the proletariat was still weak and insignificant by Western standards, not only the apostles of Marxism but the majority of its converts were middle-class intellectuals for whom it itself became a kind of romanticism, a belated form of democratic passion. It grew during the height of the populist movement, which preached the need for personal self-identification with the people and their material needs, in order to understand them, educate them, and raise their intellectual and social level, and was thus equally directed against the reactionary anti-Western party with its mystical faith in autocracy, the Orthodox Church and the Slav genius on the one hand, and the mild agrarian liberalism or socialism of the pro-Westerners, such as Turgenev and Herzen, on the other.

This was the time when well-to-do young men in Moscow and St. Petersburg, notably the 'penitent' young noblemen and squires, ridden by social guilt, threw away career and position in order to immerse themselves in the study of the condition of peasants and factory workers, and went to live amongst them with the same noble fervour with which their fathers and grandfathers had followed Bakunin or the Decembrists. Historical and political materialism—emphasis on concrete, tangible, economic reality as the basis of social and individual life, criticism of institutions and of individual actions in terms of their relation to, and influence upon, the material welfare of the popular masses, hatred and scorn of art or life pursued for their own sake, isolated from the sufferings of the world in an ivory tower, were preached with a self-forgetful passion: 'A pair of boots is something more important

than all the plays of Shakespeare', said a celebrated
revolutionary, and expressed a general mood. In these
men Marxism produced a sense of liberation from
doubts and confusions, by offering for the first time a
systematic exposition of the nature and laws of development of society in clear, material terms: its very
flatness seemed sane and lucid after the romantic
nationalism of the Slavophiles and the mystery and
grandeur of Hegelian idealism. This general effect
resembled the feeling induced in Marx himself after
reading Feuerbach forty years before: it aroused the
same sense of the finality of its solution and of the
limitless possibility of action on its basis. Russia had
not experienced the horrors of 1849, its development
lagged far behind that of the West, its problems in the
'seventies and 'eighties in many respects resembled
those which had faced the rest of Europe half a century
before. The Russian radicals read the *Communist
Manifesto* and the declamatory passages of *Das Kapital*
with the sense of exhilaration with which men had
read Rousseau in the previous century; they found much
which applied exceptionally well to their own condition: nowhere was it as true as in Russia that 'in agriculture as in manufacture the capitalist transformation
of the process of production signifies the martyrdom
of the producer; the instrument of labour becomes the
means of subjugating, exploiting and impoverishing
the worker; the social combination and organization of
the labour process functions as an elaborate method for
crushing the worker's individual vitality, freedom and
independence'. Only in Russia the method, particularly after the liberation of the serfs had enormously
enlarged the labour market, was not elaborate, but
simple.

To his own surprise, Marx found that the nation against which he had written and spoken for thirty years provided him with the most fearless and intelligent of his disciples. He welcomed them in his home in London, and entered into a regular correspondence with Danielson, his translator, and Sieber, one of the ablest of Russian academic economists. Marx's analyses were largely concerned with industrial societies; Russia was an agrarian state and any attempt at direct application of a doctrine designed for one set of conditions to another was bound to lead to errors in theory and practice. Letters reached him from Danielson in Russia, and from the exiles Lavrov and Vera Zassulich, begging him to apply himself to the specific problems presented by the peculiar organization of the Russian peasants into primitive communes, holding lands in in common, and in particular to state his view on propositions derived from Herzen and Bakunin and widely accepted by Russian radicals, which asserted that a direct transition was possible from such primitive communes to developed communism, without the necessity of passing through the intermediate stage of industrialism and urbanization, as had happened in the West. Marx who had previously treated this hypothesis with contempt as emanating from sentimental Slavophile idealization of the peasants disguised as radicalism —combined with the childish belief that it was 'possible to cheat the dialectic by an audacious leap, to avoid the natural stages of evolution or shuffle them out of the world by decrees', was by now sufficiently impressed by the intelligence, seriousness, and, above all, the fanatical and devoted socialism of the new generation of Russian revolutionaries to re-examine the issue. In order to do this he began to learn Russian; at the end of six months he had mastered it sufficiently to read sociological works[1] and government reports which his friends succeeded in smuggling to London. Engels viewed this new alliance with some distaste: he had an incurable aversion to everything east of the Elbe, and he suspected Marx of inventing a new occupation, in order to conceal from himself his reluctance, due to sheer physical weariness, to complete the writing of *Das Kapital*. After duly tunnelling his way through an immense mass of statistical and historical material, Marx made considerable doctrinal concessions. He admitted[2] that if a revolution in Russia should be the signal of a common rising of the entire European proletariat, it was conceivable, and even likely—that communism in Russia could be based directly upon the semi-feudal communal ownership of land by the village as it existed at the time; but this could not occur if capitalism continued among her nearest neighbours, since this would inevitably force Russia in sheer economic self-defence along the path already traversed by the more advanced countries of the West.

The Russians were not alone, however, in paying homage to the London exiles. Young leaders of the new united German social democratic party, Bebel, Bernstein, Kautsky, visited him and consulted him on all important issues. His two eldest daughters had married French socialists and kept him in touch with Latin countries. The founder of French social democracy, Jules Guesde, submitted the programme of his

---

[1] e.g. by Chernyshevsky, for whom he expressed his admiration, and by Bervi-Flerovsky.

[2] In a letter left unpublished by Plekhanov, who evidently thought that it was a dangerous concession to populism. It saw the light only some years after the October Revolution.

party to him, and had it drastically revised. Marxism began to oust Bakuninist anarchism in Italy and Switzerland. Encouraging reports came from the United States. The best news of all came from Germany, where the socialist vote, in spite of Bismarck's anti-socialist laws, was mounting with prodigious speed. The only major European country which continued to stand aloof, virtually impervious to his teaching, was that in which he himself lived and of which he spoke as his second home. 'In England', he wrote, 'prolonged prosperity has demoralized the workers . . . the ultimate aim of this most bourgeois of lands would seem to be the establishment of a bourgeois aristocracy and a bourgeois proletariat side by side with the bourgeoisie . . . the revolutionary energy of the British workers has oozed away . . . it will take long before they can shake off their bourgeois infection . . . they totally lack the mettle of the old Chartists.' He had no intimate English friends—he had known Ernest Jones, he worked with a good many labour leaders, he was visited by radicals such as Belfort Bax, Crompton, Butler-Johnston and Roy Lankester, he even accepted an invitation to his club from such a member of the ruling class as Sir Mountstuart Elphinstone Grant-Duff, a liberal member of Parliament, and his friend the publisher Leonard Montefiore. But such meetings touched the barest surface of his life. He did indeed, in the last years of his life, allow himself to be wooed for a brief period by H. M. Hyndman, the founder of the Social Democratic Federation, who did much to popularize Marxism in England. Hyndman was an agreeable, easygoing, expansive individual, a genuine radical by temperament, an amusing and effective speaker, and a lively writer on political and economic subjects. A light-hearted amateur himself, he enjoyed meeting and talking to men of genius, and, being somewhat indiscriminate in his taste, presently abandoned Mazzini for Marx. He thus described him in his memoirs: 'The first impression of Marx as I saw him was that of a powerful, shaggy, untamed old man, ready, not to say eager, to enter into conflict, and rather suspicious himself of immediate attack; yet his greeting of us was cordial. . . . When speaking with fierce indignation of the policy of the Liberal Party, especially in regard to Ireland, the old warrior's brows wrinkled, the broad, strong nose and face were obviously moved by passion, and he poured out a stream of vigorous denunciation which displayed alike the heat of his temperament, and the marvellous command he possessed over our language. The contrast between his manner and utterance when thus deeply stirred by anger, and his attitude when giving his views on the economic events of the period, was very marked. He turned from the role of prophet and violent denunciator to that of the calm philosopher without any apparent effort, and I felt that many a long year might pass before I ceased to be a student in the presence of a master.'

Hyndman's sincerity, his *naïveté*, his affable and disarming manner, and above all his whole-hearted and uncritical admiration for Marx, whom, with typical ineptitude, he called 'the Aristotle of the nineteenth century', caused the latter to treat him for some months with marked friendliness and indulgence. The inevitable breach occurred over Hyndman's book, *England for All*, a most readable, if not very accurate, account of Marxism in English. The debt to Marx was not acknowledged by name, a fact which Hyndman lamely tried to explain on the ground that 'the English don't like being taught by foreigners, and your name is so much detested here. . . .' This was sufficient. Marx held violent opinions on plagiarism: Lassalle had been made to suffer for far less; moreover, he had no wish to be associated with Hyndman's own confused ideas. He broke off the connexion at once and with it his last remaining link with English socialism.

His mode of life had scarcely changed at all. He rose at seven, drank several cups of black coffee, and then retired to his study where he read and wrote until two in the afternoon. After hurrying through his meal he worked again till supper, which he ate with his family. After that he took an evening walk on Hampstead Heath, or returned to his study, where he worked until two or three in the morning. His son-in-law, Paul Lafargue, has left a description of this room:

'It was on the first floor and well lighted by a broad window looking on the park. The fireplace was opposite the window, and was flanked by bookshelves, on the top of which packets of newspapers and manuscripts were piled up to the ceiling. On one side of the window stood two tables, likewise loaded with miscellaneous papers, newspapers and books. In the middle of the room was a small plain writing-table and a windsor chair. Between this chair and one of the bookshelves was a leather-coloured sofa on which Marx would lie down and rest occasionally. On the mantelpiece were more books interspersed with cigars, boxes of matches, tobacco jars, paperweights and photographs—his daughters, his wife, Engels, Wilhelm Wolff. . . . He would never allow anyone to arrange his books and papers . . . but he could put his hand on any book or manuscript he wanted. When conversing he would often stop for a moment to show the relevant passage in a book or to find a reference. . . . He disdained appearances when arranging his books. Quarto and octavo volumes and pamphlets were placed higgledy-piggledy so far as size and shape were concerned. He had scant respect for their form or binding, the beauty of page or of printing: he would turn down the corners of pages, underline freely and pencil the margins. He did not actually annotate his books, but he could not refrain from a question mark or note of exclamation when the author went too far. Every year he re-read his note-books and underlined passages to refresh his memory . . . which was vigorous and accurate: he had trained it in accordance with Hegel's plan of memorizing verse in an unfamiliar tongue.'

Sundays he dedicated to his children: and when these grew up and married, to his grandchildren. The entire family had nicknames; his daughters were Qui-Qui, Quo-Quo, and Tussy; his wife was Möhme; he himself was known as the Moor or Old Nick on account of his dark complexion and sinister appearance. His relations with his family remained—even with the difficult Eleanor—warmly affectionate. The Russian sociologist Kovalevsky who used to visit him in his last years, was pleasantly surprised by his urbanity. 'Marx is usually described', he wrote many years later, 'as a gloomy and arrogant man, who flatly rejected all bourgeois science and culture. In reality he was a well-educated, highly cultivated Anglo-German gentleman, a man whose close association with Heine had developed in him a vein of cheerful satire, and one who was full of the joy of life, thanks to the fact that his personal position was extremely comfortable.' This vignette of Marx as a gay and genial host, if not wholly convincing, at any rate conveys the contrast with the

early years in Soho. His chief pleasures were reading
and walking. He was fond of poetry and knew long
passages of Dante, Aeschylus and Shakespeare by
heart. His admiration for Shakespeare was limitless,
and the whole household was brought up on him: he
was read aloud, acted, discussed constantly. Whatever
Marx did, he did methodically. Finding on arrival that
his English was inadequate, he set himself to improve it
by making a list of Shakespeare's turns of phrase: these
he then learnt by heart. Similarly, having learnt
Russian, he read the works of Gogol and Pushkin,
carefully underlining the words whose meaning he did
not know. He had a sound German literary taste,
acquired early in his youth, and developed by reading
and re-reading his favourite works. To distract himself
he read the elder Dumas or Scott, or light French
novels of the day; Balzac he admired prodigiously: he
looked upon him as having provided in his novels the
acutest analysis of the bourgeois society of his day;
many of his characters did not, he declared, come to
full maturity until after the death of their creator, in
the 'sixties and 'seventies. He had intended to write a
study of Balzac as a social analyst, but never began it.
(In view of the quality of the only extant piece of
literary criticism from his pen, that of Eugène Sue, the
loss may not be one to mourn). His taste in literature,
for all his love of reading, was, on the whole, undis-
tinguished and commonplace. There is nothing to
indicate that he liked either painting or music; all was
extruded by his passion for books.

He had always read enormously, but towards the
end of his life his appetite increased to a degree at which
it interfered with his creative work. In his last ten years
he began to acquire completely new languages: thus

he tried to learn Turkish, with the ostensible purpose of studying agrarian conditions in those countries: as an old Urquhartite he laid his hopes on the Turkish peasantry which he expected to become a disruptive, democratizing force in the Near East. As his bibliomania grew, Engels's worst fears became confirmed; he wrote less and less, his style grew more crabbed and obscure. The second and third volumes of *Das Kapital*, edited by Engels, and the supplementary studies which formed the fourth volume, edited by Kautsky from posthumous material, are greatly inferior in mental power and lucidity to the first volume which has become a classic.

Physically he was declining fast. In 1881 Jenny Marx died of cancer after a long and painful illness. 'With her the Moor has died too,' Engels said to his daughter Eleanor. Marx lived for two more years, still carrying on an extensive correspondence with Italians, Spaniards, Russians, but his strength was virtually spent. In 1882, after a particularly severe winter, his doctor sent him to Algiers to recuperate. He arrived with acute pleurisy which he had caught on the journey. He spent a month in North Africa which was uncommonly cold and wet, and returned to Europe ill and exhausted. After some weeks of vain wandering from town to town on the French Riviera in search of the sun, he went to Paris, where he stayed for a time with his eldest daughter Jenny Longuet. Not long after his return to London, news came of her sudden death. He never fully recovered from this blow: he fell ill in the following year, developed an abscess in the lung, and on 14 March 1883 died in his sleep, seated in an armchair in his study. He was buried in Highgate cemetery and laid next to his wife. There were not many present: members of his family, a few personal

friends, and workers' representatives from several
lands. A dignified and moving funeral address was
delivered by Engels, who spoke of his achievements
and his character:

'His mission in life was to contribute in one way or
another to the overthrow of capitalist society . . . to
contribute to the liberation of the present-day proletariat which he was the first to make conscious of its
own position and its needs, of the conditions under
which it could win its freedom. Fighting was his element. And he fought with a passion, a tenacity and a
success which few could rival . . . and consequently was
the best-hated and most calumniated man of his time
. . . he died, beloved, revered and mourned by millions
of revolutionary fellow workers from the mines of
Siberia to the coasts of California, in all points of
Europe and America . . . his name and his work will
endure through the ages.'

His death passed largely unnoticed among the
general public; *The Times* did, indeed, print a brief and
inaccurate obituary notice, but this, although he died in
London, appeared as a message from its Paris correspondent who reported what he had read in the French
Socialist Press. His fame increased steadily after his
death as the revolutionary effects of his teaching became
more and more apparent. As an individual he never
captured the imagination either of the public or of
professional biographers to such an extent as his more
sensitive or more romantic contemporaries; and
indeed Carlyle, Mill, Herzen were more tragic
figures tormented by intellectual and moral conflicts
which Marx neither experienced nor understood, and
far more profoundly affected by the *malaise* of their
generation. They have left a bitter and minute account

of it, better written and more vivid than anything to be found in Marx or in Engels. Marx fought against the mean and cynical society of his time, which seemed to him to vulgarize and degrade every human relationship, with a hatred no less profound. But his mind was made of stronger and cruder texture; he was insensitive, self-confident, and strong willed; the causes of his unhappiness lay outside him—they were poverty, sickness, and the triumph of the enemy. His inner life seems tranquil, uncomplicated and secure. He saw the world in simple terms of black and white; those who were not with him were against him. He knew upon whose side he was, his life was spent in fighting for it, he knew that it must ultimately win. Such crises of faith as occurred in the lives of the gentler spirits among his friends—the painful self-examination of such men as Hess or Heine—received from him no sympathy. He looked upon them as so many signs of bourgeois degeneracy which took the form of morbid attention to private emotional states, or still worse, the exploitation of social unrest for some personal or artistic end—frivolity and irresponsible self-indulgence criminal in men before whose eyes the greatest battle in human history was being fought. This uncompromising sternness towards personal feeling and almost religious insistence on a self-sacrificing discipline, was inherited by his successors, and imitated by his enemies in every land. It distinguishes his true descendants among his followers and his adversaries from tolerant liberalism in every sphere.

Others before him had preached a war between classes but it was he who conceived and successfully put into practice a plan designed to achieve the political organization of a class fighting solely for its interests as a class—and in so doing transformed the entire character of political parties and political warfare. Yet in his own eyes and in those of his contemporaries, he appeared as first and foremost a theoretical economist. The classical premisses on which his economic doctrines rest are to-day largely superseded; contemporary discussion proceeds upon a different basis. The doctrine which has survived and grown, and which has had a greater and more lasting influence both on opinion and on action than any other view put forward in modern times, is his theory of the evolution and structure of capitalist society, of which he nowhere gave a detailed exposition. This theory, by asserting that the most important question to be asked with regard to any phenomenon is concerned with the relation which it bears to the economic structure, that is, the relations of economic power in the social structure of which it is an expression, has created new tools of criticism and research whose use has altered the nature and direction of the social sciences in our generation. All those whose work rests on social observation are necessarily affected. Not only conflicting classes and groups and movements and their leaders in every country, but historians and sociologists, psychologists and political scientists, critics and creative artists, so far as they try to analyse the changing quality of the life of their society, owe the form of their ideas in large part to the work of Karl Marx. More than half a century has passed since its completion, and during those years it has received more than its due share of praise and blame. Exaggeration and over-simple application of its main principles have done much to obscure its meaning, and many blunders, both of theory and of practice, have been committed in its name. Nevertheless its effect was, and continues to be, revolutionary.

It set out to refute the proposition that ideas decisively determine the course of history, but the very extent of its own influence on human affairs has weakened the force of its thesis. For in altering the hitherto prevailing view of the relation of the individual to his environment and to his fellows, it has palpably altered that relation itself; and in consequence remains the most powerful among the intellectual forces which are to-day permanently transforming the ways in which men act and think.

BIBLIOGRAPHY

I. ORIGINAL WORKS

THE complete edition of the works and private papers of Marx and Engels (MEGA) is still unfinished: their publication in the original languages which was commenced in Berlin under the auspices of the Marx-Engels-Lenin Institute was interrupted by Hitler's accession to power in 1933 and begun afresh after the war; 21 volumes of this edition have appeared to date (1963). All texts are in German, whatever the original language: the edition omits some documents contained in the English MEGA and adds others. Twelve volumes are still due to appear. The Russian translation simultaneously and subsequently published by the Institute in Moscow had by 1933 considerably outstripped the German edition and had reached vol. 7 in 1935. The new Russian edition begun in 1955 had reached vol. 28 (plus one unnumbered volume) in 1963; five volumes are still due. This edition does not contain variants, and is evidently coordinated with the corresponding (German) edition published in East Germany. The most important of the works not, at any rate as yet, included in this edition, is the Rough Draft (Rohentwurf, 1857-8) on which much of *Das Kapital* is based. This has now been published under the title *Grundrisse der Kritik der Politischen Oekonomie* (Moscow, 1939 and 1941, 3 vols.; Dietz, Berlin 1953, one vol.). The best-known works have been made accessible to English readers by a series of competent translations published by Messrs. Martin Lawrence (now Lawrence and Wishart). It includes, up to date: The Critique of the Hegelian Philosophy of Right; the Jewish Question; the Philosophic-Economic Manuscript; *The German Ideology* (Pts. I and III), *The Poverty of Philosophy*; *The Communist Manifesto*; *Wage, Labour and Capital*; *The Class Struggles in France*; *The Eighteenth Brumaire of Louis Bonaparte*; *Civil War in France*; *Civil War in the United States* and *Revolution in Spain* (collections of Marx's newspaper articles, letters, documents, &c.); *Correspondence, 1846–1895* (a large and well-edited selection of letters by Marx and Engels); *Letters to Dr. Kugelmann*, and

the *Critique of the Gotha Programme*; of works by Engels:
Germany: Revolution and Counter-revolution; *Ludwig Feuerbach and the Outcome of Classical German Philosophy*; *Socialism: Utopian and Scientific*; *Herr Eugen Dühring's Revolution
in Science*; *Dialectics of Nature*; *The British Labour Movement*;
and several other works. The best English translation of the
first volume of *Capital* is by E. and C. Paul (Everyman's
Library: Dent), the only available English version of Vols. II
and III is still that by E. Untermann (Chicago: C. H. Kerr
& Co.); Vol. IV (*Theories of Surplus Value*) has not been
translated into English. There are also versions of *A Contribution to Political Economy* (trans. N. I. Stone: C. H. Kerr &
Co.); *Value, Price and Profit* (ed. by E. M. Aveling, Allen and
Unwin) and *Letters on India* (ed. by B. P. L. and F. Bedi,
Lahore: Contemp. India Publications). Two useful com-
pendia, which include a good many of the works cited above,
are: *A Handbook to Marxism* (ed. E. Burns: Gollancz) and
Selected Works (2 vols., Lawrence and Wishart).

II. BIOGRAPHIES

The standard work is *Karl Marx* by Franz Mehring,
brought up to date and excellently annotated by E. Fuchs
and translated by E. Fitzgerald. *Karl Marx: a Study in
Fanaticism*, by E. H. Carr, is a lively and interesting book
based on detailed original research, which, on points of fact,
supersedes all previous authorities. An equally scrupulous
work but more sympathetic to its subject and his teaching is
Karl Marx: Man and Fighter, by B. Nicolaievsky and O.
Maenchen-Helfen, which also embodies original material,
particularly from Russian sources. Biographies exist also by
John Spargo and Otto Rühle, and shorter lives by M. Beer,
R. W. Postgate and C. J. S. Sprigge; the last of these contains
many points of interest. The standard biography of Engels is
by G. Mayer (abridged and translated by G. and H. Highet,
ed. by R. H. S. Crossman).

III. CRITICAL STUDIES

Of the immense polemical literature which surrounds Marx
and Marxism the following works, of those written in or
translated into English, are likely to be of most interest to the

general reader: *Karl Marx and the Close of his System*, by E. v. Böhm-Bawerk (this, and the works by H. W. B. Joseph and V. Simkhovich cited below, constitute the most formidable attacks upon Marx's economic doctrines). A counterattack is provided by R. Hilfferding's *Böhm-Bawerk's Criticism of Marx. What Marx Really Meant*, by G. D. H. Cole, the most competent large-scale popular exposition of Marxism, if not of Marx's own views, since Engels and Hyndman. *Towards the Understanding of Karl Marx* and *From Hegel to Marx*, by S. Hook, lucid and penetrating critical studies of Marx and his predecessors. *The Labour Theory of Value in Karl Marx*, by H. W. B. Joseph, *Marxism versus Socialism*, by V. Simkhovich (for both these, see above). *The Open Society and its Enemies*, by Dr. Karl Popper: a work of exceptional originality and power. The second volume provides the most scrupulous and formidable criticism of the philosophical and historical doctrines of Marxism by any living writer. Alexander Gray in *The Socialist Tradition*, a model of clear, at times brilliant, always entertaining, exposition. This provides a very intelligent if more personal and less detailed examination of Marxism. *Karl Marx*, by Karl Korsch, a learned but ponderously written examination of Marxism in its historical setting. *Historical Materialism and the Economics of Karl Marx*, by Benedetto Croce, an essay of arresting originality. *The Marxist Philosophy and the Sciences*, by J. B. S. Haldane, a stimulating, if not wholly convincing, discussion of the usefulness of the method of dialectical materialism in the natural sciences, based largely on the theories of Engels. *Marxism, Is it Science?* by Max Eastman, an essay of characteristic brilliance by this sharp and original critic and excellent writer, bitterly condemned as a heretic by orthodox Communists. *Darwin, Marx, Wagner*, by Jacques Barzun, a very readable essay. *To the Finland Station*, by Edmund Wilson (New York, 1940) contains a very striking intellectual portrait of Marx. *What is Marxism?* by Emile Burns, an orthodox Communist account. *An Essay on Marxian Economics*, by Joan Robinson, a characteristically penetrating study. S. H. Chang, *The Marxian Theory of the State* (Philadelphia, 1931), a painstaking treatise. *Karl Marx in his Earlier Writings*, by H. P. Adams, a competent summary of the writings before the 'London' period. M. M. Bober's *Karl*

Marx's Interpretation of History (U.S.A., 1927), a dry but useful study of this topic. A short, but exceptionally able study of historical materialism by J. L. Gray forms a chapter of *Social and Political Thinkers of the Nineteenth Century*, ed. F. J. C. Hearnshaw. The pages devoted to Marxism in *A History of Political Theory*, by G. H. Sabine, and in his *Marxism* (1958) are adequate summaries. *The Economic Doctrine of Karl Marx*, by K. Kautsky, the classical exposition of Marxist economics. *Karl Marx*, by H. J. Laski, the best short summary of Marx's achievement. The same author's *Communism* in this series is, despite its shortness, so far as is known to the writer, the best analysis of the movement and its intellectual basis. *Karl Marx's Capital*, by A. D. Lindsay, an exceptionally fair discussion of its subject. *Marx, Engels, Marxism*, by N. Lenin, a magisterial exposition and, with his *State and Revolution*, one of the texts on which orthodox Communism is to-day based. *Essays in the History of Materialism and Fundamental Problems of Marxism*, by G. Plekhanov, classical treatises by the acutest thinker and most brilliant writer among the immediate successors of Marx and Engels. A duller but solider work is *Karl Marx and Friedrich Engels*, by D. B. Ryazanov, the most erudite of all Marxists, and the most pedestrian. *The Theory and Practice of Communism*, by R. N. Carew-Hunt (London, 1950), and *What is Communism?*, by J. P. Plamenatz (London, 1947), should also be consulted.

ADDITIONS TO THE BIBLIOGRAPHY (1963)
(*works in English only are included*)

I

Capital, translated from the 4th German edn. by E. and C. Paul. 2 vols (Dent, 1957)

Capital, Vol. III, revised and corrected by E. Untermann (Lawrence & Wishart, 1960)

German Ideology, new edn. (Lawrence & Wishart, 1941)

Economic and Philosophic Manuscripts of 1844, translated by M. Milligan. (Lawrence & Wishart, 1959)

II

Leopold Schwarzschild, *The Red Prussian: The Life and Legend of Karl Marx* (Hamish Hamilton, 1948).

III

Solomon F. Bloom, *The World of Nations: A Study of the National Implications in the Work of Karl Marx* (New York, 1941).

Herbert Marcuse, *Reason and Revolution: Hegel and the Rise of Social Theory*, 2nd edn. with Supplementary Chapter (Routledge, 1955).

Paul M. Sweezy, *The Theory of Capital Development: Principles of Marxian Political Economy* (Dennis Dobson, 1946).

H. B. Acton, *The Illusion of the Epoch* (Cohen and West, 1955).

Adam B. Ulam, *The Unfinished Revolution* (Random House, 1960).

Erich Fromm, *Marx's Concept of Man* (New York, Frederick Ungar, 1962).

Robert C. Tucker, *Philosophy and Myth in Karl Marx* (Cambridge U.P., 1962).

T. B. Bottomore, *Karl Marx, Early Writings* (C. A. Watts, 1963).

T. B. Bottomore & Maximilien Rubel, *Karl Marx: Selected Writings in Sociology and Social Philosophy* (C. A. Watts, 3rd imp. 1963 London, 1956).

G. Lichtheim, *Marxism, an Historical and Critical Study* (Routledge & Kegan Paul, 1961).

J. P. Plamenatz, *German Marxism and Russian Communism.* (London/New York/Toronto, 1954).

Raymond Aron, *The Opium of the Intellectuals* (English translation, Secker and Warburg, 1957).

H. B. Mayo, *Introduction to Marxist Theory* (New York, 1962).

Eugene Kamenka, *The Ethical Foundation of Marxism* (Routledge and Kegan Paul, 1962).

INDEX

Apple Pro Training Series:

Final Cut Pro 7 Quick-Reference Guide

Brendan Boykin

Apple
Certified

Apple Pro Training Series: Final Cut Pro 7 Quick-Reference Guide
Brendan Boykin
Copyright © 2010 by Brendan Boykin

Published by Peachpit Press. For information on Peachpit Press books, contact:

Peachpit Press
1249 Eighth Street
Berkeley, CA 94710
(510) 524-2178
Fax: (510) 524-2221
http://www.peachpit.com
To report errors, please send a note to errata@peachpit.com
Peachpit Press is a division of Pearson Education

Apple Series Editor: Serena Herr
Editor: Heather Christy
Production Coordinator: Cory Borman
Technical Editor: Robbie Carman
Copy Editor: Elissa Rabellino
Proofreader: Elissa Rabellino
Compositor: James D. Kramer, Happenstance Type-O-Rama
Indexer: Jack Lewis
Cover Illustration: Kent Oberheu
Cover Production: Chris Gillespie, Happenstance Type-O-Rama

ISBN 10: 0-321-69468-6
ISBN-13: 978-0-321-69468-3
9 8 7 6 5 4 3 2 1
Printed and bound in the United States of America

Contents at a Glance

1
Overview

As part of Final Cut Studio, Final Cut Pro is the hub where your project comes to life. This book provides a lookup guide for Final Cut Pro's key features that you will use in the post-production process.

The flexibility of the application lets you develop and distribute a video project with a minimum amount of tools; or you may use all of the powerful features of Final Cut Pro, including its integration with the other Final Cut Studio applications. This chapter gives a high-level look at the Final Cut Studio post-production process. A list of new features in Final Cut Pro 7 is found at the end of this chapter.

Final Cut Studio Workflow

Various sources are ingested into a Final Cut Pro project, where they are transformed into a finished program. The finished program may include motion graphics created in Motion, sound effects and audio clean-up work done in Soundtrack Pro, and a visual sweetening pass through Color. In the end, the finished program is output from Final Cut Pro to various mastering and distribution mediums.

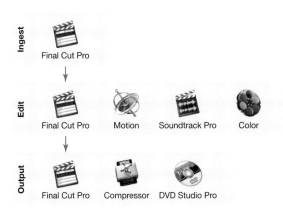

Final Cut Pro–Centric Workflow

After you break down the workflow into specifics, the central role of Final Cut Pro becomes obvious. Final Cut Pro is the application for getting material in, editing it, and getting the new revised material out. The integration of the Final Cut Studio applications allows your project to flow from Final Cut Pro to the other applications as needed for completing your project.

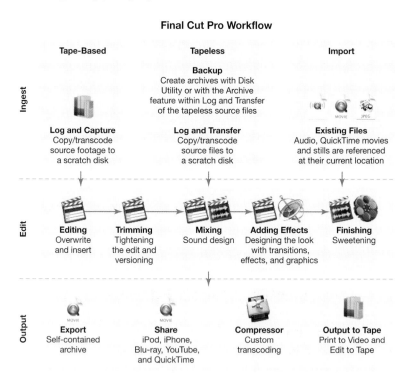

Final Cut Pro Workflow

New Features of Final Cut Pro 7

There are over 100 new features in Final Cut Studio. The following list covers only some of the new and enhanced features within Final Cut Pro 7.

Additional Apple ProRes Codecs

There's now a flavor of Apple ProRes for everyone, from ProRes 4444 with support for an alpha channel down to the offline-quality ProRes (Proxy).

Speed (Chapter 10)

The Change Speed dialog choose whether a speed change ripples the sequence. The new Speed tool is more powerful and easier to use than the former Time Remap tool. Now you can add keyframes to the Keyframe Editor's speed ticks area, which will let you create and modify speed segments within a clip.

Markers (Chapter 15)

Create and edit markers on the fly. Change the colors of markers. Command-drag markers to reposition them. Ripple sequence markers to follow ripple edits. Export marker information as a text file.

Alpha Transitions (Chapter 8)

Add transitions that utilize an alpha channel to customize the look of your production.

Global Transitions (Chapter 8)

Quickly add transitions everywhere in your sequence.

Log and Transfer (Chapter 4)

Includes a name preset function for automatic naming of clips. A new dialog helps you mount the correct volumes for reingesting tapeless media. The Automatic Transfer feature can begin ingesting as soon as a volume of raw footage is mounted.

Reveal and Match Frame Options (Chapter 15)

A new option allows you to match frame subclips to the parent master clips rather than the subclip masters. Another new option reveals all affiliated clips in the active sequence of the selected clip.

iChat Theater Preview (Chapter 15)

A remote computer is able to monitor the output of Final Cut Pro while discussing the edit with you through iChat.

Timecode Viewer (Chapter 2)

Displays a large floating window with the current timecode of the playback.

Improved Tabs

Sequence tabs in the Timeline and Canvas windows will display the color labels applied to sequences. These tabs can also be rearranged.

SD Title Safe

Title Safe in HD sequences displays tick marks to indicate the Standard Definition Title Safe and Action Safe zones.

Closed Captioning

Final Cut Pro preserves closed captioning data (including VANC) in Apple ProRes when capturing with a capture device that passes the data. Closed captioning data may be inserted during tape output and when using Compressor.

New Commands (Chapter 2 and Appendix A)

The commands now include Audio Gain (Adjust) for adjusting a selected keyframe or surround keyframes, Pre-roll Back when editing markers in real time, Close All Bins, and Close Other Tabs. Some new shortcut menu commands are available, such as Join All Through Edits for sequence-wide repair.

Share (Chapter 14)

The Share function provides easy exporting of your project with presets for various Apple devices, Blu-ray, and the web. This customizable export is a background process so that you can get back to editing.

2
Final Cut Pro Interface

Final Cut Pro's interface gives you easy access to everything you need, letting you focus on editing instead of searching menus for tools.

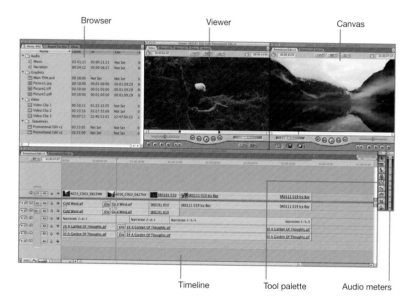

Browser   Viewer   Canvas

Timeline   Tool palette   Audio meters

Browser

The Browser provides a list or icon view of all the assets in your open projects. Since Final Cut Pro lets you have multiple projects open simultaneously, there is a tab for every open project in the Browser. Each project tab lists that project's media files and *sequences* (sequences are timelines representing your edits).

The Effects tab provides quick access to filters, transitions, and generators (including text, bars and tone, and Motion templates). Select an item from the list and drag over a clip or sequence to apply. See Chapters 8, 9, and 12 for more info about using these effects.

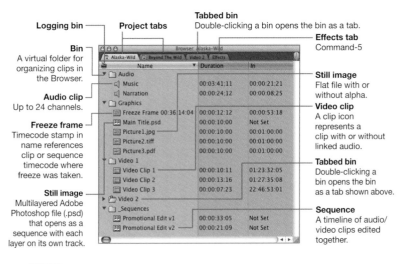

Logging bin

Project tabs

Tabbed bin
Double-clicking a bin opens the bin as a tab.

Effects tab
Command-5

Bin
A virtual folder for organizing clips in the Browser.

Audio clip
Up to 24 channels.

Freeze frame
Timecode stamp in name references clip or sequence timecode where freeze was taken.

Still image
Multilayered Adobe Photoshop file (.psd) that opens as a sequence with each layer on its own track.

Still image
Flat file with or without alpha.

Video clip
A clip icon represents a clip with or without linked audio.

Tabbed bin
Double-clicking a bin opens the bin as a tab shown above.

Sequence
A timeline of audio/video clips edited together.

TIP You can have multiple sequences in a project.

TIP You can rearrange the tab order by dragging a tab. Dragging a tab off any window lets you place the tab in another window or in a new window. In the Browser, this lets you more easily view multiple projects' assets at once or drag assets from one project to another.

NOTE ▶ Closing the Browser closes all open projects.

Viewer

The Viewer is a preview window for clips (with video, audio, or both) and graphics (such as still images or Motion projects). You can bring a clip into the Viewer in three ways:

▶ Double-click the clip in the Browser.

▶ Drag the clip into the Viewer.

▶ Select the clip and press Return.

The tabs at the top of the Viewer window will change based on the clip's properties.

NOTE ▶ When working with filters on a nested sequence or a multilayered Photoshop file (which behaves like a sequence), you can open a sequence into the Viewer by dragging it into the Viewer or by Control-clicking the nested sequence in the Timeline and choosing "Open in Viewer." See Chapter 13 for more information on nesting.

Zoom
Choose "Fit to Window" to match the Video image to the Viewer's size (Shift-Z).

Filters
Shows the parameters for video and audio filters applied to the clip.

Mono (a1), Mono (a2)
Displays the waveform of a discrete audio channel. There may be more tabs representing all audio tracks attached to a clip. Audio may also appear as Stereo (a1a2) if the clip has audio tracks that are linked as pairs.

Playhead Sync
Locks the Viewer, Canvas, and Timeline playheads. Use the Open setting when color correcting (as it automatically opens the clip under the Timeline playhead into the Viewer while keeping the playheads in sync on the same frame) or to perform a multiclip edit using the Viewer. The Gang setting locks the playheads regardless of the same-frame relationship.

Video
Displays the visual element of a clip, including In and Out points plus markers information.

Motion
Displays parameters such as opacity and basic motion.

Timecode Duration
Trimmed length of the source clip.

Current Timecode
Displays the playhead's position in the source clip.

Scrubber bar
Dragging your pointer in this white strip lets you scrub through a clip.

Jog control

In point

Generators
Provides access to generated items, such as text and Motion templates.

Shuttle control

Show Match Frame

Mark Clip

Add Motion Keyframe

Transport controls

Recent Clips
Lists the ten most recent clips brought into the Viewer.

Add Marker

View
Allows customization of the video display. Options include Image versus Wireframe, Timecode Overlays, Title Safe, and Alpha.

Mark In

Mark Out

Timeline

The Timeline is where your story comes together—you assemble your clips (trimmed from the Viewer or raw from the Browser) to create your storyline inside a sequence.

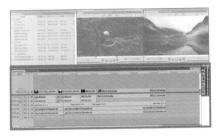

In the Browser, double-click a sequence, and the sequence opens as a tab in the Timeline window. A project may have more than one sequence. Each sequence can contain up to 99 video tracks and 99 audio tracks, and can have a maximum duration of 12 hours.

> **TIP** The terms *sequence* and *Timeline* are often used interchangeably. Technically, a sequence is where you arrange your clips to tell your story. The Timeline is a window used to navigate sequences.

Patch Panel: Source Control
Corresponds to the source content in the Viewer. When source controls are "patched" to destination controls, the source media in the Viewer flows into those destination tracks. Source controls that are disconnected will block the respective source content from use in the edit.

Current Timecode
Displays playhead position.

Time Ruler
Click in this time strip to move the playhead.

Playhead
The Timeline playhead and the Canvas playhead are synchronized.

Sequence tabs
A separate tab appears for each opened sequence. Drag these tabs to rearrange.

RT menu
Displays options for dialing in the level of playback performance.

Patch Panel: Destination Control
Identifies tracks in your sequence.

Track Visibility
Enables/disables a track during playback and export.

Lock Track
Prevents edit functions from affecting the track.

Auto Select
Specifies whether a track is included in certain functions (for example, Lift, Match Frame).

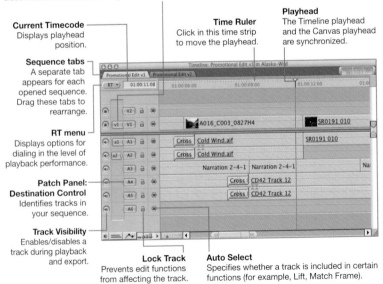

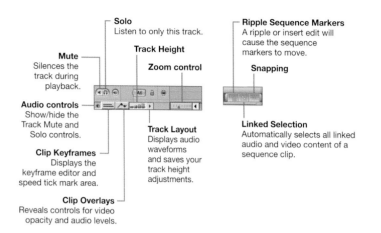

Solo
Listen to only this track.

Track Height

Zoom control

Mute
Silences the
track during
playback.

Audio controls
Show/hide the
Track Mute and
Solo controls.

Clip Keyframes
Displays the
keyframe editor and
speed tick mark area.

Clip Overlays
Reveals controls for video
opacity and audio levels.

Track Layout
Displays audio
waveforms
and saves your
track height
adjustments.

Ripple Sequence Markers
A ripple or insert edit will
cause the sequence
markers to move.

Snapping

Linked Selection
Automatically selects all linked
audio and video content of a
sequence clip.

RT Menu

The RT menu, found at the top-left corner of the Timeline window,
provides options for dialing in the level of playback performance.

Unlimited RT
Allows more effects in real time,
although an effect may exceed
your available processing power.
Rendering may not be required.
The Video Quality and Frame Rate
settings still apply.

By default, "Edit to Tape" and
"Print to Video" commands are at
Full Quality unless modified.

Safe RT
Rendering may be required to play
back certain effects in real time at
the video quality and frame rate
you specify below. If Final Cut Pro
predicts that the processing
power of your computer will be
exceeded, the Canvas will display
"Unrendered" during playback.

The default settings are Dynamic
Video Quality and Full Frame Rate
at Safe RT. You will get the most
real-time playback by choosing
Unlimited RT, Dynamic Video
Quality, and Dynamic Frame Rate.
These settings do not affect Share
or Export commands.

The two bars above the Time Ruler give the render status of the
video and audio clips in the sequence. The different colors vary
depending on processing power, RT menu settings, effects applied,
and codecs used.

The render status bars display different colors depending on a variety of factors. Pausing the pointer over the render status bars reveals a tooltip explaining the status. In this example, the RT menu is set to Safe RT, so the tooltip reveals Needs Render for the red status bar.

The top bar is the video status. The bottom bar is the audio status.

Changing the RT menu to Unlimited RT changed the red status to orange. Refer to the chart below for an explanation of the status colors.

Bar Color	Status	Description
Dark gray	None	No rendering required.
Blue-gray	Rendered	Already rendered.
Dark green	Full	No rendering required.
Green	Preview	No rendering required.
Yellow	Proxy	Some effect parameters approximated. Rendering required.
Dark yellow	Rendered Proxy	Not rendered at full quality.
Orange	Unlimited	Real-time preview (frames/quality dropped) when in Unlimited RT.
Red	Needs Render	Rendering required.

NOTE ▶ For more info about rendering a sequence, see Chapter 14.

Canvas

The Canvas displays the visual output of what you play

back in the Timeline. The Canvas window is often thought of as a Record window. You are seeing what the audience will see (except for the variety of informational overlays available in the Canvas).

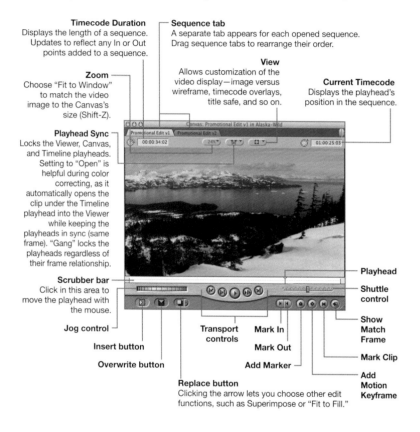

Timecode Duration
Displays the length of a sequence. Updates to reflect any In or Out points added to a sequence.

Sequence tab
A separate tab appears for each opened sequence. Drag sequence tabs to rearrange their order.

Zoom
Choose "Fit to Window" to match the video image to the Canvas's size (Shift-Z).

View
Allows customization of the video display—image versus wireframe, timecode overlays, title safe, and so on.

Current Timecode
Displays the playhead's position in the sequence.

Playhead Sync
Locks the Viewer, Canvas, and Timeline playheads. Setting to "Open" is helpful during color correcting, as it automatically opens the clip under the Timeline playhead into the Viewer while keeping the playheads in sync (same frame). "Gang" locks the playheads regardless of their frame relationship.

Playhead

Scrubber bar
Click in this area to move the playhead with the mouse.

Shuttle control

Show Match Frame

Jog control

Transport controls

Mark In

Mark Out

Mark Clip

Insert button

Add Marker

Overwrite button

Add Motion Keyframe

Replace button
Clicking the arrow lets you choose other edit functions, such as Superimpose or "Fit to Fill."

NOTE ▶ Final Cut Pro performs best when the Canvas is not zoomed in on the image during playback. If blue scroll bars are visible in the Canvas window, press Shift-Z to scale the display to fit within the Canvas.

TIP You may rearrange the tab order by dragging a tab. Dragging a tab off any window lets you place the tab in another window or in a new window. In the Canvas, this lets you view different sequences side by side.

Tool Palette

The Tool palette, located to the right of the Timeline, provides quick access to edit and selection tools. Many trimming operations you perform while editing can be accomplished with the Selection tool. However, if you want to work efficiently in Final Cut Pro, you will want to learn how to use these other powerful tools. The keyboard shortcut for each tool is listed below the tool name.

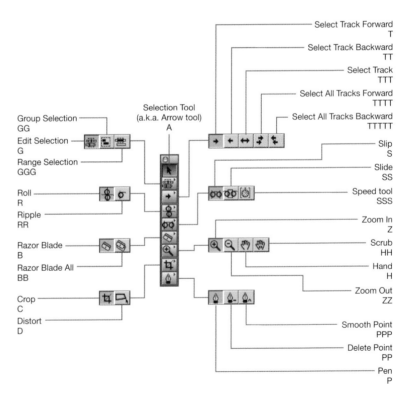

Group Selection
GG

Edit Selection
G

Range Selection
GGG

Roll
R

Ripple
RR

Razor Blade
B

Razor Blade All
BB

Crop
C

Distort
D

Selection Tool
(a.k.a. Arrow tool)
A

Select Track Forward
T

Select Track Backward
TT

Select Track
TTT

Select All Tracks Forward
TTTT

Select All Tracks Backward
TTTTT

Slip
S

Slide
SS

Speed tool
SSS

Zoom In
Z

Scrub
HH

Hand
H

Zoom Out
ZZ

Smooth Point
PPP

Delete Point
PP

Pen
P

Audio Meters

The audio meters give a visual measurement of your audio levels.
During playback, the audio meters register the audio levels of the clip
in the Viewer or the audio mix in a sequence. Each meter's scale tops
out at zero and is measured in dBFS. See Chapter 7 for more info on
using the audio meters.

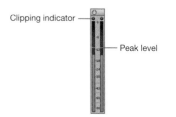

Clipping indicator

Peak level

Tool Bench

The Tool Bench, the utility window of Final Cut Pro, appears when
you choose a specialized tool from the Tools menu. These tools are
represented as separate tabs.

NOTE ▶ The Tool Bench covers the Viewer by default.

Tools	Window	Help
Audio Mixer		⌥6
Frame Viewer		⌥7
QuickView		⌥8
Timecode Viewer		^T
Video Scopes		⌥9
Voice Over		⌥0

Frame Viewer

The Frame Viewer lets you customize a split-screen view of two clips
from a sequence. You can display multiple Frame Viewers simultaneously for comparisons during color correction.

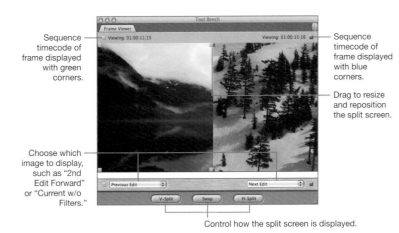

Sequence timecode of frame displayed with green corners.

Sequence timecode of frame displayed with blue corners.

Drag to resize and reposition the split screen.

Choose which image to display, such as "2nd Edit Forward" or "Current w/o Filters."

Control how the split screen is displayed.

Video Scopes

The video scopes tool set provides a variety of scales that measure the luma and chroma values of your image. Although the Canvas is literally a canvas on which you "paint" your video, you may need to measure how bright, dark, and saturated your video is before delivering to certain mediums (for example, broadcast). The tool set lets you customize a display of Waveform, Vectorscope, Histogram, and RGB Parade scopes. The update and sampling rate of the scopes is controlled via the RT pop-up menu in the top left of the Timeline.

Choose to view all four, two, or a single scope.

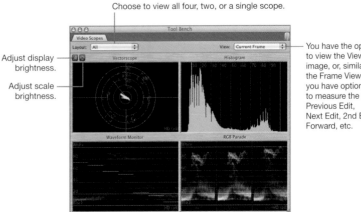

Adjust display brightness.

Adjust scale brightness.

You have the option to view the Viewer's image, or, similar to the Frame Viewer, you have options to measure the Previous Edit, Next Edit, 2nd Edit Forward, etc.

When the video scopes are displayed, these analysis-accuracy options become available in the Timeline's pop-up menu.

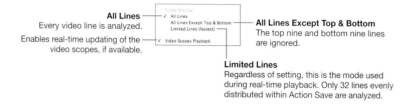

All Lines
Every video line is analyzed.

Enables real-time updating of the video scopes, if available.

All Lines Except Top & Bottom
The top nine and bottom nine lines are ignored.

Limited Lines
Regardless of setting, this is the mode used during real-time playback. Only 32 lines evenly distributed within Action Save are analyzed.

Audio Mixer

The Audio Mixer lets you adjust the level of a clip and also to record automation of that adjustment over time in both the Viewer and a sequence. The Audio Mixer can be controlled externally via the Control Surface settings within Final Cut Pro. Refer to the user manual for more information about compatibility and setup.

With Auto chosen, the Audio Mixer reflects the audio contents of the active Viewer or Canvas. You may also force the Mixer to lock to either window.

Mute/Solo   Pan

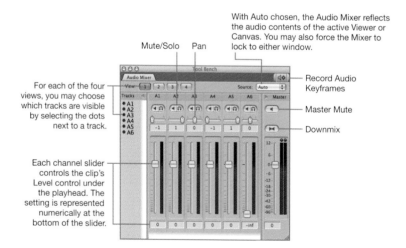

For each of the four views, you may choose which tracks are visible by selecting the dots next to a track.

Record Audio Keyframes

Master Mute

Downmix

Each channel slider controls the clip's Level control under the playhead. The setting is represented numerically at the bottom of the slider.

Voice Over

The Voice Over tool allows any audio input recognized by Mac OS X to be used as a voiceover recording microphone. See Chapter 7 for more details about using the Voice Over tool.

Start recording a take.

Displays the tool's status and provides a countdown while recording a take.

Shows in which sequence and track the take will appear.

Displays the recording level and lets you set up device settings.

Monitoring controls

QuickView

QuickView gives you the ability to preview without first rendering to your hard drive. When invoked, QuickView renders a range of time before and after the current Timeline playhead's position or between In and Out points.

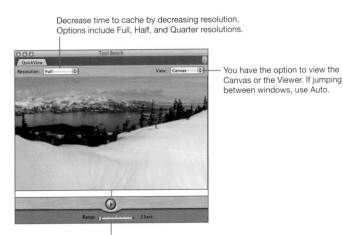

Decrease time to cache by decreasing resolution. Options include Full, Half, and Quarter resolutions.

You have the option to view the Canvas or the Viewer. If jumping between windows, use Auto.

Set the duration of the QuickView playback.

Timecode Viewer

The Timecode Viewer, a translucent floating window, gives you a large display of the playhead's current location. Choose Tools > Timecode Viewer when you need everyone in the edit suite to see the current timecode of a clip in the Viewer or the sequence timecode. The Timecode Viewer auto-updates to reflect the current timecode of the active Viewer or Canvas/Timeline and the name of the clip or sequence.

Arranging Windows

Final Cut Pro offers several window-arrangement presets. The availability of these presets varies based on the number of connected displays and their resolution. You can access the presets under Window > Arrange.

The default window arrangement is Standard. Control-U

You can create customized window settings and save them for later use.

Drag the bottom right corner of a window to resize one window.

Drag the edge between two windows to dynamically resize all adjacent windows with parallel edges.

Drag the corner junction of three windows to dynamically resize all adjacent windows both vertically and horizontally.

After you arrange the windows as desired, choose Window >
Arrange > Save Window Layout.

> **TIP** The default location for customized window arrange-
> ments is Macintosh HD/Users/[user name]/Library/Preferences/
> Final Cut Pro User Data/Window Layouts. To use your layouts
> on multiple systems, you can copy the XML files that represent
> your layouts from this location to the same location on another
> Final Cut Pro workstation.

Button Bars

Customizable button bars can be found at the top right of the Browser,
Viewer, Timeline, and Canvas. You can create shortcut interface buttons from a list of over 800 commands in Final Cut Pro. You can save
these interface customizations and share them among editing systems.
Start by choosing Tools > Button List.

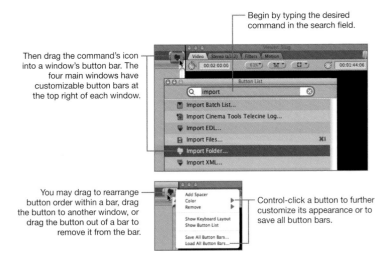

Begin by typing the desired command in the search field.

Then drag the command's icon into a window's button bar. The four main windows have customizable button bars at the top right of each window.

You may drag to rearrange button order within a bar, drag the button to another window, or drag the button out of a bar to remove it from the bar.

Control-click a button to further customize its appearance or to save all button bars.

TIP ▸ You may choose a preset button bar or your customized bars from Tools > Button Bars.

Keyboard Layouts

The Tools > Keyboard Layout > Customize menu lets you assign or reassign the over 800 commands of Final Cut Pro to multiple keyboard shortcuts. The Tools > Keyboard Layout menu also lets you choose preset or customized layouts and to save layouts.

TIP ▸ You may remove a keyboard shortcut by dragging the command's icon off the keyboard.

First, unlock the layout by clicking the padlock.　If you wish to assign a shortcut that utilizes modifier keys, select the appropriate tab.　Next, enter the desired command in the search field. The list sorts the commands as you type.

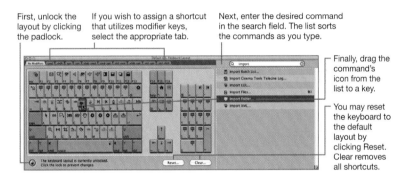

Finally, drag the command's icon from the list to a key.

You may reset the keyboard to the default layout by clicking Reset. Clear removes all shortcuts.

NOTE ▸ The Keyboard Layout window will reflect the keyboard in use with your editing system. For example, the window for a portable system will not display the extended keyboard section when you are using only the built-in keyboard.

User Preferences

The User Preferences settings (accessed by Final Cut Pro > User Preferences) are grouped by tabs. This book highlights only a few preferences. Refer to the user manual for more detailed information.

General Tab

Levels of Undo may be set as high as 99. Command-Z

You may increase the number of tracks to avoid "beeping" caused by exceeding the number of audio tracks specified here.

Use genlock for audio capture device, if capable.

Dropped frames occur when hardware is unable to process throughput at the speed required to sustain real-time playback. Deselecting allows Final Cut Pro to process as fast as the hardware is capable. This may be adequate for previewing before rendering. This preference affects playback but not export.

Leave at Low unless doing very detailed mixing or adding many audio effects. Does not affect exporting, rendering, or mixing down.

Launches Final Cut Pro with no projects open when this is deselected. This option is handy when sharing a system with a single login or for a user working on multiple projects.

The three options for handling timecode breaks are: Make New Clip (which creates a new media file at a break), Abort Capture (which stops the capture at the break but preserves the media file captured up to the break), and Warn After Capture (which captures a continuous file including any breaks).

Creates a backup copy of your project. The location of backups is specified in System Settings: Scratch Disk.

Render Control Tab

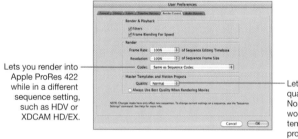

Lets you render into Apple ProRes 422 while in a different sequence setting, such as HDV or XDCAM HD/EX.

Lets you choose the quality setting of Draft, Normal, or Best when working with master templates or Motion projects.

System Settings

System settings (accessed by Final Cut Pro > System Settings) tell Final Cut Pro how to interact with the computer hardware, including how much RAM to use and where to store media files. Here are some highlights from the System Settings window. More information can be found in the user manual.

Scratch Disks Tab

The Scratch Disks tab is critical to your success with Final Cut Pro. See Chapter 3 for info on setting up scratch disks for ingesting media.

Memory & Cache Tab

If your system has limited memory and you need to run multiple applications, you can scale back how much RAM Final Cut Pro uses. A minimum value of 1 GB is recommended.

When working on a project that utilizes mostly still images, increase the Still Cache allotment to reduce the number of "Preparing Video for Display" dialogs while working in the Timeline.

Easy Setup and Audio/Video Settings

The Audio/Video Settings (accessed by Final Cut Pro > Audio/Video Settings) define how Final Cut Pro talks to your capture devices, what sequence settings to use, and how to output audio and video while editing. These settings may be modified by you or by installing a third-party capture device or video interface. To simplify the recall of these configurations, they are saved as Easy Setup presets. The Easy Setup window lists the recommended, third-party, and customized presets for quickly configuring your Final Cut Pro system.

Using Easy Setup is covered in Chapter 3. For more information about Audio/Video Settings, refer to the user manual.

3
Project Setup

Because Final Cut Pro gives you the flexibility to work with multiple internal and external hard drives, with tape-based and tapeless media, and in single- and multi-user environments, there are some important things to know when working with both new and existing projects. This chapter covers best practices in setting up your system and projects.

Setting a Scratch Disk

The scratch disk contains three folders:

▶ Capture Scratch—the destination for all captured (tape-based) and transferred (tapeless) media

▶ Render Files—for any sequence video you render

▶ Audio Render Files—for any sequence audio you render

Don't be fooled—the word *scratch* here does not refer to a temporary location.

1 Choose Final Cut Pro > System Settings from the menu bar.

2 In the System Settings window, click the first tab, General, if it isn't already open.

3 Select the scratch disk location by clicking the first Set button.

4 In the Finder dialog, choose the appropriate volume and subfolder(s).

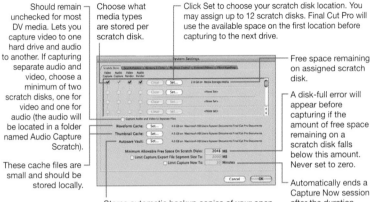

Should remain unchecked for most DV media. Lets you capture video to one hard drive and audio to another. If capturing separate audio and video, choose a minimum of two scratch disks, one for video and one for audio (the audio will be located in a folder named Audio Capture Scratch).

Choose what media types are stored per scratch disk.

Click Set to choose your scratch disk location. You may assign up to 12 scratch disks. Final Cut Pro will use the available space on the first location before capturing to the next drive.

Free space remaining on assigned scratch disk.

A disk-full error will appear before capturing if the amount of free space remaining on a scratch disk falls below this amount. Never set to zero.

These cache files are small and should be stored locally.

Stores automatic backup copies of your open projects as determined by user preferences.

Automatically ends a Capture Now session after the duration entered has elapsed.

TIP ▶ The default scratch disk is Macintosh HD/Users/ [user name]/Documents/Final Cut Pro Documents. You should choose a secondary internal or external volume suitable for media storage.

NOTE ▶ In a post-house or broadcast environment utilizing Xsan or Final Cut Server, check with your system administrator about scratch disk locations.

Final Cut Pro automatically saves captured or transferred media by project name. Simply create and choose a folder at the root level of your hard disk. Final Cut Pro automatically creates a subfolder structure, managing media for each open project.

Set your scratch disk on a secondary internal or external volume. The hard drive chosen must have a sustained data rate (write/read) higher than the ingest codec. Using partitions of a volume is not recommended. After speed, you need to consider disk space. The higher qualiity (less compressed) the ingest codec, the bigger the media files. Refer to the user manual for a formula on calculating disk space requirements.

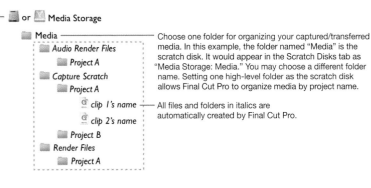

📁 or 📁 Media Storage

📁 Media ─────────────────── Choose one folder for organizing your captured/transferred
  Audio Render Files ┄┄┄┄┄┄ media. In this example, the folder named "Media" is the
    📁 Project A scratch disk. It would appear in the Scratch Disks tab as
  Capture Scratch "Media Storage: Media." You may choose a different folder
    📁 Project A name. Setting one high-level folder as the scratch disk
      🎬 *clip 1's name* ── allows Final Cut Pro to organize media by project name.
      🎬 *clip 2's name* ── All files and folders in italics are
    📁 Project B automatically created by Final Cut Pro.
  📁 Render Files
    📁 Project A

NOTE ▶ You do not need to change the scratch disk setting if you are using the same volume for multiple projects.

After a scratch disk is chosen, Final Cut Pro checks to see if that destination is available during subsequent launches. If Final Cut Pro fails to find the previously used location during launch, a warning dialog appears prompting you to resolve a scratch disk access issue.

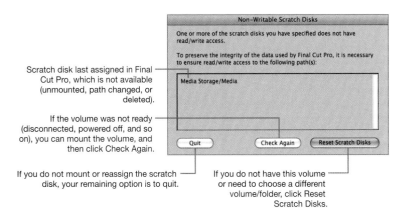

Scratch disk last assigned in Final Cut Pro, which is not available (unmounted, path changed, or deleted).

If the volume was not ready (disconnected, powered off, and so on), you can mount the volume, and then click Check Again.

If you do not mount or reassign the scratch disk, your remaining option is to quit.

If you do not have this volume or need to choose a different volume/folder, click Reset Scratch Disks.

NOTE ▶ Partitioning any hard disk for use as a scratch disk is not advised.

Changing the scratch disk location is required only if a new destination volume is necessary. Scratch disk settings are stored in the logged-in user's preferences. The user may use the same scratch disk for multiple projects (provided that the destination has enough free space).

In a shared workstation environment, individual users with separate logins can set discrete scratch disk destinations. In a shared environment with a single user login, each user must take care to either give each project a unique name not in use by other users or change the scratch disk setting to a new destination (such as a new volume and/or folder named by project or user) before capturing/transferring media.

Choosing an Easy Setup

Final Cut Pro needs to know how media is coming into your editing system, what codec you want that media to be for editing, and how you would like to monitor/output the edited media. Choosing an Easy Setup quickly gives Final Cut Pro this information. Easy Setups are made up of presets, which are predefined by Apple, third-party manufacturers of a video interface you may purchase, or you (because you can customize the presets in the Audio/Video Settings window for your particular system configuration).

Setup for Tape-Based Workflow

Choosing the correct Easy Setup is critical to a tape-based workflow.

1   Close any open projects (including any blank Untitled Projects).

NOTE ▶ Think of Easy Setup as a preference—it only affects sequences created after the preference change. It does not affect existing items. Therefore, open Untitled projects contain a sequence based on the previous Easy Setup.

2   Choose Final Cut Pro > Easy Setup in the menu bar.

3   Choose the codec you will be capturing/editing from the Use pop-up menu.

4   Click Setup.

Limits the Use options by format categories.

Limits the Use options by supported frame rates.

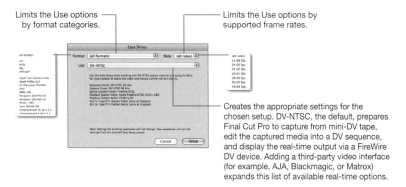

Creates the appropriate settings for the chosen setup. DV-NTSC, the default, prepares Final Cut Pro to capture from mini-DV tape, edit the captured media into a DV sequence, and display the real-time output via a FireWire DV device. Adding a third-party video interface (for example, AJA, Blackmagic, or Matrox) expands this list of available real-time options.

NOTE ▶ There are several varieties of the HD codecs. Choose the Final Cut Pro preset that matches your camera's settings.

After you choose a setup from the Easy Setup dialog, Final Cut Pro checks to see if the appropriate video interface, such as a FireWire-based camera/deck, is available. If Final Cut Pro does not detect the video interface, you will get a warning dialog.

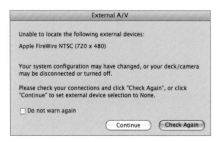

TIP Check the documentation supplied with your video interface about the optimal Easy Setup choice for your workflow.

Setup for Tapeless Workflow

Easy Setup is not as critical in a tapeless workflow as it is in a tape-based workflow. Final Cut Pro still needs to know via Easy Setup how to display external video via your video interface, if applicable. But, with the use of log and transfer and the open format Timelines (more info on these tools in Chapters 4 and 5), you may not have to visit Easy Setup.

For example, there is no Easy Setup for a workflow involving AVCHD acquired footage. AVCHD is ingested in the Log and Transfer window where the AVCHD media is transcoded to the Apple ProRes format you select, such as Apple ProRes 422 (LT). There is no Easy Setup preset for Apple ProRes 422 (LT) as the sequence codec. The first edit you make into a new sequence will give you the option to conform the sequence settings to match the settings of the Apple ProRes 422 (LT) clips.

Open format timelines, introduced in Final Cut Pro 6, let you skip using Easy Setup for choosing a sequence codec. If the sequence codec does not match the first clip you add to the sequence, this dialog appears. Clicking Yes to conform the sequence settings to the clip's settings automates part of the process you would have performed with Easy Setup.

NOTE ▶ Verify your scratch disk settings before ingesting from a tapeless medium. Refer to the prior "Setting a Scratch Disk" section.

Create a New Project

Whether you are using a tape-based or tapeless workflow, you should create and save a new project before ingest.

1   Choose File > New Project.

2   Immediately choose File > Save Project As.

Save As: Untitled Project 1 ── Click here to expand the window as shown.

Projects ── Q search

▼ DEVICES
  Macinto...
  Media St...
  iDisk
▶ SHARED
▼ PLACES
  Desktop
  fcpuser

About Stacks.pdf
Final Cut ...ocuments ▶
Projects ▶

Format: Project File

☑ Hide extension   New Folder   Cancel   Save

As soon as you create a new Final Cut Pro project, you need to save that project as a file onto your hard disk. The Final Cut Pro project file contains no media, so the file is relatively small. Where to save the file depends on your workflow.

Working on a Single Final Cut Pro Workstation

When working on a single Final Cut Pro workstation, you can save the project file anywhere on your system. But to stay organized, you may want to create a Projects folder to hold your project file and all noncaptured or transferred media.

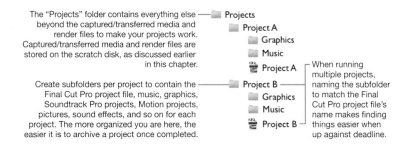

The "Projects" folder contains everything else beyond the captured/transferred media and render files to make your projects work. Captured/transferred media and render files are stored on the scratch disk, as discussed earlier in this chapter.

Create subfolders per project to contain the Final Cut Pro project file, music, graphics, Soundtrack Pro projects, Motion projects, pictures, sound effects, and so on for each project. The more organized you are here, the easier it is to archive a project once completed.

Projects
  Project A
    Graphics
    Music
    Project A
  Project B
    Graphics
    Music
    Project B

When running multiple projects, naming the subfolder to match the Final Cut Pro project file's name makes finding things easier when up against deadline.

NOTE ▶ Final Cut Pro does not copy/move media you import via the File > Import commands. Copy media such as still images or music to the project's folder before importing the media into Final Cut Pro.

Working on a Portable Final Cut Pro System

When working on a portable Final Cut Pro system, you may want to create a Projects folder on your external scratch disk. This gives you the ability to move the project from portable to portable or to a desktop system. Utilizing an external hard disk for both the project file and media also lets you efficiently archive a project.

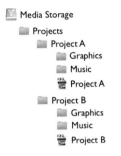

Working in an Xsan or Final Cut Server Environment

If you are part of an Xsan environment, you should utilize the project and media file locations that the Xsan administrator or the facility has assigned to you. Project files should be saved locally while you work on the project. After you complete an edit session, you should upload the project file to the assigned folder on the Xsan.

In a facility using Final Cut Server, you will upload your Final Cut Pro project to the destination device specified by your Final Cut Server administrator. You should first save and work with your project locally before uploading to Final Cut Server. For more information on integrating Final Cut Server into your workflow, refer to *Apple Pro Training Series: Final Cut Server 1.5*, by Drew Tucker (Peachpit Press).

4

Ingest

You can bring media into Final Cut Pro in three ways:

- ▶ Capture
- ▶ Transfer
- ▶ Import

Capture and transfer involve copying/transcoding media into the scratch disk. Import does not copy media—the original media, such as stills or music, is simply referenced inside the project.

> **TIP** ▶ Do not be tempted to treat the capture or transfer process as a final edit phase. Think of the entire production and post-production process as an upside-down wedding cake. You will usually be reducing the size (or duration) of a clip as it progresses from raw camera footage down to the final edited clip in the sequence.

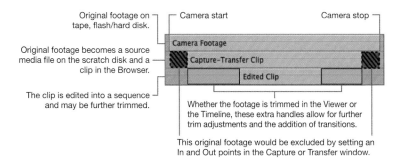

31

Capturing from Tape

You can get media off tape into a Final Cut Pro project using three capture methods:

▶   Now

▶   Clip

▶   Batch

All three result in clips for use in Final Cut Pro. The three differ in their speed and accuracy in creating those clips.

You can combine all three capture methods within the same project (although you need only use one of them).

Setup for Tape Capture

Before digging into the three methods of capturing, there are a few settings to review.

> NOTE ▶ Your capture device should already be powered on and connected before opening Log and Capture. If not, attach your device, turn it on, and then choose View > External Video > Refresh A/V Devices.

1   Choose File > Log and Capture.

2   In the top right of the Log and Capture window, click the Clip Settings tab.

> NOTE ▶ Two mono channels can be converted to a stereo pair, and a stereo pair can be broken into two mono channels.

Opens the video scopes.

When this box is selected, the clip(s) to be captured will include video. Deselect to capture an audio-only clip.

The software proc amp becomes available with some third-party digitizers.

When this box is selected, the clip(s) to be captured will include audio. Deselect to capture a video-only clip.

Input Channels is dimmed when the capture device is locked to a specific number of channels. If your capture device supports multiple settings, this pop-up menu allows you to choose from 2 to 24 channels.

Selecting Preview routes the incoming audio to the computer's speakers/line out for monitoring. If unchecked, monitor your source audio at the deck/camera.

Creates two discrete mono tracks. When editing, each channel has a separate Level control. Typical for footage shot with two lavaliers or one lavalier and a boom. In a stereo output sequence, channels 1 and 2 will be equally panned across both outputs.

Creates a stereo pair. When editing, one Level control will affect both channels. In a stereo output sequence, channel 1 will go to output 1 and channel 2 to output 2.

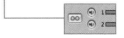

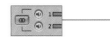

Creates one mono track. Here, channel 2 will not be captured.

3   Click the Capture Settings tab.

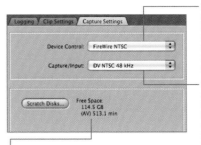

Device Control states the protocol to control your deck/camera and is initially set by Easy Setup. You may choose Non-Controllable Device to capture non-timecoded material (live feeds, consumer equipment). Check your capture device's documentation for the proper setting.

Capture/Input defines the codec for captured media files and is set by Easy Setup. Some capture devices allow you to transcode the acquisition codec to another codec. You should choose the codec that matches your source footage and/or sequence settings.

Displays the status of your scratch disk. Clicking the Scratch Disks button opens the Scratch Disk window.

4   Click the Logging tab.

Clicking a clapboard increments the last
digit or letter in the associated field.

Indicates the bin where clips will be listed
within the project. Does not indicate the
storage location on the scratch disk. See
below for more information.

Sets the logging bin up one level
in the project.

Creates a new Browser bin set as
the logging bin.

Enter the tape label in
the Reel field. The reel
should uniquely identify
the source tape.

At minimum in a
nonscripted project, you
may want to use the
Description field.
Because this data will
serve as the media's
filename, avoid the use of
special characters such
as pound (#), period (.),
ampersand (&), and
slashes (/ and \).

The name is constructed
from the marked fields
below. This will serve as
the actual filename for the
clip on the scratch disk.
With Prompt selected,
you will be prompted to
enter a clip name after
choosing Log Clip or
Capture: Clip.

When you select the
Good checkbox, a
checkmark appears in the
Browser's Good column.

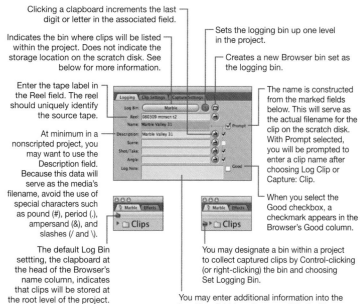

The default Log Bin
settting, the clapboard at
the head of the Browser's
name column, indicates
that clips will be stored at
the root level of the project.

You may designate a bin within a project
to collect captured clips by Control-clicking
(or right-clicking) the bin and choosing
Set Logging Bin.

You may enter additional information into the
Log Note field for reference within the Browser.

TIP ▶ If multiple projects are open, verify the Log Bin location
before capturing.

Capture Now

Capture Now is the fastest, "dirtiest" method of creating clips from
tape-based media. In essence, you are instructing Final Cut Pro to
ingest whatever audio/video feed is coming in via FireWire or supported capture device to the scratch disk.

1   In the Logging tab, enter the tape label into the Reel field, then
press Return.

TIP ▶ In the case of a live feed, you may not have information
for the Reel field.

2   Use the transport controls, or their keyboard equivalents, to cue
your tape a few seconds before the clip you want to capture.

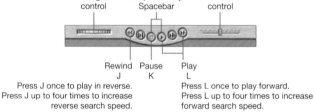

3   Enter a name for the clip in the Description field.

4   Start playback and then click the Now button in the center of the
Capture button bar at the bottom right.

TIP ▶ A large capture window will open. Your media is captured at the resolution set in Easy Setup, although it displays at a
low resolution here.

The status banner indicates that a Capture Now in progress may be stopped by pressing the Esc key. Footage captured up until the key is pressed is kept.

NOTE ▶ If you fail to start playback before clicking Capture: Now, Final Cut Pro will stall on the Capturing Clip window, displaying no video. You will have to either manually start playback on the deck/camera or abort the capture by pressing Esc (Escape).

5   When you see the desired clip finish, press Esc to stop the capture.

The clip will appear in the logging bin of the project. The Log and Capture's Name/Description fields will increment automatically, preparing you for the next capture.

6   Repeat steps 2–5 to capture additional clips.

TIP ▶ Press Command-S after capturing a few clips to update the Final Cut Pro project file.

NOTE ▶ If you change tapes, you will want to change the Logging tab's Reel field.

7   When you have finished capturing, close the Log and Capture window. Then press Command-S to save your Final Cut Pro project file.

NOTE ▶ By default, Final Cut Pro will continue a Capture Now until your scratch disk becomes full (as determined by the Free Space setting in System Settings) or the end of the tape is reached. You may set a duration for Capture Now in the Scratch Disks tab of Final Cut Pro System Settings.

You may set a duration for Capture Now sessions by selecting this box in System Settings and entering a desired time limit.

Capture Clip

Capture Clip, sometimes considered the slowest method of ingest, provides very precise clips. You mark an In point and an Out point representing the desired clip on the raw tape, and then you capture the marked media to your storage before marking the next clip. The "slow" part of the process is that you may do only one clip at a time—mark Clip A, capture Clip A, mark Clip B, capture Clip B, and so on.

Marking In and Out points
gives precision to Capture Clip.

1   In the Logging tab, enter the tape label into the Reel field, then press Return.

2   Use the transport controls, or their keyboard equivalents, to cue your tape to the beginning of the raw footage for the desired clip.

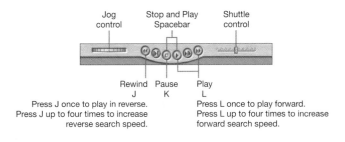

Jog control   Stop and Play Spacebar   Shuttle control

Rewind   Pause   Play
J   K   L

Press J once to play in reverse.
Press J up to four times to increase reverse search speed.

Press L once to play forward.
Press L up to four times to increase forward search speed.

TIP▶ Remember you will need handles for trimming and effects that you apply later. Cue the tape a couple of seconds before the desired footage starts.

3   Press the I key to mark an In point.

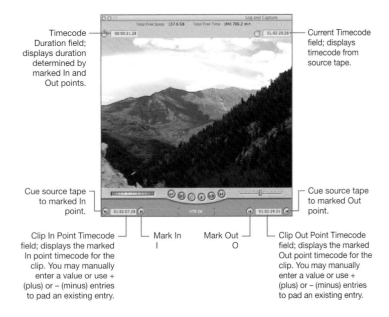

Timecode Duration field; displays duration determined by marked In and Out points.

Current Timecode field; displays timecode from source tape.

Cue source tape to marked In point.

Cue source tape to marked Out point.

Clip In Point Timecode field; displays the marked In point timecode for the clip. You may manually enter a value or use + (plus) or – (minus) entries to pad an existing entry.

Mark In
I

Mark Out
O

Clip Out Point Timecode field; displays the marked Out point timecode for the clip. You may manually enter a value or use + (plus) or – (minus) entries to pad an existing entry.

4   Cue your tape a couple of seconds after the end of the desired clip.

5   Press the O key to mark an Out point.

6   To capture the clip, click Capture: Clip.

7   In the Log Clip window that opens, name the clip, and then click OK.

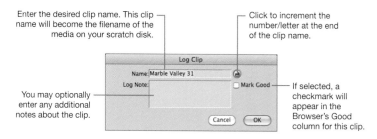

Enter the desired clip name. This clip name will become the filename of the media on your scratch disk.

Click to increment the number/letter at the end of the clip name.

You may optionally enter any additional notes about the clip.

If selected, a checkmark will appear in the Browser's Good column for this clip.

Final Cut Pro cues your tape and proceeds with capturing the marked clip onto the scratch disk. Once capture is completed, the clip is added to the logging bin in the project, and the Log and Capture's Name and Description fields increment automatically, preparing for the next capture.

8   Repeat steps 2–7 to capture additional clips.

> **TIP** ▶ Press Command-S after capturing a few clips to update the Final Cut Pro project file.

> **NOTE** ▶ If you change tapes, you will want to change the Logging tab's Reel field.

9   When you have finished capturing, close the Log and Capture window. Then press Command-S to save your Final Cut Pro project file.

Capture Batch

The process for Capture Batch, also known as batch capturing, starts with the same steps as Capture Clip. You mark In and Out points for a clip but then simply log the clip. You continue marking and logging multiple clips from one or many tapes before capturing those clips in one capture session.

1   In the Logging tab, enter the tape label into the Reel field, then press Return.

2   Use the transport controls to cue your tape prior to the beginning of the raw footage for the desired clip.

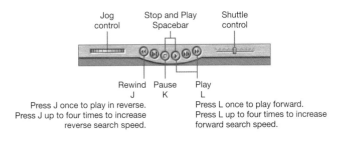

Jog control   Stop and Play Spacebar   Shuttle control

Rewind   Pause   Play
J   K   L
Press J once to play in reverse.   Press L once to play forward.
Press J up to four times to increase   Press L up to four times to increase
reverse search speed.   forward search speed.

3   Press the I key to mark an In point.

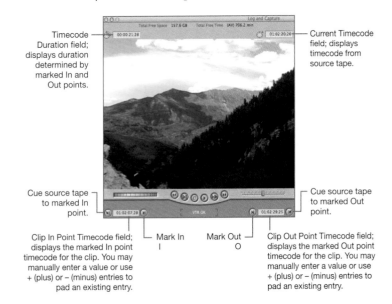

Timecode Duration field; displays duration determined by marked In and Out points.

Current Timecode field; displays timecode from source tape.

Cue source tape to marked In point.

Cue source tape to marked Out point.

Clip In Point Timecode field; displays the marked In point timecode for the clip. You may manually enter a value or use + (plus) or – (minus) entries to pad an existing entry.

Mark In   Mark Out
I   O

Clip Out Point Timecode field; displays the marked Out point timecode for the clip. You may manually enter a value or use + (plus) or – (minus) entries to pad an existing entry.

4   Cue your tape a couple of seconds after the end of the desired clip.

5   Press the O key to mark an Out point.

6   Click Log Clip to log the clip into the project.

7   In the Log Clip window that opens, name the clip, and then click OK.

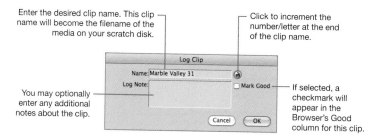

Enter the desired clip name. This clip name will become the filename of the media on your scratch disk.

Click to increment the number/letter at the end of the clip name.

You may optionally enter any additional notes about the clip.

If selected, a checkmark will appear in the Browser's Good column for this clip.

The clip becomes an offline clip in the active project.

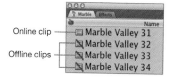

Online clip — Marble Valley 31
Offline clips — Marble Valley 32
Marble Valley 33
Marble Valley 34

8   Repeat steps 2–7 to log additional clips.

NOTE ▶ If you change tapes, be sure to change the Reel field to reflect the new tape's label.

TIP ▶ Press Command-S after logging a few clips to update the Final Cut Pro project file.

9   After you have logged your clips, select the offline clips in the project that you wish to batch capture.

10 In the Log and Capture window, click Capture: Batch.

NOTE ▶ You may invoke a batch capture by Control-clicking selected offline clips and choosing Batch Capture from the shortcut menu. You may also choose File > Batch Capture with offline clips selected in the project.

11 In the Batch Capture window that opens, verify the Total Media Time and Total Disk Space, approximate the amount of footage you desire to capture, and then click OK.

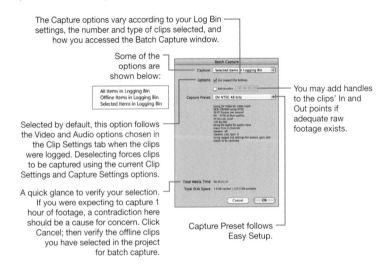

The Capture options vary according to your Log Bin settings, the number and type of clips selected, and how you accessed the Batch Capture window.

Some of the options are shown below:

All Items in Logging Bin
Offline Items in Logging Bin
Selected Items in Logging Bin

Selected by default, this option follows the Video and Audio options chosen in the Clip Settings tab when the clips were logged. Deselecting forces clips to be captured using the current Clip Settings and Capture Settings options.

A quick glance to verify your selection. If you were expecting to capture 1 hour of footage, a contradiction here should be a cause for concern. Click Cancel; then verify the offline clips you have selected in the project for batch capture.

You may add handles to the clips' In and Out points if adequate raw footage exists.

Capture Preset follows Easy Setup.

TIP If you miskeyed any In or Out point values or there were unnoticed timecode breaks, the Time and Space values may be distorted. Don't panic—you can manually adjust Media Start and Media End timecode fields for offline clips in the Browser before batch capturing.

12 Load your raw footage tape, if necessary, and then select the respective reel (tape) in the Insert Reel window before clicking Continue.

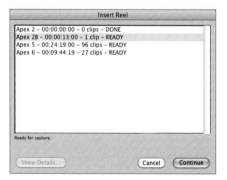

Select the tape you have loaded for batch capturing.

13 After Final Cut Pro successfully captures all clips from a reel, the Insert Reel window reappears. Load another requested tape, select the tape in the list, and then click Continue.

Insert Reel

Apex 2 – 00:00:00:00 – 0 clips – DONE
Apex 2B – 00:00:13:00 – 1 clip – READY
Apex 5 – 00:24:19:00 – 96 clips – READY
Apex 6 – 00:09:44:19 – 27 clips – READY

Ready for capture.

Show Details...   Cancel   Continue

> **TIP** ▶ Clicking Cancel aborts the batch capture process. Any clips captured prior to clicking Cancel are retained.

14 After all reels have been captured, click Done in the Insert Reel dialog.

The captured clips are updated in the Browser. Save your project.

Transferring from Tapeless Media

Tapeless acquisition is taking over the industry at all levels—from consumer video to feature film. However, tapeless devices do not yield the traditional, relatively inexpensive, tape-based camera masters. For years, these camera masters have served as backups for when a media hard drive crashes. Tapeless devices are often erased after ingest to prepare them for use on the next production, leaving no camera master. Creating cloned masters of your tapeless device before ingesting creates a "just-in-case" safety net.

Cloning Inside Final Cut Pro

You have two options within the Log and Transfer window to back up your original media: Archive to Folder and Archive to Disk Image.

1 With your tapeless device connected to your computer, the footage volume will mount.

NOTE ▶ If your footage volume does not mount, check with your device's manufacturer for any necessary software drivers.

2 In Final Cut Pro, choose File > Log and Transfer.

3 Choose Hierarchical List View.

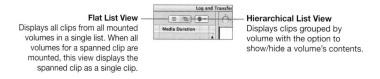

Flat List View
Displays all clips from all mounted volumes in a single list. When all volumes for a spanned clip are mounted, this view displays the spanned clip as a single clip.

Hierarchical List View
Displays clips grouped by volume with the option to show/hide a volume's contents.

4 Control-click the volume you wish to clone.

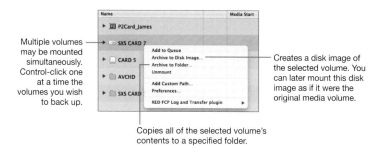

Multiple volumes may be mounted simultaneously. Control-click one at a time the volumes you wish to back up.

Creates a disk image of the selected volume. You can later mount this disk image as if it were the original media volume.

Copies all of the selected volume's contents to a specified folder.

NOTE ▶ Additional plug-ins become available as Apple expands support for additional formats in log and transfer. As shown above, this system has the RED FCP plug-in installed. Your available plug-ins may vary.

5 Choose the archive function you wish to perform.

6 Whichever you choose, you will be presented with a Finder dialog to identify the name of the disk image or folder and its destination.

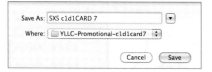

7   Clicking OK begins the archive process.

Archive to Disk Image
Creating disk image of volume "SXS CARD 7" (1 of 1)...
Cancel

You will receive an Archive Complete message to OK when done.

NOTE ▶ You will be unable to use Final Cut Pro while archive creation is in progress.

8   Eject the original footage volume, and then remove/disconnect the tapeless device.

9   If you created a disk image, double-click it in the Finder to mount the archive. For archive folders, use the Add Volume button in the Log and Transfer window to access the archive.

The clone of your original media is now available for ingest.

Cloning Outside Final Cut Pro

Due to equipment availability or location demands, you might not have time to archive a tapeless device from within Final Cut Pro. You may use the Disk Utility application, included with every Macintosh, to make a disk image of your raw footage.

Some tapeless cameras record to removable media; some record to an internal hard disk. Refer to your camera's documentation on how to mount the recorded footage on your computer.

1   Once your tapeless device is connected to your computer, the footage volume will mount.

2   Launch Disk Utility from your Applications/Utilities folder.

3   Select the volume representing your acquired media in the left
sidebar, and then click the New Image button.

4   Enter a name for the disk image and choose a destination.
Leave Image Format as compressed and Encryption set to none.
Click Save.

5   After the image is created, quit Disk Utility.

6   Eject the original footage volume; then remove/disconnect the
tapeless device.

7   Double-click the new disk image via the Finder.

The clone of your original media is now available for ingest.

Setup for Tapeless Ingest

Within Final Cut Pro, log and transfer lets you ingest a variety of tapeless media formats. Easier and faster transfers are some of the benefits of a tapeless workflow.

> **NOTE ▶** As the number of formats continues to expand and Final Cut Pro updates are released, refer to http://www.apple.com/finalcutstudio/specs/ for a list of supported formats.

1   Choose File > Log and Transfer.

Lists all clips from the mounted tapeless media volumes.

Displays a preview of the selected clip.

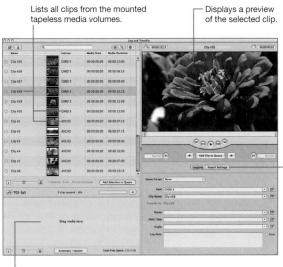

Clips you select for ingest will be listed in the queue.

Allows entry of clip information similar to the Logging tab of Log and Capture. The Import Settings tab is similar to the Clip Settings tab.

> **NOTE ▶** You may use Flat List view or Hierarchical List view. Hierarchical List view groups clips by volume, while Flat List view presents all clips from all mounted volumes in a single list. Flat List view will display a spanned clip as a single clip when all volumes containing the spanned clip are mounted.

2 Mount your media volume(s), if they are not already mounted.

If you created disk image archives, simply double-click the disk image. If you used the archive to a folder process, you may need to add the folder to the Log and Transfer window.

Click to add a volume such as an archive folder, to Log and Transfer.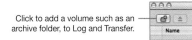

3 For some formats, you may need to click the Action pop-up menu.

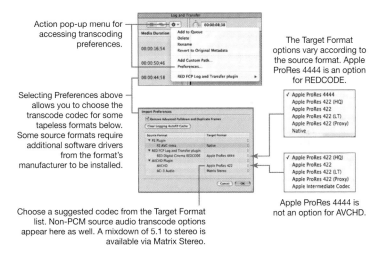

Action pop-up menu for accessing transcoding preferences.

The Target Format options vary according to the source format. Apple ProRes 4444 is an option for REDCODE.

Selecting Preferences above allows you to choose the transcode codec for some tapeless formats below. Some source formats require additional software drivers from the format's manufacturer to be installed.

Choose a suggested codec from the Target Format list. Non-PCM source audio transcode options appear here as well. A mixdown of 5.1 to stereo is available via Matrix Stereo.

Apple ProRes 4444 is not an option for AVCHD.

TIP ▶ Not every supported, tapeless format appears here. XDCAM EX is handled natively via log and transfer, so no transcode options are necessary.

NOTE ▶ Additional plug-ins become available as Apple expands support for additional formats in log and transfer. As shown above, this system has the RED FCP plug-in installed. Your available plug-ins may vary.

4 In the Logging area, click Import Settings and adjust if necessary.

The Import setting options vary
according to the selected clip's format.

Formats that record PCM audio
such as XDCAM EX and DVCProHD
allow you to set audio channel
settings much like working with
tape-based formats.

Formats that record AC-3,
such as AVCHD, are mixed
down by default.

NOTE ▶   Modifying the Import Settings is a preference and therefore affects all future transfers. You may apply specific settings to one or more clips by adjusting the settings and clicking Apply to Selection at the bottom of the Import Settings pane. Then deselect the clips and adjust Import Settings as appropriate for other clips.

The Flavors of Apple ProRes

Apple ProRes is a variable bit rate (VBR), high-quality codec. As an I-frame only codec, ProRes has lower processing requirements than Long-GOP MPEG-2 or MPEG-4 formats. Also, ProRes gives uncompressed quality with reduced bandwidth requirements compared with uncompressed formats.

ProRes Format	Target data rate of 1080i60 (GB/hr)
ProRes 4444	148
ProRes 422 (HQ)	99
ProRes 422	66
ProRes 422 (LT)	46
ProRes 422 (Proxy)	20

NOTE ▶ The target data rates shown are for estimating storage requirements. The data rates fluctuate with frame size, frame rate, and VBR compression.

Capture Now for Tapeless Ingest

When in a hurry, you can move clips en masse.

1 Select multiple clips in the clip list.

2 Click Add Selection to Queue.

All of the selected clips will be added to the queue. Final Cut Pro will begin ingesting the clips one by one, starting with the top clip.

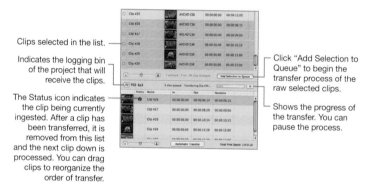

Clips selected in the list.

Indicates the logging bin of the project that will receive the clips.

Click "Add Selection to Queue" to begin the transfer process of the raw selected clips.

The Status icon indicates the clip being currently ingested. After a clip has been transferred, it is removed from this list and the next clip down is processed. You can drag clips to reorganize the order of transfer.

Shows the progress of the transfer. You can pause the process.

The clips are ingested into the scratch disk and listed in the logging bin of the project.

Capture Clip for Tapeless Ingest

When you have a little more time, you can manually add clips to the queue with specified metadata for each clip. You may also trim each clip to remove extraneous footage before ingest.

1 Select a clip in the clip list. The clip appears in the Preview area.

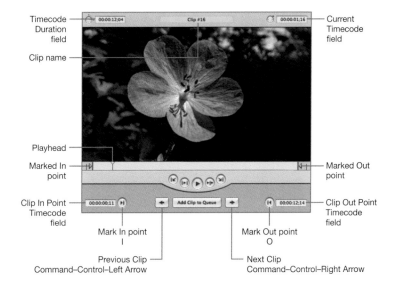

The transport controls at the bottom change slightly depending on the clip's raw format.

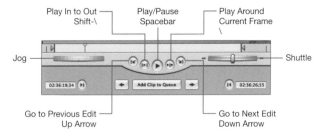

2   After previewing and trimming the clip as desired, you may click "Add Clip to Queue" or continue to the Logging tab to customize the clip's metadata.

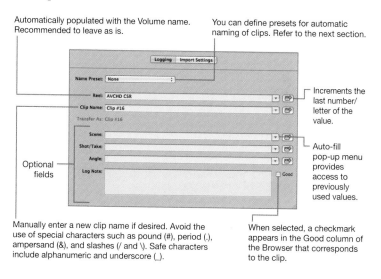

Automatically populated with the Volume name. Recommended to leave as is.

You can define presets for automatic naming of clips. Refer to the next section.

Increments the last number/letter of the value.

Auto-fill pop-up menu provides access to previously used values.

Optional fields

Manually enter a new clip name if desired. Avoid the use of special characters such as pound (#), period (.), ampersand (&), and slashes (/ and \). Safe characters include alphanumeric and underscore (_).

When selected, a checkmark appears in the Good column of the Browser that corresponds to the clip.

3   Add the clip to the queue by clicking "Add Clip to Queue" or dragging the preview to the queue.

4   Repeat steps 1 through 3 for each additional clip.

Automatic Naming and Transfer

Two helpful automation features are available in the Log and Transfer window: Automatic Naming (using presets) and Automatic Transfer.

Clicking the Name Preset pop-up menu lets you choose from the default presets, edit those presets, or create custom presets.

> ✓ None
>
> Current Name and Clip Date/Time
> Current Name with Counter
> Clip Date/Time
> Custom Name with Counter
>
> Edit...
> New...

Choosing the New option brings up the Naming Presets dialog.

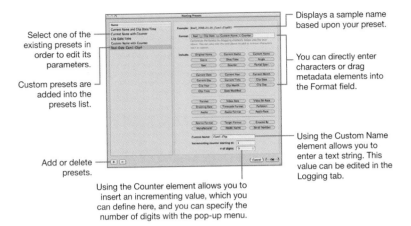

Select one of the existing presets in order to edit its parameters.

Custom presets are added into the presets list.

Add or delete presets.

Displays a sample name based upon your preset.

You can directly enter characters or drag metadata elements into the Format field.

Using the Custom Name element allows you to enter a text string. This value can be edited in the Logging tab.

Using the Counter element allows you to insert an incrementing value, which you can define here, and you can specify the number of digits with the pop-up menu.

The naming preset you define can then be used to automatically name clips and ingest them without user intervention. With Automatic Transfer enabled, log and transfer will automatically begin ingesting available footage when a media volume is mounted. If you defined a Name Preset, it will be used.

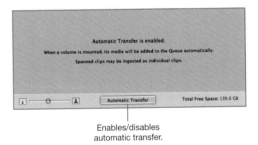

Enables/disables automatic transfer.

See the results of automatic transfer with a custom preset name once the volume labeled AVCHD was recognized.

AVCHD_2009-04-10_Cam1-Clip001
AVCHD_2009-04-10_Cam1-Clip002
AVCHD_2009-04-10_Cam1-Clip003
AVCHD_2009-04-10_Cam1-Clip004
AVCHD_2009-04-10_Cam1-Clip005
AVCHD_2009-04-10_Cam1-Clip006

New Feature

Ingesting Unsupported Tapeless Formats

Camera acquisition formats evolve quickly, and some unsupported formats may not even appear in the Log and Transfer window. For these odd formats, transcoding with Compressor is your best bet (see *Apple Pro Training Series: Compressor 3.5*). After transcoding to a supported format (such as DV or Apple ProRes), follow the Import steps in the next section.

> **TIP** If Log and Transfer, Compressor, or third-party software do not recognize your acquisition format, and your device has video/audio outputs, try the Capture Now process via a third-party capture device.

Importing Files

When media such as graphics, music, text, or supported video files already exist on your computer, use the Import command to ingest them into your project. Importing files does not make copies of the files. It only creates reference files within your project file. Remember to organize your files for the project before importing them, using the good media management procedures outlined in Chapter 3.

> **NOTE** ▶ You should only import files that are available on a locally connected drive or Xsan volumes. If a file exists on a network share (Ethernet) or removable media (flash drives, CDs, DVDs), copy the file to a locally mounted volume (internal hard disks, external FireWire/USB hard drives, or Xsan) before importing. Ethernet DAS/NAS volumes may be fast enough for some media files, but your average, in-office Ethernet network usually lacks bandwidth for real-time media playback.

Supported File Formats

Here are some examples of supported file formats for audio and stills. This list is not exhaustive. Refer to the Final Cut Pro 7 User Manual for more information.

Audio   AIFF/AIFC, WAVE, BWF
          (44.1 kHz/16-bit up to 96 kHz/24-bit)

Stills   BMP, GIF, JEPG/JFIF, Numbered Image Sequences,
          PDF, PSD, PICT, PNG, SGI, TARGA, and TIFF

Importing Individual Files

This method allows you to import an individual or group of files;
however, it will not import a folder.

1   Choose File > Import > Files.

2   In the Finder dialog that opens, choose the file(s) you wish to
    import, and then click Choose.

    TIP As in Mac OS X, you can select multiple files by
    Shift-clicking. You may choose nonsequential files by
    Command-clicking.

    NOTE ▶ You may also drag files from outside Final Cut Pro
    directly to the Browser via the Finder.

Importing Folders

This method is the same as importing individual files, except that you
may only choose a folder or folders from the Finder dialog. Imported
folders will appear as bins in the Browser's active project. The contents of the folder(s) will be inside the bin.

1   Choose File > Import > Folder.

2   In the Finder dialog that opens, choose the folder(s) you wish to
    import, and then click Choose.

    TIP As in Mac OS X, you can select multiple files by
    Shift-clicking. You may choose nonsequential folders by
    Command-clicking.

NOTE ▶ You may also drag folders from outside Final Cut Pro directly to the Browser via the Finder.

Importing from Audio CDs

1   Copy the audio track from the CD to a locally mounted volume.

TIP ▶ Add the audio track to your project's folder as discussed in Chapter 3 to practice good media management.

2   Drag the now-local audio track into the Browser.

NOTE ▶ The audio track will import at the CD-quality 44.1 kHz sample rate. Final Cut Pro will resample on the fly during play-back. If desired, you may use Compressor to resample to 48 kHz before importing.

Importing from iTunes

Every Macintosh includes iTunes. Whether you store your production music as AIFF or MP3, you will need to set iTunes to send AIFF versions to Final Cut Pro. You may choose the below settings before adding a song to the iTunes Library so that music is stored as AIFF. You may decide to store music in a compressed format and then uncompress it before importing the music into Final Cut Pro.

1   Choose iTunes > Preferences.

2   Click Import Settings.

3   From the Import Using pop-up menu, choose AIFF Encoder.

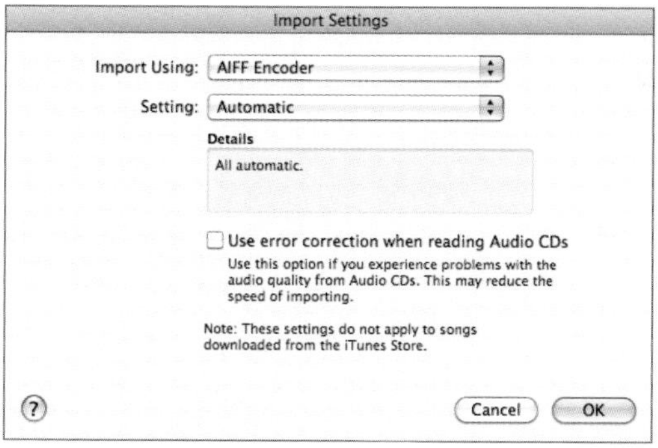

4   From the Setting pop-up menu, choose Custom.

5   In the AIFF Encoder dialog, choose the settings as shown below, and then click OK. Click OK in the Import Settings and Preferences dialogs.

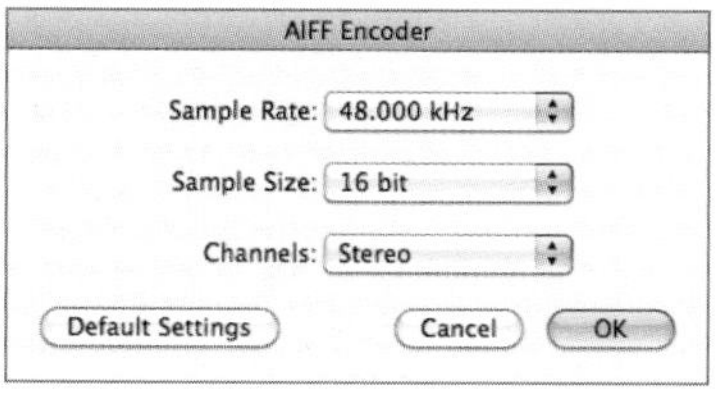

If you have not added your CD to the iTunes Library, do that now.

TIP If you have an existing song in another format, you may select the song in the Library, and then choose Advanced > Create AIFF Version.

6   Control-click the AIFF song in the Library, and choose Show in Finder from the shortcut menu.

7   From the Finder window that appears, drag the AIFF version of the selected song to the Browser's active project.

5
Editing

Three-point nonlinear editing comes down to source, duration, and location. The flexibility of Final Cut Pro lets you approach these three variables in a variety of ways. First, it's important to understand that using source and location can sometimes be like putting a square peg in a round hole. What is weird yet beautiful in Final Cut Pro is that you can.

Open Format Timelines

A sequence can play back clips of different codecs, frame sizes, and frame rates. What the Canvas displays is dependent upon the Sequence Settings (which are established by Easy Setup or modified in Sequence > Settings). When you make the first edit into a sequence, you will receive the conform dialog if the clip's settings do not match that of the sequence.

For best performance your sequence and External Video should be set to the format of the clips you are editing.

Change sequence settings to match the clip settings?

(No)   (Yes)

A best practice is to make your first edit with a clip that represents either of the following:

▶ Sequence settings that match your mastering destination

▶ Clip settings that match the majority of your clips

As mentioned in Chapter 3, clicking Yes in the conform dialog is a shortcut way around setting Easy Setup when ingesting XDCAM EX, AVCHD, AVC-Intra, REDCODE, and DVCProHD in a tapeless workflow.

> **NOTE** ▶ Though Open Format (also known as Mixed Format) timelines allow you to mix settings, your final output will generally be of higher quality if all media within the sequence uses the same settings.

Overwrite

Overwriting, the flagship of Final Cut Pro's editing functions, is the building-block tool for creating your sequence.

Duration in Viewer

The Duration in Viewer method is considered the basic "linear" way of working in Final Cut Pro.

1 Double-click a source clip in the Browser.

2 Now with the clip in the Viewer, cue the playhead to the desired start frame of the clip.

3 Press the I key to mark an In point.

4 Cue the playhead to the last desired frame, and press O to set an Out point and the duration of the source clip.

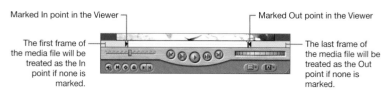

Marked In point in the Viewer ⌐   ⌐ Marked Out point in the Viewer

The first frame of the media file will be treated as the In point if none is marked.

The last frame of the media file will be treated as the Out point if none is marked.

TIP ▶ To adjust an edit point, simply move the playhead to the new location and press either I or O to mark a new In or Out point.

5 In the Timeline, cue the playhead to where you want to place the clip into the sequence.

At minimum, park the playhead at the desired timecode location. The frame at the Viewer's In point will be aligned to the Timeline playhead.

Instead of setting an In point, you may set an Out point. Whether the playhead is at the same location when you perform the edit is irrelevant. The frame at the Viewer's Out point will be aligned to the Timeline Out point.

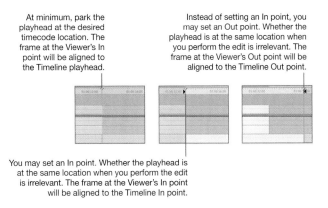

You may set an In point. Whether the playhead is at the same location when you perform the edit is irrelevant. The frame at the Viewer's In point will be aligned to the Timeline In point.

NOTE ▶ Do not set both a Timeline In and a Timeline Out point. Setting both points will override the Viewer's duration.

6 Connect the patch panel to assign the Viewer's source content to the appropriate tracks.

Connect Source patches (representing the Viewer content) to the desired Destination tracks.

Disconnect any Source patches for Viewer content that you do not want to be edited into the sequence.

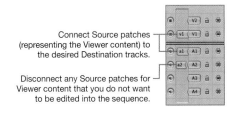

NOTE ▶ The patch panel is dependent upon the content of the Viewer clip. If the source clip in the Viewer is video only, then no audio patches (a1, a2, and so on) will appear in the patch panel.

7 Click the red Overwrite button at the bottom left of the Canvas.

Overwrite
F10

TIP There are multiple ways to invoke an overwrite edit. For example, you may also drag the Viewer clip to the Canvas and drop the clip on the Overwrite overlay.

Duration in Timeline

The Duration in Timeline method of overwriting is often used for music videos and B-roll coverage in documentaries. You have material (studio track, voiceover, narration) in your sequence that you wish to "cover" with additional audio/video.

1 Double-click the source clip in the Browser to load it into the Viewer.

2 In the Viewer, mark an In point at the desired first frame.

An Out point is not necessary, as the duration will be defined in the Timeline. If both In and Out points are marked, the Out point will be ignored.

Marked In point in the Viewer

The first frame of the media file will be treated as the In point if none is marked.

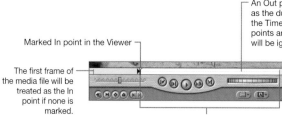

The source duration must equal or be greater than the marked Timeline duration. If an inadequate duration exists, an "Insufficient content for edit" error will result.

TIP ▶ If you wish to backtime the Viewer footage into the sequence, mark an Out point instead. Do not mark an In point.

3   In the Timeline, mark In and Out points around the sequence media to be covered.

The Timeline duration determines the amount of source footage needed. The Viewer In point will align to the Timeline In point. If only a Viewer Out point exists, it will be aligned to the Timeline Out point, and a backtime edit will occur. In either scenario, the duration of the Viewer's source clip must equal or exceed this marked Timeline duration.

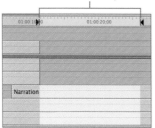

4   Connect the patch panel as needed.

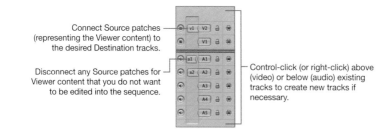

Connect Source patches (representing the Viewer content) to the desired Destination tracks.

Disconnect any Source patches for Viewer content that you do not want to be edited into the sequence.

Control-click (or right-click) above (video) or below (audio) existing tracks to create new tracks if necessary.

5   Click the red Overwrite button.

Overwrite
F10

Insert Edits

The beauty and the beast of nonlinear editing is the ability to add clips anywhere at any time. Insert edits let you jam in forgotten shots, realign a sequence for script changes, or cave in to the whims of a producer.

Duration in Viewer

With the Duration in Viewer method, the source clip in the Viewer determines the duration.

1   Double-click a source clip in the Browser.

2   Now with the clip in the Viewer, cue the playhead to the desired start frame of the clip.

3   Press the I key to mark an In point.

> **TIP** To adjust an edit point, simply move the playhead to the new location and press either I or O to mark a new In or Out point.

4   Cue the playhead to the last desired frame, and press O to set an Out point and the duration of the source clip.

Marked In point in the Viewer ⌐   ⌐ Marked Out point in the Viewer

The first frame of the media file will be treated as the In point if none is marked.

The last frame of the media file will be treated as the Out point if none is marked.

5   In the Timeline, cue the playhead to where you want to place the clip into the sequence.

At minimum, park the playhead at the desired timecode location.
The frame at the Viewer's In point will be aligned to the Timeline playhead.

You may set an In point. The playhead location is then irrelevant. The frame at the Viewer's In point will be aligned to the Timeline In point.

All clips to the right of the playhead or In point will be shifted to the right. That shift amount equals the duration of the source clip. If the playhead or In point is in the midst of a clip, that clip will split with the second section shifting right. You may avoid a split by locking tracks.

6   Connect the patch panel to assign the Viewer's source content to
the appropriate tracks.

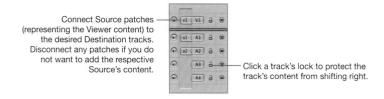

Connect Source patches (representing the Viewer content) to the desired Destination tracks. Disconnect any patches if you do not want to add the respective Source's content.

Click a track's lock to protect the track's content from shifting right.

NOTE ▶ Locking tracks that contain clip content synchronized
to content in unlocked tracks will most likely cause clips to go
out of sync.

7   Click the yellow Insert button at the bottom left of the Canvas.

Insert
F9

Dragging to the Timeline

For mouse-centric users, you can perform overwrite and insert edits
by dragging clips to the Timeline. The pointer's icon will reflect
which type of edit you are performing.

NOTE ▶ Snapping can be good or bad when dragging clips within
the Timeline. You can temporarily enable/disable snapping by
pressing the N key, even while dragging.

1   Double-click the source clip in the Browser.

2   In the Viewer, mark In and Out points as desired.

TIP ▶ If you want the raw clip durations, you can select all
desired clips in the Browser and drag directly to the Timeline,
skipping setting durations in the Viewer.

3   Connect the patch panel as desired.

> NOTE ▶ Drag-to-Timeline editing lets you semi-override the patch panel if you do not drag to the assigned tracks.

4   Drag the video from the Viewer's Video tab to the Timeline.

Drag the clip to the desired track. Ignore the thumbnail; place the clip "shadow" at the desired timecode location. Keep the pointer in the lower two-thirds of the track to get the down-arrow icon (for overwrite edit).

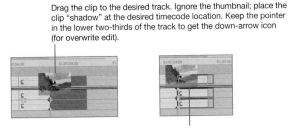

Drag the clip to the desired track. Ignore the thumbnail; place the clip "outline" at the desired timecode location. Keep the pointer in the upper third of the track to get the right-arrow icon (for insert edit).

> **TIP** ▶ To drag an audio-only clip, use the "hand over the speaker" icon in the top right of an Audio tab in the Viewer.

> NOTE ▶ Drag-to-Timeline editing does not honor Timeline In or Out points, but does honor locked tracks.

Replace Edits

The replace edit function lets you exchange an existing sequence clip for a new source clip. Replace performs the exchange by synchronizing the Viewer and Timeline playheads.

1   Load a source clip into the Viewer.

2   Cue the Viewer playhead on the frame you want to synchronize to a frame in the sequence.

> NOTE ▶ No In and Out points are necessary. Viewer In and Out points will be ignored.

3 Cue the Timeline playhead on the frame that you want to sync with the frame at the Viewer's playhead.

4 Ensure that the patch panel is targeting the desired tracks of the existing clip.

> **NOTE ►** You may disconnect patches of source content that you do not want to include (such as audio). You may also lock tracks.

5 Click the Canvas's blue Replace button.

Replace
F11

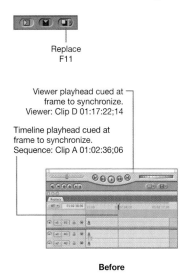

Viewer playhead cued at
frame to synchronize.
Viewer: Clip D 01:17:22;14

Timeline playhead cued at
frame to synchronize.
Sequence: Clip A 01:02:36;06

The Clip D frame at 01:17:22;14 is under
both playheads. Adequate footage must
exist on either side of the Viewer playhead
to match the sequence clip's duration
before and after the Timeline playhead.

Before   After

> **NOTE ►** If there isn't enough media on either side of the Viewer playhead to match the durations of the clip on both sides of the Timeline playhead, you will receive an "Insufficient content for edit" error.

Superimpose

The superimpose edit function is handy for stacking a clip, such as a graphic, on the next track above an existing clip. The magic is that the clip being superimposed is trimmed to the duration of the existing clip.

NOTE ▶ As with most edit functions, enough source material must exist to match the existing clip's duration. Otherwise, you will receive the "Insufficient content for edit" error.

1 Load a source clip, such as text, into the Viewer.

2 In the Timeline, park the playhead over the existing clip.

3 Ensure that the patch panel is targeting the track of the existing clip.

NOTE ▶ You may disconnect patches of source content that you do not want to include (such as audio). You may also lock tracks.

4 Press F12 or drag the clip from the Viewer to the Canvas Edit Overlay to choose Superimpose.

Before   **After**

TIP ▶ You may change the third edit button in the Canvas by clicking the arrow next to the Replace button and choosing another edit type, such as Superimpose.

Click here to change
the third button.

6

Trimming

After your rough cut, you or your client will want to make changes. Final Cut Pro's flexible trimming tools let you make changes to single edit points on a clip, both edit points on a clip, and even edit points on different clips. Mastering the trimming tools in Final Cut Pro allows you to work quickly and polish your initial edits.

Using Duplicate Sequences for Edit History

It's good practice before you trim to make backup copies of each version of your edit. This practice creates a history and also lets you go back to previous versions if you or your client reconsiders.

Rather than creating a new project, which could lead to media mismanagement, simply create a duplicate of your current sequence for each phase of the edit. No media will be duplicated, so no additional media storage is necessary.

1   In the Browser, Control-click (or right-click) your current sequence.

2   Choose Duplicate from the shortcut menu that appears.

3   Rename the "copy" sequence (give it a name like *Project Title* v5 or *Ready for Graphics*), and then double-click to open it.

Control-click the new sequence and choose
Close Other Tabs to close other sequences.

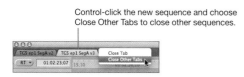

Trimming with the Selection Tool

The Selection tool lets you adjust the In and Out points of a clip, which changes the clip's duration.

1 Choose the Selection (arrow) tool.

Selection
A

2 Place the Selection tool on the edit point.

With the Selection tool on the left side of an edit point, you will be adjusting the Out point of the outgoing clip.

With the Selection tool on the right side of an edit point, you will be adjusting the In point of the incoming clip.

3 Drag the edit point to adjust.

You may cue the playhead on the desired new Out point. With snapping on, dragging the existing Out point will quickly snap it to the desired frame.

The Selection tool will only allow you to drag B's Out point left, as the next clip (C) is not adjusted.

You may cue the playhead on the desired new In point. With snapping on, dragging the existing In point will quickly snap it to the desired frame.

The Selection tool will only allow you to drag C's In point right, as the previous clip (B) is not adjusted.

Before

-00:00:14 (New Duration = 00:00:01:19)

+00:00:14 (New Duration = 00:00:01:26)

After

The Selection tool leaves a gap behind. Select the gap and press Shift-Delete (Ripple Delete) to remove the gap. Clip C and following clips will slide left. The sequence duration will shorten.

> **TIP** Adjust the audio or video content separately by Option-dragging the content's edit point. Or, deselect Linked Selection in the Timeline's button bar. A third option is to lock tracks. Be aware that these options may create an out-of-sync situation.

Trimming with the Ripple Tool

The Ripple tool lets you not only shorten a clip, but also lengthen clips (sliding the clips that follow left or right). The durations of one clip and the entire sequence are modified simultaneously.

1   Hold down the Roll tool to access the Ripple tool.

Ripple
RR

2   Place the Ripple tool on the edit point.

With the Ripple tool on the right side of an edit point, you will be adjusting the In point of the incoming clip. The "tail" of the tool points at the clip you are going to adjust, whether lengthening or shortening the clip.

With the Ripple tool on the left side of an edit point, you will be adjusting the Out point of the outgoing clip. The "tail" of the tool points at the clip you are going to adjust, whether lengthening or shortening the clip.

Placing the Ripple tool in the midst of a clip results in an "x" next to the tool. The Ripple tool can be used only when placed on an edit point.

3   Drag the edit point to adjust.

With the Ripple tool's tail pointing at B, drag to the left to shorten B.

With the Ripple tool's tail pointing at B, drag to the right to lengthen B.

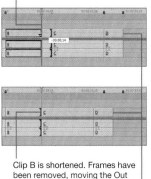   **Before**   **After**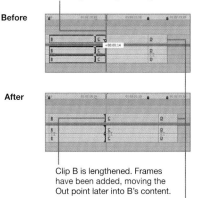

Clip B is shortened. Frames have been removed, moving the Out point earlier into B's content.

Clip B is lengthened. Frames have been added, moving the Out point later into B's content.

The sequence duration is shortened as the clips to the right side of B slide left the length of the ripple.

The sequence duration is lengthened as the clips to the right side of B slide right the length of the ripple.

With the Ripple tool's tail pointing at C, drag to the right to shorten C. Cueing the playhead to the desired In point allows you to drag and snap the existing In point for precision.

With the Ripple tool's tail pointing at C, drag to the left to lengthen C.

Only the In point is adjusted. The clip outline updates to display the resulting duration and how far D and following clips will slide.

Only the In point is adjusted. The clip outline updates to display the resulting duration and how far D and following clips will slide.

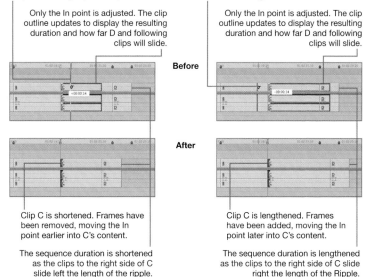

Before

After

Clip C is shortened. Frames have been removed, moving the In point earlier into C's content.

Clip C is lengthened. Frames have been added, moving the In point later into C's content.

The sequence duration is shortened as the clips to the right side of C slide left the length of the ripple.

The sequence duration is lengthened as the clips to the right side of C slide right the length of the Ripple.

NOTE ▶ The Ripple tool affects the content in all tracks to the right of the adjusted clip. You may lock tracks; however, this might affect any synchronization you've created across tracks.

Rippling the Out point of B to shorten the clip.

The second text clip is to the right of clip B.

The first text clip does not move.

The second text clip moves the ripple amount.

Before

After

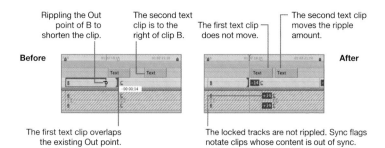

The first text clip overlaps the existing Out point.

The locked tracks are not rippled. Sync flags notate clips whose content is out of sync.

With an edit point selected by the Ripple tool, you may use a variety of keyboard shortcuts to nudge the edit point.

To adjust by a numeric value, press + (plus) or − (minus) to enter the value with the point selected.

The Out point is selected with the Ripple tool. Press the bracket keys ([and]) to nudge by one frame. Press Shift-[or Shift-] to nudge by the Multi-Frame Trim Size set in Final Cut Pro > User Preferences > Editing tab.

TIP ▶ Press U to toggle between the selected points. Pressing the Down Arrow key will advance the selection to the next edit point.

Moving an Edit Point with the Roll Tool

The Roll tool may be used to adjust two edit points at once—without affecting the entire sequence.

1   Select the Roll tool from the Tool palette.

Roll
R

NOTE ▶ If you last used the Ripple tool, hold down the Ripple tool icon to reveal the Roll tool.

2   Place the Roll tool on an edit point.

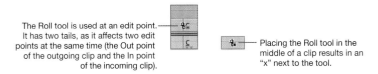

The Roll tool is used at an edit point. It has two tails, as it affects two edit points at the same time (the Out point of the outgoing clip and the In point of the incoming clip).

Placing the Roll tool in the middle of a clip results in an "x" next to the tool.

NOTE ▶ The Roll tool can be used on a single edit point (the In point of the first sequence clip, the Out point of the last sequence clip, or a clip with no adjacent clip [such as B-roll or text on a higher track]). In those cases, the Roll tool performs similarly to the Selection tool.

3   Drag the edit point to adjust.

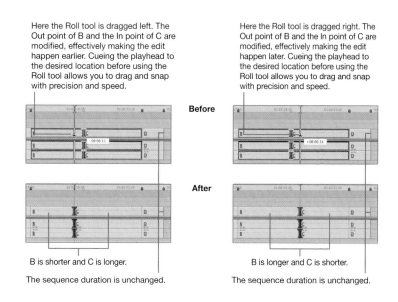

Here the Roll tool is dragged left. The Out point of B and the In point of C are modified, effectively making the edit happen earlier. Cueing the playhead to the desired location before using the Roll tool allows you to drag and snap with precision and speed.

Here the Roll tool is dragged right. The Out point of B and the In point of C are modified, effectively making the edit happen later. Cueing the playhead to the desired location before using the Roll tool allows you to drag and snap with precision and speed.

Before

After

B is shorter and C is longer.

The sequence duration is unchanged.

B is longer and C is shorter.

The sequence duration is unchanged.

TIP ▶ The extend edit feature performs a roll edit even faster. Cue your playhead to the desired location for the edit. Select the edit point with the Roll or Selection tool, and then press the E key. As long as enough media handles exist, the edit point will move to the playhead as if you had dragged it there with the Roll tool.

With an edit point selected by the Roll tool or the Selection tool, you may use a variety of keyboard shortcuts to nudge the edit point.

To adjust by a numeric value, press + (plus) or – (minus) and enter the value with the point selected.

You may press the bracket keys ([and]) to nudge by one frame. Press Shift-[or Shift-] to nudge by the Multi-Frame Trim Size set in Final Cut Pro > User Preferences > Editing tab.

TIP ▶ Pressing the Down Arrow key will advance the selection to the next edit point.

Using the Slip Tool

The Slip tool adjusts the two edit points of one clip simultaneously. Neither clips nor the sequence sees a duration change. The Slip tool is often used after trimming with other tools to "clean up" the content within a clip's new duration.

Using the Slip Tool in the Timeline

1   Select the Slip tool from the Tool palette.

Slip
S

> **NOTE** ▶ If you last used the Slide or Speed tool, hold down its tool icon to reveal the Slip tool.

2   Place the Slip tool on a clip.

3   Drag the clip to change the content without changing the clip's duration.

Before

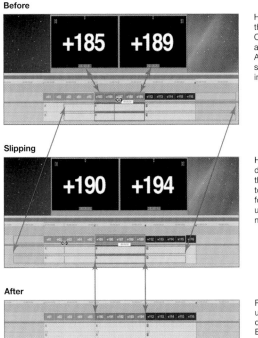

Holding down clip B with the Slip tool changes the Canvas to display the In and Out points of clip B. An outline of clip B's source media is overlaid in the Timeline.

Slipping

Here the Slip tool is dragged left. The outline of the media handles adjusts to show remaining source footage. The Canvas updates to display clip B's new In and Out points.

After

Releasing the Slip tool updates the sequence. The duration and position of clip B remain constant. Clips A and C are not affected.

TIP ▶ The Slip tool can be dragged left to reveal later footage or right to reveal earlier footage within the clip's duration and location in the sequence.

Using the Slip Tool with the Viewer and Canvas Windows

Another approach to slipping uses the Viewer and Canvas windows together.

1 Double-click the sequence clip to load into the Viewer.

The "sprockets" indicate that a sequence clip is loaded in the Viewer.

2 Drag the Viewer In or Out point with the Slip tool.

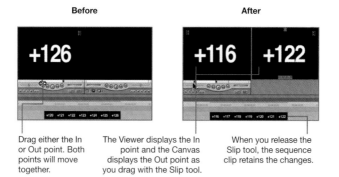

Before

After

Drag either the In or Out point. Both points will move together.

The Viewer displays the In point and the Canvas displays the Out point as you drag with the Slip tool.

When you release the Slip tool, the sequence clip retains the changes.

NOTE ▶ When you release the Slip tool, the Viewer and Canvas windows revert to displaying the frame under their respective playheads.

With a sequence clip selected and the Slip tool active, you can use a variety of keyboard shortcuts to slip the clip.

To adjust by a numeric value, press + (plus) or
– (minus), and enter the value with the clip
selected and the Slip tool active.

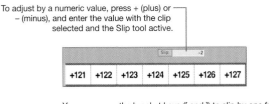

You may press the bracket keys ([and]) to slip by one frame.
Press Shift-[or Shift-] to slip by the Multi-Frame Trim Size set in
Final Cut Pro > User Preferences > Editing tab.

TIP ▸ With the Slip tool active, press Shift to select a sequence clip.

Using the Slide Tool

The Slide tool adjusts one edit point each for two clips and the position of a third clip in one move.

1   Select the Slide tool from the Tool palette.

NOTE ▸ If you last used the Slip or Speed tool, hold down its tool icon to reveal the Slide tool.

2   Drag the Slide tool on a middle clip in a group of three clips.

TIP ▸ You can use the Slide tool on a group of two clips (no adjacent third clip). The clip you slide will move, not changing content or duration, and the other clip will change duration and content.

Before

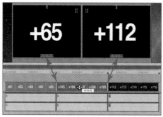

Holding Clip B with the Slide tool changes the Canvas to display the Out point of Clip A in the left frame and the In point of Clip C in the right frame.

Sliding

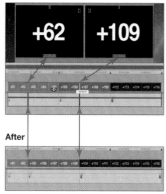

Dragging Clip B left with the Slide tool moves the outline of B without changing the content of B. Clip A's Out point is moved earlier in A's content and displayed in the left frame of the Canvas. Clip C's In point is also moved earlier in C's content and displayed in the right frame of the Canvas. Dragging Clip B right with the Slide tool would move B without changing its content. Clips A and C would change their Out and In points, respectively, to later content.

After

Releasing the Slide tool updates the sequence with Clip A's new Out point (new duration), clip B's position (same content and duration), and clip C's new In point (new duration).

NOTE ▶ When you release the Slide tool, the Canvas window reverts to displaying the frame under its playhead.

Splitting a Clip with the Razor Blade

The Razor Blade tool allows you to split a clip into two or more pieces—usually to delete the unwanted portions. There are two versions of the tool: Razor Blade and Razor Blade All. Razor Blade honors linked clips and the Linked Selection status. Razor Blade All slices through all tracks regardless of Linked Selection status.

1   Select the Razor Blade tool from the Tool palette.

Razor Blade
B

2   Move the Razor Blade tool to the desired split point.

TIP ▶ Cueing the playhead to the desired split point before using the Razor Blade tool lets you snap the tool to the playhead before clicking to increase frame accuracy.

3   Check the Linked Selection status.

4   Click with the Razor Blade tool to split the clip.

TIP ▶ Press Option before clicking to override Link Selection. Clips in locked tracks are not affected.

NOTE ▶ The red arrows that appear at the split point indicate a through edit. Reconnect the two clips of a through edit by Control-clicking the red arrows and choosing Join Through Edit from the shortcut menu. Or, choose Join All Through Edits to remove all through edits in the unlocked tracks of a sequence.

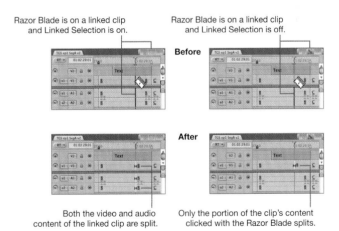

Razor Blade is on a linked clip and Linked Selection is on.

Razor Blade is on a linked clip and Linked Selection is off.

Before

After

Both the video and audio content of the linked clip are split.

Only the portion of the clip's content clicked with the Razor Blade splits.

Splitting Multiple Clips with Razor Blade All

Razor Blade All is sometimes referred to as the *super blade*. Clips under the Razor Blade All point, in any track, will be split. The only exception is if a clip is in a locked track.

1 Select the Razor Blade All tool from the Tool palett

2 Move the Razor Blade All tool to the desired split point.

> **TIP** Cueing the playhead to the desired split point before using the Razor Blade All tool lets you snap the tool to the playhead before clicking to increase frame accuracy.

3 Click with the Razor Blade All tool to split the clips.

Before	After

Razor Blade All is on a linked clip, and Linked Selection is off.

Nonetheless, both the video and audio content of the linked clip is split. The text clip in V2 is split, too.

NOTE ▶ Clips in locked tracks are not affected.

Using Add Edit to Split Clips

Add Edit is similar to Blade All but is different in three ways:

▶ It is invoked only via keyboard shortcut (Control-V).

▶ It uses the playhead.

▶ It honors the Auto Select controls.

1 Cue your Timeline playhead to the desired split point.

2 Press Control-V.

The video content of clip B is split, since the Auto Select
for V1 is active. The Auto Select for A1 is ignored, as clip
B is a stereo pair linked to A2, whose Auto Select is off.

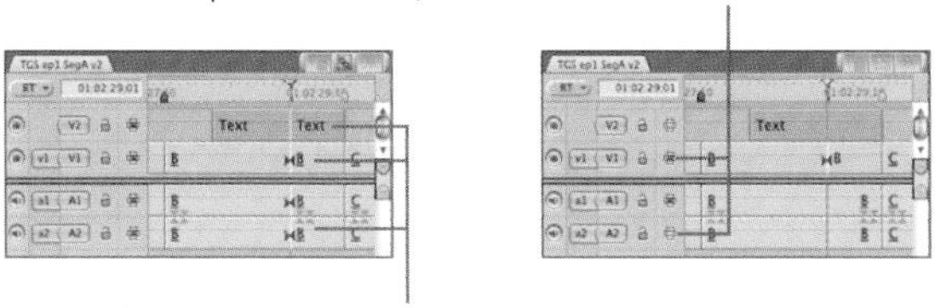

Clips in all unlocked and
auto-selected tracks are split.

NOTE ▶ Add Edit does not affect clips in locked tracks.

Repositioning Clips

While building a story line, you may want to change a shot or sound
bite to check story flow. A reposition edit in a sequence is performed
with the Selection tool and the Option key.

1 Drag a clip with the Selection tool into the new desired position,
but do not release the pointer.

TIP ▶ Snapping to the destination's edit point will perform a
clean reposition. Performing a reposition in the midst of a clip
will break the destination clip, similarly to a standard insert edit.

2 Hold down the Option key.

Drag to an edit point
to avoid splitting a clip.

Adding the Option key changes the pointer to the
reposition arrow with a small insert arrow pointing right.
Release the pointer first.

Before

After

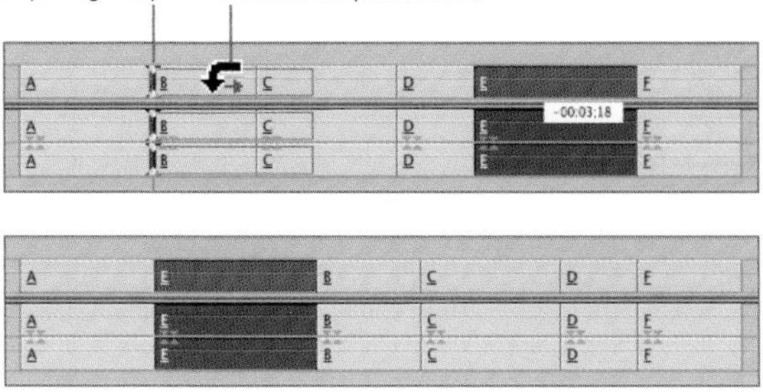

3 Release the pointer and then the Option key.

> **TIP** ▶ You can also reposition by dragging to the right in the sequence. When you add the Option key, the reposition arrow will flip, with the little insert arrow pointing left.

> **NOTE** ▶ Pointer and modifier key order are critical. Drag–Option–release pointer will perform a reposition. Drag–Option–release Option will perform an overwrite edit. Option–drag–release Option will perform a copy. Option–drag–release pointer will perform a copy and an insert edit.

7

Audio

Video is not good video without audio. Final Cut Pro includes tools for setting your mix, recording automation, and recording a voiceover.

Clip Audio Channels

Tabs in the Viewer window represent clip audio, whether linked to video content or standalone. The number of content channels and how those channels are ingested into Final Cut Pro determine their display method. A single audio channel, such as recordings from the Voice Over tool, is represented by a "Mono (a*n*)" tab, where *n* is the channel's number within the clip. Two audio channels may be linked together during capture/transfer to become a stereo pair. Stereo pairs (Ch1 and Ch2, Ch3 and Ch4, and so on) appear under one tab for each pair.

Each Mono tab has a Level slider and a Pan slider to control each discrete channel.

The Pan value defaults to 0 for a Mono tab (the content feeds both outputs in a stereo sequence), whereas the Pan defaults to –1 for a stereo pair (a1 feeds the Left output and a2 feeds the Right output of a stereo sequence).

Each Stereo tab has a Level slider and a Pan slider to control the two channels together.

Mono audio channels appear as single channels per tab (Mono [a1], Mono [a2], and so on).

Stereo pair channels appear as two channels stacked one above the other per tab.

NOTE ▶ You may make or break a stereo pair clip by selecting the audio content in a sequence and choosing Modify > Stereo Pair (Option-L).

A stereo pair clip is indicated in a sequence by two pairs of arrows pointing at each other.

Adjusting Levels with the Selection Tool

There are several ways to adjust the apparent volume of clips within Final Cut Pro. The Selection tool modifies the level for the clip's entire duration.

Changing Level in the Viewer

You can open a master clip into the Viewer to set a level before editing into the sequence. This will affect the master version of the clip for future edits until you make another adjustment. You may also open sequence clips to directly affect one instance of a clip in a sequence.

1   Load a clip into the Viewer.

2   Click the appropriate audio tab.

3   Adjust the level as desired.

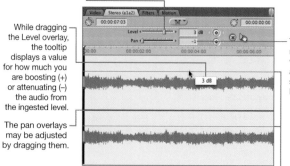

You may adjust the Level setting by dragging the slider, by clicking the small arrows at each end of the slider, or by entering a value in the Level field and pressing Return.

While dragging the Level overlay, the tooltip displays a value for how much you are boosting (+) or attenuating (–) the audio from the ingested level.

The pan overlays may be adjusted by dragging them.

The Pan setting may be adjusted with the Pan slider, arrows, or field, similarly to the Level setting.

With the Selection tool, you may adjust the level by dragging the level overlay in the Viewer. As this is a stereo pair, both a1's and a2's overlays move together.

Adjusting Level in the Timeline

Rather than reloading a sequence clip into the Viewer, you may adjust the clip's level in the Timeline.

1 Activate clip overlays by clicking the Clip Overlays control in the lower left of the Timeline.

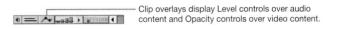

Clip overlays display Level controls over audio content and Opacity controls over video content.

2 Use the Selection tool to adjust the audio level overlay for each clip.

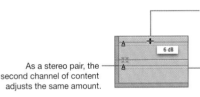

The Selection tool becomes the Line Segment tool when placed on top of the Level overlay. Drag up to boost (up to +12dB) or down to attenuate (down to –inf).

As a stereo pair, the second channel of content adjusts the same amount.

The unity line is a reference at 0 dB. All clips begin with this setting after ingest.

Modify > Levels to Adjust Multiple Levels

To adjust the Level settings of multiple clips, use the Modify menu. The Clip Overlays option is on in the below images to display the results; however, Clip Overlays is not required for making this adjustment.

1 Select the clips you wish to adjust.

2 Choose Modify > Levels.

3 Adjust as desired in the Gain Adjust dialog that appears.

As with the Level slider in the Viewer, you may drag the slider, click the small arrows, or enter a value in the field.

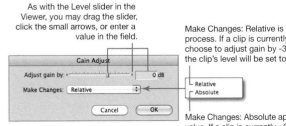

Make Changes: Relative is an add/subtract process. If a clip is currently +6 dB and you choose to adjust gain by -3 dB Relative, then the clip's level will be set to +3 dB.

Make Changes: Absolute applies a new Level value. If a clip is currently +6 dB and you choose to adjust gain by -3 dB Absolute, then the clip's level will be set to -3 dB.

Paste Attributes

You may copy and paste the Level setting from one clip to many other clips simultaneously.

> **NOTE** ▶ Although shown in the screen shots below, Clip Overlays is not required for this adjustment.

1   Select the sequence clip with the correct Level setting.

2   Copy the clip by pressing Command-C, or Control-clicking (or right-clicking) the clip and choosing Copy from the shortcut menu.

3   Select the destination clip(s) in the sequence.

4   Press Option-V, or Control-click one of the selected clips and choose Paste Attributes from the shortcut menu.

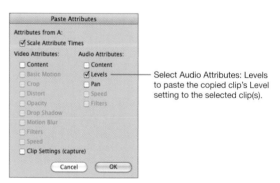

Select Audio Attributes: Levels to paste the copied clip's Level setting to the selected clip(s).

Keyframing Levels with the Pen Tool

The Pen tool lets you vary the clip's level over time. The variances are set with keyframes. The process is sometimes referred to as *rubberbanding*.

Keyframing Level in the Viewer

A great advantage to working with audio in the Viewer is the ability to zoom in tight on the audio. Final Cut Pro lets you zoom in to 1/100 of a frame when viewing an audio tab.

1   Load a clip into the Viewer.

2   Click the appropriate audio tab.

3   Zoom in to your audio, if necessary, by pressing Command-+.

> **NOTE ▶** Command-+ refers to using the keypad on an extended keyboard. On a portable, the keyboard shortcut is technically Command-=.

4   Select the Pen tool from the Tool palette (or press P).

5   Click the Levels overlay to create a keyframe. Drag the keyframe horizontally or vertically to adjust.

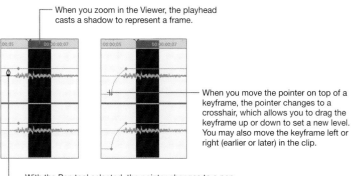

When you zoom in the Viewer, the playhead casts a shadow to represent a frame.

When you move the pointer on top of a keyframe, the pointer changes to a crosshair, which allows you to drag the keyframe up or down to set a new level. You may also move the keyframe left or right (earlier or later) in the clip.

With the Pen tool selected, the pointer changes to a pen when on top of the level overlay. Click to make a keyframe.

NOTE ▶ You must have a minimum of two keyframes to automate a level. Refer to Chapter 11 for more information on keyframing.

Keyframing Level in the Timeline
Keyframing in the Timeline lets you set keyframes in relation to other clips in the same or other tracks.

1   Activate clip overlays in the lower left of the Timeline.

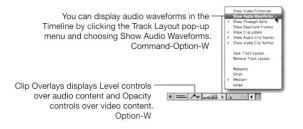

You can display audio waveforms in the Timeline by clicking the Track Layout pop-up menu and choosing Show Audio Waveforms. Command-Option-W

Clip Overlays displays Level controls over audio content and Opacity controls over video content. Option-W

2   Zoom in the Timeline, if necessary, by pressing Option-+.

TIP ▶ The Command modifer with – or + will zoom the active window (Viewer, Canvas, or Timeline). Using Option will zoom only the Timeline window, whether the Viewer, Canvas, or Timeline is active.

NOTE ▶ Option-+ refers to using the keypad on an extended keyboard. On a portable, the keyboard shortcut is technically Option-=.

3   You may increase track height by selecting a taller bar in the Track Height controls at the lower left of the Timeline.

Selecting a taller bar to increase the track height can help when adding keyframes to a sequence clip. Shift-T

4   Choose the Pen tool from the Tool palette (or press P).

With the Pen tool selected, the pointer changes to a pen when on top of the Level overlay. Click to make a

When you move the pointer on top of a keyframe, the pointer changes to a crosshair, which allows you to drag the keyframe up or down to set a new level. You may also move the keyframe left or right (earlier or later) in the clip.

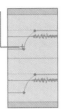

To delete a keyframe, you may click a keyframe with the Delete Point tool. Or you can use the Selection or Pen tool to drag a keyframe off the clip until you get a trashcan pointer.

TIP ▸ You can adjust two keyframes simultaneously with the Selection tool by dragging the level overlay between keyframes.

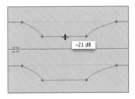

NOTE ▸ You can adjust the Level of one or two keyframes with the Gain (Adjust) commands. For example, assigning keyboard shortcuts to Gain (Adjust) -1dB allows you to adjust one keyframe when the playhead is on the keyframe. You can adjust two keyframes simultaneously by cueing the playhead between two keyframes.

Modify > Levels to Adjust Keyframes

You may still need to drop or raise the overall level of a clip after you've set keyframes. Rather than adjust each keyframe manually, use the Modify > Levels command.

1   Select the clips you wish to adjust.

2   Choose Modify > Levels.

3   Adjust as desired in the Gain Adjust dialog that appears.

NOTE ▸ You may also adjust all keyframes with the Gain +1dB (Control-=) and Gain -1dB (Control-minus) commands.

New Feature

Drag the slider or enter a value.

Make Changes: Relative is an add/subtract process. The keyframes will be adjusted by the value chosen.

Make Changes: Absolute applies a new level value that deletes the applied keyframes.

Using the Audio Mixer

Final Cut Pro includes an Audio Mixer for easily setting clip levels with a traditional audio mixer layout. The Audio Mixer lets you adjust the level of an entire clip or set keyframes.

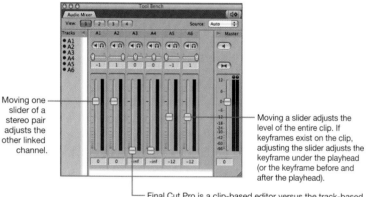

Moving one slider of a stereo pair adjusts the other linked channel.

Moving a slider adjusts the level of the entire clip. If keyframes exist on the clip, adjusting the slider adjusts the keyframe under the playhead (or the keyframe before and after the playhead).

Final Cut Pro is a clip-based editor versus the track-based Soundtrack Pro. When no clip exists under the Timeline playhead, the track's slider goes "dead."

Recording Level Automation

The Record Audio Keyframes feature lets you set keyframes while the sequence is playing back.

1   With the Audio Mixer open, click the Record Audio Keyframes button.

With Record Audio Keyframes on, any slider movement will create and then adjust keyframes.

2 Start playback of the sequence.

3 Drag the slider to set keyframes for the clip under the playhead in the respective track.

As you drag a slider, you will hear the changes before seeing them. When you stop playback, the keyframes representing your slider changes are drawn on the respective clips.

Because you can drag only one slider at a time, you will need to do multiple passes to modify additional tracks. Keyframes will be recorded only for the sliders you adjust.

Sweetening Audio

Final Cut Pro contains several filters for processing your audio. See Chapter 9 for information on how to apply and adjust filters. Final Cut Pro also has a normalization feature, but it is not applied like other filters.

Normalizing Audio

When boosting the level of a clip manually, you might raise the level too high, which would result in clipping. The Normalize feature resets the existing peak of a clip to the setting you choose.

1 Select a sequence clip or multiple sequence clips.

2 Choose Modify > Audio > Apply Normalization Gain.

3 In the Apply Normalization Gain dialog, set the "Normalize to" slider to the desired peak level.

A Gain filter will be applied to adjust the clip's peak level to the level you choose.

After you click OK, an analysis is performed on the clip's marked content to determine the existing peak before applying a Gain filter. If you trim a clip, you may need to apply normalization gain again.

Soundtrack Pro takes audio sweetening and cleanup to the next level in Final Cut Studio. Refer to Chapter 15 on how to round-trip your Final Cut Pro audio with Soundtrack Pro. For more information on Soundtrack Pro, check out *Apple Pro Training Series: Sound Editing in Final Cut Studio*, by Jeff Sobel (Peachpit Press).

Recording a Voiceover

The Voice Over tool lets you record audio directly into a sequence from any Mac OS X-compatible audio interface.

1 Choose Tools > Voice Over.

2 Set a duration and time placement in the sequence by marking In and Out points.

> **TIP** You must mark In and Out points to use the Voice Over tool in a blank sequence.

3 Verify Voice Over settings before clicking the Record button.

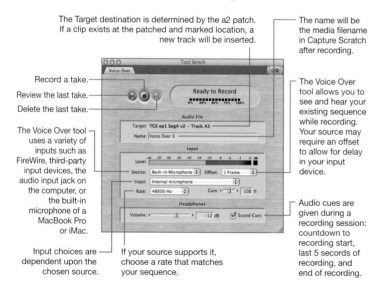

The Target destination is determined by the a2 patch. If a clip exists at the patched and marked location, a new track will be inserted.

The name will be the media filename in Capture Scratch after recording.

Record a take.

Review the last take.

Delete the last take.

The Voice Over tool uses a variety of inputs such as FireWire, third-party input devices, the audio input jack on the computer, or the built-in microphone of a MacBook Pro or iMac.

The Voice Over tool allows you to see and hear your existing sequence while recording. Your source may require an offset to allow for delay in your input device.

Audio cues are given during a recording session: countdown to recording start, last 5 secords of recording, and end of recording.

Input choices are dependent upon the chosen source.

If your source supports it, choose a rate that matches your sequence.

8

Transitions

The Effects tab and menu contain a variety of video and audio transitions. You can apply a transition to one edit at a time or to many edits at once.

Applying Single Transitions

Both video and audio transitions can be applied from a few different places:

► The Effects tab

► The Effects menu

► The Shortcut menu

► The Canvas Edit Overlay

For all transitions, at least one of the clips at an edit point must have enough source media beyond its applicable In or Out point (also known as a *handle*) to apply the transition.

From the Effects Tab

When dragging from the Effects tab, you can visually set the transition alignment (dependent upon available source media). The three transition alignments (End on Edit, Center on Edit, and Start on Edit) define how a transition interacts with the sequence clips and their handles. Knowing which handle of which sequence clip gets used depends on the alignment chosen.

1 Drag the desired transition from the Effects tab to a sequence edit point (or to a single edit point).

2 Before releasing the mouse button, adjust the transition alignment with the pointer.

Dragging a transition to the left of an edit point (End on Edit Transition Alignment) will move the In point of the incoming clip (clip on right) earlier in the source footage by the duration of the transition.

Dragging a transition to the center of an edit point (Center on Edit Transition Alignment) will move the Out point of the outgoing clip (clip on left) and the In point of the incoming clip (clip on right) by half of the transition's duration.

Dragging a transition to the right of an edit point (Start on Edit Transition Alignment) will move the Out point of the outgoing clip (clip on left) later in the source footage by the duration of the transition.

Before

After

The small x indicates inadequate source media handles. In this case, the transition cannot be applied with the End on Edit Transition Alignment.

The transition's shadow is not flowing onto the clip preceding B. An inadequate media handle exists prior to the In point of Clip B, negating the use of Center on Edit.

The only successful transition alignment in this case is a Start on Edit.

Before

After

No transition is applied when the mouse button is released.

A one-frame transition is applied when the mouse button is released.

 TIP Although Clip C will "fade to black" as the last clip in the next sequence, you should edit a slug at the end of your sequence to ensure that your exports "stay in black" once playback has completed.

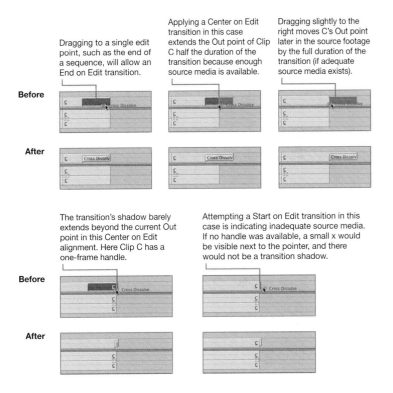

Dragging to a single edit point, such as the end of a sequence, will allow an End on Edit transition.

Applying a Center on Edit transition in this case extends the Out point of Clip C half the duration of the transition because enough source media is available.

Dragging slightly to the right moves C's Out point later in the source footage by the full duration of the transition (if adequate source media exists).

Before

After

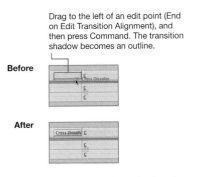

The transition's shadow barely extends beyond the current Out point in this Center on Edit alignment. Here Clip C has a one-frame handle.

Attempting a Start on Edit transition in this case is indicating inadequate source media. If no handle was available, a small x would be visible next to the pointer, and there would not be a transition shadow.

Before

After

NOTE ▶ You can apply a transition to a single side of an edit point by pressing Command before releasing the pointer.

Drag to the left of an edit point (End on Edit Transition Alignment), and then press Command. The transition shadow becomes an outline.

Drag to the right of an edit point (Start on Edit Transition Alignment), and then press Command. The transition shadow becomes an outline.

Before

After

When the mouse button is released, the transition is applied to only the Out point of the outgoing clip. During playback, the outgoing clip (preceding C) will fade to black, and then Clip C will cut or "pop" in from black.

When the mouse button is released, the transition is applied to only the In point of the incoming clip. During playback, the outgoing clip (preceding C) will cut to black, and then Clip C will fade in from black.

From the Effects Menu

Applying transitions from the Effects menu requires a pre-selection.

1 Either park the playhead at a sequence edit point or choose an edit point with the Selection tool.

 Whether the edit point was selected with the Selection tool or with the playhead, the selected transition is applied to the respective content. If a video transition is selected, then only a video transition is applied to the video content (even with Linked Selection on and both audio and video content selected).

2 Choose the desired transition from the Effects menu.

TIP ► You may also use the keyboard shortcuts: Add Video Transition (Command-T) or Add Audio Transition (Command-Option-T). Cross Dissolve and Cross Fade (+3dB) are the default video and audio transitions.

From the Shortcut Menu

The Shortcut menu method applies the default video or audio transition.

1 Control-click (or right-click) an edit point.

2 Choose Add Transition 'x,' where x is the default transition.

Control-clicking a linked clip with Linked Selection on will apply the default audio and video transitions.

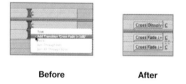

Before   After

NOTE ► See "Setting the Default Transition," later in this chapter, for more information on how to change the default transitions.

From the Canvas Edit Overlay

You can add the default transition while overwrite or insert editing into a sequence.

1   Load a source clip into the Viewer and mark as desired.

2   Ensure that your Timeline playhead and patch panel are set as needed.

3   Drag the Viewer clip to the Canvas, and release the clip on the appropriate Insert with Transition or Overwrite with Transition icon.

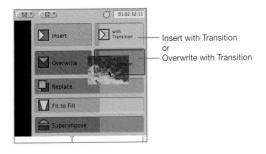

TIP Cross Dissolve is the default video transition, and Cross Fade (+3dB) is the default audio transition. Both are set to a 1-second duration.

Applying Global Transitions

Final Cut Pro lets you apply the same transition to multiple edits simultaneously.

1   Choose the edit points to receive the transition by selecting the clips or setting In/Out points around the clips.

New Feature

2 Select the transition to apply.

With sequence clips selected:

Choose a transition from the Effects menu.

Drag a transition from the Effects tab onto any selected clip (but not to an edit point).

Or, press Command-T to apply the default transition (for video).

With Timeline In and Out points set:

Choose a transition from the Effects menu.

Or, press Command-T to apply the default transition (for video).

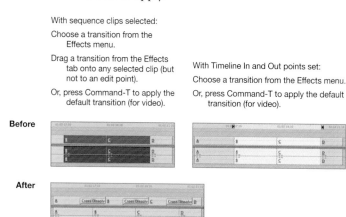

Before

After

TIP ▶ When using the Timeline In and Out points, if you set only an In point, all edit points in all tracks at and after the In point will receive the transition. If only an Out point is set, all edit points at and before the Out point will receive the transition.

NOTE ▶ If any of the selected edit points do not have enough source media, the transitions will be applied with modified durations as necessary.

Although the same transition was applied globally, the transition's duration was modified according to each clip's handles.

TIP You may select multiple edit points or junctions vertically (one per track) and use the shortcut menu to apply the default transition to both audio and video content. Using the keyboard shortcuts (Command-T or Command-Option-T) will apply only to the selected video or audio content.

| Before | After |

Modifying Transitions

All transitions let you adjust their duration (dependent upon available source media or handles). Some transitions allow you to modify other parameters, such as the color of a wipe bar or the backside of a page peel.

Adjusting Duration

There are several ways to adjust the duration of a clip.

Drag an edge of the transition away from the center to lengthen and toward the center to shorten.

Control-click a transition, and choose Duration from the shortcut menu. Enter the desired duration, and click OK in the Duration dialog that appears.

Double-click a transition to load it into the Viewer (which becomes the Transition Editor). Enter the desired duration into the Duration field and press Return.

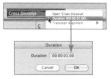

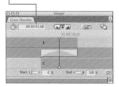

New Feature

> **TIP** As in other areas of Final Cut Pro, the pointer changes as you move across a transition. Be aware of the pointer's status (Resize on edges, Roll in the center, Selection elsewhere over the transition) before you click.

> **NOTE** ▶ Double-clicking an audio transition opens a Duration dialog rather than loading the transition into the Viewer. If you enter a duration value greater than the available handles, the dialog will give you the maximum based on the handles.

Adjusting Other Parameters

1   Double-click a video transition to load it into the Viewer (which becomes the Transition Editor).

> **NOTE** ▶ Adjusting a transition from a sequence affects only that instance.

2   Adjust the parameters as desired.

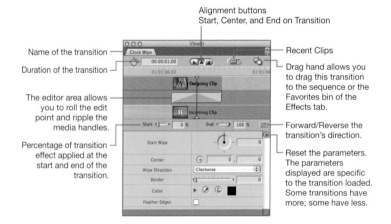

Creating a Favorite Transition

You may save a customized transition for use in other projects.

Use the drag hand to add the transition to the Favorites bin.

With the transition loaded into the Transition Editor (Viewer), choose Effects > Make Favorite Effect. Option-F

NOTE ▶ Favorites are stored inside the Final Cut Pro Preferences file. "Trashing the preferences" also deletes your favorites.

Setting the Default Transition

Setting either a standard or favorite transition as a default gives quick access to a frequently used transition.

1   Select the transition in the Effects tab.

2   Control-click the transition, and choose Set Default Transition.

   NOTE ▶ This is the transition used by the Canvas's Edit Overlay, the shortcut menu when adding a transition, and the keyboard shortcuts (Command-T and Command-Option-T). The default transition is underlined in the Effects tab.

Deleting Transitions

To delete a transition, select the transition and press the Delete (backspace) key. Do not use the Forward Delete key.

Using Alpha Transitions

Alpha transitions let you use a clip (such as a logo animation) to create the transition between two clips.

1   Apply the Video Transitions > Wipe > Alpha Transition from the Effects tab or menu to a sequence edit point.

2   Load the transition into the Viewer.

The "mechanics" part of your transition goes here to specify when and where the incoming clip replaces the outgoing clip. The outgoing clip replaces any white in the Wipe Matte clip, while the incoming clip replaces any black in the Wipe Matte clip.

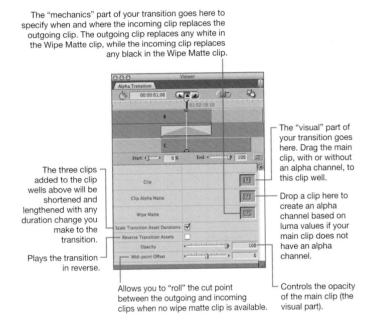

The three clips added to the clip wells above will be shortened and lengthened with any duration change you make to the transition.

Plays the transition in reverse.

The "visual" part of your transition goes here. Drag the main clip, with or without an alpha channel, to this clip well.

Drop a clip here to create an alpha channel based on luma values if your main clip does not have an alpha channel.

Allows you to "roll" the cut point between the outgoing and incoming clips when no wipe matte clip is available.

Controls the opacity of the main clip (the visual part).

TIP ▶ You can create a luma-based wipe by using only the Wipe Matte clip well.

New Feature

9
Filters

Whether you're using Final Cut Pro's built-in or third-party filters, you can apply filters quickly to one or many clips. You can also tweak and customize filters to create your own unique effects.

Applying Filters

Whether you are working with audio or video filters, there are several ways to apply filters to a clip or group of clips:

▶ From the Effects tab or menu

▶ Copy from another clip

▶ As a Filter Pack

TIP ▶ When working with visual filters, a good practice is to have the Timeline playhead cued to the clip whose filter you are about to adjust in the Viewer, so that you may see the results in the Canvas.

NOTE ▶ This book assumes that your workflow is to apply filters after you have at least a basic draft sequence. Instead, you may apply filters to master clips in the Browser if desired.

Applying Filters the Effects Tab or Menu

While you can drag a filter from the Effects tab to a single sequence clip (whether selected or not), dragging to one of multiple selected clips applies the filter to all selected sequence clips.

The same applies when choosing a filter from the Effects menu. You may have one or more sequence clips selected to receive the chosen filter. If no sequence clip is selected, then the filter is applied to the clip under the playhead in the Auto Selected track.

TIP ▶ You may also apply a filter saved as a favorite from the Effects tab or Effects menu.

NOTE ▶ If the Viewer window is active, the filter chosen in the Effects menu is applied to the clip in the Viewer. You may also drag a filter from the Effects tab to the clip in the Viewer.

You can also apply a filter to only a portion of a clip.

Use the Range Selection tool to select a portion of a sequence clip before choosing a filter from the Effects menu or dragging a filter from the Effects tab to the selected portion.

—— Range Selection tool
GGG

Copying a Filter from Another Clip

After you customize a filter on one clip, you may want to use the same filter on another clip. This method copies all of the applied audio and/or video filters from the first clip.

1 Select the sequence clip containing the desired filter.

2 Press Command-C, or Control-click (or right-click) the clip and choose Copy from the shortcut menu.

3 Select the destination sequence clip(s).

4   Press Option-V, or Control-click the clip and choose Paste
Attributes from the shortcut menu.

5   In the Paste Attributes dialog, select Filters and click OK.

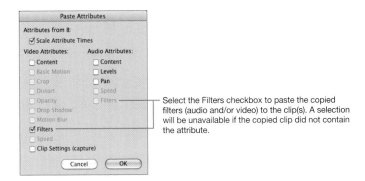

Select the Filters checkbox to paste the copied filters (audio and/or video) to the clip(s). A selection will be unavailable if the copied clip did not contain the attribute.

If you wish to copy one specific filter, use this drag method.

1   Load the clip with the desired filter into the Viewer.

2   If applying to more than one clip, select the sequence clips to
receive the filter.

3   Drag the filter's name from the Filters tab of the Viewer to the
clip(s) in the sequence.

TIP ▶ You may also save the filter as a favorite and drag the filter from the Favorites bin of the Effects tab. See the "Creating a Favorite" section, later in this chapter, for more information.

Applying a Filter Pack

You can save filters as a group or pack of favorites (see "Creating a Filter Pack," later in this chapter). Filter packs retain the hierarchical order and customization of the filters' parameters.

Apply a filter pack just as you would apply a filter from the Effects tab. Drag the bin icon to a clip in the Viewer, sequence, or selected clips in a sequence. You may drag the individual filters out of a filter pack bin; however, the end results may vary if the filter order is different than that of the pack.

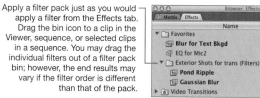

TIP ▸ Do not double-click a filter pack. This action will open the pack as a separate bin and alphabetize the filters. This may destroy the intended effect.

NOTE ▸ Filter packs cannot be applied as a pack via the Effects menu. You can choose, however, to apply the filters one at a time.

Modifying Filters

Rarely does a filter achieve the best results with its default parameter settings (an exception might be Desaturate, but even then you might not want a total grayscale clip). There are several ways to modify filters:

▸ Adjust parameters in the Viewer's Filters tab

▸ Change filter order

You can save these modified filters as favorites.

Adjusting Parameters in the Filters Tab

1   Cue the Timeline playhead to the clip whose filter parameters you wish to adjust.

TIP ▶ Cueing the playhead allows you to see the results of your adjustments in the Canvas. Alternatively, you may "rip" the Video tab out of the Viewer, after you load the clip, to monitor your progress.

2 Load the clip into the Viewer, and select the Filters tab to adjust the parameters as desired.

NOTE ▶ Make sure you have the correct filter loaded into the Viewer (the master from the Effects tab or the filter already applied to a sequence clip) before you start modifying parameters.

All filters are found in the Filters tab. Some filters, like the color correctors and the Chroma Keyer, have a graphical interface in a separate tab.

Show/hide a filter's parameters with the disclosure triangle.

Enable/disable a filter with the selection box.

The parameters available vary by filter. They may include sliders, dials, pop-up menus, text fields, swatches, or gradient editors.

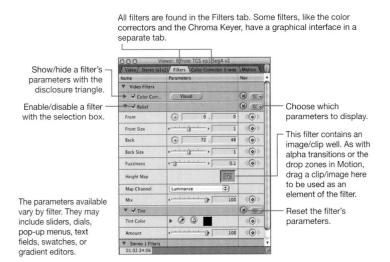

Choose which parameters to display.

This filter contains an image/clip well. As with alpha transitions or the drop zones in Motion, drag a clip/image here to be used as an element of the filter.

Reset the filter's parameters.

TIP ▶ You may adjust the master filter's settings by loading the filter from the Effects tab of the Browser to the Viewer. These modified settings will be carried over to future uses of the filter until changed; however, the master filter's settings reset to default when you restart Final Cut Pro. To preserve your changes, see "Creating a Favorite," below.

Changing Filter Order

Final Cut Pro follows a top-down compositing approach. In the case of filters, the filter listed first is applied first. The result of the first filter is then affected by the second filter listed, and so forth. For example, if you first apply a Sepia filter, the clip takes on a sepia color cast. If you then apply a Desaturate filter, the clip becomes grayscale as the second filter subtracts or "cancels" the look created by the first. Some filters add to a look, and some subtract. You can sometimes achieve different looks by reordering the entries in the Filters tab.

Drag the filter's name to the desired location. In this case, Pond Ripple is being dragged up. The insert bar is appearing above Gaussian Blur to indicate Pond Ripple's new location when released.

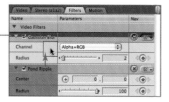

Creating a Favorite

As with transitions, you may find yourself using a particular filter regularly. You may file a filter away as a favorite for instant recall from project to project.

1   Adjust a filter's parameters as desired in the Viewer.

2   Drag the filter by its name to move the filter to the Favorites bin in the Browser's Effects tab.

Drag the filter by its name from the Filters tab to the Favorites bin in the Effects tab.

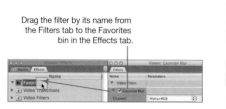

Alternatively, with a filter applied to a clip, load the clip into the Viewer or select the clip in the Timeline, and then choose Effects > Make Favorite Effect. Option-F

If the clip contains more than one filter, see "Creating a Filter Pack," below.

TIP ▶ Favorites are available from one project to the next unless you trash Final Cut Pro's preferences. Trashing preferences, however, does not affect favorites already applied to a clip. If you must "trash the prefs," or if you would like to take your favorites to another Final Cut Pro system, drag your favorite elements out of the Favorites bin to the root level of your active project's tab. Save, transfer, and open the project on another system, and your favorites are ready for use on the other Final Cut Pro system.

NOTE ▶ Although you may alter a master filter's settings, they are reset to default when you restart Final Cut Pro. Creating a favorite retains any modifications through edit sessions.

Creating a Filter Pack

Once you have created an effect with specific filters, you can save the filters as a group or "pack" for later use.

1   Load the clip with applied filters into the Viewer, or select the clip in the Timeline.

2   Choose Effects > Make Favorite Effect.

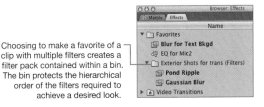

Choosing to make a favorite of a clip with multiple filters creates a filter pack contained within a bin. The bin protects the hierarchical order of the filters required to achieve a desired look.

Deleting Filters

Sometime a filter doesn't create the desired effect, and you want to remove it from a clip.

Select one filter by its name and press Delete.

Select all filters by clicking the Video Filters header, and then press Delete.

Control-click a sequence clip or group of selected clips and choose Remove Attributes. Leave Filters selected (deselect other items as necessary), and click OK.

NOTE ► You can also Control-click a filter or group of selected filters listed in the Viewer's Filters tab and then choose Cut.

TIP ► You can deselect a filter via the filter's checkbox so that you do not lose any parameter settings that you may want to use later.

Filter Playback

Final Cut Pro's filters are one of two types: FXScript or FxPlug plug-ins. The FxPlug plug-ins are part of the Motion application's architecture that utilizes the GPU (graphic card's processor) for hardware acceleration. The two filter types register themselves with Final Cut Pro during application launch, at which time Final Cut Pro determines which filters can play back in real time. The real-time performance capability of each is shown by whether or not the filter's name is in bold or plain type in the Effects tab or menu.

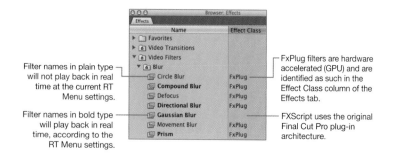

Filter names in plain type will not play back in real time at the current RT Menu settings.

Filter names in bold type will play back in real time, according to the RT Menu settings.

FxPlug filters are hardware accelerated (GPU) and are identified as such in the Effect Class column of the Effects tab.

FXScript uses the original Final Cut Pro plug-in architecture.

NOTE ► Real-time playback capabilities vary based on a system's processing power and the complexity/number of applied effects. Your system may be able to display additional effects in real time if you change the RT Menu to Unlimited RT. See the "RT Menu" section in Chapter 2.

Filter Examples

Here is a small sample of single-clip effects available in Final Cut Pro. There are audio and video filters to stylize and some to correct errors within a clip's content.

NOTE ► Another type of filter requires you to composite the pixels of one clip onto another to realize its full effect. Chapter 13 covers this kind of filter, such as the Chroma Keyer and the Four-Point Garbage Matte.

TIP ► A plethora of third-party filters are available on the web. One list may be found at www.apple.com/finalcutstudio/resources/.

Video Filters: Blur: Gaussian Blur

The blur filters let you reduce distractions of background visuals behind text. The blur is applied to the background clip and set so that the clip does not show any sharply defined content. The result is that the text "pops" visually—it is separated from the background.

Don't be fooled by the simplicity of the available parameters. Some filters need very little adjusting to have a profound effect on the clip. The Radius parameter shown here may only need a small adjustment to achieve the desired effect. As with most parameters, keyframes may be used to animate the filter.

Video Filters: Color Correction: Color Corrector 3-way

The Color Corrector 3-way has its own tab within the Viewer window. The Color Corrector 3-way allows for more precise control than the Color Corrector filter, as the color balance controls are broken down into three distinct areas of influence over the tonal range: Blacks (shadows), Midtones, and Whites (Highlights). The darkest pixels are controlled by the Blacks balance wheel, the brightest pixels by the Whites balance wheel, and the Mids wheel controls everything in between. There is quite a bit of overlap in the controls. When making a change to one area of the tonal range via one control, you'll often need to make an additional correction with one of the other controls.

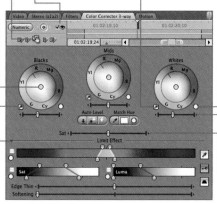

To do a quick white balance, click this eyedropper, and then click a pixel of the clip that should be white. Having the Timeline playhead cued to the clip you are correcting simplifies the process, as you can choose the "white" pixel in the Canvas.

The "eyeball" lets you quickly hide/show the corrections to give you a before/after comparison.

The drag hand allows you to copy this color corrector and its settings to other clips.

You can drag inside a color wheel to manually adjust a clip's hue and saturation. Press Command to "gear up" the control for large adjustments.

Click the Blacks eyedropper; then click a pixel in your clip that should be black to remove a tint in the shadows of your image.

At default, the Limit Effect section is hidden. Click this disclosure triangle to reveal it.

Click here to reset this color balance control. Shift-click to reset the filter.

The slider adjusts the lightness of the pixels controlled by the associated color wheel.

Controls the master saturation.

The Limit Effect controls restrict the changes above to pixels matching the settings chosen here. These controls are very similar to the Chroma Keyer, which is covered in Chapter 13.

Auto-adjusts the Whites slider to set the maximum white level of your image at 100%.

Auto-adjusts the Blacks slider to set the maximum black level of your image at 0%.

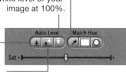

Auto-adjusts the Blacks and Whites sliders simultaneously.

Match Hue allows you to color match two shots. Begin by clicking the Match Hue Eyedropper in the Color Corrector 3-way of the non-corrected clip. Click with the eyedropper on a pixel of a corrected clip. The pixel you select should be a pixel that also appears in the non-corrected clip. Depending on the pixel chosen, the eyedropper of a color wheel in the non-adjusted clip will highlight. Click the highlighted eyedropper; then click the pixel in the non-adjusted clip.

TIP When you are outputting for broadcast and out of time, the Broadcast Safe filter is a quick safety tool for making your luma and chroma signals legal.

Video Filters: Stylize: Bad Film

The Bad Film filter is an FxPlug that "animates" or induces pixel movement on your image. After you apply the filter, play the clip, stop playback, adjust the filter, and then play again. Repeat as necessary.

With many parameters, the Bad Film filter has hundreds of variations.

TIP If Motion is not installed or is unsupported on your system, FxPlug plug-ins from Motion will not display in the Canvas.

NOTE ▶ To get real-time feedback while adjusting the filter, send the clip to Motion. See Chapter 15 for more details.

Video Filters: Video: Smoothcam

The Smoothcam filter must analyze the location of every pixel within the length of an ingested clip. This is a background process.

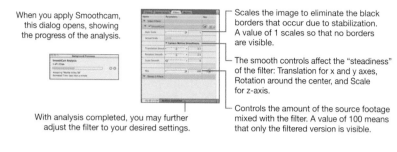

When you apply Smoothcam, this dialog opens, showing the progress of the analysis.

Scales the image to eliminate the black borders that occur due to stabilization. A value of 1 scales so that no borders are visible.

The smooth controls affect the "steadiness" of the filter: Translation for x and y axes, Rotation around the center, and Scale for z-axis.

With analysis completed, you may further adjust the filter to your desired settings.

Controls the amount of the source footage mixed with the filter. A value of 100 means that only the filtered version is visible.

TIP ▶ Smoothcam should be the first filter you apply.

NOTE ▶ Smoothcam analyzes every pixel for the entire source media of a clip. If you work with long-capture clips, trim the clip in the Viewer, and then Export the movie as self-contained with the Viewer active. Import the shorter version and apply the Smoothcam filter to reduce the processing time.

Audio Filters: Final Cut Pro: Compressor/Limiter

Dynamic range is the difference between the loudest and softest portions of a clip. The dynamic range of an audio clip may be too wide to effectively mix your audio. The Compressor/Limiter audio filter can be used to narrow the dynamic range while raising the average level of the clip to match others in your sequence.

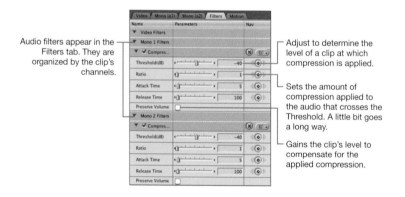

Audio filters appear in the Filters tab. They are organized by the clip's channels.

Adjust to determine the level of a clip at which compression is applied.

Sets the amount of compression applied to the audio that crosses the Threshold. A little bit goes a long way.

Gains the clip's level to compensate for the applied compression.

TIP ▶ Send your sequence to Soundtrack Pro for more control, audio effects, and sweetening options. See Chapter 15.

10

Speed

Whether you play a clip faster or slow-mo it, Final Cut Pro does not change your source media file. To achieve a speed effect, Final Cut Pro either skips frames or repeats and blends frames together.

Fit to Fill

Fit to Fill lets you cram or stretch a clip to fit into your sequence without having to do the math.

1   Either mark In and Out points in your sequence or cue the Timeline playhead over a gap/clip that you want to fill/replace with a Viewer clip.

2   Load the source clip into the Viewer, and if necessary, mark the clip's content with In and Out points.

   TIP ▶ The entire content of the source media will be used if no In or Out points are marked—no handles are necessary.

3   Patch the Source and Destination tracks to target the sequence clip/gap.

4   Perform a Fit to Fill edit.

Click the small menu button next to the
Replace button to reveal the Fit to Fill button.
Shift-F11

TIP You may also drag from the Viewer to the Canvas and choose "Fit to Fill" from the Edit Overlay.

The marked source duration.

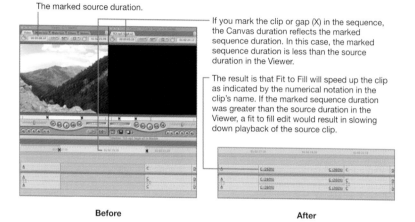

If you mark the clip or gap (X) in the sequence, the Canvas duration reflects the marked sequence duration. In this case, the marked sequence duration is less than the source duration in the Viewer.

The result is that Fit to Fill will speed up the clip as indicated by the numerical notation in the clip's name. If the marked sequence duration was greater than the source duration in the Viewer, a fit to fill edit would result in slowing down playback of the source clip.

Before   **After**

NOTE ▶ Fit to Fill edits perform constant speed changes—the speed rate is constant for the duration of the clip. Constant speed changes affect linked audio.

Modify > Change Speed

Modify > Change Speed lets you quickly apply a speed change to an entire clip.

1   Select one or multiple clips in the Browser or your sequence.

  NOTE ▶ Modifying the speed of master clips from the Browser will affect all future usage of those clips until they are modified again. Remember, however, that any speed changes made in Final Cut Pro do not affect the source media files.

2   Choose Modify > Change Speed (or press Command-J).

3   Modify the Duration or Rate and the other parameters as desired.

The Duration field allows you to define a specific new time value. The rate is calculated automatically.

The Rate field allows you to enter a specific playback rate. Greater than 100% yields faster-than-normal speed. Less than 100% results in slower playback than normal. Entering a Rate value will automatically calculate the new Duration value.

Displays the original duration of the clip for comparison. The value of the first clip is displayed if multiple clips are selected.

Reverse plays the clip's content backward. The Rate value will be displayed in red.

With Ripple Sequence deselected, the resulting duration change of the clip will not ripple-edit the sequence clips or markers to the right of this clip.

Repeats and blends the opacity of frames during playback when Rate is less than 100%.

Clip-based markers and keyframes adjust proportionately.

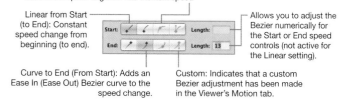

Deletes a previously applied speed setting.

Curve Centered on Start (on End): Applies a smooth speed ramp from the previous speed segment to the beginning of the current speed segment (at the end of the current speed segment into the next speed

Linear from Start (to End): Constant speed change from beginning (to end).

Allows you to adjust the Bezier numerically for the Start or End speed controls (not active for the Linear setting).

Curve to End (From Start): Adds an Ease In (Ease Out) Bezier curve to the speed change.

Custom: Indicates that a custom Bezier adjustment has been made in the Viewer's Motion tab.

Speed Tool

The Speed tool lets you perform roll and ripple edits by applying speed changes.

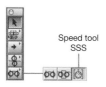

Speed tool
SSS

Rolling Two Points

This process, just like using the Roll tool described in Chapter 6, adjusts the speed of two adjacent clips at an edit point. Remaining clips in the sequence and sequence duration are untouched.

1 Select the Speed tool.

2 Drag a sequence edit point left or right.

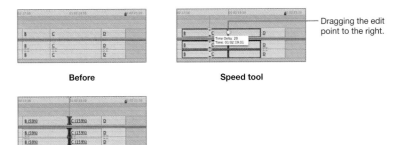

Dragging the edit point to the right.

Before   **Speed tool**

After

Rolling One Point

There is a second type of roll available with the Speed tool. The result of this second type of roll, activated by holding down Shift before dragging the Speed tool, is that one clip's speed will be adjusted. Both clips' durations will be affected.

1 Select the Speed tool.

2 Place the Speed tool on either side of an edit point.

3 Hold down Shift then drag a sequence edit point (In or Out) left or right.

> **TIP** Rolling one edit point with the Speed tool can be used on a single point—no adjacent clip required (such as at the beginning or end of your sequence).

Before   **Speed tool with Shift**

— With the Speed tool on either side of an edit point, hold down Shift, and then drag.

After

— In this case, the Speed tool with Shift was used to drag Clip B's Out point to the right. The content of Clip B remains the same, but its playback is slower, and therefore its duration is longer. The In point of Clip C is "rolled" to later in C's source footage while maintaining the same speed.

Speed Keyframes in the Timeline

With speed keyframes, you can create what are called *speed segments*. Speed segments allow different playback rates within one clip.

Creating and Adjusting Speed Segments

1   Display the Keyframe Editor by clicking the Clip Keyframes button in the lower left of the Timeline.

Clip Keyframes
Option-T

— Control-click (or right-click) in the Keyframe Editor to reveal keyframeable attributes.

Drag in this narrow column to adjust the height of the Keyframe Editor.

— The tick marks give a visual indication of speed changes. Here the ticks indicate that Clip A is playing back at its normal rate.

2   Click the speed indicator tick marks where you want to create a speed keyframe. Add keyframes to create additional segments.

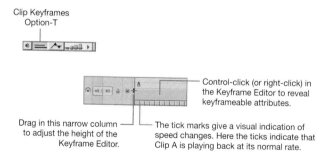

The Pen tool automatically activates when the pointer is in the tick marks area. Click to make a keyframe.

Time: 01:02:18,20
Speed: 100% for 17;29

— The tooltip displays the pointer's current location in the sequence's timecode, the current speed of the clip, and the total source media's duration.

New Feature

3 Drag a speed keyframe left or right to roll the speed of the segments on both sides of the keyframe.

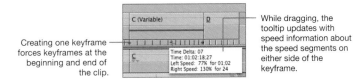

Creating one keyframe forces keyframes at the beginning and end of the clip.

While dragging, the tooltip updates with speed information about the speed segments on either side of the keyframe.

NOTE ▶ Tick marks give a general indication of playback speed. Black tick marks indicate forward playback, while red tick marks indicate reverse playback. The closer the tick marks are to each other, the faster the playback will be, compared with those tick marks that are farther apart. The absence of tick marks indicates 0 percent playback rate (which is a freeze frame).

TIP ▶ Hold down Shift while dragging a keyframe to modify the speed of one segment.

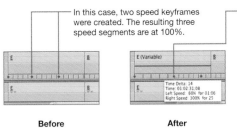

In this case, two speed keyframes were created. The resulting three speed segments are at 100%.

Shift-dragging this keyframe to the right slows the first speed segment and lengthens its duration. The second speed segment remains at 100%; its duration and content stay the same as it slides to the right. The third segment also stays at 100%, but its duration shortens as it slides under Clip E's Out point.

Before   After

NOTE ▶ Pause the pointer over a keyframe or segment to see the current settings displayed in the tooltip.

Changing Speed Segments (Keyframes)

Another way to adjust speed segments is with the shortcut menu.

1 Control-click the speed segment (between two keyframes) or the speed keyframe to the right of the segment.

New Feature

2   From the shortcut menu, choose Change Speed Segment to set
    the speed via the Change Speed Segment dialog.

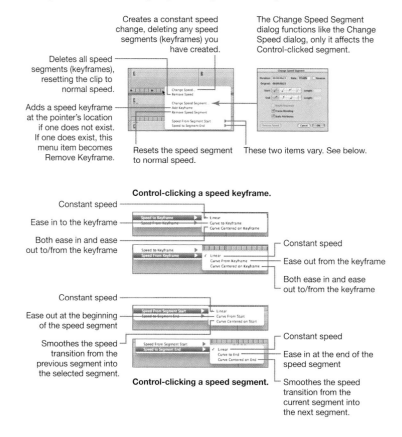

Creates a constant speed change, deleting any speed segments (keyframes) you have created.

The Change Speed Segment dialog functions like the Change Speed dialog, only it affects the Control-clicked segment.

Deletes all speed segments (keyframes), resetting the clip to normal speed.

Adds a speed keyframe at the pointer's location if one does not exist. If one does exist, this menu item becomes Remove Keyframe.

Resets the speed segment to normal speed.

These two items vary. See below.

Control-clicking a speed keyframe.

Constant speed

Ease in to the keyframe

Both ease in and ease out to/from the keyframe

Constant speed

Ease out from the keyframe

Both ease in and ease out to/from the keyframe

Constant speed

Ease out at the beginning of the speed segment

Smoothes the speed transition from the previous segment into the selected segment.

Constant speed

Ease in at the end of the speed segment

Control-clicking a speed segment.

Smoothes the speed transition from the current segment into the next segment.

Speed Keyframes in the Motion Tab

Keyframing using the Speed parameter of the Motion tab is an alternative to keyframing in the Timeline.

1   Arrange the Viewer to show the Speed keyframe graph area in
    the Motion tab.

New Feature

2 With the Pen tool or Option-clicking with the Selection tool, click the graph to create keyframes, and adjust as desired.

The *y* value equals the frame number from the source media. Zero at the bottom is the first frame. In this case, the last available frame is number 538 (shown here at the top of the y-axis).

The *x* value equals the playback time of the clip (displayed as sequence timecode for a sequence clip).

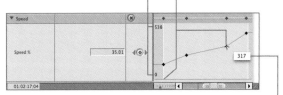

After a keyframe is created, the pointer becomes a crosshair that allows you to adjust a keyframe. Dragging a keyframe up or down, as shown here, changes the frame played at that moment within the clip's playback duration. Dragging a keyframe left or right changes when a specific frame appears within the clip's duration.

Holding down Shift while dragging displays both the playback time delta amount and the source frame number.

Control-click a keyframe and choose Smooth to create Bezier handles. These handles allow you to adjust the ease in and ease out from the keyframe. Hold down Command-Shift while dragging the blue Bezier handles to modify each independently.

Freeze frame
Flat line indicating no frame change.

Reverse playback
The steeper the angle, the faster the playback.

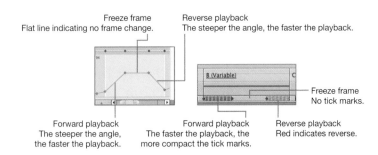

Freeze frame
No tick marks.

Forward playback
The steeper the angle, the faster the playback.

Forward playback
The faster the playback, the more compact the tick marks.

Reverse playback
Red indicates reverse.

11
Keyframing

Keyframing is the process of locking in a parameter's value at a specific point in time—that time being somewhere within the duration of a clip. Keyframes let you create an animation (or in the case of audio, automation). Start with one keyframe at a specific point in time with a parameter set to a starting value. Add a second keyframe at a different point in time with a new value for the parameter, and you have an animation. By creating additional keyframes with various values at different points in time, you can create more-advanced animations.

Keyframing in the Viewer

There are three ways to keyframe in the Viewer, through the following:

▶ Ins/Del Keyframe buttons

▶ Keyframe graph

▶ Add Motion Keyframe button

> **NOTE ▶** Refer to the "Canvas" section later in this chapter for information on the Add Motion Keyframe button.

Ins/Del Keyframe Button

Most parameters in the Controls, Filters, and Motion tabs have an
Ins/Del Keyframe button. You will also find this button in the audio
tabs and tabs specific to certain filters (for example, the Chroma
Keyer and Color Corrector).

1 Load a sequence or master clip into the Viewer.

2 Select the tab containing the parameters to be keyframed.

3 Move the playhead to the desired animation point.

> **NOTE ▶** If you have loaded a sequence clip, moving the Timeline
> playhead will move the Viewer's playhead. If this is a master clip,
> you may wish to "rip" the video tab out of the Viewer so that you
> can find the correct frame to receive the keyframe while viewing
> the parameters in the Viewer.

4 Adjust the parameter(s) as desired for the playhead's location;
then create a keyframe.

Adjust the parameter using the controls provided (slider, dial, swatch box, text field, and so on).

Click the Ins/Del Keyframe button. The diamond turns green when a keyframe exists at the playhead.

5 Cue the playhead to another point in time.

6 Adjust the parameter, and Final Cut Pro automatically creates
another keyframe.

Moving the playhead after setting the first keyframe, then changing the parameter's value, automatically creates another keyframe.

Cues the playhead to the parameter's previous keyframe.

Cues the playhead to the parameter's next keyframe (when one exists).

NOTE ▶ If you did not move the playhead in step 5, you will be adjusting the same keyframe rather than creating an additional keyframe.

7   Repeat steps 5 and 6 as necessary to create the number of keyframes required for the desired animation/automation.

TIP ▶ To create an animation/automation, you will need to create a minimum of two keyframes.

NOTE ▶ You may use the Viewer to delete keyframes as well.

Clicking the Reset button clears all keyframes while resetting parameters to their default values for the respective parameter group. In this case, keyframes and values for Scale, Rotation, Center, and Anchor Point would be reset.

Cue the playhead to a keyframe you need to delete, and then click the green Ins/Del Keyframe button. The diamond becomes clear. Also, the parameter's value changes to the value of the previous keyframe or interpolation of the keyframe values before and after the playhead. If no other keyframes exist, the value remains constant.

Keyframe Graph

Rather than using the Ins/Del Keyframe button, use the keyframe graph to create keyframes with the Pen tool.

TIP ▶ The keyframe graph is at the top of the tab for effects that utilize a separate tab (for example, the Color Corrector and Chroma Keyer).

NOTE ▶ This method may not be used on parameters that have two or more values (for example, Center and Anchor Point).

1   Load a sequence or master clip into the Viewer.

2   Select the tab containing the parameters to be keyframed.

3 Adjust the Viewer window so that you can see the keyframe graph.

In this case, a sequence clip was loaded. This time
ruler and playhead represent the Timeline's values.

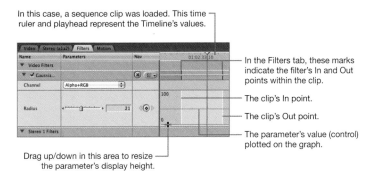

In the Filters tab, these marks
indicate the filter's In and Out
points within the clip.

The clip's In point.

The clip's Out point.

The parameter's value (control)
plotted on the graph.

Drag up/down in this area to resize
the parameter's display height.

4 Cue the playhead to the desired frame for a keyframe.

NOTE ▶ This method does not require you to cue the playhead,
but it does lend itself to more precision.

5 Create the keyframe by clicking with the Pen tool in the graph.
Set the parameter value by dragging the keyframe up or down.

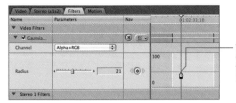

With the Pen tool or by
Option-clicking with the Selection
tool, click the parameter's control
in the graph to create a keyframe.

6 Repeat step 5 as needed to create the desired animation/automation.

There are a few more adjustments you can make, depending on the
parameter you are adjusting.

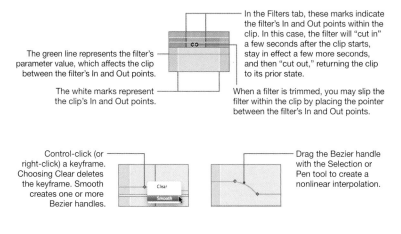

The green line represents the filter's parameter value, which affects the clip between the filter's In and Out points.

In the Filters tab, these marks indicate the filter's In and Out points within the clip. In this case, the filter will "cut in" a few seconds after the clip starts, stay in effect a few more seconds, and then "cut out," returning the clip to its prior state.

The white marks represent the clip's In and Out points.

When a filter is trimmed, you may slip the filter within the clip by placing the pointer between the filter's In and Out points.

Control-click (or right-click) a keyframe. Choosing Clear deletes the keyframe. Smooth creates one or more Bezier handles.

Drag the Bezier handle with the Selection or Pen tool to create a nonlinear interpolation.

NOTE ▶ Use the Ins/Del Keyframe button, described in the previous section, to insert or delete keyframes under the playhead.

Keyframing in the Timeline

There are two methods for keyframing in the Timeline, through

▶ Clip Overlays

▶ Clip Keyframes

Clip Overlays adjusts video opacity or audio levels directly on each clip. Clip Keyframes opens the Keyframe Editor below each clip, which allows you to choose from parameters assigned to the clip.

Clip Overlays

This method can affect only a clip's opacity or audio level.

1 Click the Clip Overlays button at the bottom left of the Timeline.

Video Opacity

Audio Level
For more about keyframing audio levels, see Chapter 7.
The process is similar to what is described here.

Clip Overlays

2 With the Pen tool or by Option-clicking with the Selection tool, click the clip's control line to create a keyframe. Repeat as necessary.

The Pen tool is visible only when the pointer is on the control line.

TIP You need a minimum of two keyframes to create an animation/automation. The distance between keyframes determines the animation/automation's speed—closer together yields a faster value change over a shorter period of time.

3 Move the pointer over a keyframe. When the pointer changes to a crosshair, drag the keyframe as desired.

When the crosshair appears, drag left or right to adjust the timing of the keyframe. As shown here, dragging up or down changes the opacity value. Press Command while dragging to "gear down" the value changes.

The opacity keyframe interpolation may be altered to give a non-linear adjustment.

Control-click an opacity keyframe and choose Smooth. Choosing Clear deletes the keyframe.

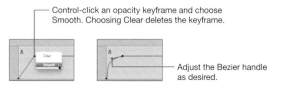

Adjust the Bezier handle as desired.

NOTE ▶ Zooming in on the clip (Option-+) can help you precisely position the keyframe. If you need to drag a keyframe free of the snapping feature, temporarily disable snapping by pressing N momentarily while dragging a keyframe.

Clip Keyframes

Various parameters may be keyframed via Clip Keyframes; however, you must choose which parameter will be keyframed, because you can keyframe only one parameter at a time.

NOTE ▶ This method may not be used on parameters that have two or more values (for example, Center and Anchor Point).

1   Click the Clip Keyframes button at the bottom left of the Timeline.

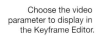

Drag up or down over this thin column to change the height of the Keyframe Editor.

Keyframe Editor

Speed tick marks (see Chapter 10 for more information)

Clip Keyframes

2   Control-click (or right-click) in the Keyframe Editor to choose the parameter for keyframing.

Choose the video parameter to display in the Keyframe Editor.

Choose the audio parameter to display in the Keyframe Editor.

NOTE ▶ If the clip has filters applied, keyframeable parameters (with single axis representation) may appear above the options shown.

3   Click the graph with the Pen tool to create a keyframe. Create
additional keyframes as needed. Adjust as desired.

The green bar with
diamonds indicates that
a filter has been applied
and keyframed. The
blue bar and diamonds
indicate that a Motion
parameter has been
adjusted and keyframed.

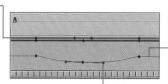

With the Pen tool or by
Option-clicking with
the Selection tool, click
the parameter's control
in the graph to create a
keyframe.

Some parameters may be adjusted by adding a Bezier
handle. Control-click and choose Smooth. Adjust the blue
Bezier handles as desired. Holding down Command-Shift
while adjusting a Bezier handle allows you to adjust one
handle independently when a pair is present.

NOTE ▶ You can delete keyframes in the Keyframe Editor.

Control-click a clip and choose Remove Attributes (Command-Option-V).
In the Remove Attributes dialog, choose the category of parameter keyframes
you wish to delete. In this case, any parameter changes made to the Basic Motion
parameters (Scale, Rotation, Center, and Anchor Point) will be cleared.

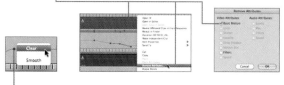

Control-click and choose Clear
to delete a single keyframe.

Keyframing in the Canvas

Keyframing in the Canvas involves using the Add Motion Keyframe
button and graphically adjusting parameters of the Motion tab, specifically Basic Motion, Crop (except for Edge Feather), and Distort.

Add Motion Keyframe Button

1   Cue the Canvas/Timeline playhead to the clip frame needing a
keyframe.

2   Choose Image + Wireframe or Wireframe from the Canvas
Display pop-up menu.

If your animation involves flying or sliding
videos on- or offscreen, you will want to
set the Canvas zoom to something lower
than the "Fit to Window" setting.

Canvas Display pop-up menu

The default image setting does not allow
the Canvas to be used for manipulating
Basic Motion, Crop, or Distort parameters.

Allows you to see the video output of the
sequence while manipulating parameters
via a wireframe box that overlays the image.

Displays only wireframes
of the clips while allowing
for parameter adjustment.

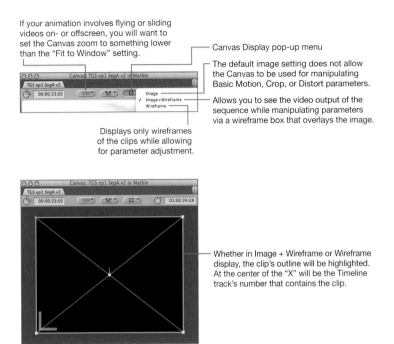

Whether in Image + Wireframe or Wireframe
display, the clip's outline will be highlighted.
At the center of the "X" will be the Timeline
track's number that contains the clip.

NOTE ▶ Wireframe mode is used here in the book to simplify
the images.

3   Select the appropriate tool, and adjust the parameters as desired.

 With the Selection tool on a wireframe's corner points, the pointer becomes a
crosshair. Drag toward the center to proportionally scale down or away from the
center to scale up. Holding down Shift while dragging changes the aspect.

 With the Selection tool to the side of a wireframe's corner point, drag to rotate when
the rotation arrow appears. Use the Distort tool below to change the anchor point
around which the rotation occurs.

 With the Crop tool (C), drag a side of the wireframe to crop one side. Command-
dragging a side changes the opposite side simultaneously. Dragging a corner point
changes the two adjacent sides, while Command-dragging a corner point changes
all sides simultaneously.

 With the Selection tool anywhere over a clip other than the edges or center, the
pointer becomes the Move tool. Drag to change the Center point.

 With the Distort tool on the center of the wireframe, drag to adjust the anchor
point. The Distort tool may also be used on corner points. Use along with the
Shift key to adjust two points at once.

4 Set a keyframe with the Add Motion Keyframe button.

Clicking the Add Motion Keyframe button (Control-K) selects Keyframe All automatically. Control-clicking the button allows you to select which parameter receives a keyframe.

TIP ▶ Parts of the clip's wireframe change color when keyframes are set. If Scale is set, the "X" goes green. When Center is keyframed, the center square of the "X" goes green. Keyframes for Distort turns the corner points green, and Crop Keyframes makes the crop lines blue.

NOTE ▶ While parked on a keyframe, Control-clicking the Add Motion Keyframe button displays a checkmark next to parameters keyframed under the playhead. Choosing a selected parameter deselects it and deletes the associated keyframe at the playhead.

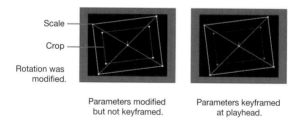

Scale

Crop

Rotation was modified.

Parameters modified but not keyframed.

Parameters keyframed at playhead.

5 Cue the playhead to the next frame for keyframing.

6 Adjust the parameters as desired. If you adjust a parameter that was previously keyframed, Final Cut Pro will automatically create another keyframe at the current frame.

NOTE ▶ If a keyframe does not exist for the parameter, you will need to set keyframes for that parameter. Cue the playhead and set the parameter as necessary; then Control-click the Add Motion Keyframe button to set a keyframe for the specific parameter.

TIP ▶ Use the Viewer's Motion tab and its various ways of setting/adjusting keyframes in conjunction with the Canvas's Add Motion Keyframe.

Modifying Motion Paths in the Canvas

When you animate the Center parameter over time, you create a motion path. Keyframing in the Canvas allows you to modify the path, adding arcs and Ease In/Ease Out, even if the animation was created first in the Viewer.

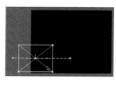

A simple motion path created by setting two center keyframes a couple of seconds apart.

Command-drag the wireframe to move the entire motion path.

Use the Ease In/Ease Out handles to adjust the rate used for the center point to arrive/depart the keyframe. The closer the center dots on the motion path, the slower the movement.

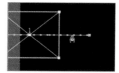

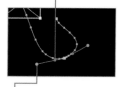

Moving the pointer over the motion path activates the Pen tool. Click to make a new center keyframe.

Drag the keyframe to a new location in the Canvas to modify the motion path.

Use the Bezier handles to adjust the arc. Command-Shift-dragging allows independent adjustment.

TIP ▶ Cue the playhead so that you can clearly see the center keyframe you wish to adjust. You may want to switch the Canvas display to Wireframe so that the keyframes are easier to see.

NOTE ▶ You can change motion path corners into curves and set deceleration/acceleration by Control-clicking the keyframe and choosing the desired option from the shortcut menu. Another option while Control-clicking is deleting a keyframe.

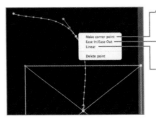

"Make corner point" removes the Bezier handles, and therefore this portion of the arc in the motion path.

Ease In/Ease Out creates a curve using Bezier handles with deceleration and acceleration applied.

Linear creates a curve using Bezier handles, but with constant speed.

12

Generators and Templates

Generators, such as black clip, text, and color bars, are created within Final Cut Pro. Some of these are utility items (such as color bars for equipment setup), while others are for creative purposes (such as creating textual lower thirds). Master templates from Motion also are accessible via the Generators pop-up menu.

If a generator has adjustable parameters, the Controls tab appears when the generator clip is in the Viewer.

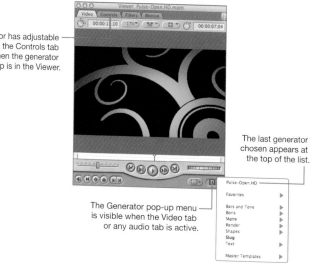

The last generator chosen appears at the top of the list.

The Generator pop-up menu is visible when the Video tab or any audio tab is active.

Using Generators

You access generators in the Effects tab of the Browser or by clicking the Generators pop-up menu in the lower right of the Viewer.

1   Click the Generators pop-up menu, and choose the desired generator or template. The item will load into the Viewer.

2   Click the Controls tab of the Viewer to modify the parameters of the generator or template.

3   Edit the generator or template into your sequence, or drag the item to the Browser to save for later use.

> **NOTE** ▶ Generators and templates are temporary items when they reside in the Viewer. Double-clicking any other clip will dump the generator or template out of the Viewer—deleting any customization you may have performed. So that you don't lose your work, edit the generator or template into your sequence, or add it to your active project.

Bars and Tone

Used for calibrating equipment, bars and tone are available in a variety of test patterns.

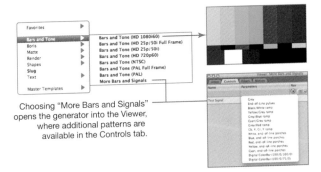

Choosing "More Bars and Signals" opens the generator into the Viewer, where additional patterns are available in the Controls tab.

> **NOTE** ▶ Most generators are automatically created at the frame size of the active sequence. Bars and tone, however, are an exception. You must choose the appropriate test pattern size.

Boris

The Boris option in the Generators pop-up menu gives access to the Boris Calligraphy plug-ins included with Final Cut Pro.

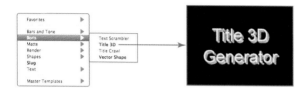

Example: Title 3D

The Title 3D option lets you create text for use in full-screen graphics or as lower thirds.

After choosing Title 3D from the Generator pop-up menu, click the Controls tab.

Then, click the "Title 3D Click for options" button to access the Title 3D interface.

The Text tab lets you make typography changes. Select the characters or word above that you wish to modify before adjusting the parameters in the tabs.

Choose your font and size from these pop-up menus and value field.

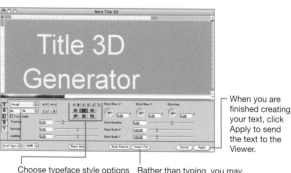

When you are finished creating your text, click Apply to send the text to the Viewer.

Choose typeface style options and global justifications.

Rather than typing, you may import a text document.

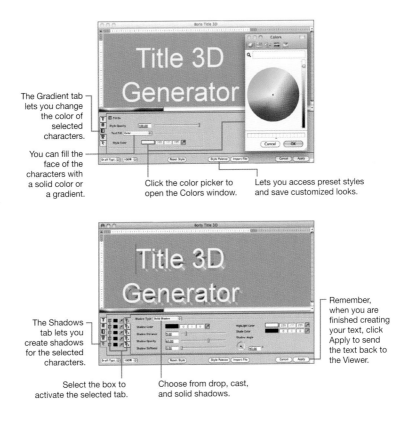

The Gradient tab lets you change the color of selected characters.

You can fill the face of the characters with a solid color or a gradient.

Click the color picker to open the Colors window.

Lets you access preset styles and save customized looks.

The Shadows tab lets you create shadows for the selected characters.

Remember, when you are finished creating your text, click Apply to send the text back to the Viewer.

Select the box to activate the selected tab.

Choose from drop, cast, and solid shadows.

TIP ▶ For more information regarding the other Boris Calligraphy plug-ins, see the Boris Calligraphy User Guide in the Documentation folder on the Final Cut Studio Install DVD.

Matte

When you need to create a solid color as a background or a background stripe (bar) to place behind text, the Matte generator is an option. There are two Matte generators: Color and Color Solid. Color is the original generator from earlier versions of Final Cut Pro. Color Solid is an FxPlug that is available when Motion is installed. Both achieve the same visual results and have the same single parameter in the Controls tab.

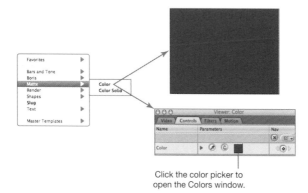

Click the color picker to
open the Colors window.

Render

The Render generators are design elements you can use for back-grounds, animations, and mattes. Each Render generator has parameters that are adjustable in the Controls tab. Some of these generators are FxPlugs and appear only if Motion is installed.

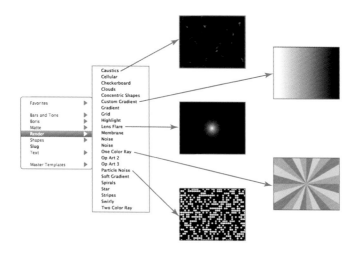

NOTE ▸ There are two Noise generators listed above. One is the original Final Cut Pro Noise generator; the second is the FxPlug version that is available when Motion is installed.

Shapes

You can create basic shapes for use as graphical elements or mattes with the Shapes generators.

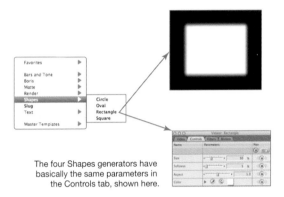

The four Shapes generators have basically the same parameters in the Controls tab, shown here.

NOTE ▶ Shapes do not contain an alpha channel. However, you may use the Luma Keyer or Travel Matte-Luma to composite these shapes with other clips. See Chapter 13 for more on compositing.

Slug

The Slug generator creates a clip with black video content and a pair of silent audio channels. Slugs can be used as a sequence clip placeholder or for fading to or from black within your sequence.

Edit a slug into a sequence as a placeholder. When you find the clip to exchange for the slug, perform a replace edit.

Before   **After**

Text

Several text generators are available, letting you quickly create simple, even animated, text.

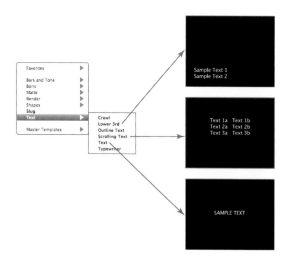

Example: Lower 3rd Text Generator

The Lower 3rd generator creates a two-line text graphic already posi-tioned on the lower left of the screen within title safe.

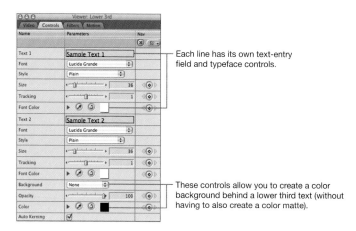

Each line has its own text-entry field and typeface controls.

These controls allow you to create a color background behind a lower third text (without having to also create a color matte).

Example: Scrolling Text Generator

This generator creates a simple, scrolling text effect often referred to as *movie-style credits*.

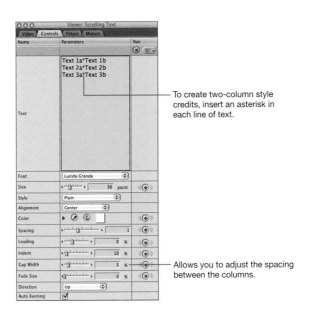

To create two-column style credits, insert an asterisk in each line of text.

Allows you to adjust the spacing between the columns.

Example: Text Generator

The Text generator lets you create simple text. This generator creates one-size, one-font, one-style text centered on the screen.

The typeface parameters apply to all characters.

To change the Origin point graphically, first click the crosshair in the Controls tab. Then, click in the Canvas or in the Viewer's Video tab.

Master Templates

Master templates are available if Motion and the Motion Content are installed. These templates let you alter parts of the template's animation, such as customizing text layers or substituting images for other layers, from within Final Cut Pro and without opening Motion.

Adding a Master Template

Accessing master templates via the Generator pop-up menu is handy if you know which template you need. To preview the master templates, choose Sequence > Add Master Template to open the Master Template Browser.

First, choose a theme from the Theme column.

Single-click a master template to view the QuickTime preview.

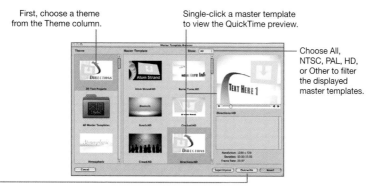

Choose All, NTSC, PAL, HD, or Other to filter the displayed master templates.

If the Timeline window is active when you open the Master Template Browser, these three options are available for editing the selected master template into the active sequence. If the Viewer window is active, click Open and the master template will load into the Viewer. You will then have to overwrite or insert edit the Master Template from the Viewer into your sequence.

Drag a video or still image clip to the clip well to replace the master template's drop zone. Drop zones only use a clip's source media (filters applied to the clip will not display).

With the master template loaded in the Viewer, use the Controls tab to customize the template's parameters.

Replace the placeholder text with your desired text.

You can modify the size and tracking of the text but not the overall design features, such as font typeface or color.

A master template or any Motion project file appears as a clip with the .motn extension in the Timeline and the Browser.

Modifying a Master Template

Design changes can be made to a master template by opening the template into Motion from Final Cut Pro. Begin by Control-clicking the clip in the sequence.

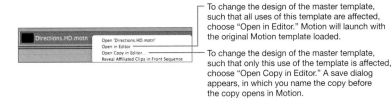

To change the design of the master template, such that all uses of this template are affected, choose "Open in Editor." Motion will launch with the original Motion template loaded.

To change the design of the master template, such that only this use of the template is affected, choose "Open Copy in Editor." A save dialog appears, in which you name the copy before the copy opens in Motion.

After you make your changes in Motion, choosing File > Save in Motion updates the master template clip(s) in Final Cut Pro.

Replacing a Master Template

A special replace edit is available to exchange templates already edited into a sequence. In some cases, you may have started with a barebones template before the look of the production's graphics was finalized. Final Cut Pro lets you update an in-use template with another template.

Start by dragging the new template from the Viewer over the existing sequence template; then pause for the overlay to appear.

Move the pointer here and release to change only this instance of a master template.

Move the pointer here and release to change all instances of this template within this sequence.

Move the pointer here and release to change all instances of this template within the active project.

13

Compositing

Having 99 tracks per sequence gives you many options for "going vertical"—stacking clips in higher tracks to create effects that blend those layers of clips together. Compositing is the act of blending clips to create an effect. Compositing can involve a combination of opacity adjustments, filters (such as keys and mattes), or composite modes.

To keep things manageable, Final Cut Pro lets you create nests that collapse a multitrack effect into a single clip.

> **TIP** When compositing in Final Cut Pro, keep in mind that Final Cut Pro is a top-down compositor. The highest clip in the Timeline is processed as the foreground. Adjusting opacity, applying a filter, or changing a composite mode is usually applied to the higher clip to reveal the background clip underneath.

Changing Opacity

A simple way to blend video clips is to make them partially transparent. You can adjust and even keyframe a clip's opacity in the Viewer or Timeline. For more details on keyframing, see Chapter 11.

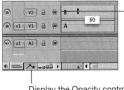

Drag the Opacity control down with the Selection tool to increase transparency, mixing the two images together. Depending on the zoom level and track heights of the Timeline, not every value may be accessible. Holding down Command while dragging the control "gears down" the step amount to show more values. Use the Pen tool to keyframe if desired.

Display the Opacity controls by turning Clip Overlays on.

Layering Filters

Final Cut Pro has filters that create or modify the transparency of a clip. This transparency (or alpha channel) specifies what portions of a clip are opaque or transparent. There are three categories of these filters in Final Cut Pro:

▶ Key filters (or keyers)

▶ Mattes

▶ Masks

Key Filters

The key filters found under Effects > Video Filters > Key create transparency based on the grayscale of an image (Luma Key) or its color values (Chroma Keyer).

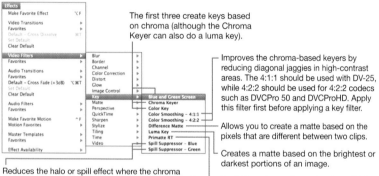

The first three create keys based on chroma (although the Chroma Keyer can also do a luma key).

Improves the chroma-based keyers by reducing diagonal jaggies in high-contrast areas. The 4:1:1 should be used with DV-25, while 4:2:2 should be used for 4:2:2 codecs such as DVCPro 50 and DVCProHD. Apply this filter first before applying a key filter.

Allows you to create a matte based on the pixels that are different between two clips.

Creates a matte based on the brightest or darkest portions of an image.

An FxPlug chroma keyer that is available when Motion is installed.

Reduces the halo or spill effect where the chroma key color leaves some fringing around the foreground image. The respective filter should be applied after the applied chroma key filter.

Example: Chroma Keyer

The Chroma Keyer is a filter that appears in the Filters tab of the Viewer once applied to a clip, but it also has its own graphical interface tab.

1 Cue the playhead over the sequence clip, and then load that clip into the Viewer.

> **TIP** If you have not stacked the chroma key clip above your intended background clip in the sequence, you may want to do that now to see the results while adjusting the filter.

2 Apply the Chroma Keyer from the Effects tab or by choosing Effects > Video Filters > Key > Chroma Keyer.

3 Open the Viewer's Chroma Keyer tab, click the Select Color eyedropper, and then click in the Canvas on the color to remove.

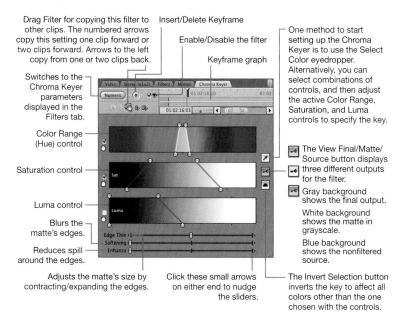

Drag Filter for copying this filter to other clips. The numbered arrows copy this setting one clip forward or two clips forward. Arrows to the left copy from one or two clips back.

Insert/Delete Keyframe

Enable/Disable the filter

Keyframe graph

Switches to the Chroma Keyer parameters displayed in the Filters tab.

Color Range (Hue) control

Saturation control

Luma control

Blurs the matte's edges.

Reduces spill around the edges.

Adjusts the matte's size by contracting/expanding the edges.

Click these small arrows on either end to nudge the sliders.

One method to start setting up the Chroma Keyer is to use the Select Color eyedropper. Alternatively, you can select combinations of controls, and then adjust the active Color Range, Saturation, and Luma controls to specify the key.

The View Final/Matte/Source button displays three different outputs for the filter.

Gray background shows the final output.

White background shows the matte in grayscale.

Blue background shows the nonfiltered source.

The Invert Selection button inverts the key to affect all colors other than the one chosen with the controls.

> **TIP** Shift-clicking with the Select Color eyedropper lets you expand the selection.

4 Adjust the Color Range, Saturation, and Luma controls as needed.

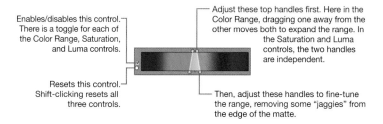

Enables/disables this control. There is a toggle for each of the Color Range, Saturation, and Luma controls.

Adjust these top handles first. Here in the Color Range, dragging one away from the other moves both to expand the range. In the Saturation and Luma controls, the two handles are independent.

Resets this control. Shift-clicking resets all three controls.

Then, adjust these handles to fine-tune the range, removing some "jaggies" from the edge of the matte.

5 Adjust the Edge Thin, Softening, and Enhance sliders as desired.

TIP Depending on your source content, you may need to add filters, such as Matte Choker or Spill Suppressor.

NOTE ▶ Although green or blue is typically used for a chroma key, the Chroma Keyer can remove pixels based on chroma or luma, allowing you to create some interesting composites.

Mattes

In some cases, you may want to create transparency based on a shape. That's when the mattes found under Effects > Video Filters > Matte are used. The mattes may be used to create or modify an alpha channel based on a custom shape or an existing matte.

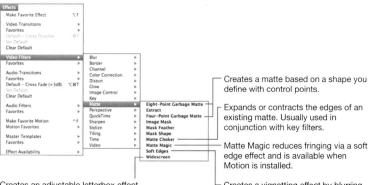

Creates a matte based on a shape you define with control points.

Expands or contracts the edges of an existing matte. Usually used in conjunction with key filters.

Matte Magic reduces fringing via a soft edge effect and is available when Motion is installed.

Creates an adjustable letterbox effect.

Creates a vignetting effect by blurring the four edges.

Example: Four-Point Garbage Matte

A *garbage matte* lets you "draw" the matte in the Viewer or Canvas. A garbage matte may be used to crop out unwanted material or to limit an effect to an area of a frame.

> **TIP** ▶ The four-point and eight-point garbage mattes are similar in operation. The eight-point garbage matte has the advantage of more control points for creating more complex mattes.

1 Cue the playhead over the sequence clip, and then load that clip into the Viewer.

> **TIP** ▶ Cueing the Timeline playhead lets you see the results in the Canvas. Otherwise, you will need to "rip" the Video tab out of the Viewer.

2 Apply a garbage matte to the clip.

3 Adjust the matte's points to enclose the "good" part of the image.

Preview displays the matte points with labels. Switching to Final removes the point overlays. Wireframe overlays the matte's edges and points over the clip.

As with most parameters in the Filters and Motion tabs, you may keyframe individual points to animate the matte.

To adjust a point, click the point's crosshair first, and then drag in the Canvas to where you want the point. You cannot pick up the point at its current location in the Canvas. If you release the point, you must click the point's crosshair in the Viewer before attempting to move the point in the Canvas.

Use these three controls to modify the matte's edges.

The matte, by default, retains content inside the matte shape by making pixels outside the matte's shape transparent. Selecting Invert reverses the areas of transparency.

Masks

Masks let you create or modify an alpha channel based on an image or shape.

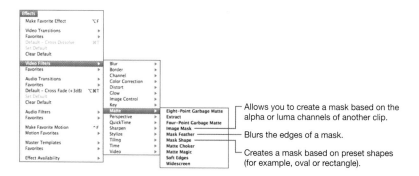

Allows you to create a mask based on the alpha or luma channels of another clip.

Blurs the edges of a mask.

Creates a mask based on preset shapes (for example, oval or rectangle).

Example: Image Mask

The Image Mask filter creates an alpha channel for a clip based on the alpha channel or luminance of another clip. This could be a video clip or a custom-drawn shape (such as a logo created in Motion).

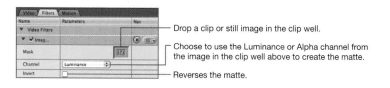

Drop a clip or still image in the clip well.

Choose to use the Luminance or Alpha channel from the image in the clip well above to create the matte.

Reverses the matte.

Composite Modes

Composite modes combine the pixels of the two (or more) clips in a variety of mathematical ways. These clips are stacked vertically within a sequence.

> **NOTE ▶** Depending on the video content, the presence of an alpha channel or matte, and the composite modes used, the effect created may pass through to affect clips stacked below. See the "Nesting" section, later in this chapter, for information on how to contain a compositing effect.

Applying a Composite Mode

Compositing clips in Final Cut Pro follows the video track hierarchical order of top-down processing—apply the composite mode to the clip on top of the clips you wish to blend.

1   Control-click (or right-click) the top clip in a stack of two (or more) clips you wish to blend.

2   In the shortcut menu, choose from the Composite Mode submenu.

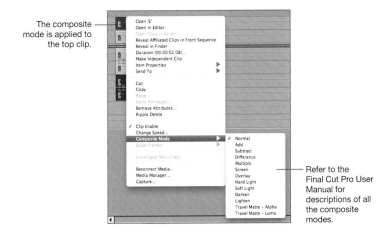

The composite mode is applied to the top clip.

Refer to the Final Cut Pro User Manual for descriptions of all the composite modes.

Example: Travel Matte – Luma

Similar to the Luma Key, the Travel Matte – Luma creates a matte based on the luma of the matte clip. In this example, the Travel Matte – Luma is used to create a gradient stripe plate for a lower third.

TIP You may use the luma of any clip as the matte. Click the Generators pop-up menu in the Viewer and look under Render for additional matte clip options (see Chapter 12 for more information).

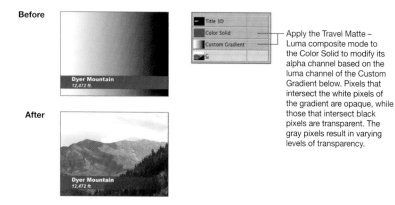

Before

After

Apply the Travel Matte – Luma composite mode to the Color Solid to modify its alpha channel based on the luma channel of the Custom Gradient below. Pixels that intersect the white pixels of the gradient are opaque, while those that intersect black pixels are transparent. The gray pixels result in varying levels of transparency.

TIP ▶ The Travel Matte – Alpha works much the same way, but the cutout is based on the matte clip's alpha channel.

Nesting

Nesting lets you group clips together into a single container within a sequence. These containers simplify moving composited effects, but also protect other sequence clips from the effects of a composite mode applied higher up. Nests can be created with clips already edited within a sequence or by dragging a sequence inside another sequence.

Clips Within a Sequence

You may wish to nest clips within a sequence in order to treat them as one clip. For example, creating a nest lets you apply a filter once to the nest, and the filter will affect all of the clips within the nest.

1   Select the sequence clips to be nested.

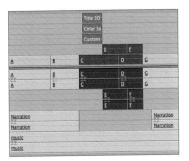

2   Choose Sequence > Nest Item(s) (or press Option-C).

3   Name the nest (sequence) you are about to create, and click OK.

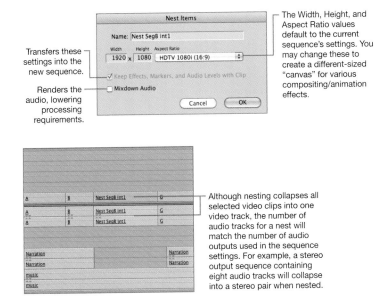

Transfers these settings into the new sequence.

Renders the audio, lowering processing requirements.

The Width, Height, and Aspect Ratio values default to the current sequence's settings. You may change these to create a different-sized "canvas" for various compositing/animation effects.

Although nesting collapses all selected video clips into one video track, the number of audio tracks for a nest will match the number of audio outputs used in the sequence settings. For example, a stereo output sequence containing eight audio tracks will collapse into a stereo pair when nested.

Double-click the nest to access the individual clips inside a nested sequence. The nest then opens into a separate sequence tab.

TIP Changes made inside a nested sequence are "hot" and will update the original "parent" sequence.

NOTE ▸ After you create a nest, you may wish to apply a filter to it. Option–double-click the nest sequence in the Browser or Timeline to load the sequence into the Viewer. Then apply filters as you would to any other clip sequence.

Sequence Within a Sequence

You can edit the scenes or segments of a project in separate sequences, and then use the nesting feature to compile the sequences into one sequence that represents the final product.

1   After creating individual sequences for various segments, create a new sequence.

2   Drag the segment sequences individually from the Browser to the Timeline to perform an overwrite or insert edit.

NOTE ▸ You may load a sequence into the Viewer to mark In and/or Out points before nesting the sequence.

TIP ▸ If you need to share an EDL/OMF of the sequence or media-manage the project, nesting may provide inaccurate timecode or mangled media. You can perform an un-nest when editing a sequence into another sequence by holding down Command while releasing the nest as an overwrite or insert edit (if dragging).

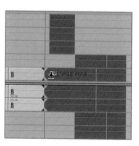

14
Output

Final Cut Pro supports output to many destination media, including iPods, Blu-ray discs, videotapes, and media files.

Rendering

Several variables affect Final Cut Pro's ability to play back a sequence in real time: RT pop-up menu settings, the editing system's hardware (CPU, RAM, video interface, and storage speed), the sequence and clip settings/codecs, and the number and types of applied effects. Whether Final Cut Pro is requiring a render or you want to force a render to see an effect at a higher quality, there are three ways to render:

▶ Render Selected

▶ Render All

▶ Render Only

> **NOTE** ▶ By default, rendering occurs at 100 percent quality and frame rate. You may alter those settings in the Render Control tab from the Sequence > Settings of the active sequence.

Render Selected

You may select sequence clips for rendering rather than rendering an entire sequence. Rendering selected sequence clips can save time during an edit session, as you specify the clips to be rendered.

1 Select the sequence clip(s) you wish to render.

2 In the Sequence > Render Selection menu, verify that the appropriate render status bar colors are selected.

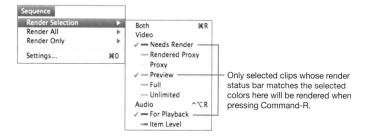

NOTE ► You may set sequence In and Out points around the clips you wish to render rather than selecting the clips.

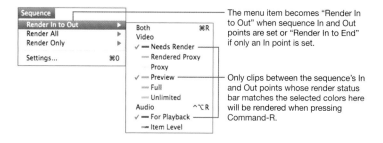

3 Press Command-R to start rendering of the selected clips.

You may cancel an in-progress render. Sequence content that has been rendered will be retained.

Render All

Use the Render All command if you need to render the entire sequence. The clips that will render must have a render status bar color that is selected in the Sequence > Render All menu.

1 Either make the sequence active in the Timeline or select the sequence(s) in the Browser.

2 In the Sequence > Render All menu, verify that the appropriate render status bar colors are selected.

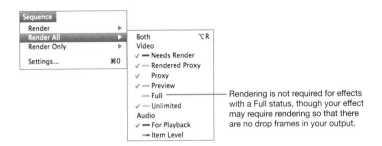

Rendering is not required for effects
with a Full status, though your effect
may require rendering so that there
are no drop frames in your output.

3 Press Option-R to start the rendering process.

Render Only

Use the Render Only command to render sequence content with a
specified render status color.

1 If desired, select sequence clips or mark In and Out points
around the content you wish to render; otherwise, clips with the
matching render status color throughout the entire sequence will
be rendered.

2 From the Sequence > Render Only menu, choose the render status bar color to start rendering.

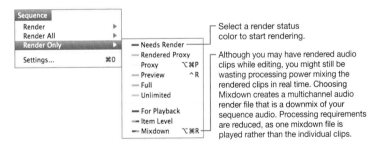

Select a render status
color to start rendering.

Although you may have rendered audio
clips while editing, you might still be
wasting processing power mixing the
rendered clips in real time. Choosing
Mixdown creates a multichannel audio
render file that is a downmix of your
sequence audio. Processing requirements
are reduced, as one mixdown file is
played rather than the individual clips.

Audio Peaks

When you get ready to output your sequence, there is a handy last-
minute check for audio that is too "hot." With no clips selected in the
active sequence, choose Mark > Audio Peaks > Mark.

1   Deselect all clips in the active sequence.

> You may perform this analysis on a master clip or sequence clip by selecting it.

2   Select Mark > Audio Peaks > Mark.

Final Cut Pro will analyze the sequence's mix level, setting Audio Peak markers in the Time Ruler and Canvas on frames where the audio peaks occur.

3   Adjust the clip levels in the sequence while monitoring the audio meters to remove the audio peaks.

4   With no clips selected in the active sequence, again choose Mark > Audio Peaks > Mark.

> You do not need to choose Clear from the Mark > Audio Peaks menu. The Mark > Audio Peaks > Mark command resets the Audio Peak markers before checking for peaks.

5   If your audio mix does not peak, you will receive a confirmation dialog. Click OK.

No audio peaks were detected.

OK

Broadcast Safe

By the time you reach this output stage, you have probably color-corrected your sequence with the Color Corrector 3-way (see Chapter 9) or the application Color (see Chapter 15). But sometimes you may be on a rush edit (like almost every edit for a newscast) and need to make some wild video "broadcast legal." Select the offending sequence clips and choose Effects > Video Filters > Color Correction > Broadcast Safe. Although not the best solution because illegal white levels are clipped off, which causes the video to lose detail, this filter will get the edit done.

Share

File > Share opens the Share window, which gives access to the batch transcoding features of Compressor. Simply choose the presets for your output type, define a destination for saving the output, and click Export. You do not have to calculate bit rates or frame sizes. Because Share is built on Compressor, you can create custom settings in Compressor that are available in the Share window of Final Cut Pro.

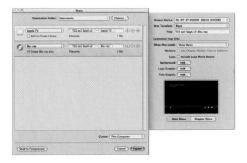

> **TIP** Once you have "shared" a sequence, you may continue editing that sequence within Final Cut Pro while the export is processing.

Starting Share with a Single Item

Before you can assign presets, you will need to define source clips or sequences for processing.

1   Make a selection of a Browser clip, a Browser sequence, or the active Timeline sequence (by making the Timeline window active with the sequence as the front, active tab).

> **TIP** Share honors any clip or sequence In and Out points.

2   Choose File > Share.

3   Modify the Share window settings as desired before clicking Export at the bottom of the window.

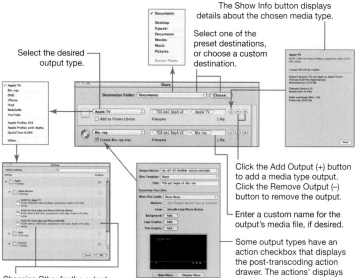

The Show Info button displays details about the chosen media type.

Select one of the preset destinations, or choose a custom destination.

Select the desired output type.

Click the Add Output (+) button to add a media type output. Click the Remove Output (–) button to remove the output.

Enter a custom name for the output's media file, if desired.

Some output types have an action checkbox that displays the post-transcoding action drawer. The actions' displays vary by output type.

Choosing Other for the output type opens Compressor's Settings window. Select the desired media type, and then click OK. Select the respective In Menu box to add the setting to the Share Output Type pop-up menu.

Example: Share for iPod

Choose iPod from the Output Type pop-up menu.

Selecting the action box displays the post-transcoding action drawer.

From the "Add to Playlist" pop-up menu, choose the iTunes playlist to which the output type's media file should be added. If a playlist does not appear, choose Refresh.

Example: Share for DVD

Choose DVD from the
Output Type pop-up menu.

Choose the destination device
for the output file: an attached
optical drive or hard drive.

Choose a menu template:
Black or White. The template
is previewed below.

Enter a title for
the DVD.

Choose a first
play action for
the DVD:
Show Menu or
Play Movie.

Create subtitles
from the Name
field of sequence
chapter markers.

Add a
background
image to the
main menu.

Selecting the action box
displays the post-transcoding
action drawer.

Previews the main menu.

Previews the chapter menu
created from chapter markers
in the sequence.

Example: Share for Blu-ray

Choose the destination device for the
output file: an attached optical drive
or hard drive. If only a SuperDrive is
available, you can burn an AVCHD
disc on standard DVD media for
AVCHD-compatible players.

Choose a menu template.
The template is previewed
below.

Choose Blue-ray from the
Output Type pop-up menu.

Enter a title for
the disc.

Choose a first
play action for
the DVD:
Show Menu or
Play Movie.

Create subtitles
from the Name
field of sequence
chapter markers.

Adds a loop
movie button to
the main menu.
Optional on
some templates.

Add a
background
image to the
menus.

Add a logo graphic to
the top right of the
main menu.

Add a graphic to the
main menu.

Selecting the action box
displays the post-transcoding
action drawer.

Previews the main menu.

Previews the chapter menu
created from chapter markers
in the sequence.

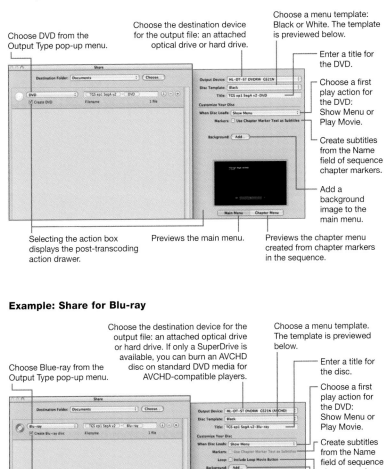

New Feature

Disc templates available for
the Blu-ray output type.

Example: Share for MobileMe

Choose MobileMe from the
Output Type pop-up menu.

Enter a MobileMe member name (do not
enter the @me.com or @mac.com domain).

Enter the MobileMe
account's passward.

Enter a name for
the movie file.

Enter a
description for
the movie file.

Denies access to
other MobileMe
Gallery files.

Makes the movie
file downloadable.

Controls access
to the movie file.
The options are
Everyone, Only
Me, and Edit
Names and
Passwords.

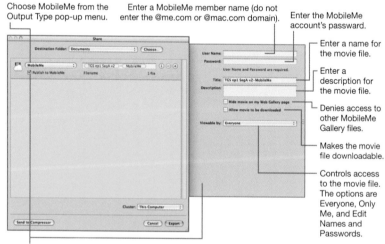

Selecting the action box displays
the post-transcoding action drawer.

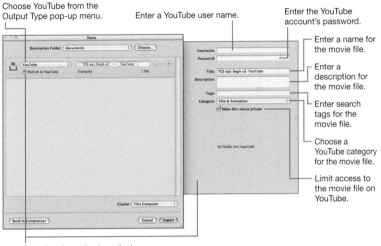

Choosing the "Edit Names and Passwords" option from the "Viewable by" pop-up menu opens this "Names and Passwords" dialog.

Clicking the Add (+) button creates an untitled user name. Double-click the user name and password fields to edit.

Add or remove user names and passwords for accessing the movie file.

Example: Share for YouTube

Choose YouTube from the Output Type pop-up menu.

Enter a YouTube user name.

Enter the YouTube account's password.

Enter a name for the movie file.

Enter a description for the movie file.

Enter search tags for the movie file.

Choose a YouTube category for the movie file.

Limit access to the movie file on YouTube.

Selecting the action box displays the post-transcoding action drawer.

Starting Share with Multiple Items

You can select multiple clips or sequences for exporting with the Share command. For best results, selected items should be of the same frame size and frame rate.

1   Make a selection of multiple clips, sequences, or bins (containing clips or sequences) in the Browser.

New Feature

2   Choose File > Share.

3   In the Share Multiple Sources dialog, choose your desired export setting, and then click OK.

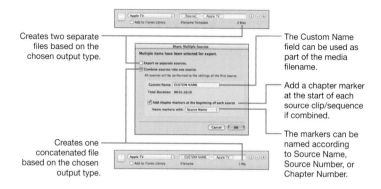

Creates two separate files based on the chosen output type.

The Custom Name field can be used as part of the media filename.

Add a chapter marker at the start of each source clip/sequence if combined.

Creates one concatenated file based on the chosen output type.

The markers can be named according to Source Name, Source Number, or Chapter Number.

4   Modify the Share window settings as desired before clicking Export.

> **TIP** See the previous section, "Starting Share with a Single Item," for more information on the Share window settings.

Exporting

The Export command (File > Export) lists several options to get media, whether one clip or a whole sequence, out of Final Cut Pro. Compared with the Share command, Export requires you to make more-granular choices within Final Cut Pro, such as codecs and marker types.

QuickTime Movie

Exporting a QuickTime movie is the "Old Faithful" of the Final Cut Pro workflow. You have the option to create either a self-contained or reference movie based on the available sequence settings in Final Cut Pro.

> **TIP** A self-contained movie is one that has a copy of the sequence footage so that this QuickTime file may play back on another system outside Final Cut Pro. As a stand-alone file,

a self-contained movie can be archived. A reference movie requires access to the original source media and render files used by the sequence. A reference movie has a smaller file size than a self-contained movie.

1   Make a selection of a Browser clip, a Browser sequence, a Viewer clip (by loading a clip into the Viewer), or the active Timeline sequence (by making the Timeline window active with the sequence as the active tab).

TIP ▶ Export honors any clip or sequence In and Out points.

2   Choose File > Export > QuickTime Movie.

3   Set up the Save dialog as desired, and then click Save.

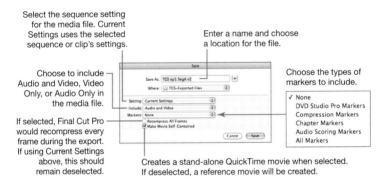

Select the sequence setting for the media file. Current Settings uses the selected sequence or clip's settings.

Enter a name and choose a location for the file.

Choose to include Audio and Video, Video Only, or Audio Only in the media file.

Choose the types of markers to include.

√ None
DVD Studio Pro Markers
Compression Markers
Chapter Markers
Audio Scoring Markers
All Markers

If selected, Final Cut Pro would recompress every frame during the export. If using Current Settings above, this should remain deselected.

Creates a stand-alone QuickTime movie when selected. If deselected, a reference movie will be created.

NOTE ▶ File > Export > QuickTime movie does not provide the best solution for transcoding. Choose Current Settings here, and then take the exported movie to Compressor.

Using QuickTime Conversion

QuickTime Conversion utilizes QuickTime components when outputting a media file. For example, QuickTime Conversion can create TIFF or JPEG formats for still images or an image sequence. Refer to the Final Cut Pro 7 User Manual for more information on using QuickTime Conversion.

NOTE ▶ QuickTime Conversion always recompresses all frames.

1   Make a selection of a Browser clip, a Browser sequence, a Viewer clip (by loading a clip into the Viewer), or the active Timeline sequence (by making the Timeline window active with the sequence as the active tab).

TIP ▶ Export honors any clip or sequence In and Out points.

2   Choose File > Export > Using QuickTime Conversion.

Choose a preset format from the pop-up menu. Third-party QuickTime Export Components may appear here. Your options may vary.

Enter a name and choose a location for the file.

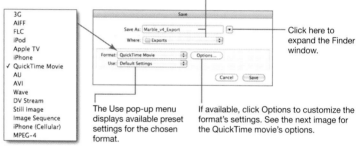

Click here to expand the Finder window.

The Use pop-up menu displays available preset settings for the chosen format.

If available, click Options to customize the format's settings. See the next image for the QuickTime movie's options.

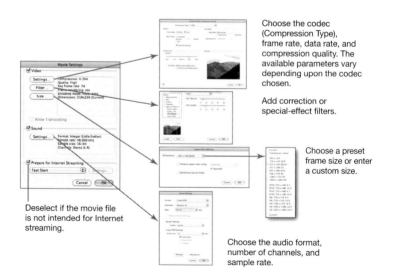

Choose the codec (Compression Type), frame rate, data rate, and compression quality. The available parameters vary depending upon the codec chosen.

Add correction or special-effect filters.

Choose a preset frame size or enter a custom size.

Deselect if the movie file is not intended for Internet streaming.

Choose the audio format, number of channels, and sample rate.

Audio to OMF

The Audio to OMF export option lets you send sequence audio to a third-party digital audio workstation (DAW). The OMF format collects your audio media files and creates a description file that allows a DAW to open your audio edits as they appear in your Final Cut Pro sequence.

> **NOTE** ▸ There is a 2 GB file size limitation for OMF.

1   In the active sequence, ensure that the desired audio tracks for export are enabled (Track Visibility is on).

2   Choose File > Export > Audio to OMF.

3   Configure the OMF Audio Export settings as needed before clicking OK.

Enter a value for media handles to be added
to sequence clips. The export will add as
much handle as is available up to this amount.

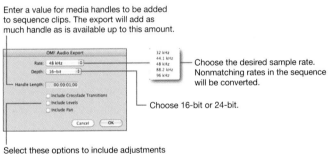

Choose the desired sample rate.
Nonmatching rates in the sequence
will be converted.

Choose 16-bit or 24-bit.

Select these options to include adjustments
made to these parameters within Final Cut Pro.

Markers List as Text

The "Markers List as Text" export command lets you create a tab-delimited text file of your marker information to share with other post-production personnel. This text file contains notes you entered for sequence or clip markers.

1   Make a selection of a Browser clip, a Browser sequence, a Viewer clip (by loading a clip into the Viewer), a sequence clip, or the active sequence (by making the Timeline window active with the sequence as the active tab).

> **NOTE** ► "Markers List as Text" is not restricted to markers within marked In and Out points but does require markers of any type to exist on the selected item.

2   Choose File > Export > Markers List as Text.

3   Give the file a name and location for saving; then click Save.

Choose the marker type to include in the text file.

Enter a name and location for the text file.

Example: Markers as Text Exported File

Name	Type	Marker Name	Comment	Start	Duration	Color
Sequence 5	Sequence	A Plain Timeline Marker	Text entered into the Comment field	01:00:07:21	00:00:00:00	Red
Sequence 5	Sequence	Another Timeline Marker	This one has been set as a Chapter Marker. <CHAPTER>	01:00:13:16	00:00:00:00	Purple
Sequence 5	Sequence	A Third Timeline Marker	Notice the last column tells you the marker's color.	01:00:16:01	00:00:00:00	Yellow
C	Clip	A Sequence Clip Marker	Clip Markers are included in the Markers List as Text export.	01:00:10:04	00:00:00:00	Red

XML

The XML export command creates a Final Cut Pro XML Interchange Format file that is readable with other applications. There are many possible uses for this file. Refer to the Final Cut Pro 7 User Manual for more information and examples of using Final Cut Pro's XML Interchange Format.

This command can help when there are project file compatibility issues. Although you can easily take a project file created in an earlier version of Final Cut Pro to the current version, that process does not work in reverse. In order to take a Final Cut Pro 7 project back to Final Cut Pro 6, for example, use the XML export command. Below is a history chart identifying the XML format appropriate for the different versions of Final Cut Pro.

1 Select all project elements in the active Project tab that you wish to export via XML.

2 Choose File > Export > XML.

3 Select the appropriate format in the Export XML dialog before clicking OK.

Apple XML Interchange
File Format | **Final Cut Pro Version**

Apple XML Interchange File Format	Final Cut Pro Version
Version 5	7.0
Version 4	6.0
Version 3	5.1.2
Version 2	5.0
Version 1	4.0

NOTE ▶ New features added to later versions of Final Cut Pro will not be interpreted correctly by earlier versions.

4 Give the file a name and location for saving the XML file; then click Save.

NOTE ▶ Importing an XML file is accomplished by choosing File > Import > XML.

Going to Tape

Final Cut Pro offers three ways to output to tape:

- ▶ Recording directly from the Timeline (or crash record)
- ▶ Print to Video
- ▶ Edit to Tape

The three methods vary in their frame accuracy when controlling the recording device.

> **NOTE** ▶ All three methods below assume you have set up a recording device that is connected to a properly configured video interface, and that View > External Video is set to All Frames.

Recording Directly from the Timeline

Also known as live-to-tape, this method lets you "crash record" your sequence to tape. Whatever you see in the Canvas is what you get on tape. This method does not guarantee a high-quality recording or frame-accurate control of the recording device.

1   Render all unrendered effects by pressing Option-R.

> **TIP** ▶ To help achieve the higher-quality output with this method, choose Safe RT from the RT pop-up menu. Leaving the RT menu set to Unlimited RT may result in lower-resolution output.

> **NOTE** ▶ Which clips are rendered is dependent on the render status bars you have chosen to be rendered in the Sequence > Render All menu. The quality of the render is dependent on the settings chosen in the Render Control tab of Sequence > Settings.

2   Cue the Timeline playhead to the desired start frame.

3   Start the record function on the recording device.

4   Start playback of your sequence.

5 Stop recording on the recording device once the sequence has passed your desired last frame.

> **TIP** Set In and Out points in the sequence and use the "Play In to Out" command (Shift-\) to increase precision.

Print to Video

Also considered a "crash record" approach, "Print to Video" offers more features, including inserting color bars, a slate, and a countdown if desired. If your recording device supports it, Final Cut Pro triggers the recording function automatically.

> **TIP** Sequence In and Out points will be honored during a Print to Video operation.

1 With your sequence active in the Timeline, choose File > Print to Video.

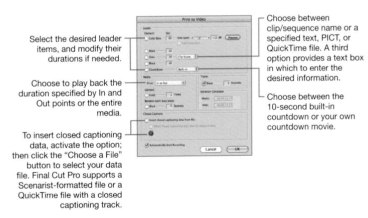

Select the desired leader items, and modify their durations if needed.

Choose to play back the duration specified by In and Out points or the entire media.

To insert closed captioning data, activate the option; then click the "Choose a File" button to select your data file. Final Cut Pro supports a Scenarist-formatted file or a QuickTime file with a closed captioning track.

Choose between clip/sequence name or a specified text, PICT, or QuickTime file. A third option provides a text box in which to enter the desired information.

Choose between the 10-second built-in countdown or your own countdown movie.

2 Choose the desired Print to Video options; then click OK.

Final Cut Pro will now automatically perform any necessary rendering according to the quality settings in the Render Control tab. Access this tab in the Sequence > Settings window.

3   When Final Cut Pro is ready to play the sequence, a dialog will
appear.

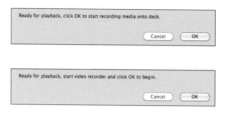

If you selected Automatically Start
Recording, the recording device
starts recording when you click OK.

If you deselected Automatically
Start Recording, start the recording
device and then click OK.

4   Stop the recording device when the sequence playback stops.

Edit to Tape

The "Edit to Tape" command is a precise method of outputting to
tape. Not all recording devices (such as a mini-DV deck) support all
of the Edit to Tape functions. Refer to the Final Cut Pro User Manual
for more information.

When in Mastering mode, lets you choose leader and trailer elements and add closed captioning.

Choose device control settings if not set up.

Mode pop-up menu

Black and Code button

Timecode Duration field

Current Timecode field

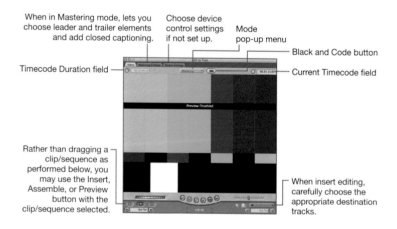

Rather than dragging a clip/sequence as performed below, you may use the Insert, Assemble, or Preview button with the clip/sequence selected.

When insert editing, carefully choose the appropriate destination tracks.

Assemble Edit

An assemble edit to tape requires an initial signal to be previously
recorded on the tape (even if only 10 seconds of black). At the In

point, all tracks (video, audio, timecode, and control track) on the tape are replaced with the output of Final Cut Pro.

> **NOTE** ► A control track break will occur at the end of the edit.

1   Choose File > Edit to Tape to open the Edit to Tape window.

2   Choose the appropriate mode.

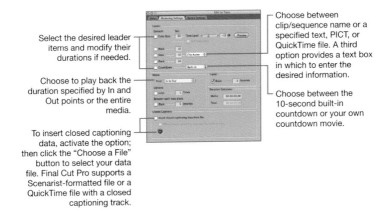

If no leader or trailer elements are needed, choose Editing.

If leader or trailer elements are needed, choose Mastering.

3   If mastering, choose the leader and trailer elements in the Mastering Settings tab.

Choose between clip/sequence name or a specified text, PICT, or QuickTime file. A third option provides a text box in which to enter the desired information.

Select the desired leader items and modify their durations if needed.

Choose to play back the duration specified by In and Out points or the entire media.

Choose between the 10-second built-in countdown or your own countdown movie.

To insert closed captioning data, activate the option; then click the "Choose a File" button to select your data file. Final Cut Pro supports a Scenarist-formatted file or a QuickTime file with a closed captioning track.

4   Cue the mastering tape, and set an In point in the Edit to Tape window.

5   In the clip or sequence you want to output, set In and Out points if needed (or clear the points).

6 Drag the clip or sequence to be mastered to the Edit Overlay of the Edit to Tape window, and release the item on the Assemble icon.

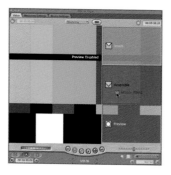

Final Cut Pro will now automatically perform any necessary rendering according to the quality settings of the Render Control tab at Sequence > Settings.

7 When Final Cut Pro is ready, a dialog will appear. Click OK.

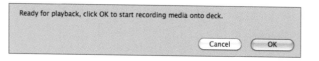

Ready for playback, click OK to start recording media onto deck.

Cancel   OK

TIP ▶ Press Escape to abort the process.

Insert Edit

An insert edit lets you surgically replace audio or video content on a tape without creating a control track break at the end of the edit.

1 Choose File > Edit to Tape to open the Edit to Tape window.

2 Choose the appropriate mode.

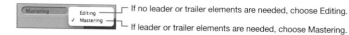

If no leader or trailer elements are needed, choose Editing.
If leader or trailer elements are needed, choose Mastering.

3   If mastering, choose the leader and trailer elements in the
Mastering Settings tab.

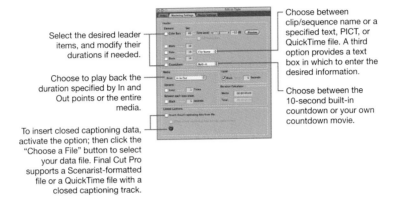

Select the desired leader items, and modify their durations if needed.

Choose to play back the duration specified by In and Out points or the entire media.

To insert closed captioning data, activate the option; then click the "Choose a File" button to select your data file. Final Cut Pro supports a Scenarist-formatted file or a QuickTime file with a closed captioning track.

Choose between clip/sequence name or a specified text, PICT, or QuickTime file. A third option provides a text box in which to enter the desired information.

Choose between the 10-second built-in countdown or your own countdown movie.

4   Cue the tape, and set at least one edit point in the Edit to Tape
window.

> **NOTE ▸** If in Mastering mode, set an In point. In Editing mode,
> you may set an In point, an Out point, or both.

5   Choose the appropriate destination tracks.

Insert Timecode

Insert Video

Click to select the destination audio tracks of the recording device.

> **NOTE ▸** Please exercise caution to select the appropriate destina-
> tion tracks. Inserting timecode will negatively affect a blacked tape.

6   In the clip or sequence you want to output, set In and Out points
if needed (or clear the points).

7 Drag the clip or sequence to be inserted to the Edit Overlay of the Edit to Tape window, and release the item on the Insert icon.

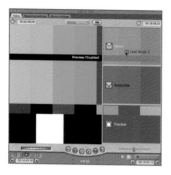

Final Cut Pro will now automatically perform any necessary rendering according to the quality settings of the Render Control tab at Sequence > Settings.

8 When Final Cut Pro is ready, a dialog will appear. Click OK.

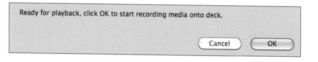

Ready for playback, click OK to start recording media onto deck.

Cancel   OK

TIP Press Escape to abort the process.

15
Specialized Workflows

Final Cut Pro includes features that speed up or simplify various parts of the post-production workflow. These features assist you when editing a multiple-camera event (multiclips), working with an off-site producer (iChat Theater preview), crafting a long-format show (markers and subclips), or utilizing the power of other Final Cut Studio applications (round-tripping).

Multiclips

You can create multiclips within Final Cut Pro to work with source footage from multiple cameras recording the same event or even when one camera records multiple takes of a repeat performance. Event scenarios that benefit from using multiclips include multi-camera recordings of music concerts, sporting events, or dramatic presentations.

> **TIP** Up to 128 angles can be combined into a multiclip.

Creating a Multiclip

You can use video and audio clips, stills, and graphics to create multi-clips. Before using audio and video clips in a multiclip, set a sync frame to identify the same moment in time within each source clip.

1   In each clip to be added to a multiclip, establish a sync frame by setting an In point (or an Out point) within each clip on a frame that represents the same point in time. This may be achieved by referencing a visible/audible action.

> **TIP** ▶ You may skip setting a sync frame in step 1 if each
> source clip was recorded with identical timecode, such as that
> from a master timecode generator.

2   In the Browser, select the clips to make up a multiclip.

3   Control-click (or right-click) one of the selected clips, and
     choose the desired multiclip option.

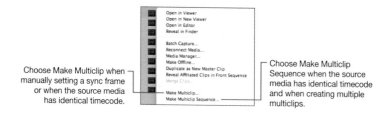

Choose Make Multiclip when
manually setting a sync frame
or when the source media
has identical timecode.

Choose Make Multiclip
Sequence when the source
media has identical timecode
and when creating multiple
multiclips.

4   In the Make Multiclip dialog, choose the sychronization method
     and click OK.

Select from In Points, Out Points, and Timecode.
The Aux Timecode options become available when
the clips contain these additional timecode tracks.

These gray areas will play back as
black for the angle because no
additional source media is available.

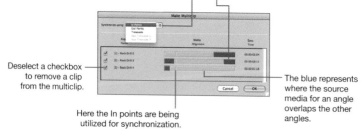

Deselect a checkbox
to remove a clip
from the multiclip.

The blue represents
where the source
media for an angle
overlaps the other
angles.

Here the In points are being
utilized for synchronization.

Using a Multiclip in Real Time

With a multiclip created, you edit the multiclip in a sequence as if
you were using a video switcher in a television production.

1   Load the new multiclip from the Browser into the Viewer.

2   If necessary, set new In/Out points to trim the multiclip.

> **TIP** As the source clips are now synchronized within the new multiclip, changing the In/Out points does not cause sync issues.

3   If necessary, you may rearrange the angle order, modify the multiclip, or change the display overlays within the multiclip.

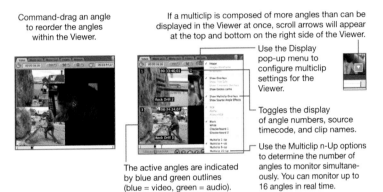

Command-drag an angle to reorder the angles within the Viewer.

If a multiclip is composed of more angles than can be displayed in the Viewer at once, scroll arrows will appear at the top and bottom on the right side of the Viewer.

Use the Display pop-up menu to configure multiclip settings for the Viewer.

Toggles the display of angle numbers, source timecode, and clip names.

Use the Multiclip n-Up options to determine the number of angles to monitor simultaneously. You can monitor up to 16 angles in real time.

The active angles are indicated by blue and green outlines (blue = video, green = audio).

> **TIP** You can slip the content of an angle by Shift-Control-dragging the angle within the Viewer. Command-dragging a nonactive (selected) angle outside the Viewer removes that angle from the multiclip.

> **NOTE** ▶ You can add additional angles or replace a nonactive (selected) angle of a multiclip.

Drag an additional master clip from the Browser to the multiclip in the Viewer. Wait a moment, and a version of this pop-up menu will appear.

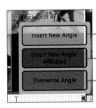

Insert New Angle — Adds this clip as a new angle to this multiclip.

Insert New Angle Affiliates — Adds this clip as a new angle to this multiclip and all affiliates of this multiclip.

Overwrite Angle — Adds this clip as an angle to this multiclip, replacing the angle on top of which the clip is dropped.

4   Edit the multiclip into a sequence. You can use the Insert or Overwrite edit buttons at the bottom left of the Canvas, or their associated keyboard shortcuts, F9 and F10.

> **TIP** ▶ If you wish to drag the multiclip to the Canvas Edit Overlay or directly to the Timeline, press Option before dragging the multiclip from the Viewer.

5   In the Viewer or Canvas, set the Playhead Sync pop-up menu to Open.

Set Playhead Sync to Open.

The default is to switch or cut Video and Audio together. You may choose to cut only Video or only Audio.

> **NOTE** ▶ The Open option for Playhead Sync will automatically open the clip under the Timeline playhead into the Viewer with the Viewer playhead cued to the same frame as the Timeline playhead.

6   Begin playback in the Canvas or Timeline.

> **NOTE** ▶ Starting playback in the Viewer does not allow for real-time switching/cutting.

7   With the sequence playing, click the angle in the Viewer that you wish to cut to. Continue cutting to additional angles by clicking the desired angle while the sequence plays.

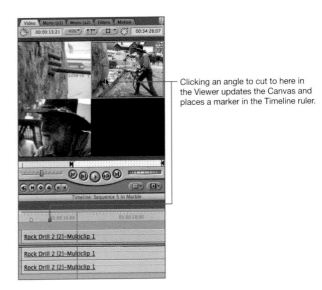

Clicking an angle to cut to here in
the Viewer updates the Canvas and
places a marker in the Timeline ruler.

TIP You can use the Tools > Keyboard Layout > Multi-camera Editing preset with an extended keyboard rather than clicking in the Viewer to cut to new angles. See Chapter 2 for more about customizing the keyboard layout.

NOTE ▶ If the active angle is not updating in the Canvas, ensure that the Multiclip Playback option is chosen in the Timeline's RT pop-up menu. If the Viewer is not updating, cycle the Playhead Sync pop-up menu to Off and back to Open.

8   Stop playback, and the sequence markers become edit points.

Refining the Multiclip Edit

Live switching the multiclip is easy, but your timing may be off, or you clicked the wrong angle. Use the switch angle command and the Blade and Roll tools to refine your edit.

> **NOTE** ▸ Exercise caution if using the Ripple tool to remove sections of a multiclip. Use of the Slide or Slip tool is fatal to the synchronization of your multiclip.

Roll Tool

You can use the Roll tool to adjust the timing of an edit point within a sequence. As the multiclip is composed of synchronized clips, using the Roll tool moves the "cut" point without affecting sync. See Chapter 6 for more information on the Roll tool.

Blade Tool

If you missed cutting to a different angle, use the Blade tool or Add Edit command (Control-V) to create an edit point within the multiclip. The Blade tool splits the clip, resulting in red Through Edit arrows on the clip. See the next topic, "Switch Angle," to change the "new" cut to a different angle.

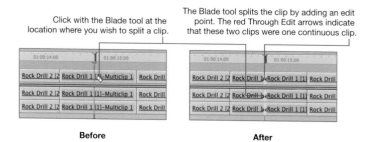

Click with the Blade tool at the location where you wish to split a clip.

The Blade tool splits the clip by adding an edit point. The red Through Edit arrows indicate that these two clips were one continuous clip.

Before   After

Switch Angle

You can exchange an edited sequence angle for another angle by clicking in the Viewer.

1   With Playhead Sync set to Open, move the Timeline playhead
     over the angle you wish to replace.

     TIP The Playhead Sync: Open option will move the Viewer
     playhead to the same point within the multiclip. This allows you
     to see what is happening in the other angles.

2   Click the desired new angle in the Viewer. Final Cut Pro performs
     a replace edit to exchange the old angle for the new active angle.

Before   **After**

Collapsing a Multiclip

Viewing and changing angles of a multiclip is very easy to do because
Final Cut Pro streams all of the angles simultaneously during playback.
However, you can protect your multiclip from inadvertently switching
angles and also improve system performance by collapsing a multiclip.

1   In the sequence, select all of the multiclips.

2   Control-click one of the selected multiclips, and then choose
     Collapse Multiclip(s).

TIP ▶ Do the reverse and choose Uncollapse Multiclip(s) to again see the other angles of the multiclip.

iChat Theater Preview

This new feature of Final Cut Pro 7 lets you share the output of Final Cut Pro during an iChat session. Now a remote client can see your active Viewer or Timeline output and comment in real time.

NOTE ▶ Though Final Cut Pro is required only on the host system, both computers must have active iChat accounts and enough bandwidth to support a video iChat session.

1   Sign in to iChat.

2   In Final Cut Pro, open a clip into the Viewer or sequence into the Canvas.

3   Choose View > iChat Theater Preview > Start Sharing.

4   In iChat, invite the remote user to a video chat session.

NOTE ▶ If the remote user does not have a camera, you may initiate a one-way video chat by Control-clicking the user in the iChat Buddy List and choosing "Invite to One-Way Video Chat."

5   After the user accepts the iChat invitation, he or she will see the output of your active Timeline or Viewer window.

Stops the output of Final Cut Pro
from feeding the iChat session.

The iChat window of the remote computer.

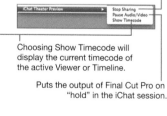

Choosing Show Timecode will
display the current timecode of
the active Viewer or Timeline.

Puts the output of Final Cut Pro on
"hold" in the iChat session.

Markers

Markers let you notate a frame or portion of a clip with production notes. These notes may be internal to you or shared externally. Markers can be given specific functionality, such as serving as scoring markers for Soundtrack Pro or as chapter markers within a QuickTime movie or DVD. There are two main categories of markers:

▶   Sequence markers

▶   Clip markers

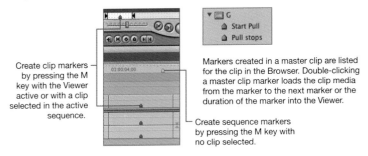

Create clip markers by pressing the M key with the Viewer active or with a clip selected in the active sequence.

Markers created in a master clip are listed for the clip in the Browser. Double-clicking a master clip marker loads the clip media from the marker to the next marker or the duration of the marker into the Viewer.

Create sequence markers by pressing the M key with no clip selected.

NOTE ▶   Clip markers on a sequence clip are not included within an exported QuickTime movie and therefore should not be used as navigation points for DVDs or web videos.

Adding Colored Markers

Beyond pressing the M key to create red markers in either a sequence or a clip, you may add a marker of a specific color by using the associated keyboard shortcut. Press Shift-1 through Shift-8 to apply markers of the respective color (Red, Orange, Yellow, Green, Turquoise, Blue, Purple, Pink). Display only certain markers within your project or customize the marker labels per color by choosing Edit > Project Properties.

New Feature

You may customize the marker labels for each color. New labels might include SFX, Insert B-roll, or Lower Third.

Toggles the visibility of markers within the project.

Navigating Markers

You can use keyboard shortcuts or shortcut menus to navigate to markers. Pressing Shift–Down Arrow moves the playhead to the next marker, while Shift–Up Arrow moves the playhead to the previous marker.

When you Control-click the Time Ruler, sequence markers are listed at the bottom of the shortcut menu.

> **TIP** Control-clicking a sequence clip displays applied clip markers at the bottom of the shortcut list.

Editing Marker Information

After you create a marker, you can edit it to customize its color or specify a name or comments.

> **TIP** The Name and Comments fields of a clip marker appear while the clip is in the Viewer. Sequence marker information is displayed in the Canvas.

NOTE ▶ You can create and edit a marker while playback is stopped by pressing the M key twice.

1   Identify the marker whose information needs to be changed.

For clip markers in the Viewer, Command–double-click the marker.

For a sequence clip marker, cue the playhead to the marker, and with the clip selected, press the M key.

For sequence markers, Command–double-click the marker in the Time Ruler or Canvas.

2   Modify the marker's information as desired.

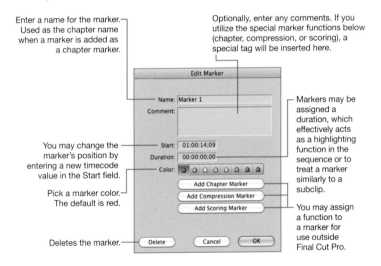

Enter a name for the marker. Used as the chapter name when a marker is added as a chapter marker.

Optionally, enter any comments. If you utilize the special marker functions below (chapter, compression, or scoring), a special tag will be inserted here.

Markers may be assigned a duration, which effectively acts as a highlighting function in the sequence or to treat a marker similarly to a subclip.

You may change the marker's position by entering a new timecode value in the Start field.

Pick a marker color. The default is red.

Deletes the marker.

You may assign a function to a marker for use outside Final Cut Pro.

Manually Moving Markers

Move Viewer and Timeline markers by Command-dragging them to a new location.

NOTE ▶ You can move any clip or sequence marker by cueing the playhead to the marker, pressing M (with the sequence clip selected, if necessary), and then entering a new Start timecode value.

Adding and Editing Markers On the Fly

Final Cut Pro 7 lets you add and edit markers while playing a clip in the Viewer or a sequence.

1 Play a clip in the Viewer or a sequence (with no clip selected).

2 Press Shift-Option-1 to add a red marker and open the Edit Marker dialog while playback continues.

3 Enter the marker's information, and then click OK.

TIP ▶ Playback continues while you are entering information. To toggle playback while in the Edit Marker dialog, press Control-Spacebar. You may also cue the playhead back 5 seconds by pressing Command-Control-Spacebar. You can change this pre-roll value in the Editing tab of Final Cut Pro > User Preferences.

NOTE ▶ Add and edit the various marker colors by pressing Shift-Option-1 through Shift-Option-8.

Rippling Markers

By default, Final Cut Pro 7 ripples sequence markers after performing an insert edit or ripple delete. Those markers to the right of the insert edit location are shifted to the right (or down) in the sequence. Markers to the right of a ripple delete edit are shifted to the left (or up) in the sequence.

 Ripple Sequence Markers is on by default. Click to toggle the function off/on.

With Ripple Sequence Markers on, it is possible to end up with two or more markers on the same frame.

"Stacked" markers display their names one above the other in the Canvas.

Command–double-click the markers in the Time Ruler, and then choose the marker you wish to edit from the Choose pop-up menu in the Edit Marker dialog.

Deleting Markers

Final Cut Pro lets you delete markers individually or all at the same time. For markers that appear in the Viewer, Canvas, or Time Ruler, hold down Command and drag the marker off the scrubber bar or Timeline ruler. To delete all markers in a clip or sequence, make the clip or sequence active and choose Mark > Markers > Delete All (or use the keyboard shortcut Control-` [grave accent]).

TIP The grave accent (`) key is sometimes referred to as the tilde (~) key, located to the left of the numeral 1 key.

Subclips

A subclip lets you break a long clip into smaller chunks. Subclips can improve your ability to search through source material, and you can rename subclips to further specify the contents of each subclip.

1   Load a master clip into the Viewer.

2   Mark In and Out points in the Viewer.

3   Choose Modify > Make Subclip (or press Command-U).

A subclip is created in the Browser and is ready to be renamed. A subclip's icon is a "ripped" clip.

NOTE ▶ You can convert clip markers into subclips. Select the markers of a master clip in the Browser and choose Modify > Make Subclip. Subclips are created that are based on the markers' names and take the duration of a marker until the next marker.

Match Frame a Subclip

A subclip restricts access to the complete original source media file from which the subclip was created. There are match frame and reveal commands to give you access to the original (or parent) source media.

With the subclip in the Viewer, choose View > Match Frame > Source File to open the source media file into the Viewer.

With the playhead parked on a subclip in the Viewer or sequence, choose View > Reveal Subclip Parent Clip. The parent clip of the sub-clip is automatically selected in the Browser.

TIP▶ You can load a subclip in the Viewer and choose Modify > Remove Subclip Limits. Be aware that this command deletes the subclip as the subclip and all affiliates become new master clips that reference the complete original source media file.

Create New Media Files from Subclips

When you capture long clips, you can use subclips and the Media Manager to create new media files. This process creates new media files based on the selected subclips and deletes the long capture media file.

NOTE ▶ This is a destructive process. Proceed with caution.

1   In the Browser, delete the master clip from which the subclips were created.

NOTE ► Select the clip and press Delete. Do not make the clip offline.

2   Select the subclips you wish to use for creating new media files.

3   Choose File > Media Manager, and set up as shown below before clicking OK.

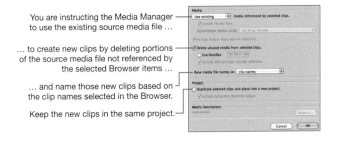

You are instructing the Media Manager to use the existing source media file ...

... to create new clips by deleting portions of the source media file not referenced by the selected Browser items ...

... and name those new clips based on the clip names selected in the Browser.

Keep the new clips in the same project.

4   If any nonselected clips in the project reference the same long capture media file, the Additional Items Found dialog appears.

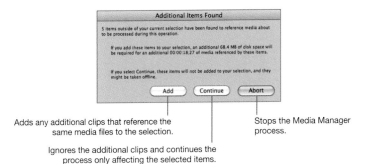

Adds any additional clips that reference the same media files to the selection.

Stops the Media Manager process.

Ignores the additional clips and continues the process only affecting the selected items.

5   A final warning appears to remind you of the destructiveness of this process. Click Continue.

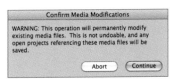

Round-Tripping

Integration of the Final Cut Studio applications lets you pass clips or sequences from one application to another. You can send material to Motion for creating motion graphics, Soundtrack Pro for audio design, and Color for visual sweetening.

> **NOTE ▶** This is a quick overview of the round-tripping process. Check out the associated Apple Pro Training Series books from Peachpit Press for more details on utilizing the other Final Cut Studio applications.

Round-Trip with Motion

You can send selected clips or a sequence to Motion to add graphics or to make optical flow speed changes.

1   In Final Cut Pro, select a sequence clip, multiple sequence clips, or a sequence in the Browser, and choose File > Send To > Motion Project.

2   In the dialog that appears in Final Cut Pro, give the Motion project a name and choose a location.

Sequence clips in Final Cut Pro are replaced with a Motion project file.

3   In Motion, design your motion graphics or apply effects to the clips. To send back to Final Cut Pro, choose File > Save within Motion.

TIP If in step 1 you chose a single or multiple sequence clips, the Motion project file within the Final Cut Pro sequence is updated to reflect your changes. If you chose to send a sequence in step 1, you will need to import the resulting Motion project file into your Final Cut Pro project.

NOTE ▶ When a Motion project file exists within Final Cut Pro, you do not need to use the Send To command to modify the file. Control-click the .motn file and choose "Open in Editor" from the shortcut menu. After you have made changes in Motion, choose File > Save within Motion to update the project file in Final Cut Pro.

Round-Trip with Soundtrack Pro

Depending on what you want to do with audio, you can send material to Soundtrack Pro in two ways:

- ▶ A single clip as an audio file project
- ▶ A sequence as a multitrack project

Sending a Clip to Soundtrack Pro

This process is handy when you have individual clips that need clean-up work or effects applied.

1   In Final Cut Pro, Control-click a clip in the Browser or a sequence clip, and then choose Send To > Soundtrack Pro Audio File Project.

2   In the Save dialog, enter a name and choose a location for the .stap file you are creating. Then click Save.

TIP The default name is the name of the clip with a "(Sent)" tag.

3   In Soundtrack Pro, modify the clip as desired.

4   In Soundtrack Pro, choose File > Save.

A dialog may appear, asking whether to save a self-contained version or save as a reference.

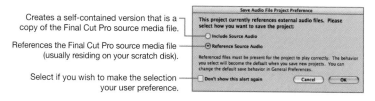

Creates a self-contained version that is a copy of the Final Cut Pro source media file.

References the Final Cut Pro source media file (usually residing on your scratch disk).

Select if you wish to make the selection your user preference.

In Final Cut Pro, the new Soundtrack Pro audio project file is added to the Browser (if you originally selected a clip in the Browser) or replaces the selected sequence clip.

NOTE ▶ When a Soundtrack Pro audio project file exists in Final Cut Pro, you do not need to use the Send To command to modify the file. Control-click the file and choose "Open in Editor" from the shortcut menu. After you have made changes in Soundtrack Pro, choose File > Save within Soundtrack Pro to update the project file in Final Cut Pro.

Sending a Sequence to Soundtrack Pro

When you are ready to add sound effects, add music, or clean up multiple clips, use the multitrack option.

1   In Final Cut Pro, Control-click a sequence in the Browser; then choose Send To > Soundtrack Pro Multitrack Project.

2 In the Save dialog, enter a name and choose a location for the .stmp file you are creating. Then click Save.

3 In Soundtrack Pro, add tracks to add music and sound effects. Modify your existing audio as desired.

4 In Soundtrack Pro, choose File > Save.

5 In Soundtrack Pro, choose File > Export to send a mixdown back to Final Cut Pro.

6 Choose your options in the Export dialog. Click Export.

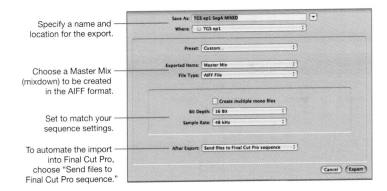

Specify a name and location for the export.

Choose a Master Mix (mixdown) to be created in the AIFF format.

Set to match your sequence settings.

To automate the import into Final Cut Pro, choose "Send files to Final Cut Pro sequence."

7 Final Cut Pro will become the active application with an Import XML dialog. Verify the settings, and then click OK.

Specify the project to receive the import (usually the active one). The options include any open project and the ability to create a new project.

Leave the other options at their defaults as shown.

8   In Final Cut Pro, you will find a new sequence in your Browser named with the filename from step 5. This new sequence contains the original audio in disabled tracks and the new mixdown audio from Soundtrack Pro in the top, enabled audio tracks.

Round-Trip with Color

Color provides powerful visual sweetening capabilities within Final Cut Studio. Any grading work done in Color must be rendered for return to Final Cut Pro.

> **NOTE** ▶ To make the round trip with Color as smooth as possible, some preparation of your sequence may be required. Refer to the document titled "Final Cut Studio Workflows" in the Final Cut Pro section at http://documentation.apple.com for more information.

1   In Final Cut Pro, Control-click a sequence in the Browser, and then choose Send To > Color from the shortcut menu.

2   Enter a name for the Color project file. Then click OK.

3   Grade your sequence as desired in Color.

4   After rendering your clips in the Render Queue room of Color, choose File > Send To > Final Cut Pro.

A series of warnings may appear if you did not render every clip. Click OK to these warnings.

5   In Final Cut Pro, a new sequence from Color appears in the Browser.

> **NOTE** ▶ Refer to the "Final Cut Studio Workflows" document mentioned earlier for information about modifying a Final Cut Pro sequence that has been round-tripped with Color.

16

Media Manager

A Final Cut Pro project may contain hundreds of clips and several sequences. The Media Manager lets you process media files in a variety of ways during the life of a project to free up media storage space or to move a project from one storage location to another. Another option in the Media Manager is to create an offline/online workflow where you may start with many hours of low-resolution media for editing, but only reingest the final durations of high-resolution media for finishing.

Using the Media Manager

This simple yet powerful feature of Final Cut Pro can clean up your media or destroy it. Be cautious while choosing your options.

1   Select the items to be managed.

The Media Manager manages selected Browser or sequence clips, selected or active sequences, or the active project. To manage an entire project, make the Browser window active with the project as the front tab; then press Command-A to select all elements of the project.

2   Choose File > Media Manager, and then select the desired options.

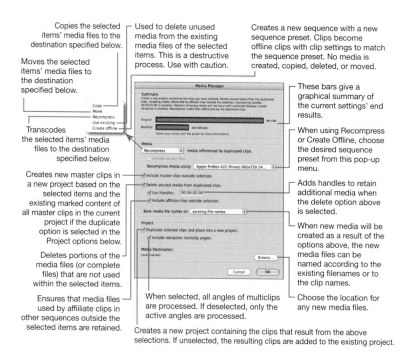

Copies the selected items' media files to the destination specified below.

Moves the selected items' media files to the destination specified below.

Transcodes the selected items' media files to the destination specified below.

Creates new master clips in a new project based on the selected items and the existing marked content of all master clips in the current project if the duplicate option is selected in the Project options below.

Deletes portions of the media files (or complete files) that are not used within the selected items.

Ensures that media files used by affiliate clips in other sequences outside the selected items are retained.

Used to delete unused media from the existing media files of the selected items. This is a destructive process. Use with caution.

When selected, all angles of multiclips are processed. If deselected, only the active angles are processed.

Creates a new project containing the clips that result from the above selections. If unselected, the resulting clips are added to the existing project.

Creates a new sequence with a new sequence preset. Clips become offline clips with clip settings to match the sequence preset. No media is created, copied, deleted, or moved.

These bars give a graphical summary of the current settings' end results.

When using Recompress or Create Offline, choose the desired sequence preset from this pop-up menu.

Adds handles to retain additional media when the delete option above is selected.

When new media will be created as a result of the options above, the new media files can be named according to the existing filenames or to the clip names.

Choose the location for any new media files.

3 Click OK.

4 Depending on the options selected in the Media Manager window, a dialog may appear in which you can specify the name and location for a new Final Cut Pro Project file.

Before processing begins, several warning dialogs may appear.

The Media Manager scans all open projects for any clips that reference the same media files that are about to be managed. If clips are found, click Add to include the additional references when calculating the media files to be managed.

Click Abort to stop the Media Manager process.

Click Continue to ignore the additional clips.

Confirm Media Modifications

WARNING: This operation will permanently modify existing media files. This is not undoable, and any open projects referencing these media files will be saved.

Abort   Continue

When your selected options will affect existing media files in a non-recoverable way, a confirmation dialog appears. Click Continue with care.

Media Manager and File Formats

Here are a few notes on how the Media Manager handles various media file formats:

▶ QuickTime movie files can be managed (transcoded, trimmed, moved, or copied). Be aware that if they do not contain time-code tracks and reel information, any reingest needed later may become impossible.

▶ Still images can be copied and moved, but their format is not affected.

▶ AIFF, WAVE, and BWF files can be copied and moved, but these audio files are not trimmed.

▶ Media files used within Soundtrack Pro Audio Project files and Motion projects cannot be managed.

Media Manager Workflow Examples

The following sample workflows highlight the most common uses for the Media Manager.

Copying a Project

This process makes it easy to copy a project to another Final Cut Pro system or to create a backup. A new project and media files will be created, while the original project file and media are unaffected.

1   In the Browser, select all of the elements to be copied (which could be everything or limited to a sequence).

2   Choose File > Media Manager and choose your options before clicking OK.

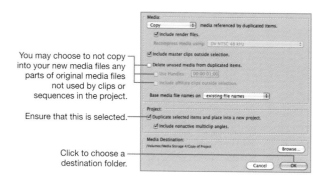

You may choose to not copy into your new media files any parts of original media files not used by clips or sequences in the project.

Ensure that this is selected.

Click to choose a destination folder.

3 Enter a name for the new project file, and choose its destination in the Save dialog. Click Save.

> **TIP** ▸ You may want to choose the same destination you designated as the Media Destination in the Media Manager window.

Moving a Project

The Media Manager can be used to move a project to a new location. This process is handy for handing a project off or to collect the source media files of a project. Clips in the current project will automatically link to the media files at the new location.

> **NOTE** ▸ Original source media files will be moved to a new destination. Any clips in other projects that reference the moved media files will go offline. Use the Reconnect Media command to link to the new location.

1 In the Browser, select all of the elements in your project.

2 Choose File > Media Manager and choose your options before clicking OK. A confirmation dialog will appear. Click Continue.

Ensure that this is not — selected.

Click to choose destination folder.

Removing Unused Media from a Selected Sequence

This process will delete portions of the master clips' media files that are not used in the selected sequence. For safety, the process also checks other sequences in any open project in order to protect the used portions of the same media files.

NOTE ▶ This is a destructive process. If multiple projects are referencing the same media, those projects will be affected. In a shared environment, such as with Xsan or a "sneaker net" external hard drive, this task will affect the projects of other users that use the same media files. Proceed with caution.

1 Select a sequence in the Browser.

2 Set the Media Manager as shown below.

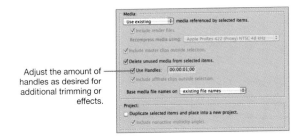

Adjust the amount of handles as desired for additional trimming or effects.

NOTE ▶ The safety features of this process may result in a smaller-than-expected amount of media being deleted. However, the portions of the media files that are deleted are not recoverable. **This is a destructive process.**

Offline/Online Version of a Sequence

When working remotely or with limited storage, you may need to work with temporary, low-resolution footage. Before finishing and outputting, you will need to reingest the media files at a higher resolution or reconnect to the existing high-resolution media files.

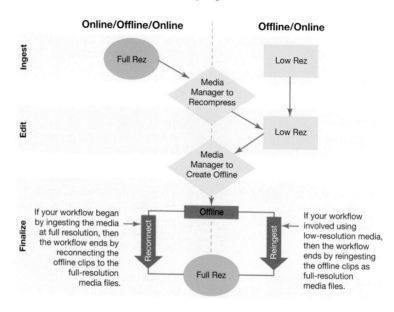

Use these settings to create the offline sequence.

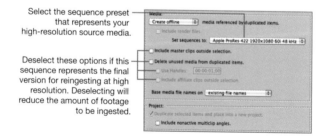

Online Bonus Chapter 17, "Troubleshooting"

This book includes a bonus lesson on common troubleshooting issues. Chapter 17, "Troubleshooting," is posted online, where it can be easily revised as Final Cut Pro is updated. Download the PDF from Peachpit Press at www.peachpit.com/apts.fcpqrg.

APPENDIX A

Keyboard Shortcuts

Final Cut Pro includes over 800 commands that have keyboard shortcuts. This appendix contains a reference for the most commonly used commands, broken down by function. Refer to the user manual for the full list of all keyboard shortcuts.

Interface

Standard	Control-U	Sets the interface to the Standard window arrangement.
Fit to Window	Shift-Z	With the Timeline active, changes the zoom setting of the Timeline to fit the active sequence's length. With the Viewer active, changes the zoom setting of the Viewer to fit the video content's frame size. With the Canvas active, changes the zoom setting of the Canvas to fit the active sequence's frame size.
Fit Selection	Shift-Option-Z	Changes the zoom setting of the Timeline to fit the selected sequence clips.
Zoom In	Command-=	With the Canvas or Viewer active, increases the zoom setting for the displayed contents. With the Timeline active, increases the zoom setting, focusing on a clip if a clip is selected or the playhead if no clip is selected.
Zoom In in Timeline	Option-=	Whether the Canvas, Viewer, or Timeline is active, increases the zoom setting of the Timeline, focusing on a clip if a clip is selected or the playhead if no clip is selected.
Zoom Out	Command- — (minus)	With the Canvas or Viewer active, decreases the zoom setting for the displayed contents. With the Timeline active, decreases the zoom setting, focusing on a clip if a clip is selected or the playhead if no clip is selected.
Zoom Out in Timeline	Option- — (minus)	Whether the Canvas, Viewer, or Timeline is active, decreases the zoom setting of the Timeline, focusing on a clip if a clip is selected or the playhead if no clip is selected.
Toggle Clip Overlays	Option-W	Toggles the Timeline display of sequence clips' Level and Opacity parameters.
Toggle Waveform Display	Command-Option-W	Toggles the Timeline display of audio waveforms within sequence clips.
Toggle Wireframes	W	Cycles the Viewer or Canvas through the Image, Image+Wireframe, and Wireframe displays.
Toggle Timeline Track Height	Shift-T	Cycles the Timeline track-height presets for the active sequence.

Continues on next page

Interface *(continued)*

Toggle Range Check	Control-Z	Toggles the Viewer or Canvas display of Range Check: Luma for the current frame under the respective playhead.

Tool Palette

Selection tool	A	Selection tool
Ripple tool	RR	Ripple tool
Roll tool	R	Roll tool
Slip tool	S	Slip tool
Slide tool	SS	Slide tool
Speed tool	SSS	Speed tool
Razor Blade tool	B	Razor Blade tool
Pen tool	P	Pen tool

Navigation

Play	K	Play/Pause.
Search Forward	L	Forward playback. Press up to four times to progressively increase speed.
Search Reverse	J	Reverse playback. Press up to four times to progressively increase speed.
Play In to Out	Shift-\	Starts playback at the In point and stops at the Out point.
Loop Playback	Control-L	Toggles loop playback.
Go to In Point	Shift-I	Cue the playhead to the In point of the Viewer clip or active sequence. If no In point exists, go to the beginning of the Viewer media or active sequence.
Go to Out Point	Shift-O	Cue the playhead to the Out point of the Viewer clip or active sequence. If no Out point exists, go to the end of the Viewer media or the last sequence clip's Out point.
Go to Next Edit	Down Arrow	Cue the playhead to the next edit point (specifically, the next clip's In point in any track).
Go to Previous Edit	Up Arrow	Cue the playhead to the previous edit point (specifically, the next In point of a clip in any track to the left of the playhead).
Go to Next Marker	Shift–Down Arrow	Cue the playhead to the next marker (clip based if a clip is selected; otherwise, sequence based).
Go to Previous Marker	Shift–Up Arrow	Cue the playhead to the previous marker (clip based if a clip is selected; otherwise, sequence based).

Ingest

Import Files	Command-I	Opens a Finder dialog to create clips in the active project without copying/moving or transcoding original source media files.
Log and Transfer	Command-Shift-8	Opens the Log and Transfer window to create clips by copying/transcoding original footage from a tapeless acquisition format to the scratch disk.

Continues on next page

Ingest *(continued)*

Log and Capture	Command-8	Opens the Log and Capture window to create clips in the project by copying/transcoding original footage from a tape format to the scratch disk.
Capture Now	Shift-C	In Log and Capture, commences recording of incoming audio/video streams received by the capture device. Device Control can be set to Non-Controllable Device for free-run sources.
Log Clip	F2	In Log and Capture, creates an offline clip in the project with the current metadata of the Log and Capture window.

Editing

Overwrite Clip	F10	Executes an overwrite edit of the Viewer clip to a sequence based on the Timeline playhead or In/Out points and track controls settings (patch panel and track locks). Must disable/reassign Exposé in System Preferences.
Insert Clip	F9	Executes an insert edit of the Viewer clip to a sequence based on the Timeline playhead or In/Out points and track controls settings (patch panel and track locks). Must disable/reassign Exposé in System Preferences.
Add Edit	Control-V	Creates an edit point under the playhead for all clips in unlocked, auto-selected tracks.
Snapping	N	Toggles the Timeline's Snapping status.
Add Audio Transition	Command-Option-T	Adds the default audio transition to the edit point under the playhead, the selected edit point(s) (can select only one per track), the In and Out points of selected sequence clips, or the edit points of clips selected by Timeline In/Out points.
Add Video Transition	Command-T	Adds the default video transition to the edit point under the playhead, the selected edit point(s) (can select only one per track), the In and Out points of selected sequence clips, or the edit points of clips selected by Timeline In/Out points.
Mark In	I	Creates an In point under the playhead in the Viewer or Timeline.
Mark Out	O	Creates an Out point under the playhead in the Viewer or Timeline.
Mark Clip	X	Creates In and Out points for the duration of a sequence clip under the playhead in the lowest unlocked auto-selected track.
Mark Selection	Shift-A	Creates In and Out points for the duration of the selected sequence clips.
Clear In	Option-I	Clears the Viewer or Timeline In point.
Clear Out	Option-O	Clears the Viewer or Timeline Out point.
Clear In and Out	Option-X	Clears the Viewer or Timeline In and Out points.

Continues on next page

Editing *(continued)*

Nudge Down	Option–Down Arrow	In the Timeline, a selected sequence clip is moved down (vertically) a track if no collisions would occur. In the Canvas set to a wireframe display, the Center parameter of a selected sequence clip is moved 1 pixel down ($y+1$).
Nudge Left	Option–Left Arrow	In the Timeline, a selected sequence clip is moved one frame left if no collisions would occur. In the Canvas set to a wireframe display, the Center parameter of a selected sequence clip is moved 1 pixel left ($x-1$).
Nudge Right	Option–Right Arrow	In the Timeline, a selected sequence clip is moved one frame right if no collisions would occur. In the Canvas set to a wireframe display, the Center parameter of a selected sequence clip is moved 1 pixel right ($x+1$).
Nudge Up	Option–Up Arrow	In the Timeline, a selected sequence clip is moved up (vertically) a track if no collisions would occur. In the Canvas set to a wireframe display, the Center parameter of a selected sequence clip is moved 1 pixel up ($y-1$).
Toggle Edit Type	U	Cycles the current edit point selection through ripple outgoing, roll, and ripple incoming.
Trim Minus	[	Adjusts the selected edit point left by one frame.
Trim Minus Many	Shift-[	Adjusts the selected edit point left by the Multi-Frame Trim Size setting in the Editing tab of User Preferences.
Trim Plus	]	Adjusts the selected edit point right by one frame.
Trim Plus Many	Shift-]	Adjusts the selected edit point right by the Multi-Frame Trim Size setting in the Editing tab of User Preferences.
Extend Edit	E	Rolls a selected edit point to the playhead if adequate source media is available.
Toggle Stereo Pair	Option-L	Disables the stereo pair status of selected sequence clips. Enables the stereo pair status of two selected sequence audio clips.
Toggle Link	Command-L	Disables the linked status of selected sequence clips. Enables the linked status of a selected sequence clip (1 video and up to 24 audio).
Linked Selection	Shift-L	Toggles the Timeline's Linked Selection status.
Clear	Delete	Executes a lift edit based on selected sequence clips or sequence In and Out points and Auto Select/Lock status.
Change Speed	Command-J	Modifies a clip's playback speed based upon user selections.
Paste Attributes	Option-V	Modifies a clip's properties by pasting user-specified attributes from a previously copied clip.
Show Match Frame	F	Loads the master clip into the Viewer, cued to the same frame and marked duration as the selected sequence clip (or the clip in the lowest auto-selected track) under the playhead.
Undo	Command-Z	Deletes the last editing function performed.

Audio

Levels	Command-Option-L	Opens the Gain Adjust dialog for relative or absolute Level adjustment of all or selected clips in the active sequence (becomes Opacity Adjust for video-only selections).
Gain -1dB	Control- (minus)	−1 dB relative gain adjustment of the Viewer clip, the selected sequence clip(s), or the sequence clips under the playhead in unlocked, auto-selected tracks. Can be used during playback (playback may pause temporarily).
Gain +1dB	Control-=	+1 dB relative gain adjustment of the Viewer clip, the selected sequence clip(s), or the sequence clips under the playhead in unlocked, auto-selected tracks. Can be used during playback (playback may pause temporarily).
Pan Center	Control-. (period)	Centers the pan of the Viewer clip, the selected sequence clip(s), or the sequence clips under the playhead in unlocked, auto-selected tracks.

Markers

Add and Edit Marker	Shift-Option-M	Creates a marker (Color 1) in the Viewer, Timeline, or selected sequence clip, and opens the Edit Marker window while playback continues. Press Shift-Option-2 through Shift-Option-8 to use the other marker colors.
Add Marker	M	Creates a marker (Color 1) in the Viewer, Timeline, or selected sequence clip. Press Shift-2 through Shift-8 to use the other marker colors.
Delete Marker	Command-` (grave accent)	Clears the marker under the Viewer or Timeline playhead. Select a sequence clip to remove a clip marker under the Timeline playhead.
Edit Marker	M	Opens the Edit Marker window for the marker under the Viewer or Timeline playhead. Select a sequence clip to edit a clip marker under the Timeline playhead.
Mark to Markers	Control-A	Creates In and Out points at the markers to the left and right of the playhead.

Render

Render All: Both	Option-R	Renders all sequence clips (audio and video) whose render status matches the selected options under Sequence > Render All.
Render Selection: Both	Command-R	Renders the selected sequence clips (audio and video) whose render status matches the selected options under Sequence > Render Selection.

Output

Export QuickTime Movie	Command-E	Creates a reference or self-contained QuickTime movie with user-specified settings.
Share	Command-Shift-E	Opens a batch exporter for transcoding Browser-selected clips or sequences or the Timeline's active sequence; based on Compressor presets (Apple devices, Blu-ray, YouTube, and so on).

Index